Malay Kingship in Kedah

Asia World
Series Editor: Mark Selden

This series charts the frontiers of Asia in global perspective. Central to its concerns are Asian interactions—political, economic, social, cultural, and historical—that are transnational and global, that cross and redefine borders and networks, including those of nation, region, ethnicity, gender, technology, and demography. It looks to multiple methodologies to chart the dynamics of a region that has been the home to major civilizations and is central to global processes of war, peace, and development in the new millennium.

Titles in the Series

China's Unequal Treaties: Narrating National History, by Dong Wang
The Culture of Fengshui in Korea: An Exploration of East Asian Geomancy, by Hong-Key Yoon
Precious Steppe: Mongolian Nomadic Pastoralists in Pursuit of the Market, by Ole Bruun
Managing God's Higher Learning: U.S.-China Cultural Encounter and Canton Christian College (Lingnan University), 1888–1952, by Dong Wang
Queer Voices from Japan: First Person Narratives from Japan's Sexual Minorities, edited by Mark McLelland, Katsuhiko Suganuma, and James Welker
Yōko Tawada: Voices from Everywhere, edited by Douglas Slaymaker
Modernity and Re-enchantment: Religion in Post-revolutionary Vietnam, edited by Philip Taylor
Water: The Looming Crisis in India, by Binayak Ray
Windows on the Chinese World: Reflections by Five Historians, by Clara Wingchung Ho
Tommy's Sunset, by Hisako Tsurushima
Lake of Heaven: An Original Translation of the Japanese Novel by Ishimure Michiko, by Bruce Allen
Imperial Subjects as Global Citizens: Nationalism, Internationalism, and Education in Japan, by Mark Lincicome
Japan in the World: Shidehara Kijūrō, Pacifism, and the Abolition of War, Volumes I and II, by Klaus Schlichtmann
Filling the Hole in the Nuclear Future: Art and Popular Culture Respond to the Bomb, edited by Robert Jacobs
Radicalism, Revolution and Reform in Modern China: Essays in Honor of Maurice Meisner, edited by Catherine Lynch, Robert B. Marks, and Paul G. Pickowicz
The "Other" Karen in Myanmar: Ethnic Minorities and the Struggle without Arms, by Ardeth Thawnghmung
A Localized Culture of Welfare: Entitlements, Stratification, and Identity in a Chinese Lineage Village, by Kwok-shing Chan
Malay Kingship in Kedah: Religion, Trade, and Society, by Maziar Mozaffari Falarti

Malay Kingship in Kedah

Religion, Trade, and Society

Maziar Mozaffari Falarti

LEXINGTON BOOKS
Lanham • Boulder • New York • Toronto • Plymouth, UK

Rowman & Littlefield
Bloomsbury Publishing Inc, 1359 Broadway, New York, NY 10018, USA
Bloomsbury Publishing Plc, 50 Bedford Square, London, WC1B 3DP, UK
Bloomsbury Publishing Ireland, 29 Earlsfort Terrace, Dublin 2, D02 AY28, Ireland
www.bloomsbury.com

Published by Lexington Books
A wholly owned subsidiary of The Rowman & Littlefield Publishing Group, Inc.
4501 Forbes Boulevard, Suite 200, Lanham, Maryland 20706
www.rowman.com
10 Thornbury Road, Plymouth PL6 7PP, United Kingdom

Copyright © 2013 by Lexington Books

All rights reserved. No part of this publication may be: i) reproduced or transmitted in any form, electronic or mechanical, including photocopying, recording or by means of any information storage or retrieval system without prior permission in writing from the publishers; or ii) used or reproduced in any way for the training, development or operation of artificial intelligence (AI) technologies, including generative AI technologies. The rights holders expressly reserve this publication from the text and data mining exception as per Article 4(3) of the Digital Single Market Directive (EU) 2019/790.

British Library Cataloguing in Publication Information available

Library of Congress Cataloging-in-Publication Data

Falarti, Maziar Mozaffari, 1975–
Malay kingship in Kedah : religion, trade, and society / Maziar Mosaffari Falarti.
pages cm.—(Asia world)
Includes bibliographical references and index.
ISBN 978-0-7391-6842-4 (cloth)—ISBN (invalid) 978-0-7391-6843-1 (electronic)
1. Kedah—Kings and rulers—History. 2. Sultans—Malaysia—Kedah—History. 3. Geopolitics—Malaysia—Kedah—History. 4. Power (Social sciences)—Malaysia—Kedah—History. 5. Kedah—Kings and rulers—Religious aspects—History. 6. Kedah—Commerce. 7. Kedah—Social life and customs. I. Title.
DS598.K28F35 2012
959.5'1—dc23

To my parents, family, teachers and everyone else that has believed in me
and the extraordinary story of Kedah!

ای نام تو بهترین سرآغاز بی نام تو نامه کی کنم باز
ای یاد تو مونس روانم جز نام تو نیست بر زبانم

(O' thy name the best to begin with, then
How one would begin his book without
Thy remembrance, the companion of my soul
Nought on my tongue but thy name)

The opening to the book *Layli va Majnun* by Ilyas Nizami Ganjavi (1141–1209 CE)

I HAD TO SEEK THE PHYSICIAN

I had to seek the Physician
Because of the pain this world caused me.
I could not believe what happened when I got there—I found my Teacher.
Before I left, he said,
"Up for a little homework, yet?"
"Okay," I replied.
"Well then, try thanking all the people who have caused you pain.
They helped you come to me."

Poem of Kabir (1440–1518 CE), in *Love Poems from God: Twelve Sacred Voices from the East and West*, translated by Daniel Ladinsky (2002: 229)

Contents

List of Figures and Maps	xiii
Foreword C. A. Trocki	xv
Acknowledgments	xix
Abbreviations	xxiii
Introduction	1
1 From Raja to Sultan: The Conversion of the Tantric Malay Ruler	35
2 The Malay Ethos: The Sultan and His Subjects	69
3 Controlling Kedah's Maritime Lines of Communication: The Sultan and the *Raja di-laut*, or Sea Lords	97
4 Bay to Gulf or Gulf to Bay: The Sultan and the Trans-Peninsular Routes of Kedah	143
Conclusion	177
Bibliography	187
Index	211
About the Author	225

List of Figures and Maps

Figure 1. A quick death at Kedah. 79

Figure 2. *Orang laut* boats in nineteenth-century Trang. 107

Figure 3. The Harbor of Songkhla. 155

Figure 4. Expedition preparing to depart from "maison de voyageurs" (i.e., a travelers lodge) in Kedah on its way to Songkhla. 156

Figure 5. Kedah River at Alor Star. 168

Map 1. World map. xviii

Map 2. Southeast Asia. 1

Map 3. Kedah in about 1810 CE. 5

Map 4. Geographical proximity of Kedah to Aceh. 42

Map 5. The Northern Corridor: Kedah's traditional maritime control at the Bay of Bengal by the indigenous *orang laut* (seventeenth to the midnineteenth century). 115

Map 6. The Malay Peninsula and Kedah's network of overland and trans-peninsular routes. 146

Map 7. The Kedah-Songkhla trans-peninsular route, as traveled by Jules M. Claine (1892: 389) in 1889–1890 CE. 160

Foreword

C. A. Trocki

Maziar Falarti's study of Kedah offers a compelling new approach to Malay history. Kedah has been the only major state of the Peninsula about which no reliable and scholarly history has been written. Moreover, its history of the past several centuries broadens our understanding of the Peninsula's place in Southeast Asian and world history as well as purely local affairs.

In many ways Kedah has been unique, as this work makes abundantly clear. Indeed, in providing yet another "model" of the traditional Malay state, Falarti challenges the rather narrow concept of the purely riverine Malay *negri*, offered by such scholars as Gullick and Milner (Gullick, 1989 #190; Milner, 1982 #929). Kedah, in some respects resembled the maritime-entrepot polities of states such as Palembang-Srivijaya, Melaka, and Johor-Riau. In other respects, however, it went beyond this model as well. The ruler not only controlled the sea coast and sea peoples, as well as the riverine hinterland, but his power stretched beyond the sources of the rivers. He exercised dominance over the trans-Peninsular routes that crossed to the east coast.

Given its unique position, Kedah was often able to control both land and sea routes between the Indian Ocean and the South China Sea. Kedah thus maintained a perennial prominence as an important node on the global trade routes between India and China, providing a regular source of income for its rulers and magnates.

The position also had its risks. Kedah was perennially vulnerable to threats from both the land and the sea. At various times in the past five hundred years, the state has faced invaders from Burma, Siam, Aceh, and Johor. In the seventh century it even came under the domination of Palembang-Srivijaya. As a result, Kedah's rulers have had to engage with sea peoples both north and south in the Straits of Melaka. At the same time, it has also been necessary to maintain relations with peasants in Kedah's rice plain as well as with the people of hills and jungles of the interior.

Historically, Kedah's royal line has been able to do what few other dynasties have managed. They have successfully made the transition from a Hindu-Buddhist monarchy to an Islamic monarchy. Despite two decades of exile following the Siamese conquest of 1821, Kedah's rulers maintained their position as the only ruler recognized by Kedah's population. The dynasty has also managed to make the transition from colonial rule to independence, where, with other Malay monarchies, it shares a ceremonial position and an important spiritual influence under parliamentary rule. This has made it one of the most durable dynasties in Southeast Asia (if not the whole Islamic world) with a lifespan of over a millennium. As Falarti shows, the sources of the dynasty's staying power are multiple. They include spiritual powers, as well as economic and strategic effectiveness.

Falarti bases his study first on a detailed and reasoned analysis of Kedah's traditional history, noting its relationship to the literature of south and central Asia. He is one of the first modern scholars who has had the linguistic competence to exploit and explain some of the key aspects of the *Hikayat Merong Mahawangsa*, Kedah's traditional hikayat. This is a document which has been largely ignored or denigrated by both colonial and more recent Malay scholars. Although often dismissed as fanciful and unbelievable, it provides a textual foundation for the spiritual legitimacy of the dynasty.

Particularly interesting is Falarti's discussion of the various conversion stories that narrate the coming of Islam to Kedah. The first, in the *Merong Mahawangsa*, naturally credits the monarch with institution of the new religion. He is pictured as a degenerate, addicted to alcohol and the descendant of rulers who engaged in a range of deviant practices including cannibalism. Until, that is, he is converted by the magical intervention of Sheikh Abdullah of Baghdad who was being transported about the world in the company of Satan. Falarti's explication of these events sheds a refreshing light on our understanding of the hikayat. The account is also a probable reference to the former Tantric practices of Kedah's Hindu-Buddhist rulers, as well as a nod to the Sufi mystics who first brought Islam to Southeast Asia.

Taking his critique of Gullick and Milner one step further, Falarti has sought out and presented alternative "conversion" stories that do not involve royal primacy. Here ordinary people and extraordinary strangers face and overcome the pre-Islamic demons and bring the new faith to the people without benefit of royal intervention. Further probing the importance of "the people" and importance of their support for the dynasty, Falarti examines the role of the traditional "social contract" which has existed between Malay rulers and their subjects. Although such a covenant is only found explicitly in the *Sejarah Melayu*, he shows that a similar understanding also existed between Kedah's ruler and its peoples.

Falarti's research is exemplary. His command of languages such as Arabic, Farsi and Turkish, not to mention Malay and English, gives him an avenue that few other scholars have explored. He has read extensively in an effort to bring together the multiple strands of Kedah's history. I have little doubt that this will stand as the standard work on the state's long history and an important contribution to the understanding of the Malay world and Southeast Asian history. It makes a number of significant additions to the historiographical trend initiated by Paul Wheatley, Oliver W. Wolters, and Anthony Reid which, place the region's history within the context of global events.

Carl A. Trocki (PhD, Cornell)
Professor Emeritus of Asian Studies
Queensland University of Technology
April 2012

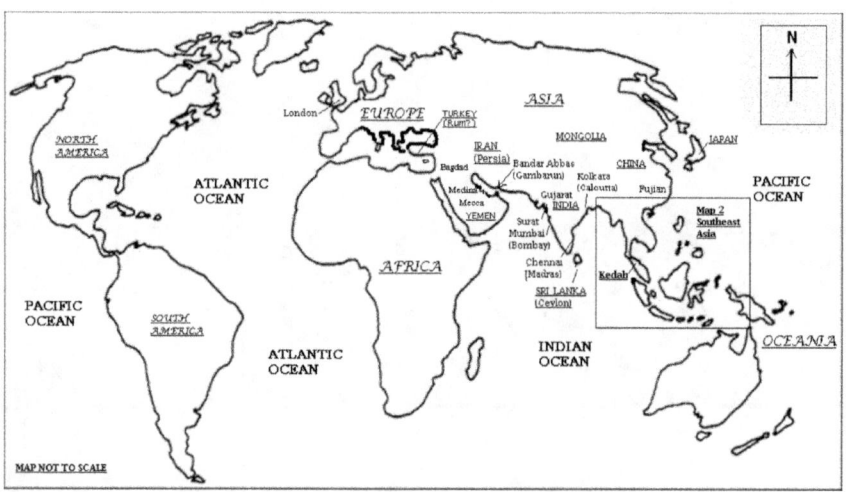

Map 1. World map.

Acknowledgments

> Sometimes the Beloved takes my pen in hand, for Hafiz is just a simple man. The other day the Old One wrote on the Tavern wall: "The heart is the thousand-stringed instrument that can only be tuned with Love."
>
> —Shams-ud-din Muhammad Hafez/Hafiz, renowned Persian lyric poet (about 1325–1390 CE), "Where Is the Door to the Tavern?" selections from *The Gift: Poems by HAFIZ the Great Sufi Master*, translations by Daniel Ladinsky 1999: 228)

I believe that the overall writing of this book into its present shape, was only possible through the generous contributions of numerous "individuals," "entities," or "lovers." Each of these contributors in their own unique ways have helped to tune or mould this volume and its various facets, just as tuning a "thousand-stringed instrument." In particular I wish to thank my mentors and teachers, Professor Carl A. Trocki and Dr. Hossein Adibi. These scholars not only oversaw the writing of my PhD thesis on Kedah a few years ago and the subsequent dawn of this book, but through their passion and love for the region inspired and nurtured a neverending affection within me for Kedah and Penang, as well as the Malay, Indian, Asian, Islamic and Persian studies/world. I further believe that Trocki's initial introduction to works, models and theories by Southeast Asian intellectuals like Professor Syed Naquib al-Attas, Luce Professor Hendrik (Henk) J. M. Maier, the late Dr. Rollins Bonney, Professor A. C. Milner, Professor Anthony Reid, Professor Cheah Boon Kheng, Professors Barbara and Leonard Andaya, and especially the eminent Professor Oliver W. Wolters (Trocki's supervisor and mentor at Cornell University) have greatly inspired aspects of this book and views of the region. Indeed I am humbled and feel a great honor to have Trocki write a foreword to this volume.

Much gratitude is given to Professor Mark Selden, Professor Henk Maier, Professor Cheah Boon Kheng, Associate Professor Timothy P. Barnard, and Associate Professor J. G. Butcher for their continuous support, interest, communication, comments and persistence for me to update, revise and publish my study on Kedah into a publishable shape. I have always admired Selden's patience and passion for the broader Asian studies and continuous guidance as the editor of the AsiaWorld Series to prepare this volume for publication. His contributions I consider have been instrumental to navigate and tune the smooth transition of the original proposal into its present contour. Indeed according to a Persian proverb "Why be troubled when the ship's captain is Prophet Noah!"

The publication of the book was also not possible without the immense assistance, technical coordination and support of the people at Rowman & Littlefield (Lexington Books), principally Justin Race and Sabah Ghulamali. I was delighted and impressed that Race regularly kept in touch with me during the course of the writing of the book and that he had personally read many editions of the book and taken a personal interest in the work with valuable suggestions.

In the course of my research, study, and field trips for the most part I relied upon financial support and a number of travel grants by the former Humanities Research Program and later the School of Cultural and Language Studies in Education (CLSE, Faculty of Education) at the Queensland University of Technology (QUT) in Brisbane, Australia. The financial help for this study was essential as I was required to take research and field trips to various locations in Malaysia, Singapore, Bangladesh, Turkey, and Iran, as well consult British and Dutch archival sources kept in Melbourne and Canberra (Australia). I would like to take the opportunity to thank former members of the Humanities Research Program, principally Professor Clive Bean, Professor Gary Ianziti, Professor Gavin Kendall, and Dr. John Synott that further contributed in their own ways to the study. A special gratitude and thanks is given to the head of CLSE, Professor Annette Patterson. She has unreservedly advised, coordinated and supported me and the book from the time I sent away the proposal to its completion and current state. The author also owes much gratefulness to the moral support and/or directions by a number of staff at the School of Cultural and Language Studies in Education during its various stages; particularly Dr. Keith Moore, Dr. Sue Keays, Associate Professor Deborah Henderson, Linda Charles, Vicki Hallett, Atholl Murray, and Dr. Radha Iyer. Lastly I like to thank members of the QUT library (principally the Document Delivery and Ms. Paula Callan).

In Canberra (Australia), I appreciated the suggestions and insights on Malay, Thai/Siamese, and Dutch history and archival sources given to me by Professor Milner, Professor Craig Reynolds, and Dr. Robert Cribb at the Australian National University (ANU). In Queensland I like to thank comments and suggestions on sources made by Associate Professor Butcher, Associate Professor Julia Howell, Dr. Roxanne Marcotte, Associate Professor Rosita Dellios, the late Dr. Maggie Gray, the late Mr. Mark Markarian (particularly on the Indian subcontinent and the Iranian-Armenian historic diaspora), Dr. Renee Worringer (particularly on her help with Ottoman sources and travel accounts), and Professor Robert Elson at the Griffith University, the University of Queensland (UQ) and Bond University. Mr. Naresh Midha's (Rugs International) generous gift of books (including some rare and reprints) imported directly from India for the study, as well as Mr. Jamshid Lakhdawala and his wife's contribution of books and discussions on the Zoroastrian or pre-Islam Persian sources and Parsi connection of Gujarat to Southeast Asia is also much appreciated. Outside Queensland, but still in Australia, I received much help from the staff at the National Library and the Menzies Library at ANU (at Canberra) and the State Library of Victoria, Royal Melbourne Institute of Technology (RMIT) and the University of Melbourne (at Melbourne).

In Malaysia and Singapore I would like to thank numerous scholars, organizations, and people who have generously helped or contributed to my research trips, aspects of the book or its writing. Each of these individuals have—symbolically—contributed to tune the various strings of this book as an instrument, in order to create Kedah's unique but striking melody. Above all in Singapore and Malaysia I thank Professor Syed Naquib al-Attas, Professor Cheah Boon Kheng and his wife, Dr. Paul Kratoska, the Dawoodi Bohra Community of Singapore and Malaysia (as well India, particularly Mr. Hozefa Rajokotwala and family), Dr. Christoph Ismail Marcincowski, the Jumabhoy family (especially the Penang branch, Datin Lubna and Datuk Mustapha), the late Datuk Rahim Khan, Mr. Taizoon Tyebkhan (and his family at Penang, Singapore and Calcutta), Mrs. Khoo Salma (Khoo Su Nin) and Mr. A. R. Lubis (much thanks to their generous time and scholarly insight of western Malaysia and Sumatra), the Mustan family, the late Mr. Mustan of Penang, the Merican family (ABC Bakery), the Merchant family, Dr. Geof Wade, Ms. Julie Yeo, the Namazi family, the Balagamwala family, Moiz Taherali (Langkawi Silks) and family, the Vasi family, the Mamaji family, the Bajuneid family, the Lim family, Professor Abu Talib and Dr. Mahani Musa, as well the staff at the School of History at the Universiti Sains Malaysia (USM). I also found the staff at *Arkib Negara Malaysia* (Penang and Kuala Lumpur), Penang Museum, USM library, and the Singapore National Archives to be of much help. In Iran I would like to thank the staff at Tabriz State Library, Isfahan University and library staff (especially Professor H. Harsij, Professor Emamjomeh and Dr. Montazerol-Qayem), Tabriz University (particularly Professor Rahimpour and family), Professor Abbasi-Shavazi and Professor Mirzaie at Tehran University, New Julfa Armenian Library (mostly Ms. Zargarian), and Dr. Jafaarian at Qum. In Bangladesh Professor Chowdhurry, Syed Zein (*Imambara Hosseini Dallan*), Mr. Martin of the New Julfa Armenian Dhakka center, the Chowdhurry family (especially Saiful, Kamrul, Mainul, Tanzina and Zuhair) also Apu and the Sicho Group (including Mr. Ahmed at Dhakka branch), the A. K. Khan family (particularly Mr. Sakandar Hayat Khan, his wife the former mayor of Chittagong and children), Haq family (chiefly Salim and Raquib), the Ispahani family, and Soheil (Diner Hossain). Separately in Turkey I gained much insight about local histories and literary sources from Dr. Ayhan Ercument and Dr. Selcuk Besir Demir (Cumhuriet University). Last but not least in Britain I personally would like to thank the immense help with primary sources and documents, as well the timely suggestion for the cover of this volume by Dr. Annabel Teh Gallop, the head curator for Indonesian and Malay in the Department of the South and Southeast Asia section, at the British Library. Indeed the choice for the cover of the book was entirely based upon her suggestion and her insight into Malay royal seals, insignia, and historic documents.

To conclude I would like to once again to thank my parents, my sister Mandana and her kids (Roxanna and Arianna), Dr. Greg Medley (my brother in law), Vahideh (especially for her help during the early stages of the book proposal and some of her translations) and Ms. Julieanne Hupalo (for her help in reading through parts of my manuscript with the intention of correcting its grammar/word choices). A special gratitude is also to my late grandmother and her brother (Ustad Abbas Ali Mozaffari Esfahani) that I attribute to have first introduced me to a general love for history. Without the help of my parents as well as their blessing, support (moral, financial and intellectual) and patience (especially in the past year) the completion of the book would have not been possible.

> Drink wine as you listen to my verse, for your jewelled cup will give to this royal pearl a different beauty.
>
> —"Ghazal 38," selections from *The Green Sea of Heaven: Fifty ghazals from the Diwan of Hafiz*, translations by T. Gray 1995: 118–119

I hope that my preliminary investigation into Kedah's premodern histiography and indigenous political systems in Southeast Asia will not only make new contributions in the field of Malay, Islamic and Asian study; but also complement or shed further light into earlier—related—studies by Dr. Bonney, Professor Wolters, Professor Maier, Professor Milner, Professor Trocki, Professor Reid, Professor Cheah Boon Kheng, Associate Professor Barnard, and others. My attempt to write the book has been to bring forth the royal jewel that is Kedah from the shadows of Malay studies; and present it openly as it is, a thousand-stringed instrument. It is thus hoped that the melody that transpires out of this study, or the tuning of the thousand-stringed instrument, would ultimately inspire new melodies to be created or alternatively lead the way to the retuning of the old melodies.

> What benefit will you derive from a basket of flowers? Carry a leaf from my garden: a rose may continue in bloom for five or six days; but this rose-garden will flourish forever.
>
> —*The Gulistan or Rose Garden by Musle-Huddeen Sheikh Saadi, of Shiraz*, translated by Francis Gladwin 1865: 104

Abbreviations

AFS	*Asian Folklore Studies*
AJMR	*The Asiatic Journal and Monthly Register for British and Foreign India, China and Australasia*
Bescheiden omtrent zijn bedrijf in Indie	*Jan Pieterszoon Coen: Bescheiden omtrent zijn bedrijf in Indie*
BSOAS	*Bulletin of the School of Oriental and African Studies*
Chau Ju-kua	*Chau Ju-kua, his work on the Chinese and Arab trade in the twelfth and thirteenth centuries, entitled Chu-fan-chi chi, translated from the Chinese and annotated by Friedrich Hirth and W.W. Rockhill*
CO 273	*Colonial Office Records (Series Straits Settlements, Original Correspondence)*
Commission of Sultan Muhyiddin Mansur Syah	*Commission Issued by Sultan Muhyiddin Mansur Syah', reproduced at length and translated by C. Skinner." In Syair Sultan Maulana 1985: Appendix E.*
Crawfurd Papers	*A collection of official records relating to the mission of Dr. John Crawfurd sent to Siam by the government of India in the year 1821*
Dagh-register	*Dagh-register gehouden int Casteel Batavia vant passerende daer ter plaetse als over geheel Nederlandts-India*
DMCMW	*The Dispatches, Minutes, and Correspondence, of the Marquess Wellesley*
Dutch Documents	*Transcripts of selected Dutch documents relating to India and the East*
Generale Missiven	*Generale Missiven van Gouverneurs-Generaal en Raden aan Heren XVII der Verenigde Oostindische Compagnie Indie*
Hadhrami Traders	*Hadhrami Traders, Scholars and Statesmen in the Indian Ocean, 1750s–1960*, edited by Ulrike Freitag and William G. Clarence-Smith

Haji Mahmud	Zaharah bt Haji Mahmud
Hikajat Potjut Muhamet	Hikajat Potjut Muhamet: An Achenese epic
HSMKP	Historical Survey of the Mosques and Kramats on Penang Island, (compiled by lecturers and members of the junior and senior history options, Malayan Teachers College)
JAH	Journal of Asian History
JAS	Journal of Asian Studies
JAIGBI	The Journal of the Anthropological Institute of Great Britain and Ireland
JAOS	Journal of the American Oriental Society
JASB	Journal of the Asiatic Society of Bengal
JIAEA	The Journal of the Indian Archipelago and Eastern Asia
JMBRAS	Journal of the Malayan (Malaysian) Branch Royal Asiatic Society
JRASBI	Journal of the Royal Asiatic Society of Great Britain and Ireland
JRGSL	Journal of the Royal Geographical Society of London
JSBRAS	Journal Straits Branch Royal Asiatic Society
JSEAH	Journal of Southeast Asian History
JSEAS	Journal of Southeast Asian Studies
JSS	Journal of the Siam Society
Koran	The Koran: with parallel Arabic text
LREIC	Letters Received by the East India Company from its Servants in the East
Mahavansi	The Mahavansi, the Raja-ratnacari, and the Raja-vali
Malay Annals	John Leyden's Malay Annals
Malayan literature	Malayan literature; comprising romantic tales, epic poetry and royal chronicles
MAS	Modern Asian Studies
Memorandum by Albinus	Memorandum by W. B. Albinus, Governor of Malacca, in 1750
MIH	Malaya in History
Muhammad Hassan	Muhammad Hassan Bin To'Kerani Mohd. Arshad

"Norton-Kyshe Cases"	Cases Heard and Determined in Her Majesty's Supreme Court of the Straits Settlements 1808–1890
OHCR	The Oriental Herald and Colonial Review
PGSC	Penang Gazette and Straits Chronicle
Phongsawadan Muang Zaiburi	Phongsawadan Muang Zaiburi (The Chronicle of Negeri Kedah)
Miscellaneous Notices	Miscellaneous Notices: The Semang and Sakei tribes of the Districts of Kedah and Perak bordering on Province Wellesley
Records of the Relations	Records of the Relations between Siam and Foreign Countries in the Seventeenth Century
Report of Governor Bort on Malacca 1678	Report of Governor Balthasar Bort on Malacca 1678, translated by M. J. Bremer with introduction and notes by C. O. Blagden."
Seventeenth-century visitors	Three seventeenth-century visitors to the Malay Peninsula, translated and edited by J. J. Sheehan
SF	Singapore Free Press
Sharifah Zaleha	Sharifah Zaleha Binte Syed Hassan
SSFR	Straits Settlements Factory Records
SSR	Straits Settlements Records
Syair Perang Siak	Syair Perang Siak; a court poem presenting the state policy of a Minangkabau Malay royal family in exile
Syair Sultan Maulana	The Battle for Junk Ceylon: The Syair Sultan Maulana
TDR	The Drama Review
The Crystal Sands	The Crystal Sands: the Chronicles of Nagara Sri Dharrmaraj, translated by David K. Wyatt
Udomsombat	Rama III and the Siamese Expedition to Kedah in 1839, The Dispatches of Luang Udomsombat

Introduction

This book proposes a new understanding of historic Southeast Asia, particularly the Malay and the Islamic world that form an important part of it (refer to Maps 1 and 2). Its focus is on the north-western Malaysian kingdom of Kedah, the oldest unbroken independent kingship line in the "Malay and Islamic world" with over 1,000 years of history. The volume highlights the impact of the Siamese invasion of 1821–1842 which devastated the state and forced the Kedah Sultan to flee to the neighboring British territory of Penang. Taking these events as a pivotal point, it examines the institution of kingship in Kedah and probes the foundations and endurance of traditional sources of power and its historical persistence in the Malay Peninsula. Thus the book examines the physical and spiritual attributes of Malay kingship together with forms of power that cemented the ruler, the peoples, and the environment. On this basis, it interrogates traditions regarding the coming of Islam to Kedah and the

Map 2. Southeast Asia.

role of the monarch among the peoples of his realm. This is a comparative study using the indigenous sources on the Islamization process and traditions in the center and the periphery of the realm. This volume also sheds much needed light on a range of important topics in Malay history including: Kedah and the northern Melaka Straits history, Britain or colonial powers expansion and rivalry, Southeast Asian history and politics, religion and society, interregional migration and the influence of the sea peoples or *orang laut*, Islamic influences as well the course of Thai-Malay relations. Beyond this, the study also takes note of Kedah's long-distance relations with states in the subcontinent and the Middle East as well as China and Europe.

Little scholarly attention has in fact been paid to Kedah's premodern history, society, religion, foundation myth, and system of government. Most Southeast Asian scholars have similarly neglected the significance of Kedah's network of overland and trans-peninsular routes, and its implications for the state's distinctive political structure. The book therefore offers a new understanding, not only of Kedah, but of the political and cultural development of the Malay world and of its relationships with the broader forces in both its continental and maritime settings. In particular, Kedah's unique geographic situation, potentially controlling both land and sea lines of communication to the remainder of Southeast Asia, is remarkable.

The book provides the first comprehensive treatment in English, or other languages, on Kedah's premodern and nineteenth century history and can provide a foundation for comparative studies of the various Malay states, Islamic history and indigenous political systems which are presently lacking. The attempt in the book to unravel the premodern sociopolitical and religious history of Kedah, as well links to the various Malay states is especially significant as the indigenous and foreign sources and reports of it are often criticized by most Southeast Asian scholars for being scanty, quasi-mythical, illogical, invented and sketchy in details and accurate dates. Similarly the ambiguity of indigenous Malay sources on names, events, royal progeny or succession and precise dates; as well their style of compilation, deliverance, narrative and mode of Islamic conversion has been further dismissed or treated with caution by most of their modern Malay readers and students. But as it will be argued in the book and discussed elsewhere by Hendrik J. M. Maier (1988), the authorship of the indigenous Malay sources, their purpose, readership, symbolism, audiences, religious significance and transformation, concept of time and morality were often significantly different to a postmodern or contemporary one. The Malay indigenous sources and their stories or events deemed as implausible or quasi-mythical in contemporary times should therefore not be dismissed or rejected, rather examined in a different light and in accordance to the time that they were written and copied or improved upon. This volume thus sifts through an eclectic number of indigenous and foreign primary sources, reports and archival documents in order to extricate and offer a number of answers to a number of key questions on the historiography of the region by:

- Fulfilling the need for a scholarly study of Kedah's pre-twentieth century history
- Challenging the commonly accepted Malay model, as conceived by J. M. Gullick and A. C. Milner
- Bringing forth Kedah as an active participant in a global economic and political system and offering a means to break through the parochialism that generally characterizes Malay studies
- The discussion of the covenant/social contract in the manuscript challenges the royalist paradigm that is part of the Gullick/Milner model and forces us to look at traditional Malay political life in a new light
- Highlighting Kedah's geographical setting by providing an innovative look at the manner in which premodern Kedah functioned as a political and social economy
- The view from within of how traditionally the Malay populace and political infrastructure viewed themselves and the spiritual-physical world around them
- Making an attempt to deconstruct and disentangle indigenous Malay sources when dealing with a complex admixture of quasi-mythical periods, personage, and events

The religious issue at Kedah is of particular interest. Not only does Kedah have the largest number of pre-Islamic Hindu-Buddhist stone structures in the Malay Peninsula but also the recent discovery of two Muslim graves at Kedah, belonging to people of presumably Persian origin, dated 214 AH (826–829 CE) and 291 AH (903/904 CE), may suggest the earliest presence of Muslims in Southeast Asia (Wan Hussein 1980: 135–137; Yatim 1985: 143–144; Bruce 1996: 73; Sheikh Niamat and Haji Wan Shamsudin 1996: 4; Allen 1998: 274; Nik Hassan Shuhaimi and Nik Abdul Rahman 2007: 47–49, 54). Furthermore, Kedah as the oldest unbroken independent kingship line in the "Malay world" is arguably the oldest in the Islamic world. With its own unique royal lineage (tracing itself to the mythical land of Rum or Persia) in the Malay world, it does not trace its founder to Alexander the Great or through the Palembang-Melaka-Johor line. The migration issue at Kedah is similarly significant since no one else has attempted to explain historic migrations of sea peoples (indigenous *orang laut* or else Bugis-Makassar, Ilanun, and Siak-Minangkabau) to Kedah and into the northern Melaka Straits.

Historic Kedah and its power structure embody many of the dynamics and developments that influenced and shaped other Malay territories along the Melaka Straits and in island Southeast Asia. Yet Kedah's geopolitical, spiritual and environmental features distinguish it from other states. It does not fit the riverine models for the Malay sultanates put forward by Gullick (1958) and Milner (1982) that have dominated much of the historic scholarship on the Malay world for the past fifty years. I believe these authors fail to sufficiently appreciate the maritime aspects of Malay states and kingship; as well the great range of variations and tensions between indigenous structures. Similarly Gullick and Milner pay little attention to what the Malay peoples saw as important limitations on royal power. Rather they analyze the indigenous political system solely from the royalist point of view.

Furthermore, the contradictions and tensions in the Malay world highlighted by Carl A. Trocki, J. N. Miksic, Jane Drakard, and Timothy P. Barnard, unique in their own way, can each be applied to Kedah. The book will therefore focus on Kedah's role as an entrepot and communications hub linking the commercial and spiritual culture of the Indian Ocean and the Bay of Bengal to that of the Malay world and the South China Sea. These variations, contradictions, and tensions are significant for further understanding and analysis of indigenous political systems persisting in the "Malay world." My findings raise fundamental questions about the historiography of the Malay world. Just how valid is the standard model? Is it even possible to come up with a single model to describe the multitude of sultanates that were scattered through the Malay world in the premodern and colonial period? This volume proposes a new conceptualization of the history and traditional political systems of the "Malay world." It is divided into four chapters dealing with Kedah's spiritual (Chapter 1), physical, and environmental context (Chapters 3 and 4) that reconceptualize Malay indigenous political systems and shows how Malay rulers traditionally maintained control of their environments and how they were viewed by their people (Chapter 2). It concludes that the ruling dynasty has historically exploited a wide range of unique environmental conditions, local traditions, global spiritual trends and economic forces to preserve and strengthen its political position.

NARRATIVE: THE 1821 SIAMESE INVASION

It was Sunday afternoon, November 12, 1821, when a large fleet of Siamese ships unexpectedly anchored off Kedah's main port of Kuala Kedah (Anderson 1824: 2–10; Newbold 1971 II: 7–8; Gullick 1983: 31; refer to Map 3). The Siamese explained the presence of this armada on Kedah's doorstep, as merely a brief stopover to procure supplies of rice for a surprise expedition against Siam's enemy, the Burmese. But the real objective of the Siamese visit soon became apparent when a heavily armed landing party slipped ashore and was then supported by more troops entering Kedah's inland frontiers from the northern and eastern borders. The audacious Siamese assault on Kedah was well coordinated, swift,

Map 3. Kedah in about 1810 CE.

and cruel. Thus began the full-scale military invasion and occupation of Kedah by Siam that ensued for the next two decades, ending in 1841.

Realizing the Siamese intention to capture him, Kedah's Sultan Ahmad Taju'ddin Halim Syah (acceded to the throne in 1803 and died in about 1845 CE, see Gullick 1983: 81n) fled for safety into the adjoining British territory of Penang.[1] The Sultan's getaway was soon followed by the flight of thousands of Kedah's native population into Penang Island and Province Wellesley.

It is believed that from 1821 to 1823 about 11,000 Kedah refugees made it to the Island of Penang, which then had a population of about 40,000, while another 9,000 settled in Province Wellesley, that had a population of about 4,000 to 5,000 (Low 1836: 125–126; Gullin and Zehnder 1905: 43; Lee Chye Hooi 1957; Ahmat 1984: 4). With their arrival, Malays then constituted the greater part of the population of Penang. These were predominantly rural Malays escaping the Siamese onslaught.[2] James Low (1836: 125–126), an English official at Province Wellesley, reports that the Malay population of the Island of Penang had jumped to 16,435, in a total population of 40,207 in the early 1830s, while at the same time they constituted a staggering 42,500 people, out of 46,880, in Province Wellesley.

The situation at Kedah rapidly deteriorated. Little is known about the precise population of pre-1821 Kedah, with estimates ranging from 40,000 to 180,000 (Newbold 1971 II: 20; Gullick 1983: 36; Ahmat 1984: 3). But by one estimate the population was reduced to less than 6,000 during the first six years of Siamese rule ("Quedah, and Tuanku Mahomed Saad" in *AJMR* 1841: 110). Low (1836: 128; 1850: 366) suggests a more realistic estimate of about 20,000 by the early 1830s, with about 70,000 Kedah Malays living at Penang. It is believed that thousands of Kedah's population either perished or were enslaved during and after the Siamese invasion of 1821.[3] Attempts by the Siamese to settle Siamese cultivators and other peoples in Kedah appear to have had only limited success (Logan 1881: 90; Banks 1983: 12–13). Hence by the time of Low's comment on Kedah's population in the 1830s it appears that only a small portion of its original population was still residing there, and that most had moved to the adjoining British territory of Penang. In an 1839 Siamese dispatch Rama III (1824–1851), the Siamese ruler, acknowledged the depopulation of Kedah and the flight of its population into Penang since the invasion: "In the case of Kedah, three-quarters of the inhabitants have gone over into British territory and we have only been able to hold on to a quarter of the population. And a lot of these have been brought up here as captives, so there aren't many left" (14th dispatch, Udomsombat 1993: 248).

According to Rama III, Kedah should not be abandoned: "If we abandoned Kedah, we would be losing a considerable source of revenue and the British would pick it up and annex it; we cannot treat the matter lightly" (12th dispatch, Udomsombat 1993: 210).

Yet several attempts by the Siamese to repopulate Kedah and reconstitute a system of government had failed miserably. In fact soon after the Siamese invasion of 1821 they replaced the Sultan with his uncle and predecessor, Tunku Diauddin or Ziaudin (died 1822), whom they had earlier deposed in 1803 (Burney 1971 II part IV: 173; Gullick 1983: 34). However, the British and the native population refused to recognize the puppet ruler and the Siamese then dispensed with him and tried to govern Kedah without Malay intermediaries until 1839 (Gullick 1983: 34).

Following a Malay uprising in 1838–1839 and the recapture of Kedah for six months, by Tenghku Mohammed Saad, the nephew of the ex-Sultan, it became necessary for the Siamese to re-examine their hold on Kedah. Rama III and his council proposed that the only way to repopulate the state and avoid further British expansion was to restore Kedah as a Malay state and recognize a new ruler. In response to a letter from the governor of Songkhla, the Siamese ruler cautioned:

> To organize the state without having anyone in authority as its ruler will simply mean that there is no state. If he expects the headman in each district to get the people now living in British territory to come back, so that every district has a population of some four to five thou-

sand people, this is something we shall never see in our life-time. (14th dispatch, see Udomsombat 1993: 249)

It was therefore acknowledged that Kedah needed a legitimate Malay ruler in order to bring about the return of its refugee population. Furthermore, Rama III maintained that these changes would end all claims to Kedah by the British and the exiled Sultan (14th dispatch, see Udomsombat 1993: 252). Thus the new ruler was to be Malay, from amongst the old aristocracy, with some repute and trustworthiness to the Siamese, hence not the ex-Sultan. Moreover, the Siamese would legitimize this new ruler with a set of royal regalia sent to him from Bangkok hoping that "now that we have sent them this sort of regalia, he can hardly fail to set it up as a state" (see the 14th and 15th dispatches, dated 28th of July and 15th of August 1839 respectively, in Udomsombat 1993: 233–261). It was thought that this would ultimately bring prosperity and people back to Kedah. There was however some concern amongst some of the senior Siamese ministers. In particular the Siamese Treasurer pointed out that " there is no Kedah Malay with any real power—there are only people with a limited amount of power—just enough to be made district headman." (14th dispatch, dated 28th of July 1839, Udomsombat 1993: 247)

Despite this, the plans went ahead. Thus Kedah was divided into four parts with Tengku Anom, a relation of the ex-Sultan, designated as the ruler of Kedah; while Tengku Hasan, Tengku Mat Akip and Said Hussein became the rulers of Kubang Pasu, Satun (contemporary Satun in southern Thailand) and Perlis respectively (Ratanapun 1961: 12; Prince Damrong Rachanuphap's 1906 addition on the "Developments subsequent to 'The Dispatches' in Udomsombat" 1993: Appendix A). The Siamese plan had little success and the idea of bringing prosperity and people back to Kedah remained wishful thinking (Asiatic Intelligence, *AJMR* 1840: 112; Gullick 1983: 50–52). According to confidential "native accounts" of Kedah under these new Malay rulers in 1840:

> Recent native accounts, confidently to be depended upon, from this ill-fated country, once the "abode of peace and plenty," represent it now to be almost deserted; that the few Malayan inhabitants still left there are in the most wretched condition and daily emigrating . . . suffering under the greatest hardship through the misrule and rapacities [sic] of the two Malayan chieftains, Tengku Anom and Tengku Hassan, who have been placed by the Siamese authorities in the temporary government of Kedah, . . . Indeed, the unfortunate inhabitants execrate their present ruler and his voracious dependants, and declare that what they suffered under the Siamese dominion were blessings compared with that which is their lot to endure now. Hence the numerous emigration which have lately taken place from Kedah to Province Wellesley and the Siamese authorities adjoining our boundaries. (Asiatic Intelligence, *AJMR* 1840: 213)

In actual fact the population of Kedah only recovered after 1842 following the Siamese decision of 1841 to permit the return of the Sultan, (Khan 1939: 43; Adil 1980: 71; Ahmat 1984: 4). Enquiries made by J. R. Logan, a British government official, during his visit to Kedah in 1850 revealed that the state had a total population of 11,300 (this figure includes Perlis and Satun, see Logan 1851: 55–56). But these figures were estimates only, and it is not clear if they included the returned Kedah Malays or those that were born outside of Kedah.[4] By contrast, in a recent scholarly study on the nineteenth century population of Kedah, Zaharah bt Haji Mahmud (1972: 96) contends that by the 1850s the population of Kedah had reached its pre-invasion level. Haji Mahmud (1972a: 193–209) concludes that unlike most other Malay states in the second half of the nineteenth century, the rise in the population of Kedah had little to do with immigration from Sumatra, China, India or elsewhere. In a separate study of Kedah in the second half of the nineteenth century, Sharom Ahmat (1970: 115–128) similarly attributes Kedah's unmatched peace, administration, and economic prosperity in the Malay Peninsula to its rulers and its large predominantly homogenous indigenous Malay population. Gullick (1983: 64), on the other hand, believes that Kedah remained "an uninhabited waste-land" until the 1850s when disturbances in other neighboring states forced people to migrate to the vacant lands of Kedah. Gullick suggests that Kedah remained depopulated since the bulk of the Malay refugees in Province Wellesley preferred to stay there rather than return to Kedah. He argues (1983: 64) that the soil at Province Wellesley was superior to that of Kedah; British rule offered protection, stability, and freedom; political uncertainty continued in Kedah despite the return of the Sultan and finally the old Kedah chiefs, the *penghulus*, were now substantial landlords in Province Wellesley hence forcing people under them (the *rakyat*[5] or peasants or common folk) to remain.

Gullick is correct to suggest that the old Kedah chiefs were, by the time of the return of the ex-Sultan to Kedah, substantial landlords in Province Wellesley. It is also likely that with the political uncertainty surrounding the return of the ex-Sultan and the distrust of the Siamese many returning Kedah refugees born at Penang or at Kedah would keep their options open by maintaining links to Province Wellesley. This would have enabled them to slip across the border back into British territory if there was a future assault on Kedah. Besides, having been born in Penang, or being resident there, would have meant that they could be considered naturalized British subjects and could exercise further legal privileges when travelling to various parts of Siam and Southeast Asia. Hence it could further be argued that many Kedah refugees would have wanted to be considered Penang residents, for political and social reasons, while living or visiting Kedah.

On the other hand, the assumption that the Kedah refugees would prefer to remain in Province Wellesley and not return home to Kedah is questionable.[6] Indeed, from the time the ex-Sultan fled to Penang in 1821 and during the subsequent revolts and uprisings of 1823–1824, 1828–1829, 1831–1832, and 1838–1839, Kedah refugees had always stood by their ruler and never deserted him in his unequivocal determination to return there (Anderson 1824; Gullin and Zehnder 1905: 43; Wheatly 1961: 388; Newbold 1971 II: 13–14, 19; Milner 1979/1980: 1–15; Osborn 1987). Indeed in the 1838 assault on the Siamese at Kedah by the ex-Sultan's nephew Tengku Muhammad Saad the *Penang Gazette and Straits Chronicle* (dated 3rd of November 1838) reported that 10,000–12,000 Malays had initially entered Kedah from all directions, while another source mentioned about 4,000 Malays in 1839, headed by several of the Penghulu Mukims, emigrating from Province Wellesley ("Quedah, and Tuanku Mahomed Saad" in *AJMR* 1841: 114). Thus it would have been strange that with the Sultan's return to Kedah in 1841–1842 the Kedah refugees at Penang would suddenly decide to remain there and not want to return.

Furthermore, Logan (1846: 318–319, 322) during his visit to Province Wellesley in 1845 reported that the price of land and rent there had fallen sharply. This he attributed principally to the return of the Malayan chiefs to Kedah. Additionally Logan (1846: 318–319) notes that other Kedah Malays were also selling their land and property cheaply (e.g., in the case of Sungei Susat) or renting their properties (particularly to the Chinese) in order to return home to Kedah. Consequently as this 1845 report by Logan indicates the departure of Kedah Malays from Province Wellesley was not solely restricted to 1841–1842 when the Sultan was allowed by the Siamese to return. Hence it is probable that many Malays in their distrust of Siamese intentions decided to delay their return to Kedah. Likewise it may be pointed out that many Kedah people upon returning to Kedah continued to keep their property at Province Wellesley and only sold it or rented it out much later. Two decades later John Cameron (1865: 331), an English visitor to Province Wellesley, notes that the Malays there were in character and disposition in "some measure of alliance with their Siamese rulers." It is likely that the Malays that Cameron met were the ex-Kedah refugees and their descendants that despite living in British territory still continued to pay allegiance to the Sultan of Kedah, now under Siamese suzerainty.

Similarly Logan in an 1867 letter addressed to Colonel A. E. H. Anson, the Lieutenant-Governor of Penang, reports on the Malays of Province Wellesley that "at present their personal devotion is chiefly bestowed on their religious leaders and on connections of the royal family of Kedah" (Logan 1885: 186).

By the 1870s, conditions in Kedah had also improved markedly and as argued by Thamsook Ratanapun (1961: 13–24), Haji Mahmud (1972a: 196–200) and Ahmat (1970: 115–128, 1984) continued well into the early years of the twentieth century. British official, Frank Swettenham, in 1874 commented that Kedah "was more advanced in its institutions in the observance of order, the well-being of its people, and in the general development of the country, than any other state in the Peninsula" (Swettenham 1906: 311).

Similarly the Thai source of *Phongsawadan Muang Zaiburi*, written predominantly in the nineteenth century, reports that in the 1870s the Siamese ruler was extremely impressed with the improvements of Kedah during his royal visit: "His Majesty saw how well Phraya Zaiburi [i.e., the Siamese official title for the Sultan of Kedah] has developed and improved the general condition of the State. There are now more than ever brick-buildings and other commercial establishments which vouch for the prosperity and happiness [of Kedah]" (1990: 102).

Kedah's royalty therefore appear to have continued to have influence and be of consequence to the Malays of Penang well after the return of Kedah's ruler in 1842. It is evident that most of Kedah's population left following the flight of Sultan Ahmad to Penang in 1821 and later returned following his return to Kedah. These circumstances testify to the depth and durability of the Kedah ruler's influence.

The core of Kedah's history is thus the extraordinary survival of the ruling dynasty, unmatched in other parts of the Malay and the Islamic world. Here we are not simply concerned with the institution of Kedah's kingship, but with a single dynasty said to be descendants of a foreign visitor "Merong Mahawangsa." A key factor in the survival of this royal line was the loyalty of its subjects. While they might be willing to dethrone an individual Sultan or to support the challenge of a pretender who claimed royal descent, they did not question the right of the royal house to rule over them. The 1771 revolt against the Sultan, by elements within his family and Bugis mercenaries from Selangor, is reported to have failed simply because people remained loyal and continued to be the ruler's "friend" (see *SSR* 35, 25th June 1772, Monckton to Ft St George). Similarly, in 1831, in recapturing Kedah from the Siamese, a number of Malay refugees at Province Wellesley justified their return to Kedah (hence avoiding "punishment" by the British) saying that they were simply "following our king in his return to our country" (*SSR* F5, 1831: 240–2, Letter from the Malay *rakyat* to the Governor of Penang).[7]

ANALYSIS OF "MODELS" OF THE MALAY "WORLD"

The contemporary Southeast Asian concept of the state as a territorial unit or a political center with clearly defined borders and divisions is believed to be a nineteenth- and twentieth-century phenomena. This is argued by Southeast Asian scholars to be a result of the rise of European concept of the nation-state, and nationalism during the period of European colonization in Southeast Asia. Scholars such as Trocki (2000) and Eric Tagliacozzo (2005) have gone as far as documenting instances in which late nineteenth century Malay rulers of the region realized the need to utilize the new European concepts of borders to their advantage. This transformation from traditional native understanding of borders, statehood and authority into a European one is significant and had much to do with expanding political and economic gains of native rulers.

Rollins Bonney (1971: 4–5) in his study of late eighteenth and early nineteenth century Kedah, has shown, how a European power (Britain) enforced its understandings of nation-state and borders and undermined the traditional Malay political concepts of borders (both at land and sea). These were far less rigid and focused more on people than on property. Conversely, it is possible that some limited understanding of manmade borders as abstract lines, similar to modern concepts of borders and nation-states did prevail earlier than the second half of the nineteenth century, at least in parts of Southeast Asia. According to an early nineteenth century Malay work from Kedah, *Syair Sultan Maulana* (1985: 236–237) written circa 1809–11, the invading Burmese army was chased and forced to retreat by both the Kedah army and their allies (as well as Siamese forces) to the *"peringgan berterat"* (translated as the "border markers"). From this passage it is not entirely clear what was the form or type of the "border markers"; nor, it is possible to conclude if this form of division was understood only in this area, or if it was practiced amongst the Malays or if its origin was a result of contact with European powers or through European advisers.[8]

Furthermore, the question of whom or what can historically be considered as "Malay" is a difficult one to answer (see the discussion by Cummings 1998: 107–121). Virginia Matheson Hooker best explain this in which:

> it should be understood, however, that the category "Malay" is a very fluid one, not defined by physical characteristics, but by language, dress, customs and, most importantly, by the profession of Islam. None of these characteristics is innate, in the sense that an individual is born with them. Each can be adopted and it is now recognized that it is possible to "become" a Malay by assuming these characteristics. (2003: 21–22)

Gullick (1991: 2–3) argues that historically this "Malay world" only covered the Malay Peninsula and the northeast of Sumatra in which a "sense of Malay-ness" created a cultural unity despite the absence of political unity. This cultural unity is according to Gullick represented in a common: "language, religion, way of life, agricultural economy, and political culture (in the sense that the presence of a Malay raja—the situation of kerajaan—was indispensable)" [sic] (1991: 3).

I would also include other regions as part of the "Malay world" which include the Cham people (in contemporary Southern Vietnam), stateless Malay seafarers (e.g., *orang laut*), most indigenous tribes (*orang asli*), all of eastern Sumatra and the kingdoms of the southern Philippines and coastal Borneo. These all show similar cultural and linguistic traits to the geographical areas mentioned by Gullick (1991). In their study of historic Barus (in the Minangkabau region) and Siak in Sumatra Drakard (1990: vii) and Bernard (2003: 5–6) have independently demonstrated the extent of ambiguity in what areas constitute conventional Malay areas and systems as argued by Gullick (1958, 1991). Thus in the study of the "Malay world" one must acknowledge the extent of what or who can historically constitute or be part of the larger "Malay world." In the words of Trocki: "Not all of them (i.e., the Malay states) were exactly the same, but they inhabited the same political and cultural universe and they were in more-or-less regular touch with one another, and thus shared a common world view" (2000).

This shared "common world view" as mentioned by Trocki (2000) can further be argued by expanding Benedict Anderson's (1983: 14–16) theory of "imagined communities" to the historic Malay population of Southeast Asia. This notion would also perhaps explain the flexibility of Malay groups in moving from one Malay kingship and polity to another without being considered a traitor or renegade from their former place of residence and authority as discussed by Milner (1995: 21–24). Nevertheless, this study accepts the idea of a hypothetical pre–nineteenth century "Malay world" encompassing the Malay Peninsula and much of island Southeast Asia.

Essentially the traditional indigenous history of the pre–nineteenth century "Malay world" can be divided into two equally significant and interrelated periods: an Islamic and a pre-Islamic or Hindu-Buddhist period.

Little is known however about the earlier period, or about the symbolism and indigenous political systems that existed prior to the arrival of Islam and Islamic influences in Southeast Asia (Wolters 1979: 15). What is known however about the early history and formation of states or political units in the "Malay world" is that they were predominantly based on the coasts and river basins. And that from about the sixth to the fifteenth century CE many of these settlements were at least for short periods of time loosely unified to form the greater Srivijaya and/or Majapahit confederacies. Pierre-Yves Manguin (1993: 24–45) suggests that these confederacies consisted of "ship-shape societies" that were coastal-based, organized into small political systems and relied upon water-borne communications and trade for food and their socioeconomic sustenance.

Furthermore, it is believed that the majority of the pre-Islam native population of these coastal settlements consisted chiefly of fishermen, mariners and seafarers practicing an admixture of Hinduism, Buddhism, Tantric beliefs, animism, or ancestor worship. Yet another aspect unique to virtually all corners of Southeast Asia was the semi-divine or near-divine attributes associated with the local kings or Rajas (Winstedt 1947: 129–139; Heine-Geldern 1956: 3, 6–8; Osborne 1997: 39–45).

The "Malay Models" of Gullick and Milner

For the past fifty years the historical scholarship on the Malay World has been dominated by a particular model of the Malay Sultanates, as discussed in detail by Gullick's 1958 study and Milner's 1982 research. Gullick is perhaps one of the earliest scholars to have studied traditional pre–nineteenth century Malay politics and Muslim society, in his book "Indigenous Political Systems of Western Malaya." This study has been scrutinized and discussed amongst more recent scholars to a great extent. Central to his model has been his discussion of traditional pre–nineteenth century "riverine states" in the "Malay world" (particularly Perak, Selangor, Negeri Sembilan and Pahang). According to Gullick (1958: 21) the largest Malay political unit was the *negeri*. The *negeri*, Gullick writes, was "typically the basin of a large river or (less often) of a group of adjacent rivers, forming a block of land extending from the coast inland to the central watershed. The capital of the state was the point at which the main river ran into the sea" (1958: 21).

Next in size came the district (translating it as *jajahan* or *daerah*). It too was founded on one or both sides of a river. Thus, Gullick (1958: 21) argues that in both instances the river was used as the main line of communication and trade.

Within any of these indigenous Malay political systems or *negeri* Gullick (1958: 44) observed, "Government was *kerajaan*, the state of having a ruler, and they visualized no other system." According to Gullick's (1958: 44–45) analysis, the ruler (referred normally as Raja, *Yang di-Pertuan* and Sultan) did not exercise substantial administrative authority, his role, rather, was to "symbolize and to some extent to preserve the unity of the State" with an "aura of sanctity and supernatural power." The "aura" of sanctity Gullick identifies in Malay as *daulat*, a quality that was exclusive to enthroned rulers. Hence, he (1958: 44–46) continues that the *"daulat"* distinguished the ruler from ordinary men, and this position was marked by a variety of prohibitions, ceremonies, and insignia which were exclusive to the ruler.

The lines of political power and control emanating from these riverine-based settlements Gullick argues were short and only extended to the nearest mountain, or hill. In addition, Gullick observed that the riverine Malay settlements generally survived through small scale agriculture, as well as depended on goods and items exchanged or purchased from the local aborigines, or *orang asli*, living in the forests and close to inland streams and rivers.

In his 1982 and 1995 studies of indigenous political systems in the traditional and colonial Malay world, predominantly Deli and Pahang,

Milner attempts to re-examine the notion of state and government. Hence from a study of historic and contemporary documents, including court-based literature, Milner (1995: 104) realized that only during the nineteenth and twentieth centuries was the term *negeri* employed for "state." This confirmed Gullick's (1958: 21) earlier argument that the Malay word *negeri* and "state" became synonymous from the nineteenth century onward. Milner however found that prior to the nineteenth century, "there had been no clear concept of 'state' as distinct from *kerajaan*; even countries outside the Malay world were described as *kerajaan*" (1995: 104).

Milner (1982: 31–32; 1995: 21–24) then concludes that the key to understanding traditional Malay politics is the concept of *kerajaan* or, as he defines it, "the condition of having a raja." Thus, the raja, rather than the *negeri*, or the territory, was central to the very notion of the Malay political system. In Milner's own words the *"kerajaan"* is not a "state" but "the condition of having a Raja. The Raja, not the Malay race or the Islamic ummat (community) was the primary object of loyalty; he was the primary object of loyalty; he was central to every aspect of Malay life" (1982: 31–32).

Milner (1982: 94–95; 1995: 24) then suggests that the indispensability of a raja in Malay life and to the survival of a polity is expressed in Malay responses to a situation of "Raja-less." In such cases of a kingdom without a raja it is equated with "utter confusion" (or in Malay referred to as *"sangatlah huru-haranya"*) and could lead to ultimate "anarchy" (Milner 1982: 104, 109; 1995: 16–24). On the other hand, Milner (1995: 21, 24) considers that the success of *kerajaan* within a traditional Malay political entity in attaining population, power, and wealth and preventing treason (*derhaka*) was in terms of its capacity to satisfy the requirements of *nama*, that is, to reputation, title or name on the part of its key subjects.

Since the publication of Gullick's and Milner's works several scholars have conceded that the above models should not obscure the existence of tensions and variations within the commonly perceived "Malay model."

Tensions and Variations in the Accepted "Malay Models"

Writing sometime later than Gullick (1958), on the state of Kedah also in western Malay Peninsula, Bonney (1971: 8–9, 9n) finds it difficult to agree entirely with the use of rivers as the main lines of communication. In a footnote he refers to this remark as an "over-simplification" since "detailed information on the subject is lacking." Nevertheless, Bonney gives an example on why one should try to avoid over-simplification, as he believed Gullick had done earlier. Referring to the Muslim period in the pre–nineteenth century "Malay world" Bonney (1971: 9n) discusses a more "intricate and dynamic system," such as a parish style division called a *"mukim"* only qualified by having a Mosque, and based largely on Muslim "ecclesiastical" divisions.

Writing several years after Bonney, Bennet Bronson (1977: 39–52) attempts to establish an overall political and economic model for any Southeast Asian coastal state, which had a riverine structure. Subsequently, he argues that the river was the main line of communication and consisted of an upriver exchange network connected with foreign trade networks at the coastal centers. Furthermore, on the lifespan of the royal centers controlling coastal polities and river-based settlements Bronson (1977: 49), in his model, is of the opinion that they were always evanescent.

O. W. Wolters (1979) has reservations about aspects of Bronson's model. According to Wolters (1979: 20) the traditional maritime centers and entrepots, such as the case of Srivijaya, did not solely rely on trade or exchange of regional riverine produce with the outside world. Likewise they did not rely solely on the nearby river systems as the main lines of communication. Rather, Wolters argues that these coastal centers were able to attract foreign goods or products, through the control of international maritime trade routes. Thus in essence these entrepots were used as meeting places and exchange centers for foreign traders, often with little dependency on local riverine products. Nevertheless, Wolters (1979: 19–20) maintains that wealth and capital generated foremost from the international maritime trade routes, from trade or exchange of local or foreign products, enhanced the prestige of the ruler. In the words of Wolters: "Foreign treasures would have enabled the ruler to maintain a glittering court and honor his entourage" (1979: 20).

Moreover, Wolters disagrees with Bronson on the overall lifespan of the royal centers in his model. Hence, he argues, "royal centers may have shifted from one river basin to another, but former royal centers would not be permanently deserted; instead they would be ruled by vassals" (Wolters 1979: 21).

Trocki, in his 1979 study of Johor argued for a further distinction in the historic "Malay world," between the riverine and maritime-based polities. Trocki (1979: xvi–xvii) is of the opinion that the maritime system or empire was essentially based on an entrepot or "trading city," with its lines of control, as discussed earlier by Wolters (1979), being the "sea routes" that "were strung out from island to island and from one river mouth to another." The "trading city" or the center of the maritime system Trocki (1979: xvi–xvii) continues was ruled by the Sultan who exercised power through a grouping of officials or chiefs. These groupings of officials or chiefs Trocki believes had at their core the "sea lords" that often dominated the office of the Sultanate as well, such as in Johor/Riau and Sulu, but were different to the actual chiefs (i.e., the *penghulus* and the *panglima*) of the tribes or the sea peoples. Moreover, the sea lords he continues exercised control over the *orang laut* or sea peoples who helped command international and local trade. Hence, by forming alliances with the *orang laut* the sea lords of the maritime state intended to dominate the riverine states and stretches of coastline with their naval forces. In return for rendering their services to the Sultan and for being and staying loyal, Trocki (1979: xvi; 2005: 10–11) maintains that both financial and symbolic rewards were bestowed upon the sea lords and the sea peoples.

The above-mentioned "sea routes" Trocki (1979: xvi–xviii) argues were indispensable to the political, social, and economic survival of the entrepot, since it was generally isolated and surrounded by dense forests and unproductive or dead lands. Consequently the "sea routes" offered the "trading city" virtually all its goods for the international trade and were its main lines of communication outside the maritime center. Moreover, the "sea routes" Trocki (1979: xvi, xviii) maintains, had a further pivotal role for the well-being and sustenance of the population of the maritime entrepot; since it was the main route through which most of its provisions entered from overseas, as well as from the nearby riverine territorial units or *negeri*, often under its political control. In both instances, Trocki (1979: xvi) comments the "sea routes" benefited both the ruler and his subjects since the trade provided "wealth to the ruler and food to his subjects."

Similarly, Trocki (1979: xvii–xviii) concedes that trade was important to both the riverine and maritime systems as a source of wealth and a standard of living. Nonetheless, drawing on Wolters (1970; 1979: 19–20; 1982: 23) insight into the significance of wealth and its redistribution within historic Srivijaya, Trocki (1979: xvii–xviii) recognizes that wealth was much more critical to the survival and endurance of a maritime, than to a riverine system, given that it was in reality what kept the "fragile" empire intact. Hence, Trocki argues that wealth generated through trade, by the center of the maritime system, greatly benefited the living conditions and sustenance of its population as well as contributing toward its riverine dependencies. In the words of Trocki with regard to Johor and the majority of Malay territories: "Any decline in trade revenues seriously endangered the state's food supply, since food for these entrepot cities had always to be imported from Siam and Java" (1979: xviii).

In addition, Trocki (1979: xvi) suggests that the attractiveness and rise of the maritime entrepot in the "Malay world" was enhanced by its "geography," located halfway along the east-west Asian trade route. Combined with the "seasonal monsoons" this "land below the wind was a natural stopping place."

In contrast to the maritime system, Trocki (1979: xvii) argues that the riverine system consisted solely of riverine territorial units or *negeri*, such as Perak or Selangor in the Malay Peninsula, that were on the periphery of the great "trading cities" like Melaka, Srivijaya, and Johor/Riau and "drew their wealth from the trade passing along their rivers." Hence, to the entrepot Trocki argues, these riverine systems were of secondary importance, with their chiefs considered as the "second level." Nevertheless, despite their political isolation Trocki (1979: xvii) believes that the chiefs in the riverine *negeri* were able to exercise much autonomy particularly when the center was weak and even could "rise up out of the hinterland" and seek "power at the centre." Herewith, it should be noted that despite the entrepot's political view of the riverine *negeri* as secondary; yet, the latter's economic and basic importance in supplying the center with various food, trade goods and even people—or perhaps labor— should not be neglected. The riverine system's ability to supply the center included its ability to conduct some form of agriculture and trade with the population, primarily subgroups of the *orang asli* or aboriginal tribes, surrounding the *negeri*. In a later work Trocki describes the population surrounding the *negeri* to be "sparsely inhabited by 'tribal' peoples, hunter-gatherers, *orang laut*, swidden farmers and even wet-rice growing peasants, most of whom were in some sort of dependency relationship with a nearby chief or raja" [*sic*] (2000, 2005).

In consequence, Trocki's study sheds further insight into traditional systems, the contrasts between the maritime systems and the riverine system, as found in the historic "Malay world." Moreover, he further draws attention to inland areas surrounding a riverine territorial unit and their economic significance.

The shortcoming of identifying the river systems as the only form of communication, as argued by Bonney (1971) and Trocki (1979, 2000) is further demonstrated in the historic case of the Minangkabau region of western Sumatra. According to Miksic (1989: 11), the traditional settlements of the Minangkabau were based in the mountain valleys with the villages (*nagari*) rather than a town or a marine polity as its center. Thus in the case of both the historic Minangkabau region and other mountain settlements of the "Malay world" it is therefore difficult to assume riverine systems as the sole forms of communication.

Drakard (1990) in principle agrees with Milner's (1982, 1995) model in giving precedence to the concept of *kerajaan* within the traditional Malay system. Yet, Drakard (1990: Preface) concedes that this model should not obscure the existence of inconsistencies within Malay culture. Since she maintains from her study of Barus in western Sumatra that its geographical and historical circumstances provoke issues which do not resolve along the lines of the conventional Malay "*kerajaan*" and which are explored and seemingly debated its indigenous literature. Thus in the case of Barus, Drakard (1990: 1) discovers two ruling families, one designated downstream (*hilir*) and another upstream (*Hulu*), in which they "ruled the kingdom, together, in rotation, or in a state where one family managed to eclipse the other for a period." Moreover, she attributes much of the survival of these ruling families to their hinterland links. With each of them deriving significant support and recognition from "different sections of the upland population and lines of loyalty existed between hinterland and coast which, in some degree, explain the survival of both families" (Drakard 1990: 24).

What's more, Drakard (1990) in the case of western Sumatra disagrees with the focus on rivers as the main lines of communication. Drakard (1990: 13) notes that, "in northwest Sumatra pathways rather than waterways provided the most important means of communication with the interior." Thus Drakard (1990) confirms Bonney's (1971) earlier argument that rivers were not the only forms of communication in the Malay political system.

In his study of seventeenth century Siak, eastern Sumatra, Barnard (2003) has shown how a number of small *negeri*, traditionally under the political control of Johor, were able to work together and henceforth unite, in principle, under the leadership of an adventurer named Raja Kecik, forming the polity of Siak, located on one of the main rivers in the area.

In addition a further aspect of Barnard's study has been the internal and external factors impacting the *negeri*'s fragile pact, systems of government and shifts amongst the Siak polity. In particular Barnard (2003) discusses historic reports, myths, and legends surrounding Raja Kecik's birth, marriages, adventures, and ability to attract a diverse base of followers, chiefly the *orang laut* or the sea peoples. This he continues made Raja Kecik an exceptional figure in regional history, as well as a contender to succeed the Palembang-Melaka and Johor dynasty following the regicide of 1699. Barnard therefore uncovers economic, social, political, and environmental motivations behind the existence and survival of both the Siak polity and its traditional political system.

Furthermore, Barnard (2003: 78–103) discusses the demise of Raja Kecik in 1735 CE largely at the hands of his rival the Johor ruler, and his powerful Bugis allies, as well as the ensuing attempt by his two sons, Raja Mahmud and Raja Alam, to inherit their father's position of leadership at Siak and amongst the sea peoples. Indeed as Barnard (2003) argues Raja Kecik, his descendants and their followers for the greater part of the eighteenth century controlled no land, and continued to shift from one island or coastal area to another, in either mainland or island Southeast Asia, creating the notion of "multiple centers of authority." Thus Barnard draws attention to an alternative model of *kerajaan* that had the ruler and his followers constantly on the move and at sea, voluntarily or forced out, often rendering their support or services to the highest bidder as a sea lord (a term first applied by Trocki 1979).

The study of the Siak polity by Barnard (2003) can perhaps be applied to other parts of the "Malay world" and is certainly reflective of alternative indigenous political system. Similarly Trocki (1979), Miksic (1989), and Drakard (1990) have effectively drawn attention to a number of variations in a number of Malay territorial units, generally seen to belong to the Malay world.

A Distinctly Kedah Model

The view of a traditional maritime or riverine structure, with few lines of communications inland, is also held to be true by Gullick, Milner and most Southeast Asian scholars for the northern Malay Peninsula, including Kedah, which was said to be in line with a distinctively common "Malay model" political system for the region.

A study of Kedah's indigenous political and power infrastructure does indeed confirm the notion that it was traditionally a *kerajaan*, as first discussed by Milner (1982). Kedah's historic lines of control, however, also included the "sea routes" that expanded to a number of river systems and estuaries within its domain, as well as several large and small islands. Furthermore, in line with Trocki's (1979: xvi–xvii) argument, Kedah was part of the maritime system in the sense that traditionally the center of power and the "trading city" were located at or close to the river-mouths, or near the coastline. Moreover, it is apparent that Kedah's "sea routes," like Johor and Siak, were traditionally controlled and defended by the ruler in conjunction with a number of sea lords and their followers, the *"orang laut,"* that were the backbone of the realm. In addition, the historic use and economic significance of overland and trans-peninsular routes at Kedah are remnants of an alternate line of communication of the type referred to in west Sumatra by Miksic (1989) and Drakard (1990).

In consequence, Kedah's traditional political structure demonstrates patterns of both a riverine and a maritime system. Conversely, Kedah's ability to be connected to a complex network of overland and trans-peninsular trade routes meant that it did not solely rely on the maritime trade routes. Kedah's unique political economy therefore demonstrates aspects that further distinguish it from distinctly maritime/riverine systems in the region. Rather it indicates a combination of systems that often drew inspirations, or were made possible, from regions and powers outside the Malay world.

What's more, Kedah's geographical location at the northern part of the Melaka Straits; its proximity to the Siamese empire, by land and sea, and proximity to Burma (or Myanmar) and Aceh by sea; its lines of communication both maritime based and trans-peninsular, its economic environment (based on both sea and land trade routes and its self-sufficiency in food and some minerals), its multiethnic population (combination of native and foreign Malays, *orang asli*, non-Malay foreigners and others), its robust literary sources and traditions, as well as its political structure and independence (arguably the oldest unbroken independent kingship line in the "Malay world") likewise show aspects that do not entirely follow, and often contradict, the commonly perceived "Malay systems." Besides the local literary version of events (i.e., *Hikayat Merong Mahawangsa*), the foundation myth and the state's political emergence contradict that of the popular *Sulalat al-Salatin* (i.e., "the genealogy of the kings"), better known as *Sejarah Melayu* or the *Malay Annals* (written outside of Kedah at the Melaka, Johor and/or Aceh court), as well the Palembang-Melaka-Johor royal progeny from which most Malay rulers claim descent.

Kedah's environmental and physical attributes were particularly instrumental in its ability to enhance the image and *daulat* of the ruler, prolong the durability of its system and attract Malay and other settlers and traders to its domain. Herewith, the problem of attracting and maintaining settlers and traders to the "thinly populated" or "population poor" pre–nineteenth century *negeri* within the Malay Peninsula, including Kedah, and island Southeast Asia must be highlighted (Trocki 1979: xvi, 1997: 86; 2000; Barnard 2003: 15). Benedict Anderson (1983: 42–44) maintains with regard to Java and Janet Carsten (1995: 327) argues in regard to the Langkawi Islands (i.e., Pulau Langkawi in Malay and traditionally considered at the fringes of Kedah's domain) the power of a ruler was traditionally revealed by the number of people they controlled rather than the geographical extent of their realm. Nevertheless, a combination of Kedah's geography, food supply, wealth, and environment combined with a prestigious royal and administrative tradition offered its inhabitants substantial opportunities. In particular its traditional abundance rice for exports, argued by Reinout Vos (1993: 104n) to be the only major rice exporting nation in the Malay Peninsula and the Melaka Straits, has given Kedah the name of "the granary" of the region (see Military background forward by C. Skinner to *Syair Sultan Maulana* 1985: 12; Sharifah Zaleha 2004: 403).[9]

Similarly Kedah's long-term relationship with such outside powers as Siam, Burma, and Aceh as well as the states of the Malay Peninsula to the south and east make it unique in the region. Kedah's geographical location, located between two powerful cultural zones, that of Thai and the Malays, as well as its trans-peninsular and maritime lines of communication may therefore explain its historic ability to shift its tributary allegiance from one area to the other. Hence in 1767 when Ayutthaya was sacked Kedah in a purely political move decided to send the tributary flowers to Ava or Burma instead of Bangkok (Anderson 1824: 151; Turnbull 1980: 85; Historical background by Skinner to *Syair Sultan Maulana* 1985: 5). Nonetheless, sometimes Kedah sent the tributary flowers to two places at the same time and sometimes it even sent tributes to the Acehnese ruler (Anderson 1824: 151; Historical background by Skinner to *Syair Sultan Maulana* 1985: 5; Andaya 2001b: 64).

CONSIDERATION OF *HIKAYAT MERONG MAHAWANGSA*: KEDAH'S MAIN INDIGENOUS LITERARY SOURCE

The *Hikayat Merong Mahawangsa* is a Malay text that only came to light outside of Kedah in the first half of the nineteenth century. Other than the fact that it was written in Kedah and was in the possession of the exiled ruler of Kedah, while he was in the neighboring British settlement of Penang in the 1820s and 1830s, there is little known about its history. Nevertheless, several scholars have speculated that it may have been compiled in seventeenth or eighteenth century Kedah by using earlier Malay sources.[10]

In his study of *Hikayat Merong Mahawangsa*, Hendrik J. M. Maier (1988) has discussed how its compilation, value, stories, and prestige has been unjustly questioned, ignored or ridiculed by most nineteenth- and twentieth-century students and scholars many of whom were produced by the British or modern educational systems. These views he continues are still paramount amongst most Malay and non-Malay scholars and this is partly due to the popularity of the English translation of the Malay work of *Sejarah Melayu* that came about thirty years earlier. Thus, Maier (1988: 30) continues that the *Hikayat* had the disadvantage of being "read against the background of the *Sejarah Melayu*, and ever since, this primacy of the Malay Annals has never been subverted."

Despite this disadvantage Maier argues that in reality the *Hikayat* could be seen as a

> fine manifestation of nineteenth century Malay culture, dominated by oral-aurality: it drew fragments from the community-shared knowledge, and combined them into a specific narrative-a play upon tradition, skilful and relevant. The *Hikayat Merong Mahawangsa* could also be used as a fine illustration of the discontinuities that emerged in the field of Malay knowledge coincident with the introduction of Western-oriented education and printing techniques: it eventually resulted in a break with the past and in a growing uneasiness among Malay intellectuals about the validity of the heritage. (1988: 157)

Kenneth R. Hall too speaks of a poor reception that the Javanese *kakawin*, or court poetry, once had to deal with:

> Traditionally, scholars were reluctant to view *kakawin* as texts that had historical merit, with the exception of the fourteenth century *Nagarakertagama*. Today, however, there is consensus among leading scholars that, if properly used, Old Javanese poetry as a whole can be a rich source, especially as it reflects on Java's physical landscape and the society and culture that occupied this space during the pre-1500 era. (2005: 7)

Sadly, the negative view of many Malay literary and historic works, such as *Hikayat Merong Mahawangsa*, discussed by Maier and Hall continues.

Writing in 1995, as a review of a recently published book on historic Malay literature, G. E. Marrison comments that "neither the *Hikayat Inderaputra* nor, the *Hikayat Merong Mahawangsa* is a typically Muslim work, nor does either achieve the standards of perfection usually implied by calling a literary text classical" (1995: 211–212).

Marrison fails to elaborate on the standards that he applied in his review in the classification of the two above-mentioned *Hikayats*. Furthermore, his comments create a number of other problems, particularly on what can be considered as "Islamic" or "classical." For the most part, if comparing stories or aspects of *Hikayat Merong Mahawangsa* and *Hikayat Inderaputra* with the more popular post-Islamic Persian or Islamic literary works (such as the tenth to the twelfth century *Shah-nameh* or the book of Kings by Ferdowsi, *Qabus-nameh* by Vashmgir Ibn Ziyar, and *Siyasat-nameh* or *Seir al Moluk* by Nezamol Molkeh Tusi) they in fact contain fewer references to pre-Islamic rulers, drinking of intoxicants, and customs of ancient times (including the correct manner of drinking wine by the aristocracy) than the latter.

Nevertheless, Marrison's remarks on the two *Hikayats* may have found support amongst more strict and orthodox Muslims. Writing about three centuries earlier than Marrison in Aceh, an orthodox Gujarati Sufi, Sheikh Nur al-Din Ibn Ali al-Raniri (died 1658 CE) expressed similar views and disgust about at least one of the two mentioned *Hikayats*. In his work *Sirat al-Mustaghim* Raniri expresses his views on the *Hikayat Inderaputra* (and *Hikayat Sri Rama*) as "worthless under Islamic canon law, such that the paper they are written on may be used for washing parts of the body, unless they incorporate the name of God" (quoted by S. W. R. Mulyadi in *Hikayat Indraputra* 1983: 44; Winstedt 1939: 98; V. I. Braginsky 1993: 53, 68, 84–86).[11] Thus, it is also possible that Raniri would have viewed stories or aspects of religion in *Hikayat Merong Mahawangsa* with little sympathy and with having little literary or religious worth.

Most nineteenth and twentieth century scholars have also unjustly questioned the reliability of *Hikayat Merong Mahawangsa* as a historic source, or been selective in their approach to Kedah's history when referring to the text. Writing only a few years after the *Hikayat* was translated into English, John Crawfurd (1856) commented: "My friend, Col. James Low,[12] translated a Malay manuscript, entitled 'Annals of Kedah,' but this production is a dateless tissue of rank fable from which not a grain of reliable knowledge can be gathered" (1856: 362).

Consequently most aspects of Kedah's history deemed to be fantastic or unrealistic, such as the conversion to Islam or the story of the tusked king (Raja Bersiung/Bersiong), as portrayed in the *Hikayat Merong Mahawangsa* have been omitted, altered, ignored or improved upon by nearly all nineteenth and twentieth century writers on Kedah (see Malay and non-Malay studies of Kedah history by: Wan Yahya bin Wan Muhammad Taib 1911; Winstedt 1938: 32; Khan 1939: 8–12, 14; Fatimi 1963: 73;

Muhammad Hassan 1968: 26–30; Adil 1980: 7–8; Sharifa Zaleha 1985; Sheikh Niamat and Haji Wan Shamsudin 1996: 1–15).[13] In fact the historic depiction of Kedah varies considerably between the more contemporary sources to that of *Hikayat Merong Mahawangsa*. For example, Wan Yahya bin Wan Muhammad Taib (1911: 3) in the earliest historical study of Kedah, in either Malay or English, without substantiating his claims has the *Hikayat* Sheikh Abdullah to be arriving in the precise Muslim year of 818 Hijri and as the student of the renowned fourteenth century North African traveler Ibn Battuta . In contrast there is no date suggested in the *Hikayat*, as well no mention of Ibn Battuta. Rather the *Hikayat* refers to Sheikh Abdullah visiting Kedah on a mystical journey and as a disciple of the Devil (Iblis/Eblis)! Maier similarly explains in his comparison of *Hikayat Merong Mahawangsa* with a popular twentieth century Malay text and source on Kedah's history, *Al-Tarekh Salasilah Negeri Kedah*:

> Kedah is no longer presented as a State which is situated between the two greatest powers in the world, and which later in the narrative will be led toward the glory and fame of Islam by its able rulers. Rather, it lies in a corner of the world, constantly invaded and threatened by external forces, vulnerable and often wounded. The Malay view on their position in the world has indeed changed. (1988: 145)

There is no doubt that many of the stories and episodes in the *Hikayat Merong Mahawangsa*, as well other indigenous Southeast Asian historic sources (and/or indeed other parts of the world) are fictions and unrealistic. Nevertheless, as Drakard (cited in Walker 2004: 218) has recently argued, the historic recitation of court texts in the Malay world did not simply seek to represent a reality, but rather to manifest it. Thus the *Hikayat* were portrayed in a context that people understood and could relate to.[14] The stories from the *Hikayat* were traditionally popular and believed according to a European observer in 1819:

> They are fond of reading; if a man gets a book he reads aloud; the neighbors on hearing him come out, and he is soon surrounded by twenty or thirty people . . . They have but few books, and they are all manuscript, chiefly Hikayat (history) as they call them, but might with more propriety be called romances; for they say very little about the character of the man, but much about his adventures, his exploits, his miracles; . . . Most of their writing are of this marvelous kind and everything is believed that is written! ("State of Education among the Malays in Malacca," Indo-Chinese Gleaner, October 1819, cited at length in *AJMR* 1820: 347)

In addition, the *Hikayat* stories were composed in such a way that complemented other popular modes of indigenous traditions (such as *wayang kulit* stories or shadow puppets), beliefs, physical objects, and oral traditions.[15] Amin Sweeney (1987: Chapter 4) and Drakard (1999: 232–238) in their respective studies and interpretations of premodern Malay literary sources argue that they have a "strong oral orientation" with composition and delivery common to poetry and ritual language. In fact it could be argued that the author/s of *Hikayat Merong Mahawangsa* cleverly incorporated indigenous traditions with those of the Indian *Ramayana* and the Safavid era (1501/1502–1722 CE) Persian *Hekayateh Simurgh*[16] or *Gheseyeh Soleyman va Simurgh*.[17] The inclusion of the Indian and Persian stories into *Hikayat Merong Mahawangsa* is indeed astounding and has never been examined. This suggests a more powerful way of enhancing the popularity of its stories both domestically and internationally. In the beginning of the *Hikayat* its author/s clearly state that the story is a continuation of the Rama story (referring to *Ramayana* but without mentioning it by name), "After the war of Sri Rama and Raja Handuman, the Island of Langka was deserted except by the bird Geruda" [sic] (Bland 1909: 107).[18] The island of Langkawi, off the coast of Kedah, was thus identified as the *Ramayana* island of Lanka, Langka, or Langkapuri. Furthermore, the story of the bet between the mystical bird and the Prophet Solomon obstructing the prince of Rum from marrying a princess from China runs almost parallel to the Persian story (Safa 1994 V Part 3: 1530–1531, 1537–1538, 1550).[19] These aspects of the *Hikayat* are significant as they can still offer us much insight into the regions' past history, especially its cultural milieu. They can also offer us alternatives in answering complex questions when dealing with aspects of Southeast Asian history. As Ricklefs forewarns of the indigenous sources in Southeast Asia:

> These are not reliable historical accounts, but in their shared emphasis upon the roles played by esoteric learning and magical powers, upon the foreign origins and trade connections of the first teachers, and upon a process of conversion which began with the elite and worked downwards, they may reveal something of the original events. (1986: 8)

SCHOLARLY STUDIES OF KEDAH'S PREMODERN HISTORY

The earliest scholarly study of Kedah's history is the Malay book of *Salasilah atau Tarikh Kerajaan Kedah*. This book was written by Wan Yahya bin Wan Muhammad Taib, nearly a century ago in 1346 Hijri (1911 CE). The author was a native of Kedah. In it he attempts to trace the history of Kedah from pre-Islamic times all the way to the early twentieth century. According to his study prior to the year 38 Hijri (621 CE) Kedah was an uncultivated place with its coastal regions populated by strange semi-human and man-eating creatures called "sea-Sakai" who were "very wicked people, they took people's life and ate their meat; they could not be taught anything" (Wan Yahya 1911: 2).[20]

Wan Yahya continues that this grim picture of Kedah and the "sea-Sakais" changed with the arrival of a wandering Persian prince (*Merong Mahawangsa*) and his entourage from the port of "Gumarun."[21] This Persian prince eventually chose to stay permanently at Kedah and came into contact with the "sea-Sakais" who invited him to rule over them as their king and ruler.

The prince having accepted the invitation proclaimed himself the hereditary ruler of Kedah and introduced new customs, traditions, and items of symbolic significance. Thus, Wan Yahya further explains that Kedah's contemporary royal family, regalia, the beating of the royal drums (*nobat*) and the government structures were first introduced by *Merong Mahawangsa* (Wan Yahya 1911: 3).

On the religion of Kedah's ruler and population Wan Yahya notes that for several generations following the death of *Merong Mahawangsa* his descendants were all Buddhists. This was however changed when a great grandson of *Merong Mahawangsa* called *Seri Peduka Maharaja Darbar* met an Arab holy man visiting Kedah from Yemen named *Sheikh Abdullah bin Ahmad Kumiri*. Following this meeting *Seri Peduka Maharaja Darbar* was converted to Islam and subsequently took the name of Muzaffar Shah. Likewise, upon the conversion of *Seri Peduka Maharaja Darbar* and the charismatic leadership of the Yemeni holy man the general population of Kedah also embraced Islam.

Wan Yahya then continues with the history of Kedah to the time of his writing. In particular he mentions these rulers in the light of their military or political achievements, succession crises, and relationships with neighboring states, including Europeans. A big portion of Wan Yahya's study is however concerned with the eighteenth and nineteenth century rulers and political developments of Kedah. Thus he describes in detail the 1724 CE Bugis invasion during continuous succession disputes of the eighteenth century, and the nineteenth century turmoil in Kedah due to the Siamese invasion in the first part of the nineteenth century. In addition Wan Yahya provides a vivid account of the more peaceful late nineteenth and early twentieth century government and policies of Kedah, a period that coincided with the writing of his book. To this account he adds a description of the court and the subdivision of government ministries of "*Menteri Empat*" and "*Menteri Delapan*" (Wan Yahya 1911: 33–35). Additionally, Wan Yahya includes a genealogical table of the king from the time of *Merong Mahawangsa* to the time of his writing.

As to the basis of his sources, Wan Yahya simply indicates a number of local traditions that he consulted prior to writing of his book. However, he neither names these sources nor refers to them specifically throughout his text. There is, however, a strong resemblance of several stories mentioned in Wan Yahya's book to those of *Hikayat Merong Mahawangsa*. Besides Wan Yahya's genealogical order and use of names of pre–nineteenth century rulers of Kedah from the time of *Merong Mahawangsa* corresponds to that of the *Hikayat Merong Mahawangsa*.

Assuming that much of Wan Yahya's sources came from stories in *Hikayat Merong Mahawangsa*, then it can be expected that he was selective in adapting these for his own book. This, of course does not only refer to the sequencing of the stories in his text, but also in their compliance with Kedah's contemporary religious dogma, politics, and customs. It is also apparent that Wan Yahya attempts to improve upon the episodes in *Hikayat Merong Mahawangsa* by making them believable and realistic. In fact the timing for the publication of *Salasilah atau Tarikh Kerajaan Kedah* and presentation of the book to the then ruler of Kedah by Wan Yahya seemed to be politically motivated. Correspondingly, the publication of the book in 1911 CE by Wan Yahya only followed the end of Kedah's tributary status from Siam (Thailand) and its acceptance of a British adviser a year later.

Wan Yahya thus portrays the origin of Kedah's ruling family from a wandering Persian prince rather than the mythical story given in the *Hikayat Merong Mahawangsa* which tells of the arrival of *Merong Mahawangsa* from the legendary land of Rum following a conflict between Prophet Solomon and Garuda. Sheikh Abdullah is named in *Hikayat Merong Mahawangsa* as the earliest propagator of Islam at Kedah and is said to have mysteriously appeared from Baghdad in the company of the Devil (Iblis/Eblis). According to Wan Yahiya, however, Sheikh Abdullah was simply a religious clergyman that arrived at Kedah alone from Yemen and subsequently converted the local ruler into Islam.

Between, 1920–1940 CE the British scholar R. O. Winstedt published several journal articles on aspects of Kedah's history, as well as romanized Malay and its translated English version of *Undang-undang Kedah*, a Malay pamphlet of seventeenth/eighteenth century Kedah (referred by him as the "Kedah Laws").[22]

In the 1920 "History of Kedah" article Winstedt discusses in length the possibility of historic reports of the port of "KALAH" by Persian and Arab navigators referred to Kedah. He also relies more on secondary sources and information he only refers to as "valuable information toward the preparation" obtained directly from Southeast Asian scholar C. O. Blagden (Winstedt 1920: 35). On the other hand, in the latter 1936 "Notes on Kedah" article Winstedt consults a larger number of both primary (particularly eighteenth century travel accounts, Dutch Governor's reports and the *Dagh-Registrar*) and secondary sources with regard to Kedah. Nevertheless, both of these articles as well as all his other articles lack an in-depth look at native social life, culture, manners, and customs, kingship, rituals, religion, etc. Rather, his works concentrate predominantly on Kedah's European trade and encounters as well as political succession crises of its rulers.

Furthermore, Winstedt gives little credit to both *Hikayat Merong Mahawangsa* and the undated *Undang-undang Kedah,* instead examining these works in the light of the *Sejarah Melayu* and the laws of Malacca (*Risalat Hukum Qanun* or *Undang-undang Melaka*).[23] This perhaps reflects his overall view that the *Hikayat Merong Mahawangsa* was "full of omissions, anachronisms and errors" and that this and the "Kedah Laws" have much in common with the writings and laws of Melaka.[24]

Nearly, two decades after Wan Yahya's Malay book, Muhammad Hassan Bin To'Kerani Mohd. Arshad published his Malay work of *Al-Tarekh Salasilah Negeri Kedah*. He too was closely related to the ruling families of Kedah and in his general assessment of its history, religion, customs, and kingship follows to a great extent that of *Salasilah atau Tarikh Kerajaan Kedah*. What's more, Muhammad Hassan follows in the footsteps of his Malay predecessor by offering no clues as to the sources of his study. Nevertheless, his overall study provides further details on Kedah's royal insignia (the *nobat*) and shows several black and white photos of coins and historic objects of Kedah reproduced from the collections kept at the Kedah Royal Museum at Alor Setar.[25]

In addition, in his *Al-Tarekh Salasilah Negeri Kedah* Muhammad Hassan attempts independently to suggest and approximate several key dates for events mentioned in *Hikayat Merong Mahawangsa* and Wan Yahya's *Salasilah atau Tarikh Kerajaan Kedah*.[26] It is difficult to accept some of these dates as authoritative yet this attempt by a native historian to bring dates to events may indeed reflect a change or a new beginning in Malay interpretation and understanding of their own and region's history.

The Malaysian scholar S. Q. Fatimi in his well researched 1963 English book *Islam Comes to Malaysia* only gives a mere four to five paragraphs about Kedah.[27] And this only refers to the legend behind the conversion of Kedah's ruler into Islam as portrayed by a story in *Hikayat Merong Mahawangsa*. Sheikh Abdulla al-Yamani asks to follow the Devil (*Iblis*) in order

> to show his ways and the snares that he lays for the gullible and the fallible of mankind. . . . Having wandered from place to place, seeing and observing without being seen, they came to "the Kafir country called Kedah" and there in the royal place an incident occurred which led to the conversion of the King and his people. (Fatimi 1963: 73–74)

In his study of the conversion of the ruler of Kedah into Islam Dr Fatimi therefore makes no reference to earlier studies on Islam at Kedah, other stories from *Hikayat Merong Mahawangsa* and other aspects of its political or social history. This approach by Fatimi may be understood by his remark that the conversion story from *Hikayat Merong Mahawangsa* is simply a myth from a book that he believes should be called a "Malayan Midsummer Night's Dream"![28]

Then again Fatimi is the first and perhaps the only scholar to note and rightfully criticize a segment of Winstedt's 1938 English translation of *Hikayat Merong Mahawangsa* on the conversion of Kedah's ruler into Islam. According to him, Winstedt's has "wrongly corrected" the converted ruler of Kedah's Muslim name from "Muzlaf Shah" into "Muzaffar Shah."[29]

Following Fatimi's work of 1963 other Malaysian scholars have continued to refer both directly and indirectly to the works of Wan Yahya (1911) and Hassan Bin To'Kerani Mohd Arshad (1927). Buyong Adil author of the 1980 Malay book *Siri Sejarah Nusantara: sejarah KEDAH* is one such scholar.

In the forward of his book Buyong Adil makes it clear that his work should be titled *Asal Negeri Kedah dan Salasilah Raja-Raja* (roughly translated as the "Foundation of Kedah and a Genealogy of its Kings"). For one thing such a title would have fit well with the contents of his book, in which he has discussed various origins of the name Kedah and each of the historic kings of Kedah to the nineteenth century separately. Likewise, he mentions both the conversion to Islam of the Kedah ruler and the arrival of the *"nobat"* in some detail.

Buyong Adil makes no reference to the sources that he consulted for his book. From the contents and layout of his arguments it can be seen that he maintains theories and framework that were seen in earlier Malaysian works on Kedah. Certainly when discussing the Persian ancestry of the royal house of Kedah, the contents and ideas behind the *"nobat"* and the conversion of the ruler "Muzaffar Shah" by a "Yemeni" Sheikh he keeps in line with his predecessors. But without any acknowledgment of his sources, Adil (1980: 20–30) gives a more or less yearly account of events in the second half of the seventeenth century. This shift in the account by Buyong Adil in those ten pages may well seem at odds with the more descriptive mode of his other writing. What he has done is to offer direct Malay translations from Winstedt's 1936 article.[30] Consequently, the use of information from Winstedt's article reflects Buyong Adil's attempt to integrate some western scholarly data and an account of events in Kedah in areas that he thought best fit.

In the same year that Buyong Adil's book was published a short Malay article by Wan Hussein Azmi dealing with the arrival and spread of Islam from the seventh to the twentieth century (titled *Islam di Malaysia: Kedatangan dan Perkembangan [Abd 7–20M]*) appeared in a Malaysian collection of articles entitled *Tamadun Islam Di Malaysia* (translated as "The Islamic Civilization of Malaysia").[31] In his study of Islam in Malaysia he believes a 1963 archaeological discovery of a Muslim grave at Kedah is the earliest indication of Islam in either Malaysia or Indonesia. The grave was dated 290 Hijri (corresponding to 903 CE) and appeared to belong to a Muslim named "Syaikh Abdul Kadir Ibn Syaikh Husin Syah Alam" (Wan Hussein Azmi 1980: 135). Wan Hussein Azmi only discusses this discovery in a mere three sentences and does not elaborate further on his sources. This article is significant since he was the first to cite the 1963 discovery of the Kedah grave and he is one of the first Malay writers that made no reference to stories brought forward by Wan Yahya (1911) or others (earlier Malay writers) from the *Hikayat Merong Mahawangsa* but instead relied entirely on archaeological evidence. Wan Hussein Azmi's article in the year 1980 seems to have similarly coincided with a new phase of historic study of Kedah by Malaysian scholars that move away from earlier works of Wan Yahya and Hassan Bin To'Kerani Mohd. Arshad.

These post-1980 studies seem better organized, better researched and have properly cited a wider variety of both Malay and English sources. One such study is the 1985 doctoral thesis titled "From Saints to Bureaucrats: A Study of the Development of Islam in the State of Kedah" by Sharifah Zaleha (Binte Syed Hassan). This work is the largest study to date of Islam and society in Kedah using both English and Malay sources. Her study of Kedah's early twentieth century and contemporary history—constituting three out of six of her chapters—deserves credit.

Nevertheless there are some weaknesses in Sharifa Zaleha's two chapters that deal with pre–nineteenth century Kedah. Aside from a couple of sixteenth century Portuguese accounts of Kedah the chapters are predominantly dominated by the more recent twentieth century secondary sources on Kedah and other parts of the Malay Peninsula. Hence when dealing with the historical aspect of Kedah there is little reference to indigenous sources, oral reports or archival sources. What's more her connection of practices, beliefs, and customs in the contemporary Malay Peninsula, or historic Melaka, to that of Kedah also lacks substantiation. For example her frequent mention that the ruling house of Kedah is traced back to Alexander the Great cannot be substantiated from her citation of *Sejarah Melayu* or other sources. Similarly, Sharifa Zaleha's belief that Islam began in Kedah solely through the fifteenth century "political ascendency of Melaka" and a visit to Melaka by the then ruler of Kedah in order to receive the royal *"nobat"* (beating of the drums) as reported in *Sejarah Melayu* cannot be verified.[32] Thus it seems she has taken as fact the popular non-scholarly beliefs about genealogy of Malay kings and their conversion to Islam through the Melaka Empire.

Similarly, out of the handful of Malay manuscripts consulted and cited by Sharifa Zaleha only two deals with Kedah at any length. The two Malay manuscripts cited most widely in Sharifa Zaleha's thesis are the *Sejarah Melayu* and the *Undang-undang Kedah* commonly referred to as the "Kedah Laws." Of these the *Sejarah Melayu* is a non-Kedah Malay work and has only a few references to Kedah; while, Sharifa Zaleha (1985: 35) believes *Undang-undang Kedah* to be of little value since in both structure and contents it follows Melaka's *Risalat Hukum Qanun* or *Undang-undang Melaka* (translated as the "Canon Laws of Malacca"). Strangely enough she has not consulted the *Hikayat Merong Mahawangsa*. Similarly she keeps aloof from notions within *Hikayat Merong Mahawangsa* and arguments brought forward by Wan Yahya (1911) and others who have made reference to "Iblis," "Garuda," "Solomon," "Rum," "Muzlaf/Muzaffar Shah" or "Sheikh Abdullah of Yemen/Baghdad/Abani." It seems that a wider variety of both Malay and non-Malay primary sources would therefore have complemented her contemporary sources used in her thesis.

Khoo Kay Kim's 1991 book *Malay Society: Transformation and Democratization* is composed of a number of his articles that deal with various historic kingly states in Malaysia. What's interesting is that these chapters deal with virtually all states and historic ruling houses of Malaysia except Kedah. Nonetheless, there are some short references to Kedah including a translation of an unusual and hard-to-get 1961 Malay article on the breakdown of the royal court (*Menteri Empat* and *Menteri Delapan*) in the fifteenth and the sixteenth century Kedah.[33]

In the 1990s the Kedah Museum (*Muzium Negeri Kedah Darul Aman*) published several books containing various articles on Kedah's history. Two of these articles deal entirely with the pre-twentieth history of Kedah. These articles are Yahya Abu Bakar's 1991 article "Kedah dan perdagangan Tradisi Di Asia Abad Ke-tujuh Hingga Abad Keenam belas Masihi" and Sheikh Niamat Bin Yusoff and Haji Wan Shamsudin Bin Muhammad Yusof's short Malay article published in 1996 titled "Sejarah dan Perjuangan Ulama Kedah Darul Aman: Suatu Muqaddimah." These articles seem to be more open in citing Malay and English secondary sources, both old and new. Nevertheless, they do not offer new Malay, English or other primary sources on Kedah. Meanwhile, they both tend to ignore the *Hikayat Merong Mahawangsa* instead citing the 1927 work *Al-Tarekh Salasilah Negeri Kedah* frequently.

It appears many that Malaysian scholars in particular have been selective in citing or relying on sources such as historic Malay books (*Hikayats*), archaeological diggings and non-Malay sources. Perhaps part of their reluctance to go beyond the common norm is partly their inability to procure appropriate sources (such as travel journals, manuscripts etc) for political/social reasons. Alternatively, it may reflect political (particularly the effect of a colonial history), social and religious changes and orthodoxy that entered the region toward the end of the nineteenth century. This transformation was noted in the western Malay states in about 1900 by R. J. Wilkinson:

> The native of the Peninsula is becoming less of a Malay and more of a Mussulman; his national ceremonies are being discarded, his racial laws are being set aside, and his inherited superstitions are opposed to Moslem belief as much as to Western science. His allegiance is being gradually transferred from national to Pan-Islamic ideals and from the local Sultans, whose fettered dignity he compares to that of a "ship in the tow of a dinghy," to the Sultan al-muadzam or Sultan par excellence. [sic] (1957: 40)

The study is even made more difficult by State and Malaysian government guidelines on what is right or wrong. An example of this may well include the 1989 guidelines given by the "National *Fatwa* Council of Kedah" to the National Museum of Kedah in one of their largest exhibitions held in that State called "Treasures from the Grave." According to the guideline the exhibition "must not glorify the religious aspect of the pre-Islamic civilization . . . whether in the display of graves or in the video shows" ("Fatwa and Archaeology" 1989).[34]

It could meanwhile be argued that the historical study of Kedah is relatively recent and only dates to 1911 CE, when Wan Yahya first published his book. This book is indeed significant as it became the groundwork for future Malay study of Kedah's history. Besides aspects of his version of Kedah's history, such as the Persian roots of Kedah's royal genealogy or the conversion mode of the ruler and the people to Islam, are now well established amidst the native population of Kedah and continue to be cited by Malay scholars.

Sadly however Wan Yahya's accounts of his sources are scanty and he does not elaborate much on the native sources that he claims to have consulted. Nonetheless, it is more than likely that in his study he was inspired to a great extent by Kedah's older indigenous source, the *Hikayat Merong Mahawangsa*. It could be further argued that he attempted to disguise, omit or rewrite aspects of the *Hikayat* that he felt were outdated and unrealistic, especially for a new breed of Malay readers and audiences. Conversely, it is possible that he obtained parts of his information from unknown native oral and archival sources. Similarly it is likely that his sources included an atypical, or unknown, version of *Hikayat Merong Mahawangsa*, or even an older source, that perhaps linked the rulers' genealogy to Persia.

Wan Yahya's arguments and aspects of his narrative have certainly inspired Muhammad Hassan (1927) in the writing of his book. In many ways it could be argued that Muhammad Hassan's book is an extension and an improvement of Wan Yahya's earlier work. Furthermore, he provides dates, figures and a wider range of information on Kedah's historic trade and commerce that were lacking previously.[35] The new approach by Muhammad Hassan and the inclusion of new information may explain the popularity of his book amongst future Malay scholars.

Following the two early works on Kedah by Wan Yahya and Muhammad Hassan other Malaysian scholars have attempted to examine alternate aspects and sources of Kedah's history. There is also a shift to more modern methods of research, study, and use of archival sources, as well as a tendency to move away from earlier works of Wan Yahya and Muhammad Hassan.

Nevertheless, it is apparent that indigenous literary sources of Kedah, particularly *Hikayat Merong Mahawangsa*, continue to be shunned or taken to be of minor significance by most contemporary scholars. Kedah's history, geography, economy, and sociopolitical structures also seem to be entirely studies in the context of its neighbors, Melaka or *Sejarah Melayu*. What's more, there is little reference, use or consultation of Kedah's unique form of oral stories (e.g., traditional story told by the story tellers of Kedah, the *selembits*) and the *wayang kulit* or shadow-puppet tradition. This is significant as these sources could further corroborate and shed light into a number of sociopolitical aspects of Kedah's history and society. Besides there is always the trap that by relying solely on Malay, European or other primary and secondary sources one's study may not fully answer the question or questions at hand. In the words of Barbara W. Andaya and her study of premodern Perak: "To ignore this text (i.e., *Misa Melayu*, an indigenous text from Perak) and write a history of Perak based purely on Dutch records might convey the impression that the Malays were concerned with little else except the alliance with the Dutch and the tin collection" (1979: 148).

NOTES

1. I use Penang to mean both the Island of Penang (*Pulau Pinang* in Malay) and Province Wellesley (or *Seberang Perai* in Malay).

2. A small number of royal courtiers, foreign traders, the king and members of his family consisted of its nonrural refugees.

3. The number of people at Kedah that were either killed or taken away by the Siamese is not known. It is believed that thousands of women and children were simply taken as slaves and taken back to Siam to be sold.

4. In the same article Logan (1851: 56) mentions meeting some of the Malays that had lived at Province Wellesley.

5. Originally a Persian word it can also be romanized into *rayat, ryot* or *ra'ayat*.

6. As will be discussed in chapter 3, there is only the possibility that the indigenous sea peoples of Kedah did not return to their former residence at the Langkawi Islands. Reasons for not returning to Kedah may vary but it is possibly due to a Siamese precondition for allowing the return of the ex-ruler to Kedah in 1841–1842.

7. In the letter they referred to themselves as "*rakyat.*"

8. Certainly the concept of individual rights to properties and boundary markings is not unusual and can be found in most historic Malay legal digests. The Kedah Laws of Dato'Sri Paduka Tuan, dated 1667 CE, has "land without boundary-marks is counted dead and belongs to the Raja," see Winstedt 1928: 9, 27. The Malay word cited in the digest for landmark is "*amarat.*" Lands or properties without landmarks were therefore considered to belong to the ruler.

9. Referring to the Mon-Khmer loan words in northern Malay dialects, including terms for wet rice fields (*bendang*) and irrigation canals (*glong*), Geoffrey Benjamin (1997: 92–93) concludes that the Malays on the Peninsula learned wet rice cultivation techniques from the early Mon population in the area following interaction between the coastal Malays and the Austro-Asiatic Mon-speaking population further inland at Kedah. The historic connection of Kedah to the Mon-Khmer speaking population, further north, is significant and raises many questions. Was the Mon-Khmer connection of Kedah restricted to the rice fields? And to what extent did the Mon-Khmer interaction with Kedah impact the indigenous political systems of the Malay Peninsula and its literary or oral traditions.

10. See the report by James Low written in 1842 and reproduced in: *Burney Papers* 1971 V: 3; Winstedt 1940: 110–111; Sarkar 1985: 296; Sharifa Zaleha 1985: 32; Andaya 2002: 33–34; Hooker 2003: 45.

11. *Sirat al-Mustaghim*, as will be discussed in Chapter 1, was one of the two books sent to the ruler of Kedah by the ruler of Aceh upon the former's conversion to Islam.

12. James Low is the first English translator of the *Hikayat Merong Mahawangsa* in 1849.

13. Maier (1988) similarly discusses a number of historic and contemporary views of the *Hikayat* by scholars and the general Malay population.

14. When, visiting Kedah, the remains of an old Hindu temple were pointed out to H. N. Evans (1926: 76), by the natives, as the palace belonging to Kedah's vampire ruler Raja Bersiung. The story of Raja Bersiung is vividly described in *Hikayat Merong Mahawangsa*.

15. Inin Shahruddin (1983) has demonstrated the three versions of the popular story of *Si Miskin*, at Kedah and Kelantan, in the forms of a shadow puppet, oral story and written text.

16. Simurgh is the Persian mystical bird (perhaps in the same context as Garuda or Girda in Hindu and Indian literature). The name *"Hekayateh Simurgh"* is the title given to the version of the story kept at Tehran National Library and Bodleian Library at Oxford, see Safa 1994 v Pt3: 1530.

17. This is kept at the British Museum. According to an added annotation the story was collected from *"majaleseh bozorgaan"* (or court of the nobles or important people) by Muhammad Kazem bin Mir K Hussein Mozaffari Sejavandi (known as Habi). The date is unknown but it likely that the stories were collected in the first half of the sixteenth century.

18. See also Low (1849: 4). Indeed the depopulation of Lanka, following the war with Ravana, is also mentioned by the Buddhist authors of Ceylon's main indigenous source of *Mahavansi* (1833: xviii).

19. In contrast in the Persian text the royal couples are referred to as the prince from the east and the princess from the west, i.e., *pesareh molkeh Mashregh va dokhtareh molkeh Maghreb*.

20. The translation cited in Maier 1988: 135–136.

21. This refers to the historic port of Gambarun/Gambaroon, the predecessor to modern day Bandar Abbas, in southern Persia, on the Persian Gulf.

22. These articles were published in the *Journal of the Straits Branch of the Royal Asiatic Society* and its later successor *Journal of the Malayan Branch of the Royal Asiatic Society*. Winstedt 1920: 29–35; 1928: 1–44; 1936: 155–189.

23. See his views on these works in a later article in Winstedt 1940: 114–115.

24. Winstedt 1938: 32; Winstedt 1940: 114–115.

25. The black and white photos can be found in page 48 of his book.

26. For example according to Muhammad Hassan the date of arrival for Sheikh Abdullah from Yemen to Kedah was in the year 531 Hijri or 1136 CE. See Muhammad Hassan 1968: 18–19.

27. Fatimi 1963: 74–75.

28. Ibid., 74–75.

29. It should be pointed out that Winstedt was not the first to do so. In fact several years earlier both Wan Yahya (1911) and Muhammad Hassan Bin To'Kerani Mohd Arshad (1927) referred to this ruler of Kedah as "Muzaffar Shah." The misspelling of Kedah's first Muslim ruler from "Muzlaf Shah" into "Muzaffar Shah" has continued to exist to this date, see Adil 1980, Khoo 1991: 47n (refer to chapter 1 for more on this issue).

30. Much of Winstedt's article consists of English translations from the existing segments of the seventeenth century Dutch Malacca Governors Reports (*Dagh-Registrar*) that deal in one way or the other with Kedah.

31. The collection contains fifteen Malay and English articles written by Malaysian scholars on aspects of religion, society, mysticism and history of Southeast Asia and has regularly been cited in later studies by Malaysian scholars.

32. A point that she maintains in a later article; in which she writes, "conversion to Islam in the fifteenth century can be attributed to the political ascendancy of Melaka" (1989: 46–47).

33. The Malay article published at Kedah in 1961 is cited by Khoo (1991: 27, 52) to belong to Datuk Wan Ibrahim bin Wan Soloh. Nonetheless, these titles seem to be virtually the same as those listed in Kedah as part of an appendix (no dates given) by Muhammad Hassan (1968: i–ii).

34. In a rather similar way a 1972 *fatwa* at Kedah states that its Muslim leaders may attend invitation by Hindu, Chinese or Christian temples, churches and schools provided "they refrain from glorifying the religious ceremony" (Hooker 1993: 98). Indeed the 1972 *fatwa* at Kedah was more relaxed than a similar *fatwa* issued at the Malaysian states of Perak and Kelantan that forbid any Muslim participation.

35. Muhammad Hassan's attempts to substantiate aspects of Wan Yahya's work by including new archival information from the 1920 article on Kedah by Winstedt.

ONE

From Raja to Sultan

The Conversion of the Tantric Malay Ruler

The English missionary Thomas Beighton (1791–1844) of Penang in explaining his unequivocal friendship and support for the exiled Raja of Kedah to his employers, the London Missionary Society of London, concluded that Malays would adopt any religion "if the Ruler orders them" (see Milner 1979/1980: 14). Milner interprets Beighton's conclusion echoing the Malay accounts of their earlier conversion to Islam.

The Malay conversion stories all agree that it was the ruler that was first converted, and subsequently his act became the catalyst for the other segments of the population to follow suit.[1] Furthermore, most indigenous Malay sources portray the conversion of the ruler as a significant event in their history. Even in instances such as in the *Hikayat Patani*, that the ruler is reluctant to convert to Islam after he does so, he becomes a more determined and zealous individual.[2] In the same way, most writers and copyists of the Malay indigenous sources, or *Hikayats*, attempt to connect their rulers' conversion stories directly to miraculous visions of the Prophet Muhammad or to Muslim saints, mystics, and descendants of the Prophet (*Syeds*) visiting the region directly from the Middle East. The conversion stories in the *Hikayat Raja-Raja Pasai* and *Sejarah Melayu* have both themes described vividly, with the Prophet Muhammad appearing to the ruler in a dream, followed by an actual visit of one or more Muslim saintly figures arriving from Mecca or Jeddah (see *Hikayat Raja-Raja Pasai* 1960: 116–120; Brown 1970: 30–33, 43–44). In both cases the ruler is instructed in his dream by the Prophet about the tenets of Islam and Muslim prayers, is circumcised and the upcoming arrival of a ship carrying Muslim missionaries is foretold.[3]

Many archaeological findings and records in Southeast Asia, such as the wordings of the early fourteenth century Trengganu inscription, are also believed by Southeast Asian scholars to be further documentation of the early conversion of the local rulers into Islam (Winstedt 1972: 34; Slametmuljana 1976: 210–213). Thus, the sources agree that traditionally the Malay rulers in Southeast Asia were viewed by their subjects as the symbolic sources of religion and were instrumental in any form of religious transformation. It is also argued that the Raja, other than having religious authority also held real political, economic, and social "power" (Milner 1982: 113). This association of the Malay Raja with religion therefore complemented his control of the economy, trade routes and the political infrastructure of the maritime and riverine systems within the *negeri*. But, as M. C. Ricklefs (1986: 6) argues it must not be assumed that once an area is known to have had a Muslim ruler, "the process of Islamization was complete since this process may indeed only symbolize the beginning of Islam amongst the populace."

The conversion hierarchy, with the ruler on top, is contested however by more recent Southeast Asian scholars. Pierre-Yves Manguin (1985: 6–7), in his study of European accounts of Southeast Asia asserts that in the case of the Malay territories of Patani, Makassar, Brunei, and Champa, the reverse process of conversion had taken place. With the native "merchant population," rather than the sovereign, of a "maritime town" being the first convert to Islam. Hence, he argues that it was these newly converted Muslim merchant classes that ultimately impelled the conversion of their non-Islamic ruler.

There is no doubt that historically the newly converted native merchants of Southeast Asia and foreign merchant visitors were instrumental in the religious shift of native Malays and their rulers into Islam (Winstedt 1972: 127; Alatas 1985: 162–175; Reid 1990, 1993).[4] Indigenous sources and traditions, in various parts of island and mainland Southeast Asia, too confirm the role of Muslim merchants in converting the local population and rulers to Islam. But most of these sources are specific and maintain that the conversion of the natives and the local rulers was at the hands of an eclectic array of Southeast Asian Muslim traders and settlers, particularly Malay speakers from Johor or Patani or Pasai or Minangkabau or Java or Champa, rather than foreign traders from the Middle East or outside this region.[5] These Muslim traders and settlers were said to have arrived in the various parts of island and mainland Southeast Asia voluntarily, for either trading purposes[6] or establishing a settlement[7] or as Southeast Asian holy men visiting the region,[8] or involuntary settlers, particularly displaced peoples (including traders) and refugees.[9]

What's more, at least in the case of Champa, Burma, Siam and Arakan there is little or no evidence that their rulers ever, or at first, converted to Islam by their large Muslim populations or merchant classes (Yegar 1972: 1–17, 19, 26–28; Mabbett 1986: 304–307; Qanungo 1988: 288–293; Setudeh-

Nejad 2002: 452; Aye Chayan 2005: 398; Thant Myint-U 2006: 74–75; Kersten 2006: 21).[10] Likewise in his study of Indonesia, Ricklefs (1986: 12) upholds the idea that Muslim traders had been present long before "significant Indonesian conversions began." Other historians have also pointed to this fact in the other parts of the Malay world, particularly Patani (see Wyatt and Teeuw 1970: 101, 174; Shaghir Abdullah 1998: 20–26; Bradley 2009: 271n). Hence, having a large and influential Muslim merchant class is not necessarily indicative of conversion to Islam.

Correspondingly, the 1940 and 1970 discoveries of Muslim coins, dating to the Abbasid period (234 AH or about 848 CE), and two Muslim graves belonging to people of presumably Persian origin, dated 214 AH (826–829 CE) and 291 AH (903/904 CE), as well as seventh to eleventh century Middle Eastern ceramics and glass types at Kedah suggests the early presence of Muslim influence in the Malay Peninsula and mainland Southeast Asia, only two centuries after the death of Prophet Muhammad (Quaritch-Wales 1940: 1–85; Lamb 1960: 106; Lamb 1961b: 13, 15; Wan Hussein 1980: 135–137; Yatim 1985: 143–144; Sharifa Zaleha 1985: 30, 34; Bruce 1996: 73; Sheikh Niamat and Haji Wan Shamsudin 1996: 4; *Kesan-Kesan Awal Islam Wujud Di Kedah* 2005; Nik Hassan Shuhaimi Nik Abdul Rahman 2007: 47–49, 54). There is also a passage in Kedah's *Hikayat Merong Mahawangsa* that prior to the ruler's conversion there were people from the city of Baghdad visiting Kedah (Hikayat Merong Maha Wangsa or Kedah Annals 1916: 112). But there is no evidence to suggest that Kedah's ruler or population had by then become Muslim. Besides, the above mode of conversion, outlined by Manguin, does not explain fully the conversion process as it moved outside of the maritime centers and into the remote river systems and *ulu* settlements of the *negeri*.

At any rate, the process of conversion of a nation, tribe or territory to a new religion, with the ruler as the first and on the top of the conversion hierarchy, is not unusual and can be documented in instances within nearly all monotheistic religions, particularly in Zoroastrianism, Manichaeism, Christianity as well as Islam. In the case of Islam, the Prophet Muhammad upon establishing himself in the Arabian Peninsula sent a letter to the Persian King, the ruler of Byzantium, and others inviting them to join the new religion. Most Arab tribes in the peninsula also became Muslims following the conversion of their chiefs.[11] In the same way, many traditions on the expansion of Islam outside the Middle East, following the death of Prophet Muhammad, draw attention to a similar conversion hierarchy with the ruler being the first to convert.[12]

It is certainly true that the Malay conversion stories, particularly those with direct links to the Prophet and the Middle East, attempt to bring prestige to local traditions and the ruler, as well as gain respect amongst neighboring nations and visitors in a methodology and language that they could best comprehend. This likely explains the fact that parallels are adapted or drawn between these conversion stories and those of China/Mongolia (the dream motif, see Laufer 1931: 209, Yi-Liang 1945: 263), India (the Garuda motif in the Sanrabone tradition), Persia (the vision and dream motif, see Frye 1964: 42, 47, Klimkeit 1982: 19), and elsewhere.

In the case of Kedah, the account of the conversion to Islam in both indigenous and scholarly sources follows a similar pattern to the rest of Malay-speaking Southeast Asia. Both sources identify Kedah's Hindu-Buddhist and Siamese styled Raja as the first to adopt Islam. Whether titled *Phra Ong Mahawangsa, Raja Ong Maha Podisat, Praong Maha Podisat* or alternatively *Seri Peduka Maharaja Darbar* it was he who adopted Islam as the official religion for himself and for his people. Thus, he changed his name to Muzlaf Shah (Mazulfulshah or Mulzutulshah, according to the *Hikayat Merong Mahawangsa* versions referred to by Low 1849: 476; Fatimi 1963: 74).[13] There are, however, significant discrepancies in the stories about the mode of conversion of Kedah's Raja between the indigenous and more recent scholarly sources on Kedah. The indigenous pre-twentieth century sources portray Kedah's religious transformation with a combination of popular stories and miraculous events. On the other hand, post-nineteenth century scholarly sources, both written locally and outside of Kedah, attribute the conversion to be simply the result of charismatic Muslim missionaries visiting the region, or alternatively that Islam was introduced with the political ascendancy of Melaka in the fifteenth century CE.

Kedah's pre–twentieth century indigenous conversion stories and their variant modes of transformation may thus suggest something about the era in which they were written. These "miraculous myths," while seemingly out of place in a rational world, tell us something about the culture and beliefs of Kedah's people in the pre-Islamic era. While modern translators have wished to delete these magical accounts, it is important for us to examine them. The question is what do they tell us about the age? Does it say something about contemporary Islam? Does it tell us something about the possible sources of the account or the literature?

Alternatively, it could be argued that this significant event in Kedah's history enables us to better comprehend the forces involved in its political survival, as well as its ability to function as a regional economic powerhouse. Indeed the Sultan's decision, as the representative of the people and the *negeri*, to convert to a new religious and belief system meant that the people soon had to follow his example and adhere to its principles. Nonetheless, the Sultan's decision meant that he had to reinvent himself within the new religious institution by handpicking pre-Islamic aspects that were popular and easily understood at various levels, e.g., court peoples, *rakyat*, sea peoples and foreigners. The socioeconomic and political divisions amongst the Sultan's peoples also meant that their expectations from him and Kedah's political entity were different. Indeed a comparison of the literary sources and oral testimony in this chapter highlights a certain cultural and moral baggage that was intentionally, but necessarily, carried into Islam.

THE LITERARY CONVERSION STORY OF KEDAH

The main indigenous source, the *Hikayat Merong Mahawangsa*, reports that Kedah's pre-Islamic ruler, *Phra Ong Mahawangsa*, noted for his great thirst for *"arak"* or spirits, and wine was the first to convert and did so under miraculous circumstances.[14] His conversion occurred through the magical appearance of a saintly Sufi disciple and mystic, Sheikh Abdullah, in the royal palace of Kedah. At the time, the mystic was accompanying Iblis/Eblis, or Satan, as part of a spiritual journey. Thus, the story according to an English translation of *Hikayat Merong Mahawangsa* unfolds as follows, cited and translated in length by Fatimi:

> Here they entered the palace of the Raja and, before he was wide awake, stood beside the bed curtains. Presently the Raja awoke and called for his usual glass of spirits.[15] The page went to fill it from one of the jars, when the wretch Iblis stepping up defiled the beverage, he being invisible. The Rajah drank it off, when Shaykh Abdullah losing his temper said to Iblis, "God bless me! Why did you defile the Raja's draught?" Iblis replied, "Did I not caution and direct you not to question or find fault with what I might do toward any of your race?" "True," said the other, "and I should not have found fault with you elsewhere, but here you have the hardihood to behave thus toward a great prince, who is about to be one of God's Viceregents." The Raja was astonished to hear people squabbling so close to him, without his being able to see them. But just at this moment Iblis got angry with his pupil and said to him, "Since you have become so clever, it is time that we should part." Hereupon he suddenly snatched his staff out of Abdullah's hand leaving him visible to the Raja, he himself departing. [sic] (1963: 74)

Here, it should be noted that an aspect of Fatimi's (1963) translation differs significantly from other versions of the *Hikayat Merong Mahawangsa* consulted in this study: e.g., R. J. Wilkinson's (1898) Jawi[16] and A. J. Sturrocks (1916) romanized version. In particular the reference in Fatimi's version to Kedah's ruler as he "who is about to be one of God's Viceregents" [sic] differs radically from Wilkinson's (1898: 98) Jawi and Sturrock's (1916: 112) romanized version of the *Hikayat* that only refer to him as *"ini ia sa-orang raja besar memegang suatu negeri"* [sic] (i.e., "this is an important king who rules a country").

This variation may reflect Fatimi's use of Low's (1849: 474) succinct English version of a possibly unknown copy of the *Hikayat*, different to the later and more popular translations. Assuming that Low was correct in translating the Malay, or Jawi, then this remark raises some important questions on how did the Sheikh know the ruler was about to be one of God's Vice-regents? Was it predestined? If so, even if the devil had not defiled the wine would this have prevented the conversion from taking place? Whatever the case may be, Low and Fatimi give few details of the version of the *Hikayat* they consulted.

With the miraculous appearance of Sheikh Abdullah, the Raja was soon induced to pronounce his *"shahadat"* or testimony, thus, becoming a Muslim (*Hikayat Merong Mahawangsa yakni Silsila Negeri Kedah Darulaman* 1898: 99–100; *Hikayat Merong Maha Wangsa or Kedah Annals* 1916: 112–113). The ruler's interest in adopting Islam and studying about the true religion, *"ajarkan ugama islam yang sa-benar itu"* [sic], was so immediate and intense that just after the two words of the confession he went so far as to dump out his jar of "arak" onto the ground and destroyed idols of wood, earth, gold and silver (Low 1849; 474–476; *Hikayat Mahawangsa yakni Silsila Negeri Kedah Darulaman* 1898: 99–102; *Hikayat Merong Maha Wangsa or Kedah Annals* 1916: 113; Winstedt 1938: 35; Fatimi 1963: 74; Sherifa Zaleha Syed Hasan 1985: 49).

The consumption of wine by the Raja is significant as doctors originally prescribed it to him as a cure for a sickness and to help strengthen his weak body (*Hikayat Merong Maha Wangsa or Kedah Annals* 1916: 94–95). The emptying of this jar of wine was therefore the last time that Kedah's Raja drank "arak" and he quit the habit.[17] Consequently, the story portrays the conversion to have been an instantaneous act on the part of Kedah's ruler. Moreover, by emptying the jar the Raja indicated his intention for others to know that he was now cured of his illness.

Furthermore, the author of the *Hikayat* makes it clear that the conversion of Phra Ong Mahawangsa to Islam was not the first such incident in the region. Earlier in the book, prior to Sheikh Abdullah's understanding with Iblis, the author refers to Tuan Sheikh Nur Al-Din Turan,[18] an *"aulia dan keramat dengan shariat"* (i.e., a blessed saintly ascetic and religious scholar), who five years after the death of Prophet Muhammad left Mecca and Medina, in the Arabian Peninsula, for the country of "Jawi," otherwise "Aceh, *datang ke-negeri Jawi ia itu negeri Aceh*," taking with him books on religious tenets, *"membawa kitab shariat agamah Islam"* (Low 1849: 471; *Hikayat Mahawangsa yakni Silsila Negeri Kedah Darulaman* 1898: 78).

The author of the *Hikayat* remains silent after this short mention of Aceh until the arrival of the news of the conversion of Kedah's ruler and its population (Low 1849: 471; *Hikayat Mahawangsa yakni Silsila Negeri Kedah Darulaman* 1898: 103; Winstedt 1938: 35). With the arrival of this piece of news, the Sultan of Aceh and Tuan Sheikh Nur Al-Din together send to Kedah two popular religious Islamic texts, that of *Sirat al-Mustaghim* and the *Bab al-Nikah*. This acknowledges the association of Aceh with Tuan Sheikh Nur Al-Din, prior to the arrival of Sheikh Abdullah, and the presence of a Muslim Sultan in Aceh at the time of Kedah's conversion. Moreover, the *Hikayat Merong Mahawangsa* with its reference to the subsequent arrival of the news at Aceh further indicates that the Kedah ruler's mode of conversion to Islam was not only a result of a spiritual experience but also a prestigious event and independent from Aceh, with direct links to the Middle East.

The naming of Aceh, rather than another regional kingdom, and the supposed arrival of two Islamic religious texts sent from there may further suggest its compelling influence in Kedah (*Hikayat Mahawangsa yakni Silsila Negeri Kedah Darulaman* 1898: 103–104; Blagden 1909: 528). Similarly it may be evidence that parts or aspects of the *Hikayat* were compiled at Kedah during the seventeenth century, when Aceh's power and influence in the region was at its peak. Indeed, the geographical location and proximity of Aceh, in Northern Sumatra, to Kedah, just across the Melaka Straits, has meant that they have traditionally been economically, politically and culturally interconnected (refer to Map 2 and 4). Furthermore, there were instances in Kedah's history when there was direct Acehnese control of its islands or the coastline centers.[19] There is also evidence of Acehnese influences at Kedah, as well the durbar or royal court (such as court titles and numerous undated Acehnese graves on the Langkawi Islands and at Perlis, see Yatim 1985: 144, 148; Andaya 2001b: 63).[20] Similarly the genealogical connection of the Kedah royal family and the land of Rum, appearing in *Hikayat Merong Mahawangsa*, is similar to several places in northern and western Sumatra (Braddell 1936: 42–44; Jessup 1990: 81; Reid 1969: 395, 2005: 69–70).[21]

Assuming this to be the case, then this may point to Aceh's historic relevance to Kedah in contrast to areas further south (there is only reference to Aceh's predecessor of Pasai in the older "Malay Annals or *Sejarah Melayu*," see Brown 1952 or 1970, *Malay Annals* 2001 and Andaya 2001a: 327).[22] This is however not to say that the authors of *Hikayat Merong Mahawangsa* were not familiar with aspects of other Malay stories popular in other parts of the Malay world. The conversion of Aceh according to the *Hikayat* took place several years after the death of the Prophet and certainly aspects of this story are in line with the older, likely fourteenth century, *Hikayat Raja-Raja Pasai* (Low 1849: 471; *Hikayat Mahawangsa yakni Silsila Negeri Kedah Darulaman* 1898: 78; Winstedt 1940; *Hikayat Raja-Raja Pasai* 1960: 32–33, 36, 116–119).[23]

In any case, the Raja's conversion to Islam was soon followed by the subsequent conversion of the king's wives, concubines, and people in the palace, as well as officials, ministers, and people in his dominion (Low 1849; 474–476; *Hikayat Mahawangsa yakni Silsila Negeri Kedah Darulaman* 1898: 99–102; Hikayat Merong Maha Wangsa or Kedah Annals 1916: 113–114). Moreover, under advice from Sheikh Abdullah, and in a daring move shortly after the initial conversion of his wives and concubines, the Raja Ong Mahawangsa asked his court servants to join in, and symbolically eat together: "*Maka titah raja Ong Mahawangsa, 'Mari juga kita makan';*

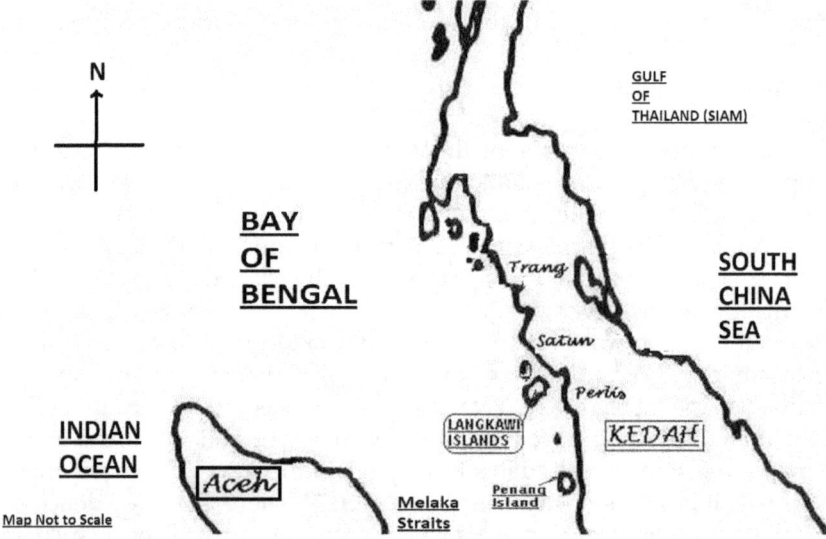

Map 4. Geographical proximity of Kedah to Aceh.

lalu makan-lah sa-hidang dengan baginda. Sa-telah itu lalu makan sireh, sambil berkata kata" (Hikayat Merong Maha Wangsa or Kedah Annals 1916: 113).

This symbolic act of the Raja eating with the Sheikh and his servants mentioned in the *Hikayat Merong Mahawangsa* was not simply a sign of newly found humility as a result of discovering Islam; but, rather one gets the impression that Islam had given the kingdom a social message of brotherhood and broke the social barriers. In particular, the eating together of *"sireh"* or "betel nut," by Kedah's ruler and his court servants is a highly significant act, uncommon in most Malay *Hikayats* or literary works (e.g., on the symbolic eating of *sireh* by native rulers only in the company of each other or with relations or court ministers or visiting traders see: *Hikayat Raja-Raja Pasai* 1960: 109, 121; Ras 1968: 282–285; *Misa Melayu* cited in Andaya 1979: 164, 189; Alexander Hamilton, 1995 II: 73, visiting Kedah in the seventeenth or the early eighteenth century, to trade, describes in detail the mode of having to chew betel-nut with the ruler).[24] Moreover, by bestowing on the servants the honor of eating together with the ruler, for their services and company, Sheikh Abdullah was likely trying to introduce new aspects and systems of government, kingship or humility to the ruler of Kedah.

In addition, it is Sheikh Abdullah that always takes the preliminary initiatives in motivating or requesting the newly converted Raja to gather the people at the palace, *"Hendak-lah tuanku himpunkan sakalian kechil besar di-dalam istani ini"* [sic], or visit the royal audience hall, *"balai rong"* [sic], and spread the message of Islam (Hikayat Merong Maha Wangsa or Kedah Annals 1916: 113). The process of religious conversion of the royal family and others in Kedah was not however entirely a result of the Sheikh's actions. Rather it was a combination of royal commands, and speeches by his majesty, or the Raja, as well as the supervision of the confession, or *"kalimah shahadat,"* and the teachings, *"ajarkan-nya,"* of its religious principles by Sheikh Abdullah. Hence working together and complementing each other was a situation of mutual benefit to the two of them.

Indeed, from the *Hikayat* it is apparent that the toughest audience to convince about the recent events at Kedah for Sheikh Abdullah and the Raja were the ministers, *"menteri hulubalang"* and in particular the four *"menteri keempat"* (Hikayat Merong Maha Wangsa or Kedah Annals 1916: 113–115).[25] The meeting with them was crucial since earlier in the story it was the four ministers *"menteri keempat,"* together with elements in the court and the queen, that had revolted and overthrown the Raja's grandfather, Raja Bersiong, who was said to have developed a vampire-like taste for human blood, liver, and hearts (Low 1849: 264; Hikayat Merong Maha Wangsa or Kedah Annals 1916: 74–75; Winstedt 1938: 34). Furthermore, the ministers were the ones that became the caretakers of Kedah government until the time they allowed Raja Bersiong's illegitimate son and the Raja's own father, Phra Ong Mahapodisat, to return to Kedah and rule (Winstedt 1938: 34). Thus, in contrast to the earlier relatively easy introduction of Islam to Kedah's royal household (who were only required to come into the presence of the Raja and the Sheikh), this time the situation was the reverse. With both the Raja and the Sheikh therefore required going to the *"balai rong."*[26] There the Raja introduced Sheikh Abdullah, sitting to his right, and then gave a long lecture on the credibility of Sheikh Abdullah, the new religion and the recent incredible, events he had experienced that day. The significance of this event may suggest that behind the Raja's honest motive for conversion to Islam and his immediate desire to forfeit his taste for "arak," there were, other more significant political reasons. The Raja was well aware of the fate of his grandfather and likely knew that ultimately the common perception of his drinking would sooner or later cause tensions and conflict with the *menteri* and other court elements. Moreover, he may have also been aware of the *menteri*'s knowledge of Islam from Acehnese sources or the previously mentioned Baghdad traders. Thus, by adapting Islam he thought it would enable him to convince his skeptics that he was a changed man. On the other hand, assuming that the wine and the blood-drinking issues were both part of Tantric rites practiced by Kedah's Rajas then they may well have been seen as attempts by them to increase their spiritual and temporal powers. Possession of these Tantric powers by the Rajas, as we shall see further below, would have been possibly seen as a direct threat to the position of the politically powerful *menteri*.

After all, converting to Islam meant perhaps a higher level of discipline and greater control over sensual desires, or *"nafs,"* especially refraining from drinking intoxicants, or other forbidden liquids (particularly urine or blood). Equally by controlling his desires the Raja was more likely to be seen by the ministers and the people to be just, "*adil* or *adel*," and become fairer, "*insaf* or *ensaf*," in his kingly duties. This is of course not to say that the Raja by accepting Islam had other ulterior, or sinister, motives in his mind. Consequently, he may well have thought that the conversion to Islam was an opportunity for him to guide, or further, his personal quest for temporal and spiritual power.

Alternatively, the Raja by openly accepting Islam may well have had the political ambition to put an end to speculations and uncertainties surrounding his physical, or spiritual, condition. It is also possible that he was attempting to prolong his rule and strengthen his position. In consequence, the Raja may well have thought that the conversion could boost his public image, at home and abroad, and result in enhancing Kedah's political stability as well as economic prosperity and commercial ties, particularly to the Muslims and visitors from Baghdad whom he earlier recalled (see Hikayat Merong Maha Wangsa or Kedah Annals 1916: 112). Furthermore, by publicly converting to Islam and visiting the *balai rong*, in the company of Sheikh Abdullah, the Raja was likely to portray himself to the powerful *menteri* to be no longer in pursuit of more power and hence a political threat, thus, seeking to reaffirm their support and allegiance.

Whatever the Raja's motivation was soon stability and prosperity, particularly in the sense of food and population increases, returned to Kedah. These signs of prosperity were certainly deemed to be key elements in the success or failure of a Malay ruler (Trocki 1979: xvi, 1997: 86, 2000, 2006; Maier 1988: 192–193; Anderson 1990: 42–44; Carsten 1995: 327; Barnard 2003: 15). For one thing, Kedah had become prosperous during the time of his father, Phra Ong Mahapodisat (placed on the throne of Kedah in an earlier incident), who proved to be both "*sangat adil dan insaf*" (Hikayat Merong Maha Wangsa or Kedah Annals 1916: 93).

The *Hikayat* therefore clearly indicates that having a just and a fair ruler was central to the prosperity of the realm. In addition, the success or failure of a ruler had necessarily nothing to do with his religion, as was the case of Raja Ong Mahapodisat, but more to do with kingly qualities of being just and the state of his mind (*akal* in Malay or *aql* in Persian[27] and Arabic). These aspects of Malay kingship, on the success or failure of the ruler, in the *Hikayat* are clearly inspired by and are in line with traditional Persian kingship, in both pre-Islamic and post-Islamic periods, which is thought to have influenced much of the traditional political systems in the region (Marrison 1955: 52–69; Lambton 1962: 91–119; Scupin 1980: 55–66; Milner 1981: 46–70; Chambert-Loir 2005: 135, 139–141; Thant Myint-U 2006: 74–75). Hence, indicating further familiarity and influences of the Kedah chronicler with non-indigenous sources and political systems.

The commendable qualities of Phra Ong Mahapodisat may likewise explain the title of Mahapodisat, the Thai pronunciation of Maha-Bodhisattva, in his name. This proclaims the king's status as a great Bodhisattva, i.e., a great Buddha-to-be, and his concern for all beings (Bennett 1929: 25). This emphasized the importance of the ruler and his realm as patrons of Tantric Buddhism (Lamb 1962: 15; Milner 1981: 50–58; Andaya 2001a: 320).[28] Being part of esoteric Buddhism and related to Mahayana (or the Greater Vehicle) sect of Buddhism, this meant that the Raja had overcome in his lifetime the four obstacles, or "poisons" [sic] (of lust, hatred, delusion and pride), as well as perfecting himself in the Ten High Virtues (or *Dasa Paramita* in Pali) in life in order to acquire a blessed, holy, and enlightened status on earth (Bennett 1929: 2–3, 24–26; Wayman 1961: 82; Luce 1969: 375).

The title Phra Ong Mahapodisat therefore confirms the notion that at least in the pre-Islamic court of Kedah the Mahayana and its Tantric form of Buddhism was observed. Indeed, the symbolic use and familiarity with the term Bodhisattva at Kedah can be traced back to the sixth century CE.[29]

This status of a divine Bodhisattva character at Kedah was of course acquired and not inherited, unlike the case of the rulers of Kotei in Borneo who claimed their origin from a God that had supposedly came down to earth (Scott 1913: 325). Thus, the portrayal of Kedah rulers in the *Hikayat Merong Mahawangsa* is not that of divine descendants living on earth, rather of individuals that had achieved higher status and were also subject to downfall. But this did not mean that God did not love and look after the rulers of Kedah even if they had not attained the status of Bodhisattva (Maier 1988: 79). Thus in the *Hikayat* Kedah's rulers may often fall from grace but then are able to once again rise and acquire their former glory, as was the case of Phra Ong Mahawangsa.

Aspects of the above story are therefore not unusual and may be familiar to Asian or Islamic scholars. In particular a parallel can be drawn with the story of Iblis or Satan in the undated Jawi text of *Hikayat Iblis*,[30] which is comprised largely of a discussion between Iblis and the Prophet Muhammad, and a symbolic dialogue between Iblis with Moaviyya, an early Muslim ruler and personality, in the thirteenth century popular Persian work of *Mathnawi* by Muhammad Jalalludin Balkhi (better known outside the Persian speaking world as Mawlana/Maulana Rumi), 1207–1273 CE. Similarly, a parallel can be drawn between this story and the Persian story of a charismatic hero, Hatem of Tai, and his wanderings with Death (*Iranskaya skazochnaya entsiklopediya* 1977 cited in Braginsky 1993: 61).[31] Hence the compilers of the *Hikayat* may well have been familiar with any of these sources.

In addition, the story of Phra Ong Mahawangsa's thirst for "*arak*" is akin to the Javanese account of king Krtanagara, of the Majapahit dynasty (thirteenth to the sixteenth century). According to the early sixteenth century Kawi text of *The Pararaton* King Krtanagara was addicted to an intoxicating drink, *"pijer anadah sajong"* or palm-wine, and was subsequently killed when the kingdom and the palace were invaded by his enemies (*The Pararaton* 1996: 98–101).[32] Thus it could well be that Phra Ong Mahawangsa was practicing a Tantric rite, rather than mainstream Buddhism. Particularly since mainstream Buddhism, such as Mahayana and Theravada, and most Buddhist texts, unlike Hinduism, strongly advise against drinking any types of intoxicants, unless it is under special circumstances or for a medicinal remedy (Hopkins 1906: 459, 459n, 461; *Fo tsu t'ung chi* and *Suvarnaprabhasa* cited in Scott 1995: 150, 158; *The Jataka* stories).

It seems that the authors or copyists of *The Pararaton* and *Hikayat Merong Mahawangsa* were therefore familiar with stories from the Buddhist *Jataka* tales (certainly characters and stories from the *Jatakas* had been appearing in both mainland and island Southeast Asia for more than 1,000 years, see Winstedt 1920b: 119–126; Luce 1969: 376–383, 386–388; and Yousof 1994: 99–100).[33] The *Jataka* stories were in line with Buddhist principles and also strongly advised against consumption of intoxicating drinks (such as the stories of *Harita-Jataka* number 431, *Kumbha-Jataka* number 512 and *Mahabodhi-Jataka* number 528). There is also a striking resemblance of one of these stories to that found in the *Hikayat*. In *Jataka* story *Kumbha-Jataka* number 512, the accidental dropping of a grain by a bird ferments the water-tank hence bringing havoc and destruction to all who unknowingly drink from it (Francis 1905: 6–11; Crooke 1906: 498–499). Later however the king, his people and animals are saved by the sudden arrival of a holy man who points to the polluted water tank as the cause of their calamities. There is especially a strong affinity between this *Jataka* story and the addiction of Phra Ong Mahawangsa. He became addicted to the wine unwillingly and was later saved by the sudden arrival of a Muslim mystic. King Krtangara's intoxication however led to his demise and unlike the Kedah ruler he did not have the opportunity to be rescued. Consequently, it is more than likely that the Muslim copyist or revisionists of the *Hikayat* agreed with the earlier Buddhist justification of the ruler's drinking habit for a medical condition.

Alternatively, the story of Phra Ong Mahawangsa's thirst for *"arak"* can certainly be connected to a continuance of an earlier story from the same *Hikayat* regarding his "vampire-like" grandfather, Ong Maha Perita Deria or Raja Bersiong, who was said to be unable to control his thirst for human blood, liver, and hearts (Low 1849: 264; Hikayat Merong Maha Wangsa or Kedah Annals 1916: 71–82; Winstedt 1938: 34). R. J. Wilkinson (1957: 14) and Braginsky (1993: 59–61) argue that the acts of cannibalism by Raja Bersiong were due to his demonic ancestry or passions that were supposedly, as the *Hikayat* maintains, tainted by several of his predecessors having married aboriginal or ogre (*gergasi*) women.[34] This echoes Hindu/Buddhist traditions that refer to *Pisitasanas, Pisitasins,* and *Naika-*

sheyas as the core of carnivorous and cannibal impulses that supposedly descended from the female line of Nikasha or Kaikasi, a female demon that was the daughter of Su-Mali (the great king of the *Rakshasa*, in Sanskrit, or *raksasa* or *gergasi*, in Malay, or ogres), and mother of Ravana, later king of the ogres, in the *Ramayana* (Dowson 1888: 214, 222, 235, 264–265, 363).[35] Indeed like Raja Bersiong, the mythological ogre king Ravana had mixed parentage, with a *Rakshasa* as his mother and a Brahman as his father, i.e., Visravas (Dowson 1888: 265, 362–363; Purnalingam Pillai 1928: 14–18).[36]

What's more, similar stories of kings and deities that were born with demonic tendencies, particularly having tusks, or had turned cruel, due to their lineage or inability to control their desire and lust for human blood, meat or brains, can also be found in other parts of Southeast Asia (*Hikayat Bandjar*, the story of Indra Barma Kala in *Hikayat Raja Babi* and folk-traditions in Philippines), China (story of He Bo, the vampire-like river god, in *Luoyang qielan ji*), South Asia (stories in the *Mahabharata*, *Vishnu Purana*[37] and *Jataka* particularly the stories of *Jayaddisa-Jataka* number 513 and *Maha-Sutasoma-Jataka* number 537), and Persia (the popular story of Zahak, referred to as the Serpent-King, and Iblis from the tenth to the eleventh century CE from A. G. Ferdowsi's or Firdausi, died 1020 CE, *Shah-Nameh* or "Book of Kings").[38] It is more than likely that the author/s and copyist/s of the *Hikayat* were familiar with any of these stories or traditions elsewhere.

Undoubtedly, the Raja's initial introduction to wine as a medication and his gradual addiction reminds one of the stories in *Shah-Nameh*. According to the *Shah-Nameh* (*The Epic of Kings or Shahnameh by Ferdowsi* 2000: 8–21) the devil (disguised as a cook) first got the vegetarian King Zahak to turn carnivore and then using treachery—before disappearing—kissed the king's shoulders implanting two live snakes there. Shortly thereafter the devil turned up again, this time disguised as a "learned man" prescribing Zahak (as a trap) to feed the snakes with human brains in order to get rid of them. This was of course the downfall of Zahak. Not only was his name tarnished, as a cruel ruler, but also misery followed in the land with people rebelling against him, and others being killed simply to feed the snakes. Similarly, the not so accidental dropping of blood on Raja Bersiong's vegetables by a servant (that initiated his cycle of destruction and downfall) and the prescription of wine to a sick *Phra Ong Mahawangsa* as a cure for his sickness are both instances in which Iblis may have had orchestrated a master plan designed for the gradual and painful destruction of the Rajas and Kedah.[39]

Then again, the cannibalistic aspect of the *Hikayat Merong Mahawangsa* could have easily entered the *text* from the mystical exorcist (*ruwatan/ ruatan* or *berjamu*) plots (*lakon*) of the "Origin of Kala" (or *Murwa Kala*) found in the *wayang kulit* or shadow-puppet tradition, popular in mainland and island Southeast Asia (the exorcist aspect of the puppet-show is very old and can be documented back to the seventeenth century, see Sears 1989: 125).[40] These mystical exorcist plots were performed prior to and after the shadow-puppet shows.

According to the exorcist plots found in Sunda (particularly *Wayang golek purwa*), Java (particularly *wayang kulit*) and the Malay Peninsula (*Wayang kulit Siam*, and *wayang gedek* unique to Kedah) Bentara/Betara Kala, or Kala or Sang Kaki, is the son of Betra/Bathara Guru (a Hindu-Javanese deity often connected to the goddess Siva), that was created because of his consort's unwillingness to have sexual intercourse (Wilkinson 1957: 34; Sears 1989: 125; Petersen 1991: 130, 132; Yousof 1994: 26, 29, 158, 160, 296; Brakel 1997: 256; Foley 2001: 1–3). The semidivine and vegetarian Bentara Kala however soon developed a voracious appetite for human flesh after having accidentally tasted blood that had dripped from the finger of his maid onto the vegetables (the maid is referred to as Mak Mabu Kelan Dermi in *Wayang kulit Siam* and as Emban Durga in *Wayang golek purwa* traditions, see Sweeney 1971: 437; Yousof 1994b: 26; Foley 2001: 9).

The Kedah author/s and copyist/s were more than likely familiar with the shadow-puppet exorcist plots, as well the story of King Zahak from the *Shah-Nameh*. Thus the incorporation of such stories in *Hikayat Merong Mahawangsa* and other premodern Malay societies would have not been unusual as argued in a detailed study by Sweeney (1987: 221–242). Certainly an episode in the life of Raja Bersiong and Kampar/Gumpar/Gampar, when the latter questioned the motives of the former, runs parallel to the story of Kaveh of Esfahan, who challenged King Zahak, and is somewhat different to the exorcist plot of the *wayang kulit* episode of Kala, whose cannibal tendencies were symbolically neutralized (Low 1849: 264–265; Sweeney 1971: 437; Petersen 1991: 130; Yousof 1994b: 135–136; *The Epic of Kings or Shahnameh by Ferdowsi* 2000: 15–18). In addition in both stories the challenge by Kaveh and Kampar resulted in the masses realizing the unjust deeds of their rulers and ultimately revolting (in both cases the ruler is also not killed). Nevertheless, it is possible to assume that the author/s of the *Hikayat* were inspired to accommodate this aspect of the *Shah-Nameh* from the *selembit*, a form of Kedah solo storytelling, as well as shadow-puppet shows (in *Wayang Gedek*, popular at Kedah stories from the Middle East were traditionally as popular as the Rama stories, see Yousof 1994: 296, 1994b: 244, 282–287). Additionally, from the type of the grammatical and spelling mistake of the Persian name of *Turan Zamin*, i.e., the land of Turan, to *Zamin Turan* by the author/s and copyist/s in *Hikayat Merong Mahawangsa* for a place that plays a pivotal role in the *Shah-Nameh* it can be argued that its author/s were not consulting a textual version of *Shah-Nameh*. Rather they were citing a place name that they had overheard (refer to the *Jawi* writing of the word by Low 1849: 165, as well as *Hikayat Mahawangsa yakni Silsila Negeri Kedah Darulaman* 1898: 35).[41] In the mid-nineteenth century J. D. Vaughan (1970:

133–134) witnessed a shadow-puppet show popular amongst the Malays of Penang, who were predominantly Kedah peoples. The story closely follows that of Rustam, representing the Iranian nation, and his son, Sohrab, representing Turan, from the *Shahnameh*. According to this report by Vaughan the hero battles his main opponent only to find out at the end that it is his own son (this report by Vaughan is also produced at length in Skeat 1900: 514–516).

Furthermore, there is the possibility that the drunkenness and blood drinking by Raja Bersiong and his great-grandson Phra Ong Mahawangsa should be considered a reference to pre-Islamic Tantric practices on the part of Kedah rulers. Indeed the drinking of wine, a soma drink (or "nectar of the Gods," made from a plant), urine, feces, and cannibalism were all parts of mystical rituals in esoteric Hinduism (e.g., Vaisnavism and practices of the Aghori Fakirs) and allowed in Tantric Buddhism, Tibetan Buddhism and by the Bauls of Bengal (influenced by Buddhism and Sufi Islam). Such practices were not unheard of and continued to be documented well into the twentieth century (Balfour 1897; Wayman 1961; Capwell 1974; Kripal 1994; Crowley 1996; Lang 1996; Mackenzie 1998). Likewise, historic Zoroastrian, Manichaean, Mitra/Mithra and Christian religions each involve the use of either urine, wine, and the drink of soma as part of religious rituals (Dowson 1888: 302; Wasson 1971: 178; Crowley 1996; Mackenzie 1998: 5, 35, 77; Norouzian 2006: 11n–12n).[42] Besides according to a 1436 CE Chinese account, by Fei Hsin in *Hsing-Ch'a Sheng-lan*, Tantric sacrifices and the offering of human blood to wooden images were popular practices during his visit to Pahang, on the east coast of the Malay Peninsula, (translated passages in Groeneveldt 1960: 136, and also the preface to *Undang-Undang Pahang* in Kempe and Winstedt 1948: 1).[43] Each of these religious rites, particularly Tantric Buddhism or esoteric Hindu sects, seems to have been practiced in the coastal and maritime centers of pre-Islamic Kedah.[44] Consequently, it is likely that the method and quantity used for drinking, either blood or wine, by Kedah's rulers went either against other locally held beliefs or more importantly, the Raja's attempt to seek more power was seen as a threat to their own, i.e., the people and the *menteris*. Alternatively, it could be that this account is simply a way for the latter day Muslim writers or copyists to cast earlier religious practices in a bad light.

What is more, it is possible that the two rulers at Kedah, Raja Bersiong, and Phra Ong Mahawangsa, attempted to go beyond the Bodhisattva or Sadhyana status and achieve a further Godlike status (Dowson 1888: 301–302; Wayman 1961: 85; Capwel 1974: 261; Bharati 1977: 242). In Hindu, Jain, and Tantric Buddhist texts and plays (e.g., *Rig Veda, Brahmayamala, Yasastilaka, Hevajra, Cetupuranam, Skanda Purana* and *Mahabharata*) drinking of ritual drinks, such as blood and wine, and eating meat is said to result in achieving immortality, pleasing the Hindu gods, in particular Shiva/Siva and Kali. One could go as far as becoming a God-like figure, such as Krishna, (Dowson 1888: 301–302, 347; Wasson 1971: 179, 181; Capwel 1974: 262n; Shulman 1976: 124, 124n; Bharati 1977: 69–70, 242, 244, 259–261; Lang 1996: 173–174; Mackenzie 1998: 41; Woodward 2004: 333). In Tantric Buddhism, as well as a Hindu ritual (still practiced in parts of Southern India) the eating and drinking of meat and liquids, often buffalo blood, involves a ritual in which the individual believes that they are feeding the goddess (the drinking of buffalo blood is popular in Southern India Shulman 1976: 128; Bharati 1977: 260–261, 267). Traditions in the orthodox Theravada school of Burma also suggests on the possibility of drinking blood solely for its medicinal purposes. According to this tradition Buddha made a physically unwell monk, whose liver was being eaten by maggots, to drink the blood of a horse in order to be cured (see "Tier E3. GI. 201" translated by Luce 1969: 382).[45] All the above sources, however, clearly stress that the consumption of the ritual drinks needs to be in moderation and within strict guidelines.

Consequently, Hindu gods (such as Agni,[46] Krishna, Indra, and Rama) are said to have loved drinking wine and soma in moderation to achieve courage and divine ecstasy and the "Right Culture of the Mind," or *Samadhi* (Dowson 1888: 123–127; Oertel 1897: 26–27, 30; Bennett 1929: 72; Wasson 1971: 181; Capwell 1974: 262n; Kripal 1994: 165–166; Lang 1996: 165, 169; Mackenzie 1998: 5, 15, 19–23).[47] Likewise, according to legends the Hindu God Ramakrishna was himself a great lover of *karana*, or wine, but only drunk it by licking it with just "a touch of a tongue" (in order to achieve divine ecstasy) and despised those that drank too much (Kripal 1994: 165–166). It is therefore possible to assume that the excessive use of blood or wine and the methods, as well the sources used to obtain them by the Kedah rulers were considered to be unjust and immoral by the people, courtiers, and priests. This objection to the excessive and irresponsible use of wine and blood, for simply attaining power and turning into a God, was likely the objective of some of the earliest non-Muslim or Hindu-Buddhist stories in the *Hikayat*.

On the other hand, the *Hikayat Merong Mahawangsa*'s later Muslim chroniclers, or copyists, may be condemning Kedah's earlier rulers for trying to go beyond the Bodhisattva's status and turning into a God-like figure that resembled aspects of Persian kingship recognized in Islam (particularly Sufism), at the time of the writing the book. Hence, Hindu and Buddhist ideas of drinking forbidden intoxicants, or other liquids, either in moderation or under strict guidelines, got little sympathy from the *Hikayat*'s authors.

The tenth to the eleventh century CE Persian book of *Shah-Nameh* further clarifies that no matter how successful or powerful, earthly men and Kings could never become Gods. For this reason, God literally "withdrew his hand" [sic] from the celebrated mythical Persian King Jamshid shortly after he was overwhelmed with pride and proclaimed himself a God and ordered images of himself to be built (*The Epic of Kings or Shah-*

nameh by Ferdowsi 2000: 7). With the end of God's blessings, King Jamshid's political and social power soon started to wane and he became destitute. This popular story of *Shah-Nameh* was likely known in Kedah.[48] Additionally, the Sufi practice of viewing oneself as "God," "pole" (or *qutb* in Persian or *kuttupu* in Tamil), or the "truth" (or *haq* in Persian and Arabic) is more to do with being one with God rather than trying to rise above God or challenging Him (John 1957, 1965; al-Attas 1963; Arberry 1969; Milner 1981; Rizvi 1986). Thus, Raja Bersiong's and Phra Ong Mahawangsa's attempts to become immortal or godlike could have been seen as a direct challenge to God. Moreover unity with God as a Sufi and the idea of becoming a "Perfect Man or *Ensani/Insani Kamil*," was very much like becoming enlightened as a Bodhisattva, and required a combination of rituals, meditation and guidelines that required effort and purity of heart, and freedom from injustice (John 1957; Milner 1981: 55–59; Nurbakhsh 1986: 73–75).

But, the most intriguing aspect of the above story is the fact that Sheikh Abdullah became agitated and broke his earlier promise to Iblis or Satan. He had agreed not to question his actions and judgments, and he kept this promise until the time when Iblis became disrespectful of Kedah's ruler by defiling his drink. From the time he left Baghdad with Iblis, Sheikh Abdullah remained silent and acted simply as a mere observer while Ibis repeatedly brought havoc and bickering amongst nations, peoples and families (*Hikayat Mahawangsa yakni Silsila Negeri Kedah Darulaman* 1898: 78–97; Hikayat Merong Maha Wangsa or Kedah Annals 1916: 100–110; Winstedt 1938: 34). Likewise, Sheikh Abdullah in an earlier episode of the *Hikayat*, during the time of Raja Peranggi Dewa, remained silent when as a result the evil-doings of Iblis many were killed following an "amok," and others became possessed by carnal and lustful desires and temptations, "*Demikian itu-lah orang yang menurut hawa nafsu shaitan*" (*Hikayat Mahawangsa yakni Silsila Negeri Kedah Darulaman* 1898: 98; Hikayat Merong Maha Wangsa or Kedah Annals 1916: 111). Furthermore, throughout the stories and events in the *Hikayat Merong Mahawangsa*, Sheikh Abdullah's orthodox Islamic views, such as the breaking of idols, and his religious zeal are evident. Thus we might expect that Sheikh Abdullah would follow his earlier routine of simply observing Satan at work and remaining cool and indifferent to what was unfolding.

So, the question arises why did Sheikh Abdullah take the dangerous road of defying Iblis by defending Kedah's non-Muslim ruler and jeopardizing his original spiritual mission? In particular Kedah's ruler was not yet a Muslim, and had not yet heard about Islam.

It is possible that Sheikh Abdullah felt his spiritual mission, in the company of Iblis, was by then complete and his destiny now lay in conversion and missionary work. This new possibility would therefore allow Sheikh Abdullah the opportunity to stay in a non-Muslim dominion, which was a fertile ground for missionary work. Similarly, the Sheikh having earlier witnessed the destruction of great nations as well as the destruction of the moral fabric of society through Iblis's evil-doings and *"hawa nafsu"* (or pronounced *"hawa-yeh nafs"* in Persian) decided that there was still time for Kedah's salvation. In the introductory words of Sheikh Abdullah to Kedah's Raja on Islam there is an explicit link between the presence of Iblis and his descendants that "come and sow chaos" together with earlier pre-Islamic religions that are untrue, *"segala ugama yang dahulu itu sesat jua tiada dengan sa-benar-nya, jangan tuan-ku tiada ketahui sebab ugama yang tiada sa-benar itu-lah dating (datang?) iblis shaitan membuat haru-biru"* [sic] (*Hikayat Mahawangsa yakni Silsila Negeri Kedah Darulaman* 1898: 98; *Hikayat Merong Maha Wangsa or Kedah Annals* 1916: 112–113; Maier 1988: 181–183). Hence, by introducing Islam, Sheikh Abdullah was in reality giving Kedah's pre-Islamic ruler an opportunity to start afresh and prevent his government from being destroyed by Satan.

In consequence, Sheikh Abdullah's intervention and conversion of Kedah's ruler results in saving Kedah from chain of catastrophic events. The author of the *Hikayat Merong Mahawangsa* makes no reference to what type of destruction would have transpired in Kedah. Nevertheless, from a description of earlier calamities outlined in the *Hikayat*, during the time of Raja Bersiong in Kedah or those orchestrated elsewhere by Iblis, it is clear that by having drank the tainted wine the unsuspecting Raja would have ignited a cycle of destructive addiction and misery for himself and chaos for his dominion. The great number of deaths would have certainly pleased Iblis, and his children and grandchildren that preyed upon their blood (*Hikayat Merong Maha Wangsa or Kedah Annals* 1916: 111; Maier 1988: 182).

Alternatively it is apparent that Sheikh Abdullah was well-aware of, or at least through esoteric knowledge knew of Kedah's pre-Islamic ruler's greatness. He also understood his legitimate status, his bright future and his noteworthy ancestry going back to the land of Rum (according to *Hikayat Merong Mahawangsa*). This can be further confirmed through the comments made by Sheikh Abdullah to Iblis (*Hikayat Merong Maha Wangsa or Kedah Annals* 1916: 112). In both the Jawi version of this event by Wilkinson (1898: 98) and the romanized version of *Hikayat Merong Mahawangsa* by Sturrock (1916: 112), Sheikh Abdullah expresses his protest at the defiling of the ruler's drink by exclaiming to Iblis:

"Astaghufur Allah al-adzim, betapa juga tuan hamba beri minum ayer kenching ka-pada raja itu? (i.e., How in the name of God can my lord give the ruler urine to drink?) (1916: 112)

Likewise, the astonished Satan responded by a question: *"Bukan-kah hamba kata dan pesan jangan tuan hamba tegur sa-barang perbuatan hamba di-atas segala manusia?"* (Roughly translated as "how can you speak and criticize a person who is above all humanity?")

In answer to which Sheikh Abdullah made his true feelings of respect for the Raja known: "*Pada tempat yang lain tiada hamba tegur, ini ia sa-orang raja besar memegang suatu negeri. Maka sampai hemat tuan hamba beri ia minum ayer kenching*" [sic]. ("In here the royal servants do not speak, this is an important king who rules a country. Thus giving the ruler to sip the tainted drink should be avoided.")

Subsequently, Sheikh Abdullah protests to Iblis because of his derogatory remarks and actions against Kedah's ruler. After all to the Sheikh, Kedah's Raja represented a grand ruler, governing a territory, and that demanded the utmost respect (Maier 1988: 182).

Furthermore there is the question of the discrepancy between the earlier and the more recent and orthodox versions of the *Hikayat*. The story of Iblis, his association with the Sheikh as part of a spiritual journey, and the conversion of Kedah's pre-Islamic ruler would be problematic to more orthodox Muslims and has thus been deleted. The scenario of a respected Muslim Sheikh accompanying Satan as part of a spiritual journey as outlined in the *Hikayat* would have undoubtedly to be eliminated because it would draw the wrath of orthodox Muslims, including many of the more institutionalized Sufi chains or "*silsila/selseleh*." Equally, it would cast some doubt about the prestige of Kedah's ruler's conversion as viewed by scholars like Fatimi: "The manner of the Rajah of Kedah's, Pra Ong Mahawangsa's, conversion is even more fantastic.[49] He was led to the Right Path by the Devil himself" (1963: 73).

No doubt then, that in later accounts of the *Hikayat Merong Mahawangsa* and more recent scholarly works on the conversion of Kedah's ruler to Islam this aspect of the story and the connection to Iblis is omitted (e.g., Wan Yahya bin Wan Muhammad Taib 1911; Khan 1939: 8–12, 14; Muhammad Hassan Bin To'Kerani Mohd. Arshad 1968: 26–30; Adil 1980: 7–8; Sharifa Zaleha 1985; Sheikh Niamat and Haji Wan Shamsudin 1996: 1–15).

However, there is more to this aspect of the *Hikayat* story and the connection of the Sheikh to Iblis. It is linked to the early Persian or Khorasan Sufi School, as well as its offspring the *wujudiya* school of Ibn Arabi, and his literary doctrine. This school displayed a strong fusion of Islamic devotionalism and Persian imagery at its roots; and the allegorical student-master relationship with Satan was acceptable.[50] This notion can be further supported by the reference to Iblis's staff, or *tongkat*, which was symbolically presented to Sheikh Abdullah, after he was admitted as Iblis's student. By holding it he showed his allegiance toward Iblis as a teacher or master (Low 1849: 473).[51] Indeed, the reference to the symbolic staff handed to Sheikh Abdullah by Iblis corresponds to that of Indian traditions in which a staff of cane, or *Sulam*, is the sign of a mystic, *Sanyase*, while in a *ranting* (or branch) story of the Malay *Ramayana*, that of *Jintan Mas Indra Bayu Rupa* and played only in some of the *Wayang kulit Siam* shows, the stick has magical qualities, *tongkat sakti* (*Ramayanam of*

Bhodhayanam 1840: 3n; Yousof 1994: 304–305).[52] Hence Persian Sufis such as Mansour Hallaj (died 922), Shahab al-Din Yahya Suhrawardi (died 1191 CE), Sana'i (died in the twelfth century), Ahmad Ghazzali (d. 1126), Sheikh Sa'di or Saadi (in his book *Boostan/Bustan* or Orchard), Sa'id Sarmad (executed 1661, who was a Persian Jew or Armenian merchant turned Sufi in Mogul India),[53] Mohammad J. Balkhi or Rumi (1207–1273 CE) and Sheikh Farid al-Din Attar Neishaburi/Neyshaburi (died 1219 CE) in their writings view Satan as an individual from whom much can be learned. Even though he was a fallen angel he was considered the greatest monotheist or lover of God (or *Khoda* in Persian). He refused to worship anything or prostrate himself in front of anyone but God, including Adam (Dehkhoda 1947; Schimmel 1975: 193–199; Attar Neyshaburi 1980; Algar 1982: 660–661; Nurbakhsh 1986; Balkhi 1987; Safa 1992/1994; Chittick 1992: 208; *Persopedia* 2011). Ghazali went as far as declaring, "Who does not learn *tawhid* (i.e., the "oneness of God") from Satan is an infidel"; while, Sarmad too advised, "Go, learn the method of servant-ship from Satan" (cited by Schimmel 1975: 195). "Iblis and Pharaoh" were likewise reputed by the tenth century Persian Sufi, Hallaj, to be the ultimate mystic masters and teachers (cited in length by Nurbakhsh 1986: 44; see also comments by Awn 1983: 125–126).[54] Sheikh Abdullah's mission with Satan and their arrival at Kedah can therefore be viewed as the highest form of a spiritual journey. At the time it was written, the account of this mystical journey of Sheikh Abdullah would undoubtedly have given further prestige to the conversion story of Kedah's ruler.

Indeed another unusual aspect of the *Hikayat Merong Mahawangsa* is the reference to the two books sent from Aceh to Kedah shortly after its conversion to Islam. Certainly *"Sirat al-Mustaghim,"* is believed to have been written by the seventeenth century Sheikh Nur al-Din Ibn Ali al-Raniri (died 1658 CE), an orthodox Sufi and self-professed anti-*wujudiya* scholar (Winstedt 1920a: 39, 1936: 157; Johns 1957: 30–35, 1965: 9; Omar bin Awang 1981: 82; Braginsky 1993: 68–69; Cheah 1993: 11; Riddell 2001: 116–125).[55] Thus, it would be expected that the author/authors or copyists of the *Hikayat* would have been familiar with al-Raniri's anti-*wujudiya* stance and followed suit in omitting aspects thought to be heretical.[56] This would have therefore been a reference to the orthodox critique of Sheikh Abdullah's association with Iblis and the subsequent conversion story of Kedah's ruler.

Beyond these stories, there are also other distinct accounts of the conversion of Kedah's ruler. These included both textual and oral reports, circulating outside Kedah's court and in the main maritime centers.

EARLY ORAL CONVERSION STORIES

Sherard Osborne, an English midshipman, while participating in the 1838 naval blockade of Kedah's coastline (against the rebels seeking the return of Kedah's exiled ruler at Penang) was given an oral account of the Raja's conversion to Islam by his native companion, "boatswain Jadee" or "*serang* Jadee," that is vastly different from *Hikayat Merong Mahawangsa*. Strangely enough, *serang* Jadee was not a native of Kedah but was rather a "Batta" (a Batak) by birth, from Sumatra, who was brought up by the Sulu people, continued to dress as an Ilanun, and later spent most of his life in Johor, Singapore and at sea in the Melaka Straits (Osborne 1987: 37, 40–44). Nevertheless, in Osborne's book he appears to be well acquainted with various aspects of Kedah's geography and traditions. Thus it is likely that Jadee had earlier visited or stayed in Kedah.

According to Jadee's account, told to Osborne on the Island of Langkawi, there were Muslim "haggis" [*sic*], (hajis) or pilgrims, that first arrived during the time of Prophet Muhammad at Kedah: "When Mahomet, — may his tomb exhale unceasingly the odour of holiness! — sent holy men to show the poor Malays the road to Paradise" [*sic*] (Osborne 1987: 353).

Subsequently, Jadee continues that it was these "hajis" that converted Kedah's Raja and advised him to stop the pre-Islamic tradition of sacrificing a virgin daughter of the royal family, "whenever a new king ascended the throne, or when war was declared with another state" [*sic*], to an "enormous boa" [*sic*] (python?) or *"Oular-besar,"* dwelling on the Island of Langkawi (Ibid.: 352–354).[57]

This advice by the hajis at Kedah, however, soon backfired and instead brought the catastrophic wrath of the *ular-besar*. Thus:

> The creature became very annoyed, and the consequence was, he almost cleared the Island of Langkawi of its population and cattle. All schemes failed to check its wrath, prayers were offered up in all the mosques, but for our previous sins the Oular-besar still lived, and still kept swallowing up Malays, until the fields were left untilled, and the country was fast becoming one great forest. [*sic*] (Ibid.: 353)

Following the devastation of property and people by the *ular-besar* "Allah's," or God's, salvation came once again to Kedah with the arrival of a holy man, an Arab Sheikh, that "exhorted all the people to remain firm in their new faith, for some of them were backsliders. He pointed out to them, that the wrath of the Oular-besar was only a means to test their faith; but that now Allah was satisfied, and had sent him to put a stop to their sorrow" [*sic*] (Osborne 1987: 353–354).

The Arab Sheikh then, in the company of the people from Kedah, proceeded on boats to challenge the enormous python at its residence on the Island of Langkawi. Upon arriving on the Island, "the holy man performed his ablutions, said his prayers, put on his green turban, and balancing the Koran on his head, landed at once either to drive the Oular-besar away or to die" [sic] (Osborne 1987: 354).

The unsuspecting *ular-besar* at the sight of the Sheikh attacked him and swallowed the "haji" whole. Consequently, when the *ular-besar* was digesting the "Haggi a violent fury seemed to seize it; its whole body writhed in a perfect frenzy, it raised its head high above the loftiest trees, its eyes flashed lighting and for a few minutes the creature seemed upon the point of dashing into the sea" [sic] (Ibid.: 354).

With these signs of agitation and discomfort the snake proceeded toward the nearby mountains and disappeared, never to be heard or seen again. At the same time, with the disappearance of the *ular-besar* from Kedah the Sheikh also disappeared and he too was never seen again. Consequently, with the end of the monstrous python of Langkawi, and the reconfirmation of the Islamic faith in Kedah, by the deeds of the visiting Sheikh, the territory continued to prosper. Moreover, other snakes on the island no longer ate humans, or Kedah folks, but only animals. With this concluding remark Jadee ended the story to Osborne.

Jadee's conversion story differs radically from that of *Hikayat Merong Mahawangsa*, and other Malay texts mentioned in the introduction. It suggests that Muslim missionaries were sent during, and not after, the time of Prophet Muhammad. To a certain extent this aspect of the story has more in common with the conversion traditions found in southern China. According to the Fujian version of the story two Muslim saints, Imam Sayid and Imam Wagga, were sent during the time of the Prophet Muhammad from Medina and shortly arrived in the area (Gladney 1987: 498). This link to China is significant and may indeed indicate an alternate origin of the Langkawi tradition.

The arrival of a second Muslim missionary and the renewal of Islam is also a motif that is lacking in *Hikayat Merong Mahawangsa*. This aspect of Jadee's story is however similar to the *Hikayat Raja-Raja Pasai, Sejarah Melayu* and conversion stories in Southern Sulawesi in which the Prophet appears in a dream or physically and is followed by actual missionaries visiting the region.

On the other hand, there are some similarities between Jadee's account and that of the *Hikayat Merong Mahawangsa*. In both accounts of the story Muslim missionaries from the Middle East are paramount in the religious conversion of the ruler and his people. Moreover, the destructive wrath of the snake at Langkawi reminds one of a similar parable in Biblical and Muslim literature of the destructive nature of the devil and satanic lust in the form of snakes or serpents (e.g., *The Epic of Kings or Shahnameh by Ferdowsi* 2000: 9, 11, 16, 20; *Masnavi i Manavi* 2001: 179, 247). Thus perhaps indicates a similar origin of the two stories.

Alternatively, the snake in Jadee's report may well represent the Naga, or the pre-Islamic earth/water spirit, that figured largely in traditional South Asian and Southeast Asian religions and mythology.[58]

According to Hindu and Buddhist, as well as Southern Indian Dravidian (particularly Pallava legends), Funan, Khmer, and Cham traditions the Naga is the deity of fertility and the guardian of the life-cycle of the land, nature, soil, rain, rulers' reigns, disease (particularly skin related diseases),[59] mineral wealth and agricultural processes and could not be destroyed.[60] The Naga's destructive powers and temperament could only be controlled by the ruler, as well as -in accordance with Buddhist traditions (particularly in the Theravada traditions) by the Buddha, or a monk or through the presence of his "shadow," i.e., stupas and relics.

The Naga tradition and worship in Southeast Asia is indeed very old and can be documented to the Srivijaya era inscriptions of the seventh and eighth centuries CE (namely the carved seven Naga heads on the top of the Telaga Batu inscription, transcribing an oath of allegiance from all of the king's subjects and listing punishments for failing them, found near Palembang, South Sumatra, believed to date from about 686 CE and the Wiang Sa, or Ligor, inscription of 697 Saka, or 775 CE, that mentions the ruler as the "patron of *nagas*," see Coedes 1918: 23–25; Jessup 1990: 61; Zakharov 2007: 140). The Naga also features regularly in Malay indigenous sources and traditions.[61]

In the case of Kedah the word Naga is intertwined with historic place names; individual names and the zodiac (see the numerous references to the word Naga in the early nineteenth century epic *Syair Sultan Maulana* 1985: 102–103, 212–213, 239, 276). The power of the king over the Naga was also traditionally invoked as part of rice planting and other agricultural rites (see the call for the blessing of the king of the Naga's in mid-twentieth century Sam Sam village of Titi Akar at Kedah, see Archaimbault 1957: 87, 91). Moreover, the royal residence and the royal cemetery at Kedah, likely dating to the seventeenth century, were also located at a place referred to as Naga (Winstedt 1936: 157; notes by Skinner in *Syair Sultan Maulana* 1985: 269n).

Furthermore, the founder of the Kedah kingship, according to *Hikayat Merong Mahawangsa*, has the title of Merong Mahawangsa. This title is indeed a combination of Siamese, Sanskrit/Pali and Malay words meaning the "great snake/dragon dynasty/race," with Merong (also Maroni) signifying a great snake or dragon in Thai (Crawfurd 1830 II: 32; Roberts 1837: 309; Echols and Shadily 1994: 354, 612; Kaempfer 1998: 70).[62] Undated Siamese sources likewise refer to Kedah having the emblem of a Merong or big snake as one of the cities under the hegemony of Ligor (i.e., modern day Thai province of Nakhon Si Thammarat/Dhammarat/Dharrmaraja, see Chand Chirayu Rajani 1974: 176–178; *The Crystal Sands* 1975: 84–85). Thus the connection of Kedah's dynasty and its agricultural rites to a Naga is a further distinction to that of Jadee's story, which has Kedah's rulers attempting to inhibit the forces of the Naga. The distinction is significant as it raises fundamental questions on development and the historic origin of the two traditions in Kedah's continental and island settings. In fact this aspect of Jadee's account is similar to Sumatran local folklore and literary sources, which refer to the slaying of a powerful snake by a local personality, founder of the dynasty and/or the descendant of Alexander the great.[63] Moreover, it also indicates the historic replacement of Naga worship, popular in Tantric and Mahayana Buddhism, with the eleventh and fifteenth century arrival and revival of the more orthodox Theravada Buddhism at parts of Southeast Asia (see Gosling 2001: 76–78; Thant Myint-U 2001: 85–86).[64] This transformation quite often was followed with violence and suppression of esoteric teachings, practices, and competing Buddhist doctrines (Chandler 1974: 207–222; Mirando 1985: 15; Barua 1991: 150; Gosling 2001: 77; Thant Myint-U 2001: 86).[65]

Then again, Jadee's account of the powerful snake may not necessarily have indigenous roots. Indeed the story is very similar to the Chinese, Sung dynasty (960–1279 CE), story of *Baishe zhuan*, a popular Ur-myth, of Madame White Snake and her companion the little green snake that became popular in traditional Chinese theatre (Chao 1979: 201; Lai 1992: 52–53, 64; Wessing 1997: 335).[66] In this early version of the story an unsuspecting man, Hsu-Hsuan, marries the snake demon. But upon realizing his mistake he seeks the assistance of a monk that overpowers the demon and casts her away to be trapped under a pagoda (Chao 1979: 201–202; Lai 1992: 52–53). In a later edition of the same story, likely Ming era (1368–1644 CE), a Taoist and later a Buddhist monk fail to defeat a powerful snake-woman who lived on an island in a lake (Lai 1992: 53). Hence, the Bodhisattva Guanyin/Kuan Yin is summoned and succeeds in defeating the demon successfully and banishing it under the weight of a pagoda forever. A similar story is also thought to exist in Japan that in many ways is similar to Jadee's account and the Chinese story. According to the story an eight-headed and eight-tailed serpent devoured a maiden every year until the god Susanoo slew it and married the last of the destined victims (Daniels 1960: 145, 159).

Another aspect of Jadee's story in which the holy man is swallowed by the snake has certain affinities to the *Ramayana* story in which the monkey god Hanuman once purposely allowed *Sinhika*, an ogre, to swallow him in order to rend her body to pieces and in a later episode Hanuman was swallowed whole by Su-Rasa, an ogre and mother of the Nagas, but he managed to escape by distending and shrinking his body until he was able to escape through her right ear (*Vishnu Purana* 1864: cxxxiii; Dowson 1888: 293, 310).[67] Hence, it is more than likely that the pre-Islamic traditions of Naga were by Jadee's time intertwined with those of Islam. Besides it is noteworthy that the Jadee account leaves little room for action by the ruler, who has almost no role at all in the removal of the snake.

Consequently, the story of a powerful and immortal giant snake acting as the custodian of the Langkawi Islands, as well as living on land and sea corresponds well to that of a Naga. Furthermore, the *ular-besar*'s attempts to seek inducements directly from the ruler, particularly asking for the virgin princess, and its ability to bring havoc to the island's peoples, animals, and environment are further proof of its position as a powerful Naga. Indeed the custom of sacrificing a royal virgin may reflect earlier agreements between the Naga and the ruler's ancestors that supposedly continued. Certainly the theme of a Naga asking for tribute from the ruler in return for political power is not unusual and is a popular one in South Asian, as well as Khmer, Cham, Burmese, and Mon traditions. The sudden arrival of a green turbaned Sheikh meanwhile suggests the power of Islam over the old traditions. The color green indicates that the priest came from Prophet Muhammad's tribe or that he was one of his descendants (Osborn 1987: 74–75).[68] He came just in time to prevent the snake from causing havoc and destruction. At the same time, the priest's challenging the snake and the subsequent disappearance of both run parallel to Buddhist stories (e.g., *Jataka*, *Dipawamsa*, *Vinaya*, and *Mahawamsa*) discussing the appearance of Buddha, or Buddhist monks, to inhibit the destructive forces of a Naga. In contrast *Hikayat Merong Mahawangsa* (Low 1849: 473) has the devil rather than Sheikh Abdullah dressed in green thus perhaps indicating its author's orthodox view to distance the book from popular pre-Islamic traits, connecting the color green to Rama or other deities, found amongst the general population.

On the other hand, the Naga aspect of the story of the *ular besar* and its devouring of maidens, people, animals, and the environment at Langkawi was likely created or adapted in response to local beliefs, as well as in *Hikayat Merong Mahawangsa*, that the island was home to the mystical bird Garuda, Gerda or Geroda (Low 1849: 4, 8n; Maxwell 1887: 31–32; Thomson 1991: 161; Stokes 2000: 14–16). Indeed, Garuda according to South Asian, particularly *Padma-Purana* and *Mahabharata*, and Angkor traditions is, on the one hand, the cousin, or the step-brother to the Naga King Vasuki[69] and, on the other hand, the main enemy of the Nagas and snakes (Low 1849: 4n; Bastian 1865: 82; Dowson 1888: 109, 233; Bloomfield 1924: 227; Grancsay 1937: 147; Dimock 1962: 313, 313n; Reck 1983: 84–87).[70] What's more in the more popular, South Asian version of the *Ramayana* (as well as those found in Tibet, Laos, Thailand, *Hikayat Sri Rama*, and other parts of Southeast Asia) only refer to the Naga king residing under the ocean in his subterranean Naga-Loka or *Patala* world and capital called Bhogavati or Put-Kari (a similar folk-story is also reported from Sarawak, see comments by A. H. Hill in *Hikayat Raja-Raja Pasai* 1960: 200n). Similarly in Pagan and Thai sources the island of Lanka is traditionally home of the Naga king.[71] Hence to the narrators of the story, it would have been strange to acknowledge that Langkawi held the powerful Naga while the island was considered the home of Garuda.

Nevertheless, this aspect of the story may in fact point toward a version of the *Ramayana*, in textual form, or the Rama story used in the shadow-puppet plays that identified Lanka, or Langkapuri, as the island home of the "Naga-Raja," rather than the ogre king Ravana.[72] Indeed according to the Buddhist *Sussondi-Jataka* (number 360), the Naga's adversary, the Garuda, resided on the Naga Island.[73] On the other hand, in the Mongolian, Japanese, and most Chinese versions of the story the "Naga-raja" like Jadee's account resides on the island, and not under the ocean (Dowson 1888: 54, 213, 179, 233; De Jong 1994: 171–173; Hara 1994: 340–356; Sahai 1994: 226–227, 1996 II: 100b, 258b). This connection of Jadee's account to that of East Asia is significant particularly in understanding China's impact and relations to historic Kedah and the Malay world. It may also suggest that relations with China were not based solely on economic terms and that it had deeper roots and connections, e.g., social and political.

CONCLUSION

In consequence, from the above reports of Kedah's conversion to Islam it appears that many aspects of both sources are distantly related. These stories and traditions were probably fully absorbed into the local cultures through the popular storytellers, customs, poetry, and performances of *wayangs*. In the *Hikayat*, or the court version of the conversion, the entire focus is on the ruler. He is central to the theme of the conversion story and the authors of the text ensure that no matter how cruel, fallible, or unjust the rulers become yet they cannot be blamed for their actions. Hence, the ruler is the only source of power in the land that is favored by God. They can temporarily fall from grace but can easily rise and reclaim their true position and status. Furthermore, the ministers are portrayed as powerful entities that complement the ruler in the sense that they monitor his conduct and ensure that the monarchy can be maintained under the laws.

Conversely, in the oral report there is little emphasis on conversion or powers of the ruler and the ministers. Rather the emphasis is on the religious conversion and belief of all the peoples, including the ruler. The destructive power of the snake or the advice by the religious missionaries to stay steadfast in their beliefs are all addressed to the people and do not distinguish the ruler as a separate entity. Nor is the snake's destruction solely directed toward the ruler for refusing to sacrifice a member of his household. Instead, the snake brings havoc to all the land, peoples, and animals. The ruler meanwhile appears powerless to stop the snake and if it were not for the sudden appearance of the sheikh then the destruction would have certainly continued.

It is conceivable that the nineteenth century court, or textual, versions of Kedah's conversion to Islam is a compilation of numerous foreign, as well as native sources and stories, such as those from the shadow-puppet stories. In particular, the use of complex and often contradictory sets of Islamic and pre-Islamic imagery and events may in reality suggest the eclectic nature of the various *Hikayat Merong Mahawangsa* authors and copyists over the years. Nonetheless, the authors of the texts attempt to distinguish between the pre-Islamic and Islamic period of Kedah's history. In both cases the symbols or practices associated with the former religious traditions are demonized and defeated by representatives of Islam.

Prior to converting to Islam the rulers easily fall prey to the devil's mischief and temptations. These events result in a chain reaction that ends in destruction of the land, peoples, and food resources. Yet, with the conversion of the ruler to Islam, prosperity, wealth, and tranquility returns to Kedah and from that period there is no mention of the devil's attempts to return. Similarly, the text attempts to suggest that prior to Islam there was no pragmatic belief system at Kedah. Hence there is no specific reference to Buddhism, Naga or any Hindu or Buddhist God.

Indeed aspects of the *Hikayat* closely follow and resemble those of, Persian, South Asian, and other Southeast Asian sources. Hence, indicating an attempt by its authors to construct a text and a theme from several sources that would appeal to the court bureaucracy, natives, and foreign visitors without compromising Kedah's unique position and prestige in its regional and international sphere of influence. The text was therefore meant to preserve aspects of Kedah pre-Islamic history, and to remind people of the ancient roots of the royal line, that were deemed by its authors as essential and relevant but in a methodology that was better suited to the time and accepted amongst native and regional courts and scholars. For example the smashing of statutes by the Muslim ruler of Kedah represents a popular theme of breaking idols found in Islam and other monotheistic religions (particularly in Christianity and Manichaeism, see Norris 1849: 462; Thompson 1916: 383–388; Pfeiffer 1926: 211–222; Croix 1963: 21, 29; Buddensieg 1965: 44–65; Klimkeit 1982: 21; Waszink and Winden 1982: 15–23; Adler 1987: 95–117; Goldberg 1991: 3–11; Scott 1995: 145; Smit 1997: 40–53; Sprunger 1997: 36–53). Likewise, it is possible that this aspect of the story was to provide a further explanation for the large number of pre-Islamic Hindu and Buddhist statutes and temples found at Kedah.[74] Indeed worshippers of trees and rocks, "*menyambah kayu-kayukan atau menyambah batu*," in the rural villages, were denounced as committing treason, *derhaka*, and a great sin toward the Raja, Allah, and Prophet Muhammad as late as 1667 CE in the Kedah Laws of Dato'Sri Paduka Tuan (Winstedt 1928: 8, 27). Hence indicating the survival of pre-Islamic practices (perhaps replacement of statues with rocks and trees), as well as the growth of religious fervor in villages and rural centers.

In the case of the oral tradition from Langkawi however the power of Hinduism and Buddhism in the folk tradition proved tenuous, and was easily transformed when the orthodox supporters were withdrawn. Thus, Islamic ideas and stories gradually replaced or were intertwined with those of earlier times. Indeed what are intriguing are the similarities between the snake and conversion story of the Langkawi Islands to that of China, Japan, and Mongolia. Were these connections deliberate? Or were they unintentional? For one thing the connections between Kedah and East Asia are unprecedented, even though they may remain fully unexplained. Alternatively, it is possible that the whole aspect of the great snake story was to warn against the revival of Naga worship and the old religion. Hence such a warning would not have been necessary if such backsliding was not occurring.

NOTES

1. Refer to conversion stories in *Hikayat Raja-Raja Pasai*, *Sejarah Melayu* or *Sulalat al-Salatin*, *Hikayat Patani*, *Detik-detik Sejarah Kelantan*, *Hikayat Bandjar*, *Hikayat Marong Mahawangsa*, *Misbana Mengkaji Sejarah Trengganu*, *Hikayat Aceh*, as well as traditions amongst the Makassarese in South Sulawesi (Gowa, Tallo and Sanrabone), Kutai and in the Southern Philippines.

2. In cases that the ruler chose not convert to Islam, members of his family later became Muslims and played an important role in the regional conversion stories. Hence the ruler of the Sunda kingdom of Pajajaran, in West Java, refused to convert to Islam. But one of his daughters, Kean Santang, later brought Islam into West Java; whilst his other daughter, the mythical Nyai Lara Kidul, became the mother of the Muslim mystic *Sunan Gunung Jati* (see Brakel 1997: 254, 266; Wessing 1997: 318, 320). Similarly in *Sejarah Banten* the local ruler refused to convert to Islam. Yet his grandson, Sunan, converted and soon became a Muslim mystic as well the driving force behind the propagation of Islam in Giri, Java (Ricklefs 1986: 10).

3. Somewhat similar traditions can also be found in Tallo and Sanrabone, both in Southern Sulawesi, see Jones 1979: 149–150; Cummings 1998: 112–113.

4. Traders and learned men are also said to have been instrumental in the spread of Islam in Southern India and various parts of Africa, see Horton 1971: 86; Kokan 1974: 1–2.

5. Refer to the conversion stories in *Hikayat Patani*, *Hikayat Bandjar*, as well numerous indigenous literary sources and oral traditions found amongst the Makassarese in south Sulawesi island, and of the Ternate ruler and peoples in Maluka island, eastern Indonesia (refer to a number of Islamic conversion stories by R. Jones 1979: 149–150, 152; W. Cummings 1998: 110–115, 119). The conversion to Islam of the Cambodian king, Reameathipadei I, in the seventeenth century is also attributed to the Malays and Champa peoples living there see Kersten 2006: 1–22.

6. Such as the case of the Javanese merchant "Datu Mula Hussein" in Ternate in Maluku, eastern Indonesia; see Jones 1979: 152.

7. For example the permission given to Raja Bongsu of Pasai by his brother in law, the Majapahit ruler, to establish a settlement in *Hikayat Bandjar*, see Ras 1968: 416–421; and the Pasai settlement at Patani, see *Hikayat Patani*, see Wyatt and Teeuw 1970: 148–152.

8. The conversion of the Tallo ruler and people in south Sulawesi was through the arrival of the Minangkabau mystic Dato ri Bandang, see Jones 1979: 149–150.

9. Such as the Melaka, Johor and Patani Muslim peoples living in Southern Sulawesi (especially at Gowa, Tallo and Sanrabone), see Cummings 1998: 110–115, 119.

10. It is thought that ultimately a Champa ruler may have converted to Islam in about 1676 CE, see Kersten 2006: 10n. The fourteenth to the sixteenth century rulers of Vijayanager, Southern India, similarly continued to remain Hindu despite employing a large Muslim workforce, as well the presence of powerful Muslim mercantile community there, see Wagoner 1996: 851–880.

11. Personal communication with Dr. Roxanne Marcotte (University of Queensland).

12. Examples may include the fourteenth century conversion of the Mongol territory of Chaghadai and the Turkic tribes in Central Asia, as well Islamic conversions in Africa, see *Conversion to Islam* 1979; Bone 1982: 128; Hua Tao 1993: 107; Biran 2002: 742–752).

13. The name Muzlaf Shah is according to Fatimi (1963: 73–75) wrongly romanized by later scholars, namely Muhammad Hassan Bin To'Kerani Mohd Arshad (1927, 1968) and Winstedt (1938), as Muzaffar Shah. Nevertheless, following this note by Fatimi later scholars, e.g., Adil Buyong (1980) and Khoo (1991: 47n) have continued to romanize the name as Muzaffar Shah. G. M. Khan (1939: 14) however mentions that the pre-Islamic ruler of Kedah changed his name to Mulzuful Shah upon conversion and Wan Yahya (1911: 3) refers to him as Sultan Mahamud Shah. The Thai source of *Phongsawadan Muang Zaiburi* (1990: 94), written predominantly in the nineteenth century, also refers to Kedah's ruler, Phra Ong Maha Wangsa, changing his name to "Sultan Muzafar" after converting to Islam.

14. *Hikayat Merong Mahawangsa* is a Malay text that only came to light, outside of Kedah, in the first half of the nineteenth century. Nevertheless, several scholars have speculated that the book may have been compiled between the seventeenth and eighteenth centuries by using earlier sources (see the 1842 Report by Low in *Burney Papers* 1971 V: 3; Thomson 1865: 167; Winstedt 1939: 110–111; Sarkar 1985: 296; Sharifa Zaleha 1985: 32; Andaya 2002: 33–34). In this study I have consulted R. J. Wilkinson's (1898) Jawi version procured by him at Penang, A. J. Sturrock's (1916) romanized version and Low's (1849) succinct translation of *Hikayat Merong Mahawangsa*.

15. In the *Hikayat* versions consulted in this study, Kedah's ruler consumed "*arak tadi*" or "coconut wine" rather than "spirits" since it was not distilled.

16. The Malay Muslim era language (written in the Perso-Arabic letters or scripts).

17. In a later episode in the text, when having dinner with the Sheikh, Kedah's newly converted Muslim ruler only drank coffee and tea (Low 1849: 475).

18. Persian legends, such as those contained in the eleventh century *Shah Nameh*, mention Turan as a neighbor. In the pre-Islamic era it was a region bordering Persia, in contemporary northern and western Pakistan (Eggermont 1993: 113; Sayles 1999: 75–76; Vogelsang 2001: 160; Potter 2004: 304; Frye 2004: 39–44). But during Islamic Persia it has often been mistakenly associated with the Turkic peoples of Central Asia.

19. The earliest presence of Aceh perhaps dates to an Acehnese fort at Perlis in 1570 CE that was reportedly disbanded five years later, see Turnbull 1980: 47. Nonetheless, Aceh directly ruled Kedah and the Langkawi Islands circa 1619–1621 (Fort Jakarta to the yacht "Cleen Hollandia," 2nd of June 1619, in *Bescheiden omtrent zijn Bedrijf in Indie* 1920 II: 560; *Phongsawadan Muang Zaiburi* 1990: 95; Reid 2005: 7; Andaya 2001b: 41, 44).

20. It is possible that some, or all, of these graves belonged to the early eighteenth century settlement of Kedah as reported in the Acehnese epic *Hikajat Potjut Muhamat* 1979: 7, 168–169. It is also possible that some of the grave stones were simply imported to Kedah from Aceh.

21. According to the west Sumatran indigenous source of *Tromba Minangkabau*, the Raja of Rum, has the title of Sri Maharaja Alif, and is one of the three royal brothers descended from Alexander the great (*Tromba Minangkabau* translated and cited at length in Moor 1837: 262). *Hikayat Indraputra* (1983: 210–222), an undated work com-

piled in Sumatra before the seventeenth century, meanwhile refers to Nabat Rum Syah as the son of the king of the Islamic jinn's and that his sister, Jumjum Ratnadewi, married the hero of the story Indraputra.

22. Pasai is also featured in Patani's conversion in the *Hikayat Patani*. It is difficult to say if it predates *Hikayat Merong Mahawangsa* or was written around the same time as each other. Nevertheless the mention of the name Pasai in *Hikayat Patani* raises a number of questions and possibilities with regard to Kedah and Patani. What does this tell us about the context for Kedah's conversion? That it happened later? Or merely that the story was written later and the author/s conveniently asserted claims of authority and purity by referring to the Acehnese connection?

23. In both cases Muslim missionaries were dispatched to Southeast Asia after the death of Prophet Muhammad for the propagation of Islam.

24. According to the *Sejarah Melayu* with the beat of sovereignty, i.e., the *nobat*, "*sireh*" was accordingly given to the people of the court according to rank and status as it was a custom that began when an earlier ruler, Sultan Muhammad Shah, established the ceremonial of the court (see Brown 1970: 44, 48; Leyden 2001: 104). In Javanese courts too, chewing *sireh*, spelt *sirih*, was highly symbolic and offered to honored guests, see Jessup 1990: 150, 154.

25. Similarly in the *Hikayat Patani* the ministers play an active part in the tale, showing that the authors did not reserve sole authority and agency for the ruler (see Bradley 2009: 272).

26. In contrast, Low's (1949: 475) English translation has Kedah's ruler sending for the ministers to come to the hall. This discrepancy to the other versions of the story is significant as Low may have been translating a different version of the *Hikayat* that was given to him by the Sultan or a member of Kedah's court. This may also explain the previously mentioned reference by him to the Kedah's ruler as "one of God's Viceregents."

27. Or Farsi, Parsi, Dari, and Tajik.

28. In Bengal, during the Pala period and Chanda rule from the eight to the twelfth century CE, and Burma, from the early Pagan dynasty rule to the twelfth century, Tantric Buddhism gained royal patronage see Luce 1969: 375; Qanungo 1988: 85–88.

29. Several sixth to the twelfth century clay tablets with representations of the Bodhisattva as Avalokitesvara, as well as other Hindu-Buddhist icons and Tantric prayers were found in the mid-twentieth century in a north Kedah cave, at Perlis. See Sastri 1954: 13, Lamb 1960: 88, 93, 1962: 14–19, and Wolters 1970: 134. Similar tablets to those found at Perlis have also been found at several caves to the north of Kedah in Trang, contemporary southern Thailand and historically part of Kedah, see Steffen and Annandale 1902: 177–180.

30. The undated *Hikayat Iblis*, found—likely—in island Southeast Asia and now kept in Berlin, Germany. Interestingly, *Hikayat Iblis* too follows a mystical aspect formulated in a similar manner as the early Persian, and probably Indian, Sufi perspective.

31. Certainly a story attributed to Hatim Tai is given in a seventeenth century Acehnese text by Sheikh Nur al-Din Ibn Ali al-Raniri, *Taj-i-Salatin* or *Makota Raja-Raja*, see a translated version of the text by Starkweather 1901: 183–189.

32. Krtangara's practice of Tantric Buddhism is well documented, e.g., Nihom 1986: 485–501. Hariani Santiko (1997: 225n), believes that Krtangara's drinking was part of a religious ritual belonging to *cakra* Tantrism. Additionally it is possible that Krtanagara was trying to imitate Kumbha-Karna, full brother of Ravana in the *Ramayana*, who drank 2000 jars of liquor and subsequently defeated and captured the monkey god Hanuman (Dowson 1888: 170–171).

33. The *Jataka* tales appeared first in canonical form and was collected in Sri Lanka around four century CE, Behm 1971: 31.

34. *Hikayat Merong Mahawangsa* (Low 1849: 3, 9) is somewhat ambiguous in making a statement if the *raksasas* or the *gergasis* were considered as friends or foes of the human race. The founder of the dynasty, i.e., Merong Mahawangsa, is cited by the

Hikayat to have married a girl at Rum, whose father was a *"gergasi"* while his mother was descended from a *"raksasa."* Hence the royal courtiers were said to have "dreaded his preternatural powers." Then at Kedah the *gergasi* visited Merong Mahawangsa in order to invite him to become their Raja "because we have not established a Raja over this place." Merong Mahawangsa accepted their invitation and "encouraged them by speaking to them in a soft tone of voice" since he "knew the *Caste* of these Girgassi" [*sic*]. The obscurity may suggest the significance and influence of the indigenous peoples of Kedah to the later Malay migrants. It may similarly suggest the attempt of the author/s of the *Hikayat* to highlight the political power of Kedah's rulers amidst the indigenous population.

35. Similarly in *Hikayat Si Miskin* (a popular folk-tale that exists at Kedah and Langkawi as an oral tradition, a text and as shadow-puppet plays; see Shahruddin 1983: 20–28, Appendix 1) the demonic appetite of the *raksasa* is further portrayed when princess Cahaya Khairani was kept as a prisoner in order to be fattened-up and eaten later.

36. Ravana also kept Brahman traditions e.g., knew Sanskrit, Vedic rituals and was burned with Brahman rites; see Purnalingam Pillai 1928: 14–18.

37. Belonging to the *Vaishnava* branch of Hinduism.

38. Refer to van der Tuuk (1887: 34–35), Dowson (1888: 144–145), Blagden (1917: 47–48), Winstedt (1938: 31, 1939: 110), Quaritch-Wales (1940: 82, 85), Sullivan (1957: 289–295), Ramos (1969: 243), Ferdowsi (1988); Lai (1992: 55, 63), Braginsky (1993: 60–61), *The Epic of Kings or Shahnameh by Ferdowsi* (2000: 8–21), and *Persopedia* (2011).

39. In the *Jataka* story of *Samugga-Jataka*, number 436, an unsuspecting woman is fed first on ghee, then rice, fish and finally flesh by a demon in order to woo her. Similarly in *Vishnu Purana* a vengeful *raksasa* transforms itself into a cook and prepares human flesh for the unsuspected *Vasishta* (that earlier had offered a sacrifice for the king). *Vasishta* discovers what he has done and hence curses the king for a specific period during the day for twelve years. The king, nicknamed as *Kalmasha-Pada* or spotted feet, devours many during the twelve years (Dowson 1888: 143–144). Folk traditions in the Philippines also report that an individual acquires a cannibal taste by having eaten food that was spat on or licked by a "weredog" [*sic*] or a "viscera sucker," see Ramos 1969: 243.

40. Certainly in the case of *Hikayat Bandjar* the young prince Ratu Anom, has a jinn for a mother and is therefore born with tusks, hence he is referred to in the text as a *"buta/bhuta,"* i.e., to be blind or giant or demon or beast of the forest, a term peculiar to the *ruwatan* aspect of the Sunda and Java *wayang kulit* (see Kempe and Winstedt 1948: 7, 34; Wilkinson 1957: 13–14; Ras 1968: 504–505). Similarly, *buta* was a standard component of the *wayang kulit* of Java and Sunda with a scene known as the "flower battle," *perang kembang*, from a story from the *Mahabharata* (Petersen 1991: 129–130). In Malay folklore *buta-ranggas* are also identified as ghosts or birth-spirits (Wilkinson 1957: 12). Indeed in the original Sanskrit version of the *Jataka* story of *Maha-Sutasoma-Jataka* number 537 the cannibal is referred to as the *kala*, or black, *bhuta* (see *The Jataka* 1963: 465). Meanwhile, *Vishnu Purana* (1864: 83) has the *buta's* as "fierce beings, who were denominated goblins and eaters of flesh" (also Dowson 1888: 55; Skeat 1900: 102, 105).

41. The same grammatical error of the name can be found in the Malay version of *Hikayat Amir Hamza* (1987). For comparative purposes I have consulted the undated Berlin version of the Persian edition of *Hamzeh-Nameh* or the Amir Hamza story, edited by Jafaar Shoaar (1982).

42. Likewise, in Mitra traditions the drinking of wine, symbolizing the blood of the holy bull, was an opportunity for the order's members to conclude a social contract amongst themselves and the deity (Norouzi 2006: 11n).

43. The mention of wooden, rather than stone or metal, statues could be significant. According to *Hikayat Bandjar* (Ras 1968: 238–241) an Indian trader upon establishing a settlement at Bandjar decided to have two sandalwood statues built temporarily, to represent a king and a queen, since he was not of royalty and could not proclaim himself as one.

44. Refer to the studies by Earl (1863: 122–123), Quaritch-Wales (1940: 1–85), Hindu-Buddhist Civilisation in South Kedah (1958: 34), Lamb (1959a, 1959b, 1960, 1961, 1962), Colless (1969), Peacock (1970), Treloar and Fabris (1975), Christie (1988/1989: 41–49, 51–52), Santiko (1997: 209–226) and Nik Hassan Shuhaimi Nik Abdul Rahman (2007: 41–59).

45. G. H. Luce (1969: 380) believes that these stories in Burma have their origin in Theravada teachings and texts, particularly *Mahavamsa* and its continuation in *Culvamsa*, of Sri Lanka.

46. He had many attributes amongst which he was the Fire God and the divine messenger of the Hindu Gods.

47. Indra did however become overly intoxicated at least once on soma-juice, during a celebrated sacrificial ritual performed by Marutta, a monarch see Dowson 1888: 205.

48. Certainly aspects of *Shah-Nameh* are drawn or cited in sixteenth century to eighteenth century Malay works such as the *Bustan al-Salatin, Taj as-Salatin, Hikayat Iskandar* and *Sejarah Melayu*, as well in the Siamese royal book of *Iran Rajadhamma* or *Nithan Sibsawng Liam* and in King Chulalongkorn's 1878 tale book, *Lilit Nithra Chakhrit*, that often deals with aspects of Persian kingship (see Wilkinson 1901: Introduction, ii, 1957: 20–21; Winstedt 1939: 49; Marrison 1955: 60; Muhammad Ibn Ibrahim 1972: 80–85; Scupin 1980: 66; Milner 1981: 46–70; Braginsky 1993: 60; Rutnin 1996: 109–111; Chambert-Loir 2005: 135). What's more the Chinese classic of *Feng-Shen-Yen-I* has many stories that run parallel to *Shah-Nameh* see, Brewster 1972: 115–122

49. More fantastic than the conversion story from *Sejarah Melayu*.

50. For a similar discussion for the association of Islam, Kings or Sufis with wine and other intoxicants in Persian Sufi imagery, see Yarshater 1960: 43–53, Eaton 1996: 257–258; Norouzi 2006: 7–12.

51. The symbolic touching and holding of objects as an oath, or allegiance, in historic Malay world is not unusual. For example in the case of Prince Muhammad and the influential *uleebalang* in the mid-eighteenth century Acehnese epic of *Hikajat Potjut Muhamat* 1979: 22, 151–163, the swearing of the oath was simply taken "on the bullet" [sic].

52. In *Hikayat Bandjar* the conversion of most people in the Majapahit capital is attributed to the newly arrived Raja Bongsu. Upon arriving and founding his settlement on the Majapahit coastline Raja Bongsu had a walking stick, or *tongkat*, made from the local *gading* cane. Possession of the walking stick appears to have contributed toward his aura and prestige amongst the indigenous population of the area that believed Raja Bongsu to possess "greater radiance than the king of Madjapahit" [sic], see Ras 1968: 416–421. Likewise, in *Hikayat Raja-Raja Pasai* (1960: 74, 134) a powerful Yogi performs magic with his walking stick in front of Sultan Ahmad. But his magic was overpowered by the Sultan's sanctity and hence he converted to Islam, in return giving Sultan Ahmad the title of *Perumudal Perumal*.

53. For more on Sarmad see a recent article by Nathan Katz (2000: 142–160). The Armenian origin of Sarmad was reported to me by Mr. Martin of the Dhaka Armenian Church, at Arminotola (Bangladesh), in 2001.

54. Hallaj in the same account continues that "Iblis was threatened with fire; yet he did not retract his position. Pharaoh was drowned in the sea; yet he did not disavow his claim. Neither of them accepted any intermediaries."

55. *Sirat al-Mustaghim* (translated as the "straight path" from the Arabic) deals entirely with the rules of Islamic ritual see Riddell 2001: 119. It is difficult to speculate on the authorship or origin of *Bab al-Nikah* (translated as the "Chapter on Marriage" from the Arabic). There are several books from the Middle East, as well the Malay World that includes a chapter by that name. It could even be a work written by Raniri, or that it was simply a chapter by that name from *Sahih Bukhari* (one of the main six canonical *hadith* collection of Islam by the ninth century Persian scholar Muhammad Ibn Ismail al-Bukhari).

56. Similarly A. J. Arberry 1969:113 discusses the seventeenth century Islamic orthodoxy toward allegorical imagery in Persia.

57. *"Oular-Besar"* must be read as "python," not "boa." Pythons are indigenous to Asia and Africa; boas are not.

58. For South Asian and Southeast Asian studies of the Naga see: Brown 1921: 79; Le May 1929: 219; Maung Htin Aung 1931: 79–82; Dimand 1933: 124–125; Dupont 1950: 39–62; Briggs 1951: 243–244; Visser 1956: 374–377; Wilkinson 1957: 29–30; Dimock 1962: 307–321; Ramos 1969: 242; Bloss 1973: 36–53; Bharati 1977: 94; Stutley 1977: 198; Woodward 1980: 157, 163–165, 170–174; Reck 1981: 85–86; Duran 1990: 41; Wessing 1990: 240–241, 243–244, 248, 1997: 321, 324–326, 332; Gaudes 1993: 333–358, 342, 348–349, 352–353. Similarly there are many related snake and dragon stories in East Asia, for Japan see Daniels 1960: 145–164; China, Chao 1979: 193–203; Sahai 1996 I: 19. Snakes and serpents are also central to other historic civilization, particularly the Australian aborigines and in Africa (e.g., ancient Egypt).

59. In twelfth century Pagan artwork of king Rajakumar's temple there is a symbolic reference to a Naga followed by a story of Buddha curing an enemy, a leper (*tamnim*), by taking out a snake from his mouth; see "Tier E3. GI. 201" referred and translated by Luce 1969: 382. In Malay literary sources the Naga is also a dragon, see the reference to a "horned" dragon in the eighteenth century *Syair Perang Siak* 1989: 158–159.

60. See Hindu and Buddhist texts of *Rajatarangini, Dipawamsa, Vinaya, Mahabharata, Jataka, Mahavamsa* and *Si-yu-ki* cited by Vincent 1878: 239–240; Bharati 1977: 94; Irwan 1982: 349n; Wessing 1990: 247, 1997: 321, 324–325, 332–334, 336; Gaudes 1993: 348; Jordaan 1997: 302–303.

61. Naga is commonly referred to in the seventeenth century *Hikayat Bandjar*, see Ras 1968: 120, 127, 308–311. According to *Hikayat Bandjar* having a loud voice like a "naga" was indicative of having a good genealogy, as was the case of Ki Mas Lana whose voice had the ability to make "women wild with desire" [sic] (Ras 1968: 364–365). The sea naga is similarly an important aspect of the story of *Hikayat Koris* of Sumatra (Wilkinson 1957: 15). Furthermore, a Jambi tradition has the three hills of Palembang, Jambi and Minangkabau to have been formerly three parts of a powerful snake (reported by locals to Andaya 1993: 254n). *Hikayat Indraputra* (1983: 225) likewise compares the body of a monstrous snake (called *mamlud*), slayed by the hero of the story into two parts, to a hill. The nineteenth century indigenous work of *Tuhfat al-Nafis* (Ali Haji Ibn Ahmad 1982: 46) has the five legendary Bugis brothers travel west and seek their fortunes (from their place of residence at Siantan and Cambodia) based on a dream by one of the brothers Opu Daeng Menambun that the "penis of his brother, Opu Daeng Cellak, had stretched out and become a serpent, whose head reared up toward the west and Johor" [sic]. Hence the brothers interpreted the dream of the serpent pointing westwards as a good omen and thus the travel went ahead.

62. Merong is also used in Thai sources to signify the "dragon" year as an astronomical sign in the *naksat* or twelve-year animal cycle, see Low 1849: 11n.

63. Examples may include the popular Sumatran folklore of slaying the great serpent Si-katimuna by Sang Seperba [sic] as reported in Wilkinson 1957: 14, the killing of the *"lambu* snake" by Tun Beraim Bapa in the fourteenth century *Hikayat Raja-Raja Pasai* 1960: 151, 199n–200n, the slaying of the *mamlud* snake by Indraputra in *Hikayat Indraputra* (1983: 225) and the *Sejarah Melayu* story of the slaying of the snake Sacatimuna by Raja Sangsapurba in the Minangkabau region of Sumatra, see Malay Annals 2001: 38–39. What's more, according to the indigenous source of *Tromba Minangkabau*, included in the royal regalia of Minangkabau was the sword that allegedly wounded the great serpent "Sicatimuna" [sic] (Moor 1837: 262). There is also a story in *Hikayat Deli* (cited by Milner 1982: 73, 105) that has a similar undertone and may be related. According to this Mohammed Dalek, the hero of the story arrives at Aceh learning that a powerful ascetic, by murdering the inhabitants, is creating havoc in the interior. Dalek then successfully kills the ascetic, on behalf of the Sultan Iskandar Muda of Aceh, and in doing so he is bestowed a title.

64. It is believed Theravada Buddhism first entered Southeast Asia in the sixth century and was popular amongst the Mons. But it only gained wider popularity and royal patronage following the conversion of the Pagan rulers, through Sri Lankan missionaries, in the mid-eleventh century. Furthermore, a further revival of Theravada Buddhism came in the fifteenth century through the Burmese and Siamese connection with the court of Kandy, Sri Lanka, as well as Siamese incursions into Cambodia and Laos.

65. David P. Chandler (1974: 207–222) has discussed Theravada Buddhism's historic attempts to end human sacrifice practices in parts of Indo-China and the bizarre continuation of Cambodia's Siva cult practice of human sacrifice, often with royal consent, well to the nineteenth century. Indeed one may only wonder if the destruction of Buddhist statutes and icons in Southeast Asia had more to do with the suppression of Tantric and Mahayana inspired Buddhist doctrines than Islam, although in contemporary Southeast Asia Mahayana practices persist quite peaceably, even in Theravada monasteries and temples.

66. The earliest version of this story is thought to have originated in the Shao-Hsing reign, 1131–1162 CE, after the removal of the emperor and his court to the south of China.

67. The swallowing aspect of Jadee's story is also similar to the *Si Miskin* (for various versions of the story see Shahruddin 1983: 20–28) tradition of Kedah and Kelantan. According to which prince Marakarma is swallowed whole by a shark, *Ikan Nun*, but later "steps out" when an old woman puts rice-grass on the shark's belly. This aspect of the *Si Miskin* story, with the main character swallowed by a sea creature has certain affinity to the story of Jonah of the Old Testament. *Sejarah Melayu* too mentions the spewing of a man, Bath or Bat'h or Bard or Ba'th, from a white cow, see Winstedt 1938b: 2, 55–57; Brown 1970: 15; *Malay Annals* 2001: 22.

68. Alternatively, in *Ramayana* traditions, the color green corresponds to that of Rama, as an indicator that he was a reincarnation of the demigod *Dewa Berembun*, see Sweeney 1972: 41, 65. Similarly Bengal and Javanese traditions refer to the female deities of Tara and Nyai Lara Kidul having green colors, see Jordaan 1997: 286–289, 304.

69. Also referred to in Indo-Chinese sources as Phaya Nang or Bhujangendra, see Gaudes 1993: 334, 342.

70. See also the *Jataka* stories of *Kotisimbali-Jataka* number 412, *Pandara-Jataka* number 518, *Bhuridatta-Jataka* number 543, as well the *Ramayanam of Bhodhayanam* 1840: 7, 7n.

71. In the Burmese sources Lanka is the home of *Nagadipa*, or *Naga-diva*, rulers, as well as the *Nagavana*, i.e., the Nagas forest, in which was visited by Buddha to settle a dispute (see twelfth century "Tier A I. GI. 185" and "Tier B" ink glosses, in the entrance to Rajkumars's temple, referred and translated by Luce 1969: 380). Thai sources likewise, in line with earlier Sinhalese sources, discuss the visit of the Naga king to Buddha's tooth relic when it arrived at Lanka (*The Crystal Sands* 1975: 67n, 67–73). According to Sri Lankan traditions the Jaffna Peninsula was traditionally *Nagadipa* which was visited by Buddha (Codrington 1970: 6). But other South Asian sources sometimes connect the Andaman and Nikobar group of islands to the story (Gerini 1909: 381, 383).

72. In Malay sources Langkawi is often believed to be one and the same as Lanka or Langkapuri mentioned in Indian sources (e.g., *Ramayana*, and *Bhagavata Purana*), see Low (1849: 8n), Maxwell (1881: 32), Dowson (1888: 208), Sweeney (1972: 65–80, 1972b: 258), Maier (1988: 92–93), Braginsky (1993: 59), and Stokes (2000: 14–16).

73. For a shorter version of the *Sussondi-Jataka* story (without the use of the word Naga or Naga Island), see *Kikati-Jataka* (Number 327).

74. This was also true for regional Malay kingdoms. According to *Hikayat Patani* the pre-Islamic ruler of Patani would sometime swear by the idols he worshipped, or in another version of the same story he swore by the "image of the Lord Buddha," see comments by D. K. Wyatt the passage in *Hikayat Patani* (1970: 43, 73–74).

TWO

The Malay Ethos

The Sultan and His Subjects

According to the Malay indigenous source *Sulalat al-Salatin*, or *Sejarah Melayu*) three brothers, all descendants of Alexander the Great, appeared miraculously near Palembang, Sumatra. The brothers were then visited by neighboring dignitaries, with the youngest invited to the city of Palembang by its chief, Demang Lebar Daun (Brown 1970: 15).

At Palembang Bichitram Shah, or Nila Utama (according to W. G. Shellabear's version), the youngest of the three brothers, was then magically given the title of Sri Tri Buana, or Sangsapurba Trimarti trib'huvena [sic], by a person named Bath or Bat'h or Bard, who was himself created out of the spew of a white cow (Winstedt 1938b: 2, 55–57; Brown 1970: 15; *Malay Annals* 2001: 22).[1]

Sri Tri Buana then decided to marry and was presented with a number of princesses as potential brides. But, all attempts to find a suitable consort for Sri Tri Buana ended up in utter failure. The marriage failures and the reasons behind it are worded somewhat differently in the two popular versions of *Sejarah Melayu*. In the Leyden version, these girls "were not of proper rank for such a noble prince, as soon as they associated with him they were stricken with a leprosy, as with a plague sent as a curse" (*Malay Annals* 2001: 25).

This is portrayed somewhat differently in C. C. Brown's version of the *Sejarah Melayu*. According to Brown's version, the young Sri Tribuana took one of the local girls as his consort, "but when she had slept with the king, she was found by him the following morning to be stricken with chloasma (*kedal*)[2] as the result of being possessed by him, whereupon he abandoned her" (1970: 15–16).

In both Leyden and Brown's version of *Sejarah Melayu* the young Sri Tribuana fails 39 times to find a suitable match and hence resorts to asking Demang Lebar Daun to give him his own daughter, Wan Sendari or Wan Sundaria, in marriage. Demang Lebar Daun who like Sri Tri Buana shares the ancestry of Alexander the Great, agrees. But only on the condition that they should enter into a solemn and sacred covenant with each other. Hence, the story in both versions of *Sejarah Melayu* unfolds as follows:

In Brown:

> Sri Tri Buana said: "What is it that you wish of me?" And Demang Lebar Daun replied: "All my descendants shall be your highness subjects and they must be properly treated by your highness' descendants. If they do wrong, however greatly, let them not be disgraced or insulted with evil words: if their offence is grave, let them be put to death, if that is in accordance with Muhammadan law." And the King replied, "I will give an undertaking as you wish but in return I desire an undertaking from you . . . that to the end of time your descendants shall never be disloyal to my descendants, even if my descendants are unjust to them and behave evilly." And Demang Lebar Daun replied, "So be it, your highness." And that is why it has been granted by Almighty God to all Malay rulers that they shall never put their subjects to shame: however greatly they offend, they shall never be bound or hanged or insulted with evil word. If any ruler puts his subjects to shame, it is a sign that his kingdom will be destroyed by Almighty God. Similarly it has been granted by Almighty God to Malay subjects that they shall never be disloyal or treacherous to their rulers, even if their rulers should behave evilly or inflict injustice. (1970: 16)

In Leyden's version:

> these conditions were, that on Sangsapurba marrying his daughter, all the family of Demang Lebar Dawn would submit themselves to him; but that Sangsapurba should engage, both for himself and his posterity, that they should receive a liberal treatment; and in particular, that when they committed faults they should never be exposed to shame nor opprobrious language, but if their faults were great, that they should be put to death according to the law. Sangsapurba agreed to these conditions, but he requested, in his turn, that the descendants of Demang Lebar Dawn should never move any treasonable practice against his descendants, even though they should become tyrannical. "Very well," said Demang Lebar Dawn, "but if your descendants break your agreements, probably mine will do the same." These conditions were mutually agreed to, and the parties swore to perform them, imprecating the divine vengeance to turn their authority upside down who should infringe these agreements. From this condition it is that none of the Malay rajas ever expose their Malay subjects to disgrace or shame; they never bind them, nor hang them, nor give them opprobrious language; for whenever a raja exposes his subjects to disgrace, it is

the certain token of the destruction of his country; hence also it is, that none of the Malay race ever engage in rebellion, or turn their faces from their own rajas, even though their conduct be bad, and their proceedings tyrannical. (*Malay Annals* 2001: 25–27)

By consenting to the solemn covenant Sri Tri Buana married Wan Sendari and soon it becomes apparent that she has effectively escaped the curse. Sri Tri Buana is then, according to Leyden's (*Malay Annals* 2001: 29) version, installed by Demang Lebar Daun as the king of Palembang (in Brown's, 1970:15, version Demang Lebar Daun decided to abdicate, or *turun* i.e., "step down," in favor of Sri Tri Buana, appointing himself as the chief minister shortly after that the other two of the three brothers got married and left Palembang).

In consequence, celebrations were held at Palembang for forty days and forty nights for the newly installed royal couple. Furthermore, Demang Lebar Daun assumed the role of *mangkubumi* (i.e., regent), or *Bendahara*, and the country grew and prospered (Winstedt 1938b: 56; Brown 1970: 17–18; Josselin de Jong 1986: 221; Kratz 1993: 75; *Malay Annals* 2001: 29; Chambert-Loir 2005: 149).[3] From here on, the sacred covenant between Sri Tri Buana and Demang Lebar Daun, and his peoples, pervades the rest of the *Sejarah Melayu*, and it is held to be valid no matter what the circumstances. In particular the covenant becomes an important factor in the social and political functions of the Melaka Sultanate of whom Sri Tri Buana was the ancestor of the rulers and Demang Lebar Daun of its *Bendaharas* (Kratz 1993: 76; Chambert-Loir 2005: 141).

Little is known about when the covenant myth of *Sejarah Melayu* was written or created and there not much is known about the sources that were influential in compiling it.[4] This is especially interesting since there are no other similar "covenant" myths to be found in other parts of the Malay world and Southeast Asia (or indeed elsewhere in the Indian subcontinent and the Muslim world).[5] In the Muslim world the most detailed forms of covenants are found in the Sufi, i.e., the mystical aspect of Islam, as well as the Shiite school and are generally attributed to the time of Imam Ali (599–661 CE).[6] Following their examples other Shiite dynasties, particularly the Fatimid dynasty (909–1171 CE) in Egypt, also stressed the importance of a covenant, see Imam Ali's letters in *Nahjul-Balagha* (2001) and a Fatimid mirror, translated by G. Salinger (1956: 24–39).[7] But these covenants are generally instructions on how best to look after the subjects, rather than statements of the people's own rights and duties. Likewise, there is no archaeological evidence of a symbolic or sacred covenant between the ruler and the peoples in the Malay world in pre-Islamic times, although the covenant between Sri Tri Buana and Demang Lebar Daun is set in a pre-Islamic time.

Yet the clarity of the terms between Sri Tri Buana and Demang Lebar Daun, as well as the mode and nature of the covenant between them, as equivalent if not equal, is significant. Particularly since it not only outlines the Raja's demands from his subjects, but most importantly it directly states what the people themselves requested, in return, from their ruler. J. H. Walker (2004: 220), in his study of Brown's version of *Sejarah Melayu*, further suggests that in the text of the contract there are in fact two versions of the "compact" with, "the second, absolutist version effectively undermining the original, social contract by making the ruler accountable not to his followers, but to God." Walker (2004: 247), referring to Brown's version, suggests that the "social contract" occurs chronologically in the text prior to Melaka's ruler becoming Muslim thus the references to the laws of Islam suggest later interpolation. To this insight it can be added that the pact between Demang Lebar Daun and Sri Tri Buana likewise made the people's relationship with their ruler accountable to God. Nevertheless, this divine aspect of the covenant is to be found only in Brown, and not in Leyden's version. Thus perhaps, indicating a later religious influence and an addition to the original pre-Islamic text of the covenant.

This foundation myth in the *Sejarah Melayu*, as in other Malay texts, indicates that the ruler, important as he may be, is nothing without a people, and that it is the people and their traditional leader/s who choose their ruler, and who decide freely to whom they offer their total obedience. There is of course a price that the two parties have to pay. The sacred covenant between the ruler and the subjects puts conditions on the political powers exercised by the ruler on the one hand, and at the same time it dictates the duties and actions of the peoples. And if both sides failed to observe its terms, then it had the potential to lead to chaos and confusion. Thus when the ruler shames, disgraces or humiliates his peoples then it is a clear sign that his kingdom would soon fall and/or disaster and ruins would strike the realm.[8] The people are consequently advised not to take matters into their own hands, or act against the ruler, since a greater power (that of the "Almighty God" according to Brown 1970: 16) is already at work and that justice would ultimately prevail. Nevertheless, the dire prophecy of the covenant was fulfilled in *Sejarah Melayu* at the time of Sri Tri Buana's grandson, Sultan Iskandar Shah of Singapore, when he had one of his inferior wives impaled in the marketplace (Winstedt 1938b: 81; Brown 1948: 731, 1970: 41; *Malay Annals* 2001: 86–87). This harsh punishment of his wife by Sultan Iskandar was based on nothing more than a mere suspicion. Thus, the outraged and deeply humiliated, i.e., "*terlalu malu*," father of the girl commented: "*Jikalau sunggoh sa kali pun anak hamba, ada berbuat jahat, bunoh ia sahaja; mengapatah maka di-beri malu demikian itu*" (i.e., "If my daughter is really guilty, let her be merely executed. Why put her to shame like this?"). And in revenge, the same father-in-law of Sultan Iskandar betrayed him by allowing the invading Javanese forces inside the Singapore fort thus ending Sultan Iskandar's rein. The house that he shared with his wife was then turned into rock, as a divine retribution for committing *derhaka*, i.e., "*crimem laesae maiestatis*" or a crime of high treason, against Sultan Iskandar (Maitland and Pollock 1898: 165; Mawson and Ehrlich 1987: 81).[9] Consequently Sultan Iskandar and his father-in-law both failed the terms of the covenant's agreement. Sultan Iskandar, without proper investigation, wrongfully accused and then publicly shamed and humiliated his wife. On the other hand, his father in law's action of taking revenge by betraying the kingdom to the Javanese was a clear violation of the terms of the covenant.

In general, the notion of what the Raja and his officials demand from their subjects, as well as what they think the people anticipated in return are not difficult to find in most Malay literary sources. But none of these Malay sources follow the *Sejarah Melayu* in giving a voice to the common people, discussing their needs and expectations from the people in the authority. Similarly, a general overview of the structure of power of several Malay states by Gullick (1958), Milner (1982), and Khoo (1991) do not draw attention to these features that serve as pointers to what the Malay peoples themselves saw as important limitations on royal power. Rather they analyze the indigenous political system solely from the royalist point of view.

The question is then, did such a social contract, similar to the one outlined in the *Sejarah Melayu*, exist at Kedah, as well as other parts of the Malay world? And if so to what extent was it known or invoked and implemented? Furthermore, what aspects of the covenant did the people deem significant? And what were their expectations from the rulers?

FOUNDATION STORIES ELSEWHERE

The *Sejarah Melayu* was compiled at Johor, and perhaps Aceh, between the sixteenth and early seventeenth century and deals chiefly with the history of the Melaka/Johor Sultanate (Winstedt 1939: 58, 106–109; Roolvink 1967: 301–324; Wolters 1970: 110; Braginsky 1993: 58; Walker 2004: 215; Chambert-Loir 2005: 136). R. Roolvink (1967: 301) has labeled it as "the most important Malay historical work." Although Roolvink's observation can be argued as excessive, yet the *Sejarah Melayu* does offer further insight into Malay society, culture, and political systems in areas surrounding Kedah. In particular, the text is significant when dealing with Malay polities that connect their foundation story to the historic Palembang and Melaka dynasty (such as Pahang, Perak, Johor, Selangor, Jambi, Siak, and Riau, see Wilkinson 1957: 77; Andaya 1993: 2, 8) or Johor's *Bendahara* (such as in Terengganu, Pahang, and modern Johor, see Khoo 1991: 8–9). Drakard (1999: 243) has further argued that the foundation myth in *Sejarah Melayu* closely resembles traditions and characters in historic western Sumatra, thus effectively linking the Melaka genealogy to that of the Minangkabau-Melayu.

At any rate, the fluidity of the terms and the social contract between Demang Lebar Daun and Sri Tri Buana does appear to be unique to *Sejarah Melayu*. But this does not necessarily mean that the covenant story, or aspects of it, was not prevalent elsewhere in the Malay world or Southeast Asia. In fact several Malay sources quote stories and passages from the *Sejarah Melayu* and it appears that they were familiar with the story of Demang Lebar Daun and Sri Tri Buana.

Raja Ali Haji Ibn Ahmad in his nineteenth century *Tuhfat al-Nafis*, or "Precious Gift," at Riau retells fragments of Melaka's history, and interprets anecdotes of *Sejarah Melayu* as the demonstration of a cosmic law (Ali Haji Ibn Ahmad 1982: 17, 312; Chembert-Loir 2005: 143, 143n). The fall of Melaka, for instance, to the Portuguese, in 1511 CE, is seen as the result of divine vengeance on Sultan Mahmud's government for his unjust murder of the *Bendahara Seri Maharaja*.

Additionally, the *Tuhfat al-Nafis* refers to the events in the life of Sultan Iskandar Shah in Singapore, noticeably worded differently to that of *Sejarah Melayu* (Ali Haji Ibn Ahmad 1982: 13–14). According to this the secondary wife of the Sultan was commanded to be "beheaded" at a public place, because of rumors of her infidelity. Following the beheading, her father felt "humiliated" and so commented that, "if she was in fact guilty, she should have been killed secretly. Since she had already been made important, she should not have been placed in the centre of the town for all to see her disgrace" (Ali Haji Ibn Ahmad 1982: 13–14).

Thus not only similar stories from *Sejarah Melayu* were told at the nineteenth century royal court of Riau, but were also interpreted with the terms of the covenant in mind. Furthermore, the comments by the father-in-law of Sultan Iskandar confirm the notion that amongst the Malays it was disgraceful and uncommon for people of high status to be publicly executed (see a note by Virginia Matheson and Barbara W. Andaya, in their translation to Ali Haji Ibn Ahmad 1982: 312n).

Similarly an episode in the eighteenth century *Siak Chronicles*,[10] cited and translated at length by Leonard Y. Andaya (1975: 186–188), has Johor's Sultan Mahmud II summoning and then killing a pregnant woman, by cutting open her stomach, after she had eaten a piece of his jackfruit while he was asleep.[11] The husband of the woman then hears of the shocking murder of his pregnant wife by the Sultan and is outraged. He therefore decides to take vengeance on the Sultan by committing *"derhaka."* In planning the revenge the husband found support and help from virtually all the court officials, as well as the *Bendahara*, except one "incomparable *hulubalang*" called Sri Bija Wangsa. Sri Bija Wangsa argued that he couldn't take part in any plot against the Sultan since "there was no custom of subjects committing derhaka against their lord and that the contract between the people and their lord could not be retracted. He then allowed himself to be krissed" [sic] (Andaya 1975: 186–188).

The author/authors of the *Tuhfat al-Nafis* and *Siak Chronicle* were therefore aware of a historic pact between the ruler and his subjects. Similarly in another text attributed to Siak, *Syair Perang Siak*,[12] there is reference to the "ancient covenant." According to this passage: *"Tidaklah boleh sahaya katakana, kehendak Allah sahaya sukarkan. Di mana boleh kita cintakan janji dahulu ditepatkan?"* ["I cannot relate more, the will of God oppresses me. Where may we expect the ancient contract to be fulfilled?"] (*Syair Perang Siak* 1989: 206–207).

Donald J. Goudie (see footnote in *Syair Perang Siak* 1989: 207) believes that the passage is a reference to the covenant between Sri Tri Buana and Demang Lebar Daun regarding the relationship between a royal house and its subject people. It can also be argued that the authors of these texts had ulterior motives in keeping aspects of their works in line with *Sejarah Melayu*. Principally since both these regions attempted to represent themselves in the Malay world as descendants of Alexander the Great, and/or the true heirs of the Melaka/Johor Sultanate after the confusion and controversy of the 1699 murder of Sultan Mahmud Shah II, the childless king of Johor (for more on this see: report by Hamilton 1995 II: 95–98, 1997: 74–76, of his visit to Johor in 1695; 1703 CE respectively; also Winstedt 1932: 50, 1979: 49–50; Andaya 1975: 182–191; Ali Haji Ibn Ahmad 1982: 41–43, a note by Matheson and Andaya in Ali Haji Ibn Ahmad 1982: 323n; Walker 2004: 253n).[13] It also seems that these texts tend to skip over what was expected from the rulers by their subjects. Rather, they underline loyalty of subjects toward the rulers and what was demanded of them. *Tuhfat al-Nafis* does in fact refer to the relationship between Demang Lebar Daun and Sri Tri Buana; but it fails to mention the covenant between them. According to this:

> *Sebermula adalah Raja Seri Teri Buana itu kerajaan di Singapura adalah menterinya yang bernama Demang Lebar Daun yang datang bersama-sama dengan dia dari Palembang. Adalah Demang Lebar Daun itu raja Palembang jadi mertua kepada Raja Seri Teri Buana itu.* [When Raja Seri Teri Buana set up a kingdom in Singapore, he had a minister named Demang Lebar Daun who had accompanied him from Palembang. Demang Lebar Daun, the King of Palembang, had become Raja Seri Teri Buana's father-in-law.] (Ali Haji Ibn Ahmad 1982: 13)

Sejarah Melayu stories are also corroborated in the first part of the 1815 CE *Silsilah Raja-Raja Perak I* (i.e., the "Perak book of Descent"), better known as Maxwell 105. The text intends to emphasize that members of the Perak line were the only legitimate heirs to the great Melaka dynasty and contains a brief version of the *Sejarah Melayu* as found in Winstedt (1938b) and Brown's (1970) version (see Roolvink 1967: 310–317; Ceridwen 2001: 43, 46–49, 51–52, 79–83, 103).

Nevertheless, despite the resemblance of the contents of *Silsilah Raja-Raja Perak I* to that of *Sejarah Melayu* it does not give details of the covenant between Demang Lebar Daun and Sri Tri Buana. Rather it mentions in passing that the two men simply took an "oath" of mutual loyalty prior to the marriage-taking place (Ceridwen 2001: 82, 103).[14] According to this:

> Maka baginda dengan Demang Lebar Daun pun bereguh-teguhan janjinya; barangsiapa mengsubahkan janjinya dibalikkan Allah Subhanahu wa Ta'alla bumbungannya ke bawah kaki tiangnya ke atas dan negeripun binasa, itulah setianya dinugerahkan Allah Subhanahu wa Ta'alla pada segala raja-raja Melayu. Setelah sudah puas perjanji[an]nya baginda dengan Demang Lebar Daun maka anaknya pun dipersembahkannya baginda. [Then his majesty made an agreement with Demang Lebar Daun promising that whoever violates the pact then the almighty God will destroy them and that their house will be overturned and the country destroyed. After the agreement with Demang Lebar Daun then his peoples also became devoted to his majesty.] (Ceridwen 2001: 82, 103)

Was the attempt by the author/s of *Silsilah Raja-Raja Perak I* to avoid the details of the covenant deliberate? And if so what did they intended to gain from this? Equally, why did the author of *Tuhfat al-Nafis* as well as other Malay texts fail to mention a sacred covenant between Sri Tri Buana and Demang Lebar Daun in their texts?

It is difficult to answer the above questions. Although there is the possibility that the court oriented author/s and copyists of *Silsilah Raja-Raja Perak* and other Malay works compiled their texts to be read at the court or presented to the ruler and officials.[15] Hence, the compilers of these texts omitted what they held to be inappropriate and/or irrelevant. But this did not mean that the rulers and the subjects traditionally did not acknowledge a pact, or a form of covenant, amongst themselves.

On the other hand, there is the question of why the numerous versions of *Sejarah Melayu* and its author/s, or copyists, preserved the contract story.

This perhaps was due to the compilation of the book in the sixteenth and seventeenth century, after the defeat of the Melaka Sultanate by the Portuguese in 1511. Hence the nostalgic author/s of *Sejarah Melayu*, and their descendants residing at Johor, intended to highlight and/or maintain the moral and ethical aspects of the Melaka Sultanate. Or, perhaps they offered a moral explanation to the downfall of the Sultanate.[16]

Indeed in one of the clauses of *Undang-Undang Melaka* (i.e., the Laws of Melaka; likely first compiled during the reign of Muhammad Shah I, 1424–1444 CE, the third ruler of Melaka, see Khansor 1999: 131) there is a reference to the Arabic *"yaum al-mithak,"* translated as the "Day of the Covenant" (Liaw 1976: 170).

According to the reference from *Undang-Undang Melaka*:

> *Dan barangsiapa memalu hamba raja tiada dengan salahnya, maa iaitu salah kepada "yaum al-mithak." Jikalau ia salah, sekalipun tangkap, bawa kepada orang yang memegang dia. Jikalau patut mati, iaitu mati.* [Whoever beats a royal slave without any fault on the part of the slave, has violated (the agreement made at) the day of the Covenant. If he is guilty, arrest him forthwith and bring him to the person who has control over him. If he (the slave in question) deserves death, let him die.] [sic] (Liaw 1976: 170–171)

A similar clause from *Undang-Undang Melaka* is also reproduced at length in a late sixteenth century legal digest from Pahang that suggests its contents are valid in Pahang, Perak, and Johor.[17] Roolvink (see notes in Liaw 1976: 192n-193n) suggests the passage refers to the violation of the symbolic covenant between Demang Lebar Daun and Sri Tri Buana. Roolvink is correct to speculate on the historic significance of this passage, as well as the existence of a mutual covenant between the Malay ruler and their subjects. Indeed *"barangsiapa memalu hamba raja,"* translated by F. Y. Liaw (1976: 170–171) as "whoever beats a royal slave," can further be translated as "whoever has shamed/disgraced/humiliated (i.e., *memalu*) a royal servant/subject" and resembles the covenant myth, as found in *Sejarah Melayu*. Likewise, in an earlier section of *Undang-Undang Melaka* there is a clause (chapter 1.2) that is very similar to Sri Tri Buana's demand from his peoples (Liaw 1976: 66–67). According to this clause, on the qualities (i.e., *"syarat"* [sic]) required of the ruler's subjects, it is demanded that the *"hamba raja"* always abide to the commands of the ruler; whether he is tyrannical or not.

Regardless, there is no indication in the quoted passages, as well as in other parts of *Undang-Undang Melaka* (or from Pahang's legal digest) of a covenant between the persons of Sri Tri Buana and Demang Lebar Daun. Nor do these passages shed further light on the topic of the "day of the covenant" and why it is referred to in the Arabic language, with no Malay equivalent (the question arising is that did they intend to furnish the covenant with an Islamic or religious coloring).[18] Conversely, the covenant myth between Sri Tri Buana and Demang Lebar Daun could have been the remnant of a historic pact or oath that was held between an unnamed Srivijaya or Malay ruler with the chief of the sea peoples, or *orang laut* (see comments on the historic absorption of *orang laut* into the realm by Wolters 1982: 36; for the significant link of this pact and oath to that of the Minangkabau and earlier traditions see Drakard 1999: 49, 241–243).[19] Hence, it is possible that the author/s of *Sejarah Melayu* endeavored to reaffirm the bargain, covenant or alliance made with the sea peoples and to rally them, behind the defeated Melaka Sultans and their descendants at Johor.

COVENANT AT KEDAH AND ELSEWHERE

In 1838 CE Inchi Laa [sic] was an associate, or "Secretary" [sic], of Tengku Mohamed Said, a nephew of the exiled king of Kedah that had recaptured parts of the land from the invading Siamese. On meeting Sherard Osborn (1987: 154–164), a British ship captain helping the Siamese blockade Kedah's coastline, Inchi Laa explained the reasons for the native Malay population opposing the Siamese wholeheartedly and in wanting to escape to Penang. Inchi Laa vividly described the Siamese atrocities against the natives at Kedah and then:

> he swore by Allah no Malay man had ever been known to wantonly torture women and children, as those devils did. "If," said Inchi Laa, "the woman and the child, because they are our country people, deserve death—let them die! But, beyond death or slavery, there should be no punishment for those who cannot help themselves." [sic] (1987: 162)

There is no doubt that during their invasion of Kedah, 1821–1841/1842, the Siamese dealt oppressively with the people (see reports and studies by Anderson 1824; Tomlin 1831: 62; Begbie 1834: 132, 446–448; *AJMR* 1834: 176–177; Earl 1837: 170–173; Low 1837: 101–103; *SFP* dated 29 August 1839, and 12 September 1839; Malcom 1840: 34; Maxwell 1876: 43; Beighton 1888: 13–17; Bonney 1971: 156–167; Newbold, 1971 II: 8–16; Thomson 1991: 156–159). Yet as Inchi Laa points-out the Siamese manner of punishment (particularly torture) and forms of social control were considered atypical amongst the local Malay population and aspects of it were unquestionably viewed as being humiliating, disgraceful, and shameful. This fuelled resentment and opposition to the Siamese invading forces at Kedah. Certainly about three decades earlier when a detachment of Siamese forces from Songkhla visited Kedah their method of punishment used against local Kedah officials was viewed as so severe and disgraceful that Kedah's ruler was extremely annoyed (i.e., "*baginda murka tiada terkira*") and contemplated going to war, also the Datuk Maharaja and his brother plotted to avenge the disgrace offered them, i.e., "*memalas malu hendak dikira*" (*Syair Sultan Maulana* 1985: 70–73).

In addition, Inchi Laa makes it clear that the Siamese practice of torturing women and children was uncommon amongst the Malays. Moreover, the ideas of prolonging people's death by torture were socially unacceptable to the native population and considered as appalling (see Figure 1 for a common form of execution at historic Kedah). Thus, he argues that the only form of punishment acceptable to the Malays is a quick death, "deserve death—let them die!" [sic] or slavery.

The discourse by Inchi Laa closely resembles examples from *Sejarah Melayu*, *Siak Chronicle*, *Tuhfat al-Nafis* and *Undang-Undang Melaka* that highlight a quick, respectable and low-key death for their subjects by the

Figure 1. A quick death at Kedah. Claine, J. (1892). Un an en Malaisie, 1889–1890. *Le Tour Du Monde* **(Paris), 63, 369–400.**

ruler. But unlike the examples from *Undang-Undang Melaka*, *Siak Chronicle* and *Tuhfat al-Nafis*, that specifically refer to the ruler's mistreatment and unjust killing of a person of high status and/or a person connected to the raja (i.e., a *hamba raja*, see Liaw 1976: 170–171); Inchi Laa's remark is similar to that of *Sejarah Melayu* which is a statement of the rights of all the populace, including commoners and royal slaves.[20] Hence, this passage indicates a familiarity at Kedah with a likely prototype of the covenant tradition that held those with power should not abuse or humiliate their peoples, no matter if they were royal subjects or not.

A similar desire for a quick death rather than the humiliation of torture is also expressed by Munshi Abdullah bin Abdul Kadir (1970: 94–95; a Melaka-born person of South Indian and Arab Muslim ancestry with connections to Kedah, Melaka, Johor, and Singapore, see Abdullah 1970: 31–32; Thomson 1991: 323–332), a contemporary of Inchi Laa. Writing on the Dutch and their use of various appalling forms of torture in their former colony of Melaka (1644–1824 CE) Abdullah remarks that "so far from inflicting such tortures imprisonment in itself is enough, for is not the very stigma of prison well-known and a sufficient humiliation? What good is it then to torture a servant of Allah for if his crime merits death it is better for him to be put to death at once?" (1970: 94).

Similarly in the mid-1830s a British officer, Low (1972: 239–240), reports on the negative attitude of convicted Malay prisoners at Penang of being kept alive until the time of their sentence. Hence Low continues that a Malay, that was arrested and imprisoned on charges of murder at Penang, was heard to exclaim "what is the use of fattening me up; better hang me at once!" [sic].

Colonel Nahuijs, a Dutch visitor to Singapore, conveys a similar report about the Malays of Singapore in the 1820s (Miller 1941: 195). They were upset about the treatment of the body of the Pahang trader "Syed Yasin"[21] who had gone amok and then been killed and mutilated after he had stabbed the British Resident, Major William Farquhar (Cameron 1865: 259; Buckley 1902 I: 97–100; Low 1972: 296; Trocki 1979: 50–51; Spores 1988: 37–40).[22] Despite strong opposition from native authorities, on the grounds that "the evil doer had given his life against other lives" thus "all further punishment terminated," Sir Stamford Raffles had the body tried in the court the next day, and then had the corpse publicly hanged in chains and later displayed on a metal bar for all to see ("Indian and Colonial Intelligence" in *OHCR 1824* I: 171; Miller 1941: 195). But the Malay people became upset with Raffles's humiliating public display of Syed Yasin's body. The prospect of an uprising by the Malays on the non-Malay segment of Singapore was averted when Raffles judged it wiser to have the body taken down and handed over to the Sultan for proper burial after just three days.[23] Indeed the offence offered to the dead body of Syed Yasin by the British authorities, and the fact that he was a considered a descendant of the Prophet, as a Syed, may have been likely reasons for his grave to be later considered a *Keramat*, or shrine, by the natives and Muslims of Singapore well to the 1860s when it was visited by J. T. Thomson (see footnote by Hill in Abdullah 1970: 174n; also Buckley 1902 I: 97–100; Trocki 1979: 51).[24] Equally the public display and the hanging of the dead corpse of To'Janggut (i.e., Old Long Beard) by his feet, as the leader of the 1915 Kelantan rebellion reportedly outraged the public and were interpreted by them as degrading and "a form of humiliating by the colonial authorities" (*Detik-Detik Sejarah Kelantan* 1971: 115–121; Cheah 2006: 44).[25] In his recent study of To'Janggut 1915 Kelantan rebellion, and events surrounding his death Cheah Boon Kheng concludes that "the hanging of his corpse was meant to serve as a lesson for rebelliousness and to end his invulnerability cult, yet contrary to expectations, it was such a shocking spectacle that it evoked great sympathy and support for him among the populace, and turned him into a hero" (2006: 130).

In consequence, the demand for a quick death, indicated by Inchi Laa and others, as well as the respectful disposal of the body of the dead Syed Yasin and To'Janggut suggest that the Malay peoples acknowledged a covenant between themselves and their rulers and that this had become embedded within indigenous political systems.[26] But it is likely that if such a covenant existed it was based on indigenous customs and traditions. There is no evidence that it was ever rigorously formalized, since only a few Malay legal digests support it.[27] In reality most sources advocate that the officials, royal household and people serving the ruler, the *hamba raja*, could not be punished by being publicly disgraced, shamed, executed in a debased fashion or having their deaths prolonged by impalement or other forms of torture. But this prohibition did not apply to the common people, or *rakyat*. Hence, in the case of Kedah Port Laws, or *Undang-Undang*, of 1650 CE (Winstedt 1928: 7, 25) a person (*rakyat*) of untitled father running off with the daughter or debt-slave of another was to be impaled and a gong beaten for three days. But for a similar crime involving the son of a dignitary (e.g., a *hulubulang*) he should be only punished "*taazir/ta'zir*" for seven days or be punished at the discretion of the Raja.

In the same way in the 1681–1684 CE commission issued by Sultan Muhyiddin Mansur Syah of Kedah, in the Bugis-Makassar incursion and the ensuing civil war, a person of high rank was to "be stripped of his rank and punished as appropriate, i.e., with a club or mace or the like" but soldiers and people with no rank were to be punished by the "sword, impalement, [trampling underfoot by] elephants, chains, and fetters or the prison case" when refusing to follow and obey orders (see *Commission of Sultan Muhyiddin Mansur Syah* 1985).

An anonymous European writer equally reports a comparable system of dealing with slaves and people of wealth and influence, in the early nineteenth century Savu/Sawu Islands.[28] According to this:

> Their punishments are very severe, being slavery for petty offences, and death for many crimes amongst the lower classes; but with those who are possessed of property, it is in general commuted to fines proportioned to the means of the delinquent; not having any fixed sum as an equivalent for the life of a man, as on Celebes and Sumbawa. [sic] (See "Short Account of Timor, Savu, Solor, and c" cited at length in *AJMR* 1822: 530)

Indeed the report from Savu is of interest since the chiefs were said to have been converted to Christianity only recently and that the general population were "heathens" with no "single convert to Islamism on the island" [sic] (Ibid.).

This notion is also supported by Portuguese sources. Tome Pires, the sixteenth century Portuguese visitor to the Melaka Straits, asserts that the Malays only publicly execute "commoners" and not people of higher status (Cortesao 1944 II: 262). Consequently, a person's *nama*, or title, ancestry, and relationship to the ruler was crucial in making decisions about their crime, arrest, and punishments.

In most literary and oral traditions however the covenant between the ruler and subject was true for all levels of Malay society, including religious mystics, officials, and traders. This is highlighted in two versions of the mid-eighteenth century Acehnese epic *Hikajat Potjut Muhamat* that "refined people are not blamed, and believers are not lost" (Siegal 1979: 88) and that "well-mannered people are never put to shame, people trusting in God will never perish" (i.e., "*Ureueng meudjeulih hantom kandjaj, ureueng teewakaj hantom binasa*" [sic], see *Hikajat Potjut Muhamat* 1979: 106–107, 140–141).[29]

COVENANT IN LITERARY AND ORAL TRADITIONS

The public executions as well as the humiliating and improper disposal of the bodies, of a Minangkabau trader and Muslim mystic named Sheikh[30] Gombak and his pupil, Abdulmu'min, by the order of the Patani ruler is reported in *Hikayat Patani* (composed during the period 1690–1730 CE, see Cheah 1993: 9; Bradley 2009: 268, 273, 290). The *Hikayat Patani* signals that Muslim holy men, traders and their pupils were also to be treated with dignity and respect. According to the story (*Hikayat Patani* 1970 I: 76–77, 152–154, 227–228) the Patani king banned the sale and export of copper for three years. But Sheikh Gombak attempted to sell a small quantity of copper to a Melaka ship. The port attendants became aware of the sale and despite the fact that Sheikh Gombak's pupil admitted to the fault and fully cooperated with the ensuing investigations the king ordered them both to be killed at the "Elephant Gate at the foot of the Kedi Pier" after which the corpses were thrown into the moat. Under "God's decree" [sic] and miraculous circumstances, the dead bodies were later found standing upright on the water. Both the bodies were then recovered from the bay and buried.

The disgrace offered to these two men by the king was revealed when their recovered corpses from the moat suddenly "began gently to extend themselves, a thing which had never happened to human corpses before" [sic] (*Hikayat Patani* 1970 I: 154).[31] Furthermore, it took another three years, after the burial of the Sheikh and his pupil, for the Patani ruler to finally be able to successfully cast and fire the copper cannons. It seems that the failure of the cannons is the moral point of the story, suggesting that the king was punished for unjustly executing the Sheikh and his pupil, and shamefully disposing of their bodies. Hence the disgrace of Sheikh Gombak, as a person of repute, went against native traditions. What's more the severe order of the Patani ruler to murder the Sheikh and his pupil was also a violation the indigenous political system that matters had to be properly investigated and justice rendered.[32] Thus, the fact that the Sheikh was not a native of Patani and that the ship was also from a fellow Muslim territory could have indeed made a difference if the Patani ruler had further delayed and investigated the issue. Furthermore, the severity of the order to publicly kill the Sheikh and his pupil, merely for a small quantity of copper, went against local customs that preferred a life be spared by the generosity of the ruler unless it was for murder. Indeed *Undang-Undang Melaka* is very specific that only people who killed someone, even without a fault (e.g., if provoked), were to be put to death by the law of God (Liaw 1976: 68–71).[33] Preferably however a ruler normally revoked a death sentence and either charged a fine or forced the subject instead to become a royal slave, even if he had murdered a *hamba raja* (Kempe and Winstedt 1948: 7, 10, 25–26, 33, Liaw 1976: 70–71).[34] Consequently, it would have been expected that the ruler of Patani would fine or warn the Sheikh rather than have him executed.

A parallel to the story of Sheikh Gombak can also be drawn with that of Tun Jana Khatib in *Sejarah Melayu* (Brown 1970: 39–40; *Malay Annals* 2001: 82–83); the execution of Mahsuri at the island of Langkawi (Kedah) and Syed Asmayu'd din in *Hikayat Raja-Raja Pasai* (1960: 69–73, 129–133). Tun Jana Khatib was a visiting Muslim mystic from Pasai who was wrongly accused by the Raja of Singapore, Paduka Sri Maharaja, and then publicly executed. In this case the Raja was jealous because the mystic had apparently performed some magic in front of the window of one of his wives. During his execution a clot of the mystic's blood incredibly turned the lid of a cake-maker's pan into stone and his body was then miraculously "spirited to Langkawi."[35] Soon after this incident Singapore's shore was inexplicably attacked by a species of swordfish (or *todak* in Malay, see *Malay Annals* 2001: 83), and panic took over the island, described vividly in *Sejarah Melayu* (Brown 1970: 40) as "Like rain came the swordfish and the men they killed were past numbering." Hence it is likely that the wrongful accusation of Tun Jana Khatib of immoral behavior without proper investigation and his subsequent murder was considered shameful and humiliating. Moreover, the swordfish attack is an indication of the divine retribution, for the ruler having violated the terms of the covenant.[36] In the case of Mahsuri however she was not a foreign visitor but rather a local princess that was wrongly accused of infidelity, by the ruler or the island's chief, and hence put to death (see note by Skinner in *Syair Sultan Maulana* 1985: 269n–270n; Bird 1989; Lynch and

Talib 1994: 91, 96; Yousof 1994b: 157–158; Northam and Olsen 1999: 332; Stokes 2000: 12–16).[37] Upon her public execution her innocence became clear after white blood spilled out of her wounds and she is then reputed to have cursed the island for seven generations.[38] A further intriguing aspect of Mahsuri's story is the moral explanation of her unjust and humiliating death. Her execution was soon followed by the 1821 Siamese invasion of Langkawi Island, as well as the justification for the boost in the island's economy in the 1980s is similarly attributed to the end of Mahsuri's curse (Bird 1989).

In a similar way Syed Asmayu'd din (*Hikayat Raja-Raja Pasai* 1960: 69–73, 129–133), as the chief minister, was wrongly blamed by Sultan Maliku'l Mahmud of Pasai, for the fault of his own brother, Sultan Maliku'l Mansur, and then punished harshly. The punishment of Syed Asmayu'd din by the Sultan Maliku'l Mahmud was twofold. First he was not allowed to accompany his superior (Sultan Maliku'l Mansur and his other followers) when banished from Pasai, and finally Syed Asmayu'd din's own request to be executed only by beheading was observed in part when Sultan Maliku'l Mahmud ordered the severed head to be thrown into the sea and his headless body publicly desecrated by being impaled at Kuala Pasai. But, the treatment of the corpse of the dead Syed Asmayu'd din was the beginning of miraculous events. His head was soon recovered at sea by Sultan Maliku'l Mansur after it had miraculously left Pasai and followed his ship. Sultan Maliku'l Mansur then asked his brother for the impaled body of his chief minister to be returned to him and then had it joined to the head before giving it a proper Islamic burial. Soon however another miracle happened when a voice from inside the grave of Syed Asmayu'd din spoke to Sultan Maliku'l Mansur notifying him of his own upcoming death. In consequence, miraculous events after the tragic death of a wrongly accused and humiliated person in Malay tradition were also a further indication of their innocence.

Kedah's indigenous historical source, the *Hikayat Merong Mahawangsa* is similarly in line with *Sejarah Melayu* and other indigenous sources in suggesting that the violation of the covenant on the part of a ruler could cause his downfall. Accordingly (Low 1849: 263–269) the infamous cannibal (and tusked) ruler of Kedah, Raja Bersiong, secretly continued his cannibalism by sentencing prisoners and innocent people to death so that he could maintain his supply of hearts and livers. This practice by the Raja went unchallenged by the people until a mysterious and sly man named Kampar/Gumpar, who was known for practicing black magic, suddenly left his residence in the mountains, called as Sri Gunnong Ledang, and came to the capital.[39] Kampar then knowingly had himself arrested by the Raja's men. When brought to the Raja he was immediately sentenced to be executed. Kampar then uttered to the court: "This Raja does not justly examine into cases, but sits quietly down and orders people to be slain" and later to the Raja "Is Raja Bersiong mad, that he wished to inflict punishment before he has examined the charge against me?"

These challenges to the Raja's ruling then became the catalyst for the ministers, the queen and others at the court to consolidate forces and to confront the Raja's tyranny and rule, without committing *derhaka*. The point here is that the raja violated the indigenous Malay requirement for basic justice by not investigating the cases before deciding if a person was guilty. What's more, the court ministers and peoples by remaining loyal and not revolting against Raja Bersiong's tyranny, prior to the appearance of Kampar, may suggest their part in fulfillment of the covenant agreement. Kampar's sudden appearance, his supernatural abilities, and his verbal challenge of the ruler were, however, interpreted by the people to signal the divine retribution for the Raja's violation of the covenant and his demise.

Without proper investigation Malay indigenous sources specify that punishment did not serve justice and that it was an abuse of power. Hence the Kedah indigenous legal source of *Qanun Law of Dato'Kota Star* (undated but likely from mid-eighteenth century; for a succinct translation and the complete Malay text see Winstedt 1928: 10, 34) states an immutable rule for the ruler to inquire into offences "*menyuroh pereksa tentukan kesalahan sa-orang*" [sic]. Similarly at Bandjar its temporary ruler, Ampu Djatmaka, advised his two sons as a deathbed wish to "Always inquire first and do not be quick-tempered; do not be spiteful toward people" (i.e., "*Dan baik-baik lawan kulawarga dan lawan rakjat; pareksa-pareksa, djangan mamakai puaka dan djangan dangki lawang orang*" [sic]) (Ras 1968: 266–267). It can further be argued that the indiscriminate killing of the people by Raja Bersiong, to satisfy his bloodlust, violated the covenant between the ruler and his subjects. A similar violation of the people's rights, as well as their proper social relationships may further explain the historic downfall and replacement of Patani kings with queens. Writing in the late 1680s Nicholas Gervaise, offered the following explanation for the rise of queens in Patani: "It is said that its people were weary of obeying kings who maltreated them, and shook off their yoke. Having forced him who was reigning to descend from the throne, they put in his place a princess to whom they gave the title of queen, without giving her any authority" (Nicholas Gervaise cited at length by Cheah 1993: 8).

Consequently the replacement of kings at Patani, as well as the downfall of Raja Bersiong highlights instances in Malay indigenous political systems in which the subjects resorted to removing a ruler, without committing *derhaka*, and violating the basic terms of the covenant contract. Furthermore the above stories further signal the historic existence of a prototypical covenant myth amongst the Malay people outside areas often associated to the Palembang, Melaka and Johor royal line. Conversely, assuming that the people had not resorted to removing the ruler by force it was thought that divine vengeance would ultimately prevail in removing the tyrant. Visiting the Langkawi Islands and Perlis about three years after the devastating Acehnese attack of 1619, the French Admiral Beaulieu (1705: 245, 247) reports on an indigenous view of why the invasion occurred and the moral justification of the downfall of the monarch. According to this information:

> The Customs and Imports at this place were very moderate, till the Father of the present King came to Reign, who was a perfidious and cruel Tyrant, and by Divine Vengeance (as the Natives will have it) was carry'd off in Captivity by the King of Achem about three Years ago. In earnest, this place bears several Marks of the Divine Wrath; for about four Years before it was subdued, two thirds of the Inhabitants amounting to above 40000 Souls, were carried off by a Plague. [sic] (Beaulieu 1705: 246)

Consequently, an unjust ruler would fall from grace and his/her actions would have a negative effect on the realm and suffer a loss of population. The ruler was thus responsible for his/her actions as by default it could simply spark a chain of disaster and havoc, as reiterated in the indigenous source of *Tuhfat al-Nafis* (Ali Haji Ibn Ahmad 1982: 141) they would be "Struck by the Lord's curse."

There is an early eighteenth century report by an English sea captain, Alexander Hamilton (1995 II: 95–98, 1997: 74–76), surrounding the demise of the previously mentioned Sultan Mahmud Shah II of Johor, circa 1690–1699, that related atrocities similar to those of Raja Bersiong. According to Hamilton, who went to Johor in 1695 and again circa 1703, Sultan Mahmud was "intolerable" [sic] and acted as a tyrant toward his people and visitors.[40] Additionally from events witnessed during his stay at Johor, Hamilton (1995 II: 95–96) continues that the Sultan was "a great *Sodomite*, and had taken many of his *Orankays* or Nobles Sons, by Force into his Palace for that abominable Service" [sic]. The Sultan's mother then decided to take matters into her own hands and hence cure her son. Thus she asked a young woman to visit the Sultan in his bedchamber.[41] But the Sultan quickly had his guards enter the room and break the girl's arms, although she had earlier explained to him that his mother had asked her to visit him. The Sultan then sent a guard the next morning to bring in the head of the girl's father, but "he being an *Orankay* did not care to part with it, so the Tyrant[42] took a Lance in his Hand, and sware he would have it; but, as he was entering at the Door, the *Orankay* past a long Lance through his Heart, and so made an End of the Beast" [sic].

This act of regicide by the nobleman against the Sultan was not simply an act of outrage or revenge. Indeed if the nobleman wanted to take revenge on the Sultan, he would have instead taken the initiative and gone to murder him when he heard the news about the breaking of his daughter's arms. He was thus within the bounds of the terms of the covenant. However, it appears that the Sultan was the one that was outraged and wanted to kill the nobleman.

THE COVENANT AND THE SHAMING OF THE MALAY RULER

There are rare instances in which the rulers would argue that they were publicly shamed and humiliated by the subjects. Fernao Mendes Pinto (1989: 31–33), a Portuguese visitor to Kedah in the 1520s, reports on the brutal execution of Khoja Ali, the agent of the captain of Portuguese Melaka, as well as the arrest of other merchants by the ruler. According to Pinto (1989: 31–32) a royal proclamation was circulating at the time of his visit to Kedah to the effect that no one was to discuss, or question, the controversial circumstances surrounding the recent regicide of the old ruler (by his son, the new ruler) and the subsequent marriage of the young ruler to his mother, whom he had earlier gotten pregnant.[43] Khoja Ali together with a number of his friends and Patani relations were arrested after being overheard gossiping about the controversy in Kedah by the ruler's men. They were therefore brought to the young ruler who explained to Pinto that he felt humiliated and shamed thus ordering the prisoners to be at once executed by "*gregoge.*"[44]

Similarly there are instances in Malay literary sources in which the Malay rulers would feel humiliated, or shamed, by his subjects, neighbors or visitors. In these occasions the Malay ruler would not get directly involved, rather he/she would seek the assistance of a loyal subject to counter the person/s that had shamed or humiliated them.

According to *Hikayat Hang Tua*[45] and *Sejarah Melayu* Sultan Mansur Shah of Melaka felt humiliated after one of his warriors, Hang Kasturi/Casturi or Hang Jebat, committed high treason against him, by occupying the royal palace and sleeping with the Sultan's women attendants, or concubines (Wolters 1970: 247n–248n; Kratz 1993: 77–78; Khansor Johan 1999: 133n; *Malay Annals* 2001: 184–192; Hooker 2003: 67). Sultan Mansur Shah then exclaimed that if his loyal warrior Hang Tua, thought to be dead, were still alive "he would have quickly removed my disgrace" (*Malay Annals* 2001: 185). After realizing that Hang Tua was still alive and in meeting him then the Sultan symbolically presented him with a *kris* and said "with this wipe off this stain from my face" (*Malay Annals* 2001: 187).[46] Malaysian scholar Zakaria Ali (1993: 383) argues that the *kris* performs more than just symbolic and practical functions in the story. It conveys the message that no one should ever revolt against the Sultan because that violates the Malay ethos.

On the other hand, Malay literary sources imply that when foreign visitors humiliated the ruler it was customary not to kill them but rather to expel or exile them. Hence *Hikayat Patani* (1970 I: 253–257) continues that when a Johor official, the *Yang Di Pertuan Muda*,[47] "violated" the

Queen of Patani and then had a love affair with her maid, named Dang Sirat, he was simply expelled while the maid was executed.

Hikayat Raja-Raja Pasai relates a similar story in which a number of physically strong Kalinga buccaneers publicly insulted and humiliated Sultan Ahmad of Pasai. According to the chronicle when the Kalinga men arrived at Pasai:

> So they asked the man of Telok Teria "What are the things which in this city it is lawful only for the ruler to do?" The man of Telok Teria replied "The only thing which may not be done, except by the king himself, is to sit in the big audience-hall at the royal park and to undo one's hair, with legs dangling and swinging from side to side. This is forbidden in this place." When the buccaneers heard this they said "Very well. That is exactly what we will do." (*Hikayat Raja-Raja Pasai* 1960: 136–137)

The story then continues that the Kalinga buccaneers entered and sat in Pasai's royal hall while "letting down their hair with their legs dangling and swinging from side to side" (*Hikayat Raja-Raja Pasai* 1960: 137).[48] This was certainly a challenge to Sultan Ahmad and felt insulted. Thus Sultan Ahmad requested his most loyal and powerful subject, incidentally also his son, Tun Beraim Bapa and instructed him to "rid me of my shame" (*Hikayat Raja-Raja Pasai* 1960: 141). The Kalinga men were then defeated in a match by Tun Beraim Bapa and returned to their ship "hanging their heads in shame" (*Hikayat Raja-Raja Pasai* 1960: 142).

The reality of treatment of foreigners might however be very different to what has been portrayed in the above stories from *Hikayat Raja-Raja Pasai* and *Hikayat Patani*. For example Dutch sources discuss the treatment of Johor's *Yang Di Pertuan Muda* very different to that of *Hikayat Patani*. According to the Dutch account the Queen's supporters made an attempt on the life of the *Yang Di Pertuan Muda* who managed to escape, but his followers were massacred (Andaya 1975: 67–68, 192n; Cheah 1993: 9). Furthermore, there is the report by Pinto (1989: 31–33) on the brutal execution of Khoja Ali and his Patani relations at Kedah, whereby the Sultan showed no mercy toward them.

CONCLUSION

From the references in *Undang-Undang Melaka* and *Hikayat Raja-Raja Pasai* it seems certain that there was traditionally a covenant myth surviving amongst the population and that it predated the *Sejarah Melayu*. Furthermore, it seems the author/s of *Tuhfat al-Nafis, Silsilah Raja-Raja Perak I, Siak Chronicle, Syair Perang Siak* and possibly other areas that connected themselves to the Melaka and Johor lineage, were familiar with the covenant story from *Sejarah Melayu*. In particular, *Tuhfat al-Nafis, Silsilah Raja-Raja Perak I* and *Siak Chronicle* tend to be in line with *Sejarah Melayu* in voicing their opposition to public and humiliating punishments of people by their rulers. However, most authors avoid reproducing the terms and conditions of the covenant myth. There is also little reference in Malay legal digests to the covenant, or aspects of it. While in the reference to "the day of the covenant" in *Undang-Undang Melaka* it does not elaborate further on what it was and between whom. Nevertheless, the short reference in *Undang-Undang Melaka* to the covenant is significant as it suggests that the agreement was real and that it was widely acknowledged and understood, amongst the Malay population. Similarly the Islamic coloring given to the covenant passages in *Undang-Undang Melaka* and *Sejarah Melayu* (the version used by Winstedt and Brown) suggest the cementing of the historic pact with a religious undertone. Alternatively, the Malay concept of a covenant as reiterated in *Sejarah Melayu* and highlighted in other literary and oral reports is particularly of wider interest since it is unique with no equivalent or similar tradition known to exist elsewhere.

On the other hand, from oral and literary reports at Kedah and other areas it appears that there was a familiarity with the covenant, or aspects of it, between the Malay rulers and their subjects. This further highlights the persistence of a historic covenant prototype outside areas traditionally associated with Palembang-Melaka and Johor royal lineage and their foundation myth. Underlining that in a general way there was uniformity in the demands of the Malay peoples and their rulers from each other.

The understanding of what constituted humiliation, or shame, thus appears to have been well embedded into the Malay mind and became an integral part of their political and social worldview. Hence the tradition of a covenant between Demang Lebar Daun and the Sri Tri Buana may also highlight the historic loyalty of the Malay subjects, as well the sea peoples, i.e., the *orang laut*, toward their rulers. The Malay rulers are also portrayed by the literary sources to demand respect, loyalty and not to be humiliated or shamed. But their limits and mode of countering their insults is somewhat different to the subjects. In particular they never seek to act alone and rely on the assistance of their loyal subjects. It is likely that this aspect of Malay literary sources is an attempt to give a moral explanation for the failures of the ruler's—supposedly—powerful curse, as well as in distancing them socially and politically from actual violence.[49]

The examples from the territories of Melaka, Penang, Kelantan and Singapore are similarly unique as they reiterate the notion that the Malay peoples would still continue to adhere to its values and expect the same level of treatment from any ruler whether Malay, Siamese, or European. This attitude in fact appears to be deeply embedded within Malay mind, traditions, and indigenous sources. Most sources show that the historic pact was between the local chief and a foreign prince that was invited to ruler over them. In fact the never-ending opposition to the Siamese methods of social control and coercion in the aftermath of the 1821 invasion of Kedah (and elsewhere in the Malay world) may further suggest the Siamese failure to realize that their Malay subjects were to be treated differently to their other conquered peoples, e.g., treatment and enslavement of the Laotians and their ruler Prince Chow Van Chan (see *AJMR* 1834: 175–176; Gullick 1983: 34; Wyatt 1984: 171; in particular Laotian children were taken as slaves to Bangkok, see an eyewitness report by Jacob Tomlin 1831: 62). It also signals the lack of Malay experts or advisers at the royal court of Siam and that the Malays were perhaps simply treated as just another tribe that happened to be Muslims. Hence the frequent appointment of Muslim dignitaries, ministers, or advisers many of whom had foreign ancestry, particularly Persian, in dealing with Siam's southern Muslim provinces made little progress, as they were unaware of a distinct Malay culture and sociopolitical worldview.

In reality the Malay rulers expected an equal level of treatment, loyalty, and respect toward themselves and their subjects in their tributary relationship with the Siamese and others. In discovering the 1909 Siamese transfer of Kedah to the British, without his prior consultation and knowledge, Kedah's then ruler Sultan Abdul Hamid Halim (1881–1943) seemingly remarked to Sir George Maxwell (the British advisor to Kedah): "My country and my people have been sold as one sells a bullock. I can forgive the buyer, who had no obligation to me, but I cannot forgive the seller" (Letter to the editor by Sir George Maxwell, *The Straits Times* dated 16th of May 1957).

Furthermore, the public resentment shown toward Sir Stamford Raffles's treatment of the dead body of the Pahang trader "Syed Yasin" at Singapore, reiterates a similar reaction to that of the Siamese treatment of the Malays and the covenant. Thus the Malay population of Singapore interpreted Raffles motives differently to its intended objective and saw it as a violation of people's rights by those in authority. Raffles also outraged the Muslim population of Singapore, composed chiefly of East Indians, as they considered the victim to be the Prophet's progeny. To Raffles and other British officers meanwhile the treatment of Yasin's body, after his death, was warning to the native population as an indication of the treatment if they were attacked. These tactics were common in Europe and were considered a success strategy by officers in other British colonies, particularly India. This event also heralds the fact that at the time the British considered the Malay colonies and their subjects simply as an extension of British India.

The tradition of the covenant in Kedah is an important part of the book because it suggests that a historic pact existed between the ruler, the people, and the land. The Kedah rulers in particular were to historically benefit and use various aspects of the covenant to their own advantage in legitimizing and prolonging their rule. Thus by conveniently highlighting aspects of the covenant Kedah's rulers could ensure support and an unconditional loyalty from their subjects. The people were consequently advised not to revolt or commit treason against the ruler even if he becomes a tyrant, as this would be a direct violation of the historic agreement.

In return for their unquestioning loyalty the people traditionally held the ruler accountable for not publicly humiliating or disgracing them. An example of this would have been the historic right of the people to have a low-key and quick death. This delicate relationship can be further demonstrated in the story of Raja Bersiong and popular outrage at his mistreatment of his subjects. *Hikayat Merong Mahawangsa* maintains that there was no revolt against him until it became publicly evident, through Kampar that he was contravening the law by his mistreatment of the people and failing to investigate their alleged crimes. The ministers were also instrumental in his removal suggesting that they were representative of the people, as was Demang Lebar Daun in *Sejarah Melayu*. In the case of the Siamese invasion of Kedah in 1821 however it is evident that Kedah's ruler continued to receive continuing support from his exiled subjects. The invasion of Kedah was thus not viewed or understood by the people as an example of a tyrant being destroyed due to divine retribution, as was the 1619 Acehnese invasion of Kedah as reiterated by the locals to Beaulieu (1705: 245–247). Hence this may further explain why the people chose to remain loyal to the ex-ruler, his cause, and to assist him in retaking Kedah by force. Indeed in an 1831 English report, of the Malay success in capturing Kedah from Siam, by Robert Ibbetson, Resident of Singapore, he was amazed that the planned attack was kept a secret: "Not a single individual among the many hundreds of the Malays living in British administered settlements . . . came forward to give intelligence" (cited in length by Milner 1982: 10–11, 124n).

NOTES

1. In J. Leyden's version of the text this title was bestowed, upon Bichitram Shah, by a man emerging from the vomited foam of a bull prior to his meeting with Demang Lebar Daun, see *Malay Annals* 2001: 23–24. But in another version of the story, translated into French by mid-nineteenth century Ed. Dulaurier, Bichitram Shah accompanies the three brothers as their half brother, see Winstedt 1938b: 2n.

2. There is some disagreement in translating the Malay word *"kedal"* into English. It has been translated by Wolters (1970: 132) as "skin discoloration"; Amelia Ceridwen (2001: 82–3, 103) as a "rash"; and as "a skin disease" by Henry Chambert-Loir (2005: 144). But it is possible that the Malay version consulted by Leyden had leprosy (i.e., *kusta* in Malay) rather than *kedal*.

3. *Hikayat Bandjar* also has the local chief ceding his power to his son-in-law and then assuming the position of *mangkubumi*, see Ras 1968: 120. Similarly Mohammed Dalek, the hero of the story in *Hikayat Deli* (Milner 1982: 79), arrives at Percut, east coast of Sumatra, and its ruler then offers him his daughter, in marriage, as well as the territory of Percut.

4. The marriage aspect of the story has some similarity to traditions in South India, Cambodia and Bandjar (Ras 1968: 120; Harman 1985: 411–430; Gaudes 1993: 333–358). It is possible that these sources may have influenced each other.

5. Pre-Islamic Persian inscriptions generally depict the ruler carrying a symbolic ring. This is thought to signify a sacred covenant between the ruler and God, rather than the people. The goddess Mitra, often connected to preside over contracts in historic Persia, is only thought to have only symbolically be involved be social contracts between individuals, e.g., marriage or a business venture, see Frye 1964: 38–39, 38n, Nabarz 2005: 1–2, 166; Norouzi 2006: 11n.

6. Imam Ali was the son-in-law of the Prophet Muhammad, his spiritual successor and the fourth caliph. There is a reference in the Koran/Quran, verse or *Sura* 7:172, to *"yaum al-mithak"* as the "day of the covenant." It refers to a momentous covenant between the children of Adam and God. Most mystical schools within Islam, particularly Sufi orders and Shiites, refer to this verse and the covenant as the day of *alastu*, the "primordial time," in which the human heart truly "witnessed" to its Lord, see Nurbakhsh (1987: 126–129), *Koran* (1990: 319), Webb (1994: 93, 106), Ibn Al-Farid (2001: 24), Douglas-Klotz (2003: 267) and Kadi (2005: 49). Most Sufi orders as well as Shiites, citing Sunni or Shiite traditions, refer to the day of the appointment of Ali as his successor by Prophet Muhammad, at a small oasis known as *Ghadir Khumm* (i.e., the pool of Ghadir) as *"yaum al-mithak,"* see Lawson (2001: 106).

7. Originally written in Arabic, *Nahjul-Balagha* (i.e., "The Peak of Eloquence") was first compiled and published in the eleventh century, see Bill and Williams 2003: 153n.

8. The Arabic and Persian usage of the word *"fadzhihat"* in *Sejarah Melayu* (the MS. No. 18 of the Raffles collection, Winstedt 1938b: 55–56), to indicate the "public humiliation" of the peoples at the hand of the ruler, rather than a Malay equivalent is highly imperative. Thus highlighting the Islamic or religious undertone of the contract in which the parties involved were symbolically answerable to God.

9. The Malay word *"derhaka"* is derived from the Sanskrit word of *"drohaka"* and its usage can be documented to the seventh century CE "Kota Kapur" (or Bangka) inscription of Srivijaya, see the Romanised version of the inscription and its translation in G. Coedes (1918: 54–56) whereby the word is mentioned 6 times.

10. Also referred to, as *Hikayat Siak* or *Hikayat Raja Akil*; see Milner 1982: 160.

11. *Tuhfat al-Nafis* reports this aspect of the story differently. According to this story the prior to assassinating the ruler, Sultan Mahmud, Megat Seri Rama, had Sri Bija Wangsa, the faithful servant of the ruler, lured away and killed, see Ali Haji Ibn Ahmad 1982: 41–42.

12. The text is believed to have been written in 1764 for Raja Mahmud of Siak's children in exile, see comments by Donald J. Goudie in *Syair Perang Siak* 1989: 71, as well as Barnard 2003: 105–106. *Syair Perang Siak* is different to the *Siak Chronicle* as it does not link Siak's ruler, Raja Kecik, to that of the royal house of Johor or Melaka (Barnard 2003: 66). Rather it connects Raja Kecik to the Minangkabau region, as well as his genealogy to Alexander the great through one of the three brothers in the "Bukit Siguntang" tradition (*Syair Perang Siak* 1989: 89, 137, 209).

13. According to *Siak Chronicle* the Johor Sultan was not childless as he managed to get a woman pregnant, under miraculous circumstances, a day before he died in 1699 CE, see Andaya 1975: 258. A similar story to the *Siak Chronicle* is reiterated in the nineteenth century indigenous source of *Tuhfat al-Nafis*, from Riau, by its author Ali Haji Ibn Ahmad (1982: 42).

14. According to *Silsilah Raja-Raja Perak I* Sri Tri Buana had already married 40 times, rather than *Sejarah Melayu's* 39 times, prior to his wedding to Demang Lebar Daun's daughter, see Ceridwen 2001: 82–83, 103. For further differences between the two texts see Wolters 1970: 248n.

15. Besides each of these indigenous sources have a historiographical significance to the compilers of the text and the specific polity it describes. For example *Silsilah Raja-Raja Perak* and *Hikayat Siak* take great efforts to link the ruler's genealogy to the Johor-Melaka-Srivijaya line, while the *Tuhfat al-Nafis* attempts to highlight the Johor-Riau polity and its royal link.

16. Similarly in a recent historical study of *Hikayat Patani*, Francis R. Bradley (2009: 267–293) argues that the text was written in a way to re-establish a moral order through writing during an era of political and social collapse.

17. A passage at the end of the clause however suggests that it dates from an order by Sultan Muzaffar the son of Sultan Mahmud, the last ruler of Melaka; see Kempe and Winstedt (1948: 3, 21, 24, 30).

18. The reference to the Arabic usage of the Quranic words of *"yaum al-mithak"* (Sura 7: 172) is highly significant (refer to an earlier note on the usage of term in Islam, particularly within Sufism and Shiism). Particularly it points out to its adaptation into indigenous Malay context and usage.

19. Demang Lebar Daun can be translated as "Chieftain Broad/wide Leaf/oar blade/ paddle," see translation of the name by Harvey 1884: 64n and the words in Winstedt (1964: 47, 109) and Shadily and Echols (1994: 133, 137, 333). Trocki believes this title could indeed refer to the chief, or forefather, of the sea peoples. But Brown believes that the name signifies chief of "Lebar Daun," a place in Palembang, and offers no translation of the latter words nor does he make a connection to the sea peoples, see his notes in Brown (1970: xxxii). Indeed in the Southeast Asian context it is not unusual to find sea captains or maritime chiefs connected to the name "leaf," which may symbolically refer to the oar blade or paddle. According to the tenth century Chinese work of *Tai-ping-yu-lan* the female sovereign of Funan, named Liu-ye, under miraculous circumstances failed to capture and plunder a trading boat and then submitted herself to a devout Brahman passenger that later became Funan's first king (Gaudes 1993: 339–340). Southeast Asian scholar Rudriger Gaudes (1993: 340) has translated the name "Liu-ye" as a "willow leaf," according to the Chinese characters.

20. *Sejarah Melayu* makes it clear that the covenant is valid between Demang Lebar Daun, Sri Tri Buana, their families, descendants, as well all Malay rulers and subjects, i.e., *hamba Melayu*, see Winstedt 1938b: 57.

21. The translator of Nahuijs's account spells his name as "Sayid Yasin."

22. John Cameron refers to this incident as Singapore's first case of amok.

23. Munshi Abdullah reports this differently. According to Abdullah (1970: 171–174), the body was displayed for ten days or a fortnight, at Tanjong Malang, and then handed over to the Sultan who had buried it with "lustration and prayers."

24. For more discussion on Malay *keramats* see Skeat 1900: 61–71; Winstedt 1925; Wilkinson 1957: 12.

25. I would like to thank Dr. John Butcher (Griffith University) and Professor Cheah Boon Kheng for drawing my attention to this aspect of the life and death of To'Janggut.

26. There was traditionally a system of executing and disposing of bodies according to rank, status and religion. For example in the case of Tuk Mir, who had committed high treason against Patani's ruler, the indigenous source of *Hikayat Patani* (1970 I: 195–196) points out since he was a Syed and descendant of the Prophet thus his blood should not be shed and he was thus executed by being drowned at sea. In consequence, it would have been expected that no further disgrace be offered to Syed Yasin after his initial death.

27. The rulers were also more lenient when family or relations were involved. Thus Sultan Iskandar of Perak's treatment of his enemies in the second half of the eighteenth century contrasts sharply with the relative leniency he showed to members of the royal family (Andaya 1979: 247).

28. It is located to the west of the Timor Island, in the Indian Ocean, and is part of Indonesia's East Nusa Tenggara province.

29. The text describes the epic struggle between the sons of Sultan Ala'ad-din Ahmad Shah, the first ruler of the Bugis dynasty of Aceh, and Sultan Jemal al-Alam Badr al-Muni, in about 1735 CE, see Lee 1995: 5.

30. In another version of the same story he is referred to as a *Nakhoda*, or sea captain, rather than a Sheikh, see comments by D. K. Wyatt to the *Hikayat Patani* (1970: 33).

31. The extension of a person's corpse, grave and grave-posts are a mark of achieving sainthood. Several Malay *keramats* at Penang, Perak and Kedah are attributed to be similar (I would like to thank Mr. Merican, a practicing Sufi, and former owner of ABC bakery at Penang, and his son-in-law (Mr. Jafar Sadik) for taking me to visit several of Sufi shrines, including some with extended grave-posts at Penang). When visiting Patani in 1899 W. W. Skeat (1900: 75) recalls a grave belonging to a local saint of "Cape Patani" that his grave-posts were believed to miraculously make "prophetic movements" [sic].

32. Similarly oral traditions in the Langkawi Islands in attempting to explain Mahsuri's curse and the Siamese invasion of the island point out that in sentencing Mahsuri the chief had failed to investigate allegations brought forward against her (Mohamed Zahir Haji Ismail 2000: 10, 121–125, 128). Her innocence and rights were thus violated.

33. There were however certain exceptions to the rule e.g., when the person was a *hamba raja* (i.e., a dignitary or a person of good background according to *Majellis Aceh*), someone running amok, the murder was committed with the knowledge of the king or an official and/or if the murder happened in darkness during the night-time see Braddell (1851: 27), Winstedt (1928: 5, 9, 22, 30), Kempe and Winstedt (1948: 21, 58–59), Liaw (1976: 68, 70–71, 74–75) and Khansor Johan (1999: 134–135).

34. *Undang-Undang Pahang* rules that a murderer could survive a death sentence by becoming a royal servant due to an old tradition *"kaul kadim hukum resam,"* see Kempe and Winstedt 1948: 33. T. J. Newbold (1835: 297–298) however reports that in 1805 a Kedah man, Sali, had murdered one of his slaves and hence was executed by the chief, *penghulu*, of Naning, in the contemporary Malaysian state of Negeri Sembilan, according to Minangkabau customs, *Adat Minangkabau*, as he was unable to pay a fine. There is no record that Sali was offered to become a royal servant by the chief of Naning.

35. Langkawi is often believed to be the same as Lanka or Langkapuri mentioned in Indian sources (e.g., *Ramayana*, and *Bhagavata Purana*) and Malay traditions where Mount Meru and celestial spirits were found, see Low (1849: 8n), Maxwell (1881: 32), Dowson (1888: 208), Sweeney (1972: 65–80, 1972b: 258), Maier (1988: 92–93), Braginsky (1993: 59), Drakard (1999: 237), and Stokes (2000: 14–16). This may explain the spiriting away of Tun Jana Khatib. Furthermore, according to Burmese Buddhist sources the spirits at Lanka were about to fight each other, at *Nagavana* (i.e., Nagas garden), when Buddha intervened, see translation of twelfth century "Tier A I. Gl. 185 and 186" ink glosses, in the entrance to Rajkumars's temple, by Luce 1969: 380.

36. The reference to swordfish is significant. Indeed swordfish play an important part in the conversion story of Kutai (East Kalimantan) peoples to Islam (cited at length by R. Jones 1979: 149–150). According to the story Tuan Tunggang Parangan (i.e., "the Gentleman astride a swordfish") arrived at the island riding a swordfish. Hence it is possible that the author/s of *Sejarah Melayu* were familiar with the swordfish's story from Kutai, or another similar story, whereby their presence had divine aspirations and they were instrumental in assisting holy men in their quests.

37. According to a version of the story Mahsuri's parent were originally from Phuket but had decided to migrate to the Langkawi Islands about two hundred years ago, see Lynch and Talib 1994: 91; Stokes 2000: 13. There is a shrine in contemporary Langkawi Island attributed to Mahsuri and is popular with visitors. It is believed that her family and child returned to Phuket and that her descendants still continue to live there, see Mohamed Zahir Haji Ismail 2000: 129–132.

38. The story of Mahsuri is thought to date from the eighteenth or the nineteenth century. Nonetheless, the theme of "white blood" and its significance is much older and widespread in Southeast Asia, see *Hikayat* Raja-*Raja Pasai* (1960: 112), *Hikayat Patani* (1970 I: 197, 261–262), *The Crystal Sands* (1975: 44–46), Gresick (1995: 42, 42n) and Cummings (2002: 14, 94–163). Southeast Asian scholar David E. Sopher (1977: 286) argues that the white blood theme may have its origin at Kedah and then travelled to the other parts of Thailand.

39. In Indian and Malay traditions the hill and mountains are often inhabited by celestial spirits and mystics, see Dowson 1888: 208; *Hikayat Indraputra* 1983: 49–277. According to the mid-eighteenth century Acehnese epic of *Hikajat Potjoet Moehamat* most people living in the mountain have great power of invulnerability, as well the power of deception, "without your knowing they deceive you" [*sic*], see Siegel 1979: 33, 113.

40. For example the Sultan tested a pistol given to him by Hamilton as a gift "on a poor Fellow on the Street, how far they could carry a Ball into his Flesh, and shot him through the Shoulder" [*sic*] (Hamilton 1995 II: 95). The tyrannical rule of the Sultan is also corroborated in Dutch sources. Shortly after his assassination, the Dutch in Melaka were told that the Johor nobles had carried out the regicide because of the ruler's tyranny, his arbitrary killings, and his outrageous practices toward their wives (Andaya 1975: 186).

41. The matrilocal nature of marriages and relationships in historic Southeast Asia is particularly relevant at that period, see Reid 1993b: 147; Li 1998: 149.

42. The tyrant here is meant the Sultan.

43. The controversy surrounding this marriage must have continued well beyond sixteenth century Kedah. Hamilton (1995 II: 74; 1997: 50–51, 51n) reports the same story in the early 1700s that according to him happened "Some Ages ago" [*sic*]. But in reality it is likely that the young Sultan married his stepmother and not his true biological mother.

44. Pinto (1989: 31–32) describes this execution as "sawing a live man to death, starting with the feet, then the hands, the neck, and the chest, all the way down the back to the bottom of the spine, which is the way I saw them all afterwards"[*sic*].

45. *Hikayat Hang Tua* likely dates back to the fifteenth century (Reid 1994: 282). Nonetheless, aspects of the text may suggest that it existed much earlier.

46. This remark by Sultan Mansur Shah is quite significant. The Maranao (Muslim in the Lanao province in Southern Philippines and related to the Malays) similarly believe that a person that has been shamed, or *maratabat*, has "dirt on his face"; see Saber, Tamano and Warriner 1960: 14–15.

47. Likely the brother or a cousin of Johor's Sultan (Cheah 1993: 9). The marriage was dissolved sometime around 1642–1643 (*Dagh-register* [1643–1644] 1902: 32).

48. Traditionally people's hair and heads were considered, in Malay culture, as sacred (Winstedt 1947: 137). According to *Hikayat Bandjar* (Ras 1968: 337) people were not allowed to wear "long hair without permission from the king." *Hikajat Potjoet Moehamat* (Siegel 1979: 113) meanwhile highlights that only the mysterious people living in the mountains (practicing black magic) were having "long hair."

49. The use of a curse by the ruler was symbolically a powerful weapon against an enemy and the preferred method of execution. Accordingly in the inscription of Kota Kapur (Bangka), dated circa 686 CE, the Srivijaya ruler issued a powerful curse against Java for not being devoted to Srivijaya (cited and translated at length by G. Coedes 1918: 54–56). In a similar manner the sixteenth century *Undang-undang Pahang* (Kempe and Winstedt 1948: 21–22, 57) commands a criminal to be killed using a curse and if in case it fails then he/she to be executed using a weapon. Drakard (1999: 6, 49, 153, 157, 222, 235, chapter 9) suggests that in the Minangkabau region the royal curse, i.e., *besi kawi*, remained popular well into the nineteenth century.

THREE

Controlling Kedah's Maritime Lines of Communication

The Sultan and the Raja di-laut, *or Sea Lords*

In Trocki's 1979 study of Johor, he raised the issue of a distinction between the maritime and riverine systems. Since then, there has been relatively little scholarly attention paid to the manner in which the Malay rulers actually controlled the maritime and riverine routes. Likewise the role of the powerful sea lords and their followers has not been fully explored.[1] For example it is not known if the mode of control suggested by Trocki was common across the Malay world or if there were regional variations. Hence, a study of historic Kedah can shed further light into how the Malay rulers traditionally maintained their control of the maritime domains.

The control of maritime and riverine routes was in fact an integral part of the political and economic structure of Kedah. Kedah was part of the maritime system since its centre of power and the "trading city" was located at or close to the river-mouths, or near the coastline. Moreover, its historic lines of control included the "sea routes" that also extended to a number of river systems and river estuaries within its domain, as well as several large and small islands.

In line with Trocki's (1979: xvi–xvii) argument, Kedah's sea routes were controlled and defended, at least from the seventeenth to the nineteenth century, by the ruler in conjunction with a number of "sea lords" or *raja laut* and their followers, the "sea peoples" or *"orang laut,"* that were the backbone of the realm's navy.[2] Moreover, Kedah's rulers also bestowed economic incentives and symbolic rewards upon the sea lords. Furthermore, like Johor the sea lords of Kedah served as court officials such as the Laksamana (i.e., the admiral) or other individuals of that rank. The Laksamanas in particular acted as Kedah's undisputed sea lords for much of the seventeenth to the early nineteenth century. Furthermore, they were related to Kedah's ruler by blood and family connections at least from the second half of the eighteenth century onward. Indeed, in the indigenous sources of Kedah the Laksamana is referred to as *"panglima laut"* or *"raja di-laut"* [sic], a notion that corresponds to Trocki's earlier term of sea lord.[3] Hence, in contrast to Aceh, as argued by Andaya (2001a: 53), the Laksamana's position at Kedah resembles that of a similar position at the Johor courts, and its predecessor Melaka, which entailed the direct command of the *orang laut* and their chiefs.

In spite of the many similarities with Johor, there are however aspects of Kedah's traditional control of its maritime and riverine lines of communication that draw attention to alternative indigenous political systems, or models, and shed further light into indigenous modes of control current in the Malay world. Some of these trends and variations may well have been current in Johor, as well as other parts of the Malay world, but evidence is less definite.

The seventeenth century Kedah was dominated by the indigenous or Melaka Straits-born *orang laut*, who are thought to have come originally from the southern half of the Malay Peninsula. And the eighteenth century saw the rise in importance of chiefs and sea people originally from Sulawesi; the Southern Philippines; Siak and their Minangkabau allies from central Sumatra and *orang laut* groups from the Mergui Archipelago. The recruitment of the sea lords and the naval power of the sea peoples thus chiefly helped to prolong the security and stability of Kedah's international maritime routes from foreign or pirate attacks, as well helped to direct shipping to its ports. It also enhanced the ruler's prestige, aura or *daulat* and his control over his riverine and island-based territorial units, district chiefs, and neighboring political centers.

Many of these sea peoples and *sukus* (i.e., clans of sea peoples) were often led collectively under sea lords or chiefs that were not home-grown, or were like wandering sea lords, that had their own ulterior motives for staying and operating in or around Kedah. These were *anak rajas* (i.e., royal progeny) or powerful chiefs, such as in the case of Siak and Bugis-Makassar, that had left or been driven from their former *negeri* by political, financial, or strategic reasons and roamed Southeast Asia seeking allies, employment, political ascendancy, wealth, and booty (Andaya 1975; Andaya: 1976: 163–186; Trocki 1979, *Syair Perang Siak* 1989; Barnard 2003, 2007).[4] This therefore meant that they could be politically at variance with each other and in competition for power, wealth, and employment. Eighteenth century Kedah witnessed many reported instances in which wandering sea lords were employed temporarily, or for longer periods, by the highest bidder during succession problems and domestic turmoil by its warring factions.

In addition, economic and symbolic enticements were not the only channels that cemented mutual trust, confidence, support, and loyalty between Kedah's rulers and the sea lords. Rather, marriages or blood relationships between Kedah's royalty and elites to influential sea lords, as well the persistence of a covenant or foundation tradition were also powerful means to further bonds, unity, and could politically, or symbolically, benefit the two parties. This inexorable attachment and loyalty shown toward Kedah's royalty can be further demonstrated in the *bakti* (i.e., unconditional devotion, commitment or homage in Sanskrit) or the unconditional devotion of the sea peoples and their chiefs to the self-exiled Sultan and other officials during the 1821–1841/1842 Siamese occupation of Kedah. Indeed during this period it is doubtful that the Sultan was capable of seeking support from his subjects solely through financial or symbolic incentives (*SSFR* 113, 19th of January 1826, General Letters: Raja of Kedah regarding delays in payment of pension; Beighton 1888: 16–17; Gullin and Zehnder 1905: 43; Newbold II 1971: 16–17; Gullick 1983: 39–43; Wu 2003: 28). He was often unable to pay his own debts incurred at Penang or Melaka and was three times forcibly moved by the British (from Penang to Province Wellesley and hence to Malacca).[5] Hence the intangible and traditional forms of connections, between the ruler and the sea lords, must have supported Kedah's monarchy.

With the end of the Siamese occupation of Kedah in 1841 and 1842 and the return of its Sultan and officials however nothing is heard from the sea people, their chiefs and the wandering sea lords. The return of the Sultan may indeed suggest the beginning of an end to such indigenous systems and relationships at Kedah and elsewhere in the Malay world, between the ruler and the sea peoples. It may also herald a weakening position of the Laksamana and the need for wandering sea lords, amidst the growing Siamese and colonial consolidation of their powers in Southeast Asia. In consequence, the Laksamana's position at Kedah became merely a symbolic appointment, rather than a position held by a man of influence, power, and prowess.

THE UNSEEN POWERS OF THE SULTAN AND THE COMMAND OF THE LAKSAMANA

The perceived prestige and the unseen power of the ruler, as well the likelihood of the royal curse may explains why the *penghulu* or chief of the Langkawi Islands in 1621 CE refused to sell pepper to the French Admiral Beaulieu (1705: 245, 247) unless he could produce a license from Kedah's heir apparent who was then hiding at Perlis on the Malay Peninsula. Beaulieu was thus required to travel from the Langkawi Islands all the way to Perlis in order just to procure the required paperwork and return to the island to purchase pepper.[6] This harsh requirement by the *penghulu* took place against a backdrop of a loss of 600 of his 700 people because of Acehnese attacks on Kedah and the Langkawi Islands a few days earlier. There were also rumors of more upcoming attacks on Kedah and its islands by the Acehnese (Beaulieu 1705: 245–246; Winstedt 1920: 31; Bonney 1971: 15–16; Turnbull 1980: 49, 84; *Phongsawadan Muang Zaiburi* 1990: 95).

David J. Banks (1983) and Carsten (1995) in their studies of the outer Kedah districts of Sik and the Langkawi Islands further argue that Kedah's ruler had little political or economic control in the periphery of his realm. Reflecting back on Beaulieu's account of his visit to the Langkawi Islands in 1621 and the conduct of its *penghulu*, it appears that Banks's (1983) and Carsten's (1995) assertion about control in the periphery was of a physical rather than a perceived and an unseen notion of control.

One would therefore suppose that by acknowledging a ruler and his political infrastructure, the villages, towns, riverine territories, and islands, such as the Langkawi Islands, would in return be protected from piratical attacks and other misfortunes (including environmental disasters). Hence, the control of Kedah's coastal regions, riverine systems, and other maritime routes would be protected by the sea lords; but, foremost by the sanctity and power surrounding its *kerajaan* a notion that was deeply embedded within indigenous Malay culture (Gullick 1958: 44–45; Milner 1982). In the words of, Logan: "Without protection from the rulers, the coasts are unguarded, and villages there would be very vulnerable to piratical attack" (1970: 756).

Theoretically the sea lords at Kedah and their followers, the sea peoples, in return for offering their services to the ruler and by remaining loyal to him, expected to actively participate and prosper from their association. Conversely, the sea lords were able to collectively hold together the sea peoples and their chiefs by lobbying and looking after their interests at the court, as well ensuring the customary redistribution of acquired booty, plunder, and prisoners to the sea peoples by their chiefs. In the case of the wandering or foreign born sea lords or powerful chiefs that only stayed at Kedah for short intervals, such as those from Siak, it is unlikely that they were actively working as court officials or personally held the position of the Laksamana. Yet it is likely that they were given official titles and ranks, or *nama*, and symbolic rewards were bestowed upon them by Kedah's ruler. Nonetheless, it is to be expected that many of the chiefs and the sea peoples, working for the wandering sea lords and operating out of Kedah, had their conduct, or movements, monitored by the Laksamana or other high ranking officials. These court officials were often related by blood or marriage to the wandering sea lords and their relations. Indisputably marriage and "playing" relatives between members of the royal Kedah household with the sea lords or the Laksamana further cemented political alliance with "sea peoples" and their chiefs (Andaya 1976: 166–167, 1979: 300–301; Trocki 1979: xvi–xvii, 2005:

5; Day 1996: 384–409; Barnard 2003: 3). It also ensured further loyalty and leverage amongst the sea peoples toward Kedah's ruler and his *daulat*. This form of alliance, therefore, best explains the 1722 or 1724, royal wedding between Tengku Masuna, a niece of the Kedah ruler, and Raja Kecik (or Kechil) the great sea lord and chief of Siak as well as claimant to the Palembang-Melaka-Johor throne (Winstedt 1936: 177; Andaya 1975: 301–303, 318–319n; Trocki 1979: 8–9; Ali Haji Ibn Ahmad 1982: 332n; Bassett 1989a: 14n).[7]

From various historical records it is evident that the Laksamana at Kedah monopolized the position of the sea lord at the royal *balai*, or court, for much of the seventeenth to the early nineteenth century. The Laksamana's undisputed political position at sea is even equated to that of a Raja on land. In the words of a Kedah document, *"Bunga Mas, Alat Kerajaan Pada Masa Tabal, Orang Besar-Besar, Adat Meminang"* (written in about 1222 Hijri/circa 1807 CE): *"Shahadan kebesaran Laksamana itu: takala ia keluar ka-laut, di-suroh Raja: barang Siapa di-hukum-nya atau di-bunoh tiada-lah taksir, kerana ia ganti Raja pada ketika itu"* [sic] ["At sea the Laksamana can sentence or slay whom he will, because he takes the place of a Raja there"] (Reproduced at length and partly translated by Winstedt 1928: 11, 41).

In addition, it is apparent that the position of the Laksamana at Kedah's court became a hereditary position by the second half of the eighteenth century and their political ascendancy and power continued after marrying into the royal family in 1772.[8] The marriage of the Laksamana to the ruling family of Kedah was a significant development in the history of Kedah and may further explain the relentless loyalty and support of the sea peoples toward the political institution of Kedah well into the first half of the nineteenth century.[9]

Other than controlling or dominating the maritime lines of communication the sea lords in the historic "Malay world" further expected to gain politically by their alliance with the Sultanate. It is also possible that a large quantity of the timber imported to Kedah for the local construction, repair, and sale of various trading, fishing, and war boats was under the control of the Laksamana (Hervey 1885: 132; Bowrey 1905: 257n, 282–283; *Report of Governor Bort on Malacca 1678* 1927: 134–135; Gopinath 1950: 86; Gibson-Hill 1954: 147, 165; Andaya 1975: 44–51; Trocki 1979: xvi; Hall 1985: 11; Subrahmanyam 1990: 310n, 310–311; Barnard 2003: 28).[10] This may further explain the residence of the Laksamana at the river based town of Limbong on the Kedah River and close to Langgar, the royal capital, at least from the seventeenth century onward, were the Limbong Kapal dockyard was located (*SSFR* 99, 18 February 1825, Memorandum of a conversation with the Ligor Envoys; Dobby 1951: 290, 308; Alor Star Through the Ages 1953: 4; *Burney Papers* 1971 II: 46; *Syair Sultan Maulana* 1985: 84–87; Bassett 1989a: 12–13).[11] Hence the Laksamana's position also meant that he was likely, with the help of the sea peoples and other officials, in charge to oversee the construction, refitting, and repair of trading ships, as well as boats belonging to the sea peoples.

At Kedah the sea lords not only procured the required timber for the maritime entrepot from the riverine systems and the *orang asli* but also from across the Melaka straits in Sumatra, whereby it was traditionally acquired, possibly for construction of houses and boat building, and often re-exported it to Melaka and China for financial gain (Harper 1997: 3; Soon 2001: 133; Andaya 2001b: 325). Additionally, other forms of economic advantage including access to fishing grounds, forest products, prisoners, loot, and keeping all or part of war booty were bestowed by Kedah's ruler upon the sea lords (*Commission of Sultan Muhyiddin Mansur Syah* 1985; Barnard 2003: 91; Trocki 2005: 10–11). Among these must be included an elaborate and well-monitored pearl fishing industry controlled by Kedah and reported by the Dutch in 1644 CE (4th of May 1645 entry in *Dagh-Register* (1903): 78–79; Winstedt 1936: 162).[12]

Furthermore, at least in the eighteenth century the Laksamana was one of the few natives in Kedah allowed to own ships and trade directly with other areas (including Sumatra and East-Indian ports) in tin, elephants, and cloth (Bassett 1989a: 11, 23, 1990: 38, 50, 53).[13] He was also the only court official responsible for control of the birds' nest islands, as well together with Kedah's ruler to have the monopoly of purchasing and selling opium (*SSR* 2, 12th September 1786, Francis Light to Governor General of India; Winstedt 1936: 179; an account of Kedah given by James Low and reproduced in *Burney Papers* 1971 V: 69–70; Bassett 1989a: 11, 1990: 38, 50).

Besides, a further duty of these sea lords was the collection of dues and tolls from the shipping traffic or the tin trade at a number of ports and hence overseeing its safe transfer and passage to Kedah's *kota*, or the royal seat of power, and the treasury. Indeed in collecting the tolls and dues the Laksamana was traditionally entitled to receive a share as was reported in the case of Kuala Kedah by Monckton, a British official, in June 1772 (see the contents of the letter by Monckton to Du Pre in Bonney 1971: 50).[14] Consequently the grant by Kedah's ruler to the English, in the early 1770s, to collect port dues, monitor shipping, and provide security, at the two ports of Kuala Bahang[15] [sic] and Kuala Perlis, can be seen as rooted in the indigenous political and economic system, and not unusual (Bassett 1990: 70–71, 76; Lee 1995: 44).[16] This entitlement and grant by the Kedah ruler may indeed herald a common Malay view to consider the British, and other European powers, as merely another wandering sea lord.

The sea lords at Kedah also provided and guarded boats that carried people and property when required and ordered to do so by the ruler.[17] Hence sea peoples and their chiefs from Kedah, particularly Wan Mali (the son of the ex-chief of Langkawi), were believed to be behind the transportation, repopulation and return of Malay refugees, scattered at various locations on the Malay Peninsula and Sumatra in the Bay of Bengal, to the Langkawi Islands and Kedah between 1837–1839 when the islands were recaptured back from the Siamese (Adil 1980: 69–70; 2nd dispatch, Udomsombat et al. 1993: 86).

The service of the sea lords and sea peoples was not however restricted to defending or operating in the coasts and islands of Kedah. It was also offensive in nature and involved attacking targets in areas traditionally not controlled by Kedah.[18] Thus it appears that according to indigenous systems it was expected from the wandering sea lords and the *orang laut* chiefs to agree unreservedly to a defensive, as well as offensive pact or oath with the ruler. Consequently there are numerous reports in the seventeenth to the nineteenth century whereby the assistance of the sea lords was procured in order to utilize their power to attack, ambush or intercept boats and ports (in the Bay of Bengal and the Straits of Melaka) that at the time belonged to Kedah's enemies. This may include the 1661 instance of a daring ambush and assault by two Kedah vessels on the Dutch stronghold at Melaka (Winstedt 1936: 166). According to the Dutch governor's report, the motive behind this attack was to capture some of the Dutch alive; and since it failed, the "Kedah vessels" were still able to seize two ships from Deli. Similarly the 1789 attack on Songkhla by Syed Ali, the Siak sea lord, was more than likely orchestrated on behalf of the Kedah Sultan. According to one account Syed Ali and his Ilanun allies attacked Songkhla, burned the city, seized two Chinese junks, and carried off a large number of people (*SSFR* 2, 17 July 1789, Francis Light to Governor General; Warren 1981: 158; Barnard 2003: 154).[19] Furthermore, there are numerous reported attacks on Dutch, Indian or native ships at various localities on the Perak coastline by boats belonging to Kedah (referred to as "Quedaze pirates" [sic] in *Dagh-Register*), in the seventeenth and eighteenth century (Winstedt 1920: 32–33; Bassett 1990: 38, 50).

Undeniably, much of the sea lords' accumulated wealth, tolls, booty, dues, and economic incentives ultimately benefited the sea peoples. Their respective chiefs, the *penghulus* or the *panglimas* (i.e., their commanders) chiefly distributed this to the sea peoples. The commission issued by Sultan Muhiyiddin Mansur Syah (written circa 1681–1684) instructs that the captured loot, plunder, and prisoners from the Bugis-Makassar at Kedah were to be distributed to the troops by the *panglima*, or commanders, according to the "*adat*" (i.e., custom) with only selected portions of it kept for the Sultan (*Commission of Sultan Muhiyiddin Mansur Syah* 1985). Thus, it appears that there was a local custom on the distribution of captured wealth at Kedah according to rank and status.[20] Correspondingly, the Bugis-Makassar sea lords and their chiefs in order to be enticed to render their mercenary services in Kedah's succession crises of 1713–1715, 1722–1724, and perhaps during 1770–1771 were promised cannons, a considerable quantity of milled dollars (or ringgit, e.g., the promise of fifteen *bahars* of ringgit in 1721–1722) or tin in return and the assurance that they would be allowed to unreservedly plunder Chinese and Indian ships at the captured ports (Bastin 1964: 147n, 146–147; Lewis 1970: 120–121, 1975: 39; Bonney 1971: 29–40; Andaya 1975: 229–231, 301, 36; Turnbull 1980: 80; Ali Haji Ibn Ahmad 1982: 147–150).[21] Francis Light, Penang's governor, alleged in 1791 that in order to obtain the services of Syed Ali, the Siak sea lord, and his Ilanun allies, against the British at Penang, Kedah's Sultan had promised them a sum of 20,000 dollars (*SSFR* 2, 5 January 1791, Francis Light to Fort William).

Regardless, of the above economic or political benefits Kedah's rulers were able to further procure the loyalty of sea lords and their followers through symbolic means. Thus, it is more than likely that traditionally oaths were exchanged or taken. And royal concessions (i.e., *ampun kurnia*), titles (i.e., *nama*), and symbolic gifts (such as robes of honor) or gestures (such as royal drumbeats or *nobat*) were also bestowed upon the sea lords (Marsden 1975: 242–243; Wolters 1979: 18; Hall 1985: 88; Drakard 1990: 181, 181n; Barnard 2003: 12–13; Sharifah Zaleha 2004: 404). The mode of oath-taking was highly symbolic and a powerful mode of seeking loyalty particularly amongst sea lords and the chiefs of the *orang laut*.[22] Undoubtedly the oath taking ceremony at Kedah was quite an elaborate process and was symbolically taken over an object, item or the royal regalia.[23] In the case of Kedah's southern neighbor Perak, witnessed by Low (1971: 273–274) in 1827, the rajah administered the oath of allegiance to his chiefs. All the chiefs in the realm were therefore seated in the royal court, or *balai*, with a Koran placed on a low stool in front of the assembly, and beside it stood a large jar filled with water, which the Rajah consecrated by dipping into it that portion of the regalia which consisted of arms and armor.[24] The arms were then placed leaning against a pillar, and a small regal crown of gold was put over the mouth of the jar. The chiefs then swore fidelity on these regalia. On the other hand, there were traditionally more powerful modes of seeking loyalty and enticing the support of the *orang laut* and their chiefs. O. W. Wolters (1970: 124) in his study of fourteenth century Srivijaya history suggests that Parameswara, the fifteenth century founder of the Melaka dynasty, had earlier undergone in Srivijaya an *abhiseka* ceremony, in which "a consecration rite was performed and accompanied by the prince's assumption on a new name identifying him with a god." Leonard Y. Andaya (1975: 48–49) further speculates on the possibility that the *orang laut* in the sixteenth and seventeenth century Johor responded whole-heartedly to the performance of the *abhiseka* ceremony and believed less in the promise of "robes of honor" than in the "special powers acquired traditionally by the rulers in this ceremony." It is possible that an *abhiseka* type ceremony involving the sea peoples and their chiefs was traditionally held by the Kedah rulers, although it is not clear if this practice was designed solely for its indigenous sea peoples and their chiefs (rather than the foreign born sea lords and sea peoples).

On a similar note, the act of loyalty by the sea lords, as well the *orang laut* and their chiefs toward the Malay ruler was viewed as an act of *bakti* without any expectations of financial gain in return. It was also seen as a religious obligation (see the definition of *bakti* as a religious action by Sharifa Zaleha 1985: 68), as well according to an early nineteenth century indigenous source *Syair Sultan Maulana* (1985: 74–75, 112–113, 180–181, 252–253), a public acknowledgement of obtaining a reputation for royal service, or *"nama kebakti"* and a "duty for the interests of the realm." For this reason, the loyalty shown toward Kedah's Raja by the previously mentioned *penghulu* of Langkawi, by directing Beaulieu to Perlis to acquire a royal permit to purchase pepper, may be further explained as an act of *bakti* on his behalf, and not for immediate financial gains from the young Sultan in hiding. Indeed the concept of *bakti* was traditionally a powerful component in the indigenous political system and was interwoven in the subject-ruler relationship.[25] In a late sixteenth century legal digests from Pahang, (i.e., *Undang-Undang Pahang,* see the Malay text and a translation by Kempe and Winstedt 1948: 18, 53) a traitor, or a person committing high treason, could in fact be pardoned, by a just ruler, through the process of *kebaktian*.

Furthermore, the *orang laut* and their chiefs would traditionally show *bakti* and their desire to protect and follow the ruler, and possibly the Laksamana, by an annual contribution of men, or volunteers, and boats to the royal seat of power. In the case of early nineteenth century Savu/Sawu Islands[26] it is reported that sea peoples "appear to be of the Badju, or Orang Laut tribe" [sic] living on the coastline and the islands annually sent one hundred volunteers, to the capital at Kupang (west Timor), to acknowledge its "government"[27] [sic] (see "Short Account of Timor, Savu, Solor, and c" cited at length in *AJMR* 1822: 534). Similarly, Tome Pires, the sixteenth century Portuguese visitor to the Melaka Straits, reports that the new ruler of Melaka in the fifteenth century sent "all the *Celate* mandarins to live on the slopes of the Melaka hill to act as his guards" [sic] (Cortesao 1944 II: 238). Hence, indicating the protection of the ruler by the *Celate* a term denoting sea peoples, as well as their willingness to move there. In consequently it is highly likely that a similar, or larger, contribution of sea peoples were committed by the sea peoples and their chiefs to Kedah's capital or its main entrepot as guards, as well as a further sign of their devotion to the dynasty and the ruler.

In the 1681–1684 commission issued by Sultan Muhiyiddin Mansur Syah, reports an act of *bakti* toward Kedah's Sultan by the chiefs, officials, and other was to be symbolically well rewarded. In consequence: *"barangsiapa mengerjakan kebaktian, adalah kami hadirkan baginya balas kebajkan daripada martabat gelar dan persalin dan kurnia yang sepatutnya dengan kebajikan seperti firman Allah taala"* [sic] ["Anyone who performs his duty (*kebak-*

tian) in meritorious fashion, we shall reward his service by granting him rank and title and robes (of state), according to his service, in accordance with what God Almighty has decreed." See *Commission of Sultan Muhyiddin Mansur Syah* 1985].

This was in contrast to any acts of sabotage, weakness or treachery on the part of Kedah chiefs and the court officials that were to be dealt severely with no mercy shown. Hence, there was to be no sympathy granted to the Bugis-Makassar, and their Kedah collaborators, since the commission clearly indicates that they had committed the crime of high treason, or *crimem laesae maiestatis*, and the highest form of disloyalty *"derhaka kepada kita"* [*sic*]. To the English in the 1770s and their 1786 lease of Penang Island, however, other than solely economic benefits, the latter symbolic and indigenous forms of recognition by Kedah's ruler were of little consequence.[28] Hence this view by the English and the mistaken expectations of Kedah's ruler, from what he normally would have expected in the case of sea lords, may also be a further reason behind their continuous mistrust, frustrations and failed dealings toward one another. Indeed, the reluctance of the British authorities in 1772 to agree to an offensive agreement with Kedah, particularly in partaking in a joint attack on the Bugis at Selangor, was a key decision by Kedah's ruler and officials to terminate the continuation of a recently built British commercial factory (operating from April to August 1772), as well as other forms of agreements, including the return of a hundred Indian sepoys for defensive purposes provided by the British for Kedah (Bonney 1971: 47–48, 48n; Mills 1971: 25; Lee 1995: 42–44, 51, 54, 60n).

HISTORIC CONTROL OF KEDAH'S COASTLINE AND MARITIME LINES OF COMMUNICATION

From the various reports and studies of the eighteenth century western Malay Peninsula it appears that Siak and Bugis-Makassar sea lords and sea peoples dominated much of Kedah's maritime lines of control. But these sea lords and their followers are thought to have entered Kedah's political scene in the early 1680s. Earlier reports and accounts of the seventeenth century however highlight the presence of other sea lords and their followers at Kedah as distinct from the Siak and the Bugis peoples. In particular they suggest importance of *orang laut* at Kedah (Bowrey 1905: 237–238, 237n, 261–262; Winstedt 1920: 32–33, 1936: 168; *Report of Governor Bort on Malacca 1678* 1927: 182; Hogan 1972: 205–235; Bassett 1989a: 1; Hamilton 1995 II: 68–69; Dhiravat Na Pombejra 2003: 277). Thus there was a distinction between the seventeenth and the eighteenth century origins of Kedah's sea peoples. With the seventeenth century maritime lines of communication dominated by the indigenous *orang laut* (see Figure 2) and the eighteenth century seeing the importance of Bugis or Siak chiefs and peoples along the southern coast of Kedah.

This shift of the origin of the sea lords and their followers in Kedah appears to have been very much in line with events in the rest of the Malay Peninsula. In an article on the *orang asli* in the Malay Peninsula, T. N. Harper (1997: 3) suggests the *orang laut* were replaced in the eighteenth century by the Bugis in the Malay Archipelago. Nonetheless, he ignores the centrality of the Siak sea lords particularly at Kedah and the western Malay Peninsula. Likewise, he fails to cite the earlier 1681 or seventeenth century reports of Bugis-Makassar and Minangkabau's at Kedah and the northern Melaka Straits.

Remarkably, the Dutch had earlier commented on the origin of the "*Salleeters*" [sic] found throughout the Melaka Straits and especially menacing shipping at Phuket, Kedah, Perak and Sumatra (*Dagh-register*

Figure 2. *Orang laut* boats in nineteenth-century Trang. Crawfurd, J. (1830). *Journal of an Embassy from the Governor-General of India to the Courts of Siam and Cochin China Exhibiting a View of the Actual State of Those Kingdoms* (2 vols.). London: Henry Colburn and Richard Bentley; Smyth, W.H. (1898). Journeys in the Siamese East Coast States. *The Geographical Journal*, 11 (No. 5, May), 465–489.

[1640–1641] 1887: 427, 431, [1644–1645] 1902: 61, 78–79). In 1643–1645 Dutch reports on the continuous forays against Dutch ships at Phuket and nearby "Bangkhli" [sic] (also spelt Bang Khli or Bangkeri/Bangeri to the north of Phuket), as well as at pearl fisheries at "Poulo Mottia" [sic] (Pulau Mutia to the north west of Ko Talibong or Talibong Island, see Map 5), and "Mabangers" [sic] to the north of Kedah, it identified the *"Johorse Saletters"* [sic] as the culprits of the attacks (May 1645 entry in *Dagh-register* (1644–1645) 1902: 78–79; *Syair Sultan Maulana* 1985: 44, 273, 281, Appendix B; *VOC* 1158, Verbael, by Johan Verpoorten, of October 1645 cited in parts by Dhiravat Na Pombejra 2003: 283, 298n). Assuming that *"Johorse"* meant that these peoples originated from the Malay territory of Johor, then it is possible that the *"Saletters"* at both Phuket and Kedah had their origins further south.[29] But whether they were recruited by the Kedah's ruler, the Laksamana, sea lords or that they independently moved further north, it is impossible to say. If they did come on their own, then it is possible that these *orang laut* were independent of the Johor ruler (following the 1623 succession crisis at Johor and the departure of several *orang laut sukus* to Jambi to be with the two year old claimant to the throne, see Andaya 1975: 84–85). The assumption that the reported seventeenth century *"Johorese Saletters"* were operating independent of Johor, to the north of the Melaka Straits, would indeed make sense. There is a report that with the defeat of Jambi in 1679, Sultan Ibrahim of Johor sent envoys to Kedah to demand the return of some forty Johor refugees living there (see Andaya 1975: 128).[30] Hence it is plausible that the sea peoples that were met by the Dutch were remnants of *sukus* that had earlier shifted north to Kedah from Johor, and offered their services to the ruler of Kedah (perhaps pursing a joint anti-Johor alliance together with Jambi).[31] Then again it is possible that they were sent there intentionally by Johor's Laksamana as part of reconnaissance missions, pirating, intercepting unfriendly shipping (such as those from Jambi, Dutch, Siamese, Acehnese, and others) or directing/accompanying ships to its own ports at the south of the Melaka Straits.[32]

The formation of an alliance with the *orang laut* at that juncture in history would indeed make political sense for Kedah.[33] In 1644 the Dutch reported that Siamese war plans against Kedah were recently averted (Dutch Records [volume 14], 13 October 1644, Jeremias van Vliet to Governor Arnold Heussen, cited at length in *Records of the Relations* 1915/1917 II: 6). This followed a recent visit to Siam by Kedah envoys and the acknowledgement of its newly ascended "Raja" for his mistake of ascending the throne without their approval. But then two years later in 1646 Kedah decided to join Songkhla and declare war against Ayutthaya and hence attack Phattalung, as well as coastal settlements to the north of Trang (Entry for May 1648 in *Dagh-Register* [1647–1648] 1903: 70; Governor General Gerard Reynst to the Heren XVII, 24th of December 1655, in *General Missiven* 1968 III: 19–24, also Correspondence for 1676, 1969 IV:

160; Smith 1977: 32; Choungsakul 2006: 45). Additionally, the presence of the *orang laut* in seventeenth century Kedah would have helped to further protect and defend its maritime routes against a potential Portuguese, Dutch, Johor, Siamese, Acehnese or a piratical attack (especially after the 1619 Acehnese attack on Kedah and their influence and continuous presence at Perak well into the 1660s, see Andaya 1979: 41–49). The services of the sea peoples were also used in the second half of the seventeenth century when Kedah reportedly attacked Dutch shipping at various localities traditionally outside its own lines of communication in the Straits of Melaka (e.g., the 1661 sea attack by Kedah vessels on the Dutch headquarter at Melaka or the continuous attacks on the Perak coastline, see translated passages from *Dagh-Register* cited by Winstedt 1936: 166–173).

Conversely, it is entirely possible that some of the reported sea peoples in and around seventeenth century Kedah and in the north of the Melaka Straits were unrelated to or distinct from the Johor *sukus*. Thus it is possible that the reported sea peoples and their chiefs were indigenous to Kedah or that they had their origin in the islands or coastlines further north in the Bay of Bengal or in areas that were considered outside of Johor's sphere of influence in the southern half of the Melaka Straits, or the island of Sumatra.

In fact, according to a tradition amongst the *Orang Laut Kappir* (*Kafir/Kaffir* is an unbeliever in Arabic) and the *Urak Lawoi* or *Orang Lonta* of Ko Lanta Yai (or Pulau Lantar in Malay) and the Trangphura district (that included both Trang and Talibong Island) in contemporary Thailand, they originally came from *Gunong* Jerai (i.e., Mount Jerai also known as the Kedah Peak) or the island of Langkawi in Kedah, but, later moved north fleeing from "opposition and trouble they were experiencing" (oral report by an old *Urak Lawoi* man to Hogan 1972: 218–219) or according to other reports they left since they did not want to adopt "Islam" as their religion (Annandale and Robinson 1902: 411–412; Annandale and Robinson in 1903 cited by Sopher 1977: 65, 67; comments on historic Trang by Skinner in *Syair Sultan Maulana* 1985: 44, 268, 271, 283; Granbom 2005: 41; Wongbusarakum 2007: 9–10).[34] Assuming that there was indeed a migration north from Kedah by the *Orang Laut Kappir*, the correct date of this migration is not known. In the same way, it is not possible to determine if their disagreement over religious conversion was with Kedah's ruler, the Laksamana or another high ranking official (e.g., the *Kathi*, or Muslim judge). Also, it is not clear if historically the *Orang Laut Kappir* and the *Saletters* constituted a larger group of sea peoples but were later separated over the question of converting to Islam.[35]

There is also the possibility that the previously mentioned pearl fisheries controlled by Kedah in the 1640s were run by the *Selung*, a group related to the Moken (linguistically and, perhaps, ethnically distinct from the *Urak Lawoi* and the *orang laut* subgroups of southern Thailand and the Malay Peninsula) sea peoples (for more on the *Selung*, see Anderson 1890;

White 1922: 56–57, 155, 161–162; Hogan 1972: 206–207). They are said to have historically controlled all of the pearl fishing in the Mergui Archipelago, particularly in the Tavoy area (modern day town of Dawei, and the nearby islands in southeastern Burma), all the way to south-western Siam (Anderson 1890: 5, 21–22; Smyth 1895b: 522–523, 532). Thus, it is likely that they were pearl fishing for Kedah for some time in the 1640s but were somehow replaced or driven out of the area and moved elsewhere.[36] There are also other subgroups of the Moken, such as Moken Pulaw and the Moken Tamab, and related groups, e.g., the Moklen, scattered along the southern coastline of Thailand in the Bay of Bengal, Andaman Sea and the Adang Archipelago, about eighty kilometers west of Satun district in southern Thailand, that may have at one stage provided their services to the Laksamana of Kedah (Hogan 1972: 210, 222–224, 229; Aporn Ukrit cited in Wongbusarakum 2007: 19n).[37]

Reasons behind gradual loss of control over the *Saletters* by Kedah's ruler in the 1670s and their replacement by non-native sea lords and peoples are complex and diverse. According to an eyewitness account by Thomas Bowrey (1905: 261–263, 283), an English visitor to Kedah circa 1669–1679, the King's instruction to the *"Saleeters"* [sic] not to attack British ships, considered as friends and rivals to the Dutch, had fallen on deaf ears and was soon followed by a savage attack in 1675 off the coast of Kedah. Bowrey (1905: 262) continues that Kedah's ruler had therefore attempted in vain to arrest and sentence the "Ringleaders or Common people" [sic] of the *"Saleeters"* [sic] but they avoided being captured by using Kedah's extensive network of islands and rivers as refuge. Herewith, Bowrey's reference to "ringleaders" undoubtedly corresponds to the *panglima* or chiefs or commanders of the "sea people." Similarly, the term may be a reference cited by Bowrey, in English, to the "Palimajatti" [sic] observed by Genaelli Careri (Seventeenth century visitors 1934: 103) in the 1690s, as a term denoting the "chiefs" of the *"Salittes"* [sic].

The 1675 attack on the British ship and the Kedah ruler's subsequent decision to collectively punish the *Saletters* thus may reflect deeper divisions and rifts between the two parties. So much so that the sea peoples and their chiefs were prepared to disobey the ruler. Foremost, as in the case of the previously mentioned *Orang Laut Kappir* tradition it is likely that a demand by Kedah's ruler to convert to Islam was a key factor for several of the *orang laut* chiefs or their sea lords to act independently and shift their allegiance away from Kedah. In addition, disagreements over work or payments to the *orang laut* by Kedah's ruler or the sea lords may have further widened a rift between the two parties. This was likely the result of the presence of other recently arrived sea lords and their sea peoples at Kedah. Hence, as the events of the 1681–1684 civil war at Kedah indicate there was by then a growing tendency to utilize the services of the Minangkabau and the Bugis-Makassar sea lords, likely at the expense of the local *orang laut*. It is also possible that the *Saletters* viewed their collective punishment by the ruler of Kedah as unnecessary and as humiliating, after all the attack on the English ship could have been simply a mistake in identifying the Dutch as English ships.

There are other possible factors that must have aided the seventeenth century rift between Kedah's ruler and the *Saletters*, or other *orang laut* groups. For one thing the 1660s onward witnessed numerous devastating attacks and a blockade of Kedah's coastline and its maritime routes by the Dutch and the Siamese, especially in 1665–1668, 1670, 1673–1674, 1677, and possibly 1681. To complicate things further there were also Dutch boats that constantly sneaked into Kedah's sea routes to gather intelligence and spy on the English and others trading ships (e.g., in 1672; *Dutch Documents* [M 546], 14th of May 1672, Letter to the Governor General from Masulipatnam and the Council for India).[38] There presence may have also alerted the *Saletters* to be extra sensitive to European boats.

The most disastrous Siamese-Dutch attack meanwhile came in 1673–1674, when a fleet consisting of twenty three boats and ships (three Dutch and twenty Siamese), attacked Kedah supposedly because of its delay in sending its triennial tribute, the *Bunga Emas dan Perak*, to Siam (*Original Correspondence* (No. 3917), 1st of January 1674, Kedah General to Surat). The Dutch in particular were eager to unite with the Siamese to attack and plunder Kedah in response to the establishment of an English factory in about 1669, as well as the deterioration of relations between the two since the 1642 treaty (*Dutch Documents* [M 546], 17th of May 1673, Letter to the Governor General and the Council for India, for the General Dutch Chartered Company at Batavia; Winstedt 1936: 163–176).[39] During this period the Dutch were also at war with England and were competing against other Europeans to monopolize the tin and other trade in the Melaka Straits (Bassett 1989b: 628–642).[40]

The 1674 attack was however only a partial success since Kedah's timely defense preparations and political events in Siam, likely the 1671–1690 war with Pegu, forced the Siamese boats to return, leaving two of the three Dutch ships to continue blocking Kedah's coastline (*Original Correspondence* [No. 3917], 1st of January 1674, Kedah General to Surat; Bonney 1971: 20–21).[41] Interestingly, the Dutch did continue to blockade and patrol Kedah's coastline well into the 1680s though they often admitted the difficulty in achieving their objectives or in being able to get rid of British or other traders there (Winstedt 1936: 161). Nevertheless, with the end of Siamese blockade in 1674 Kedah had little to celebrate. A devastating fire the previous year in February is reported to have destroyed in just two hours half of Kedah's main trading entrepot and the main *bazaar*, or market (*Original Correspondence* [No. 3917], January 1674, Francis Capell and Joshua Burroughs at Kedah to Surat).[42] The Dutch manipulation of Kedah's maritime trade and economy in this period is similarly significant. Not only did they block the sea routes and attempt to divert native Asian traders and or European shipping to their own ports but also they tried indirectly to disrupt the market and trade there. They may have also forced the Siamese to restrict and pressure Kedah since their own attempts to reason with the ruler had failed.[43] For example in order to keep the British out of Kedah in 1671 the Dutch allowed Muslim and native traders to enter Kedah without any hindrance (*Dutch Documents* [M 546], 29th of August 1671, Letter to the Governor General and the Council for India). This was according to the official Dutch document solely intended to "discourage" British trader at Kedah since "these Moors being dangerous competition" [sic]. But nearly a decade later the Dutch in reviewing their failed policies in controlling the tin trade (to the "coast of Coromandel, Surat, and Persia") or stopping Kedah's maritime trade, to their dismay discovered that the British were obtaining "large quantities of tin from Kedah in their own or Moorish vessels" (*Dutch Documents* (M 546), 19th of May 1679, Letter to the Governor General, Rycklof van Goens, and the Council for India). This letter then concludes that the Dutch should consult with the ruler of Siam in order to forcefully bring Kedah's "king into submission" and "forcing him to allow us the monopoly of the tin trade and the right to seize, any vessel of whatever nation."[44]

Then again, in 1677, and perhaps 1681, there were further Dutch-Siamese attacks against Kedah thus forcing Kedah's ruler and his family to take refuge in the mountains (Bowrey 1905: 256–257, 276; Bassett 1990: 7; Dhiravat Na Pombejra 2003: 293–294). Albeit, peace was restored with Siam briefly in 1679, but a decade of turmoil and destruction had left behind a devastated and politically weak Kedah. The tribulations of Kedah may have therefore prompted a division between Kedah's ruler, his brother (Dato" Padang Seri Jana), the court officials and possibly the *orang laut* in 1681 when the Bugis and Minangkabau were eventually called in.

On the other hand, Bowrey (1905: 262–263) and the *India Office Records* tended to view the 1670s anarchy at Kedah and the subsequent divisions by pointing their finger toward the control of the ports and trade. The King's *prahus* and shipping foremost was in the hands of several influential Chulias or South Indian merchants, particularly one named Deria (*Original Correspondence* [No. 3917], January 1674, Francis Capell and Joshua Burroughs at Kedah to Surat; Bassett 1989a: 3). These were said to control the economy, politics, held real power and complicated the affairs of trading at Kedah. It is therefore likely that the enormous power accumulated by these adventurous Indian settlers' further complicated local politics and hence somehow forced the "*Saletters*" out of Kedah.

In consequence of attacks by the Dutch and the Siamese, misfortunes in the 1670s, the succession crisis and the domination of the royal court by powerful merchants it seems that Kedah's ruler had lost control over much of his traditional maritime routes and the *orang laut*. Furthermore, there is a strong possibility that events to the north of Kedah (particularly at Phuket and Bang Khli) impacted and alleviated the estrangement between Kedah's monarchy and the *orang laut*. According to passages in the Dutch governors report, the *Dagh-Register* in January 1680 a Siamese official ("Oya Berquelang" [sic] likely Phraya Phraklang) informed the Dutch Governor at Melaka of their inability to grant them the tin at Phuket and Bang Khli since the inhabitants were "turbulent and incited by Kedah Malays" and that attempts by the Siamese to take the area had failed (see translation of passages in *Dagh-Register* dealing with Kedah for the period 1680–1682 in Winstedt 1936: 174–175).[45] These tin mines were important to the Dutch as they believed by controlling these and those on the Malay Peninsula they would be able to have a monopoly of the trade (see letters dated 16th of May 1676 and 11th of May 1677 in *Dutch Documents* [M 546], Letter to the Governor General and the Council for India). Then in October of 1682 the *Dagh-Register* continues that the Siamese had sent forty war boats to recapture Phuket, with another seventy to follow. It appears that the Siamese naval attack to recapture Phuket was a success.[46] But the Siamese were eventually able to control the area in about 1681 with the help of the native population, at Phuket and nearby Takua,[47] and perhaps the refusal of the sea peoples to assist the Muslim governor sent there earlier by Kedah.[48]

Little is heard about the *Saletters* following the 1681 civil war at Kedah. It is likely that they migrated elsewhere, probably north and west to the area extending from Aceh to the Mergui Archipelago. In traveling to the Mergui Archipelago, Bay of Bengal (including Kedah) and south to the Malay Archipelago, at turn of the seventeenth century Hamilton noted encountering the *Saletters*:

> Between Mergui and Junk Ceylon (i.e., contemporary Phuket) there are several good harbours for shipping, but the sea-coast is very thin of inhabitants, because there are great numbers of freebooters, called *Saletters*, who inhabit islands along the sea-coast, and they both rob, and take people for slaves, and transport them for Aceh, and there make sale of them, and Junk Ceylon often feels the weight of their depredations. (Hamilton 1995 II: 68–69)

Consequently Hamilton reports on the *Saletters* in an area geographically much further away from Kedah and the Straits of Melaka. Furthermore, he continues that the *Saletters* would only travel south to Aceh to conduct trade. It is possible that the *Saletters* reported by Hamilton were traditionally the *sukus* that operated to the north of the Straits of Melaka and were for a period of time rendering their services to the rulers of Kedah. But by the 1670s their services and loyalty to the ruler of Kedah, or the Laksamana, was terminated forcing them to move out of the area offering their services elsewhere (such as Aceh) or taking shelter in the complex network of islands in the Mergui Archipelago whereby they could live unmolested.[49] This possibility may thus explain the *Saletters* desire, at the time of Hamilton, to travel south and trade at Aceh, an area previously familiar to them and traditionally significant for their trade (such as procuring yams and sago that were central to their diet).[50]

Alternatively, due to their naval know-how and sea powers, it is entirely possible that the rising number of *anak rajas* in the Malay Archipelago, particularly the Siak and Bugis-Makassar recruited some of the sea peoples at Kedah. Hence, the attachment to the *anak raja* at that juncture in the seventeenth century by the *orang laut* was to a great extent economic rather than for attaining symbolic royal rewards.

It seems that by the mid-eighteenth century the *orang laut* and their chiefs were once again recruited by the Laksamana of Kedah. In particular the *orang laut* assisted in farming the birds' nest islands, between Kedah to the Mergui Archipelago, on behalf of the Laksamana and the ruler of Kedah. It is estimated that the Laksamana required approximately 1,000 boats and a workforce of about 4,500 people, most of whom were sea peoples (Begbie 1834: 443; Bonney 1971: 10). Although quite extensive, it was Kedah's ruler that ultimately benefited financially from the collection of taxes and sale of the birds' nests (a yearly profit of about fifteen thousand Spanish dollars in the 1780s), as well as enjoying the prestige associated with possession of the islands (*SSFR* 2, 12 September 1786, Francis Light to Governor General of India; Winstedt 1936: 179; an account of Kedah by Low reproduced in *Burney Papers* 1971 V: 69–70). Furthermore, it is plausible that the *orang laut* also assisted Kedah's royalty and the Laksamana, in the second half of the eighteenth century, in briefly annexing Phuket (particularly in the 1770s) and several islands in southern Siam (Anderson 1824: 69; Clodd 1948: 39; Simmonds 1963: 596; background and notes by Skinner in *Syair Sultan Maulana* 1985: 3, 5, 289n; Gerini 1986: 56–57, 132).[51]

But in contrast to the seventeenth century, when the indigenous *orang laut* were reported to be active in controlling an area extending from Phuket to Melaka, in the eighteenth century they were only active south as far as the Kedah River. This perhaps reflects the entrance of foreign born sea lords and their peoples that were recruited to control and defend as barrier against intrusions to Kedah's southern maritime lines of communications. Kedah was then divided into two corridors or zones. With the northern half controlled by the *orang laut*, with their epicenter in the Langkawi Islands (see Map 5), and the southern half controlled directly from the entrepot through a succession of foreign sea lords.

KEDAH'S NORTHERN CORRIDOR: THE LANGKAWI CONNECTION

In a dispatch dated 26th of April 1839 and sent during the 1838–1839 Malay rebellions at Kedah, the Siamese ruler, Rama III, warned of a looming Malay assault on the Siamese forces: "They are poised to attack us; [they are as close to us as the nose on our face] with Langkawi ready

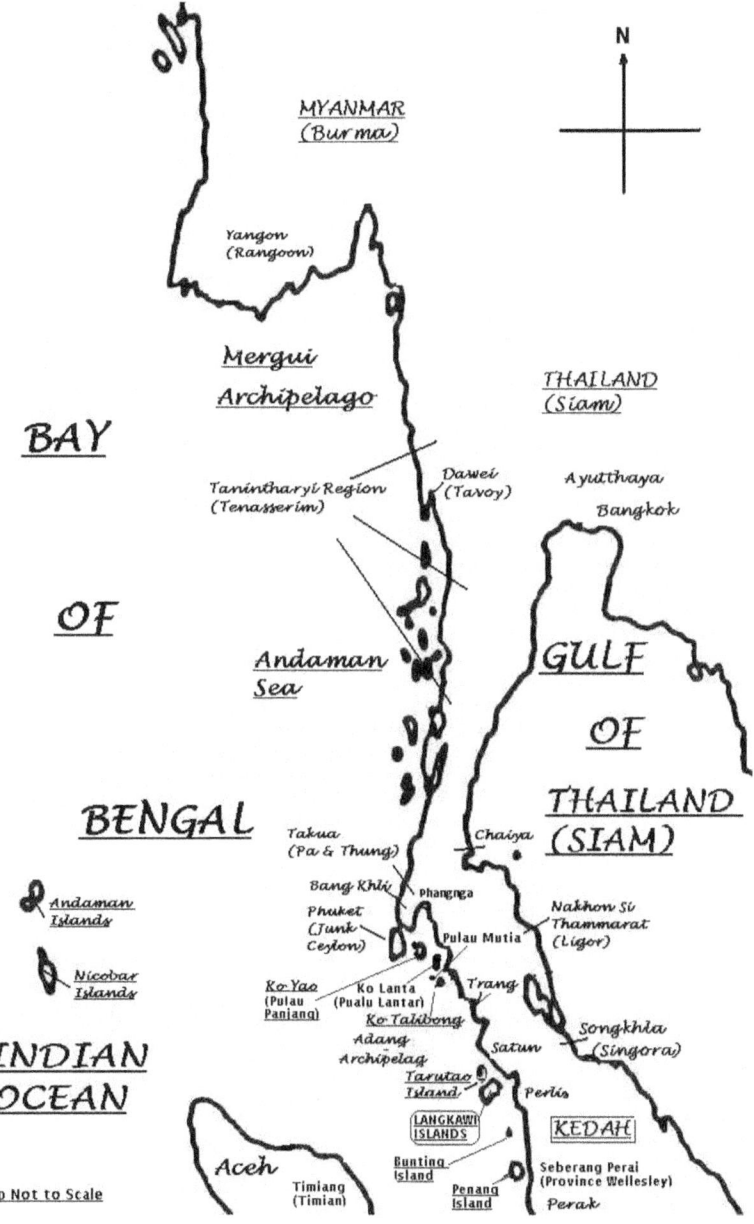

Map 5. The Northern Corridor: Kedah's traditional maritime control at the Bay of Bengal by the indigenous *orang laut* (seventeenth to the mid-nineteenth century).

to plug up our left nostril and Perai ready to plug our right nostril—they're just waiting for a chance to stop us breathing" [sic] (5th dispatch, dated 26th of April 1839, Udomsombat et al. 1993: 142).

Consequently it was thought that there would be two separate sources of attack on the Siamese troops at Kedah. With one attack anticipated by land originating from Perai (i.e., Province Wellesley) and the second from the sea from the Langkawi Islands.[52] The acknowledgement of a looming sea attack originating from the Langkawi Islands is indeed noteworthy. It not only shows that the exiled Sultan was able to rally his peoples for a joint land and sea attack on Kedah; but also the fact that to the Siamese the assault by sea was seen as an equal threat to the land assault.[53] Furthermore, it raises the question of who was coordinating the Malay sea attacks on Kedah. Were the attacks organized by foreign born sea lords, or even recruited pirates, acting on behalf of the exiled Sultan or the Laksamana of Kedah? Or was the assault on the Siamese composed and organized by the indigenous sea peoples? Then there is the question of why did the attacks come from the Langkawi Islands?

The Thai source of *Phongsawadan Muang Zaiburi* (1990), written predominantly in the nineteenth century, similarly discusses the 1838–1839 Malay revolt, including the maritime attack by the population of the Langkawi Islands, against the Siamese forces at Kedah. *Phongsawadan Muang Zaiburi* (1990) is more specific about the main instigators, giving dates and leaders of the ensuing attack, than the previously mentioned dispatch by Rama III, According to this information:

"In the Year of the Dog, Samrit Saka, J.S. 1200,[54] Tengku Muhammad Saad, a son of Tengku Daud who was a younger half-brother of Chao Phraya Zaiburi Pangeran, together with Wan Ali incited the Malays of Pulau Langkawi and the Kedah Malays to revolt. They were successful and were able to capture Muang Zaiburi[55] temporarily" [sic] (*Phongsawadan Muang Zaiburi* 1990: 97).

Phongsawadan Muang Zaiburi (1990) then goes on to say that a year later in the "Year of the Pig, Ek Saka, J. S. 1201" [sic] (i.e., 1839 CE) news arrived from Kedah that "Tengku Muhammad Saad and Wan Ali had retreated from Zaiburi" [sic]. Hence, suggesting that Tengku Muhammad Saad and Wan Ali together were behind the 1838–1839 land and sea attacks.

From court documents, reports, and other indigenous sources the Thai historian Prince Damrong however suggests that Tengku Muhammad Saad was not involved. Rather he claims that the revolt was led by Wan Mali, or Che Mali, whom commanded the ex-Kedah naval fleet and was in fact the "chief of the Malay pirates on Ko Yao [Pualu Panjang] in the Phuket area" (Historical background by Prince Damrong, dated 1906, in Udomsombat et al. 1993: 20).

In consequence, the Siamese sources that deal with the Malay revolts in the aftermath of the 1821 Siamese invasion of Kedah are in contrast to the non-Thai studies of the same period that only refer to the land assault (e.g., Malay and English studies by: Wan Yahya 1911; Winstedt 1936; Khan 1939; Muhammad Hassan 1968; Banks 1982; Gullick 1983; King 2006). What's more, the contemporary scholarly sources only refer to Tengku Muhammad Saad, the nephew of the ex-Sultan, as the acknowledged leader of the 1838–1839 uprising as well as his later arrest by the British and subsequent exile to Calcutta. But fail to mention other key individuals, other than the Sultan, that were prominent in resisting the Siamese invasion of Kedah, and avoided capture by the British or the Siamese. Thus little significance, if any, is given to the elaborate sea attacks by the Malay rebels during the Siamese invasion.

It is correct to presume that Muhammad Saad was the symbolic leader of the 1838 uprising. He was a brilliant strategist and was instrumental in capturing much of Kedah's mainland, parts of Siamese territories and defending the inland areas.[56] Siamese sources too acknowledge the charismatic leadership of Saad, as well as his command of the land assault and its subsequent defense. All the same, it is premature to consider Wan Mali and his followers merely as pirates. Indeed Ko Yao, its surrounding islands and the Mergui coastline are traditionally *orang laut*, or *Urak Lawoi*, areas (Hogan 1972: 205–235; Ivanoff 1997).[57] Besides, Wan Mali appears to have remained faithful to the ex-Sultan by joining in the campaign with Tengku Muhammad Saad against the Siamese.[58]

Wan Mali according to a number of Siamese royal dispatches of 1839 had a considerable force of about 95 boats under his command. With this force he had swiftly captured the Langkawi Islands (earlier in 1837)[59] and then Perlis, Satun, and Trang (Supplement to Asiatic Intelligence in *AJMR* 1837: 48; Burney 1971 IV: 161–162; Udomsombat et al. 1993: 37–40, 86, 92, 148, 213, 222–223). Additionally Wan Mali controlled and disrupted all Siamese sea lines of communication in the Bay of Bengal or Siam's western coastline for most of 1837–1839.[60] After which he was reported to have escaped from the Langkawi Islands, following the recapture of Kedah by the Siamese, and then was spotted heading with his followers, for an island off Mergui Archipelago, never to be heard of again (13th and 14th dispatches in Udomsombat et al. 1993: 217, 242).[61]

What is intriguing is that Wan Mali was indeed a native of the Langkawi Islands (Khan 1939: 41). In a nineteenth-century report by Low (cited by Skinner in Udomsombat et al. 1993: 28n) Wan Muhammad Ali is referred to as the son of the former Chief of Langkawi. Wan Mali is further identified as a nephew to the ex-Sultan of Kedah (see Skinner's comment in Udomsombat et al. 1993: 322n).[62] Hence he was related to the Sultan of Kedah on his father's side, although it is likely that he was connected to the sea peoples by birth, e.g., on his mother's side, or by marriage. It is possible that following the Siamese capture of Langkawi, in late 1821, he had taken refuge amongst the sea peoples. Nevertheless, he seems, together with his followers, to have continued rendering their services to the ex-Sultan of Kedah. A number of letters, communicated to the ex-Sultan of Kedah by the Burmese ruler in 1824, refer to recent visits by "Che Lanang"[63] and "Muhammad Ally" [sic] who were relations of the ex-Sultan, and that they acted as his emissaries (two letters reproduced at length in Anderson 1824: Appendix).[64] It is thus possible that Muhammad Ally was one and the same as Wan Mali and that he acted as ex-Sultan's emissary to the court of Burma.

In addition, it appears that by the time of the 1838–1839 uprising Kedah's ex-Sultan had appointed Wan Mali as the chief of the Langkawi Islands (it is likely that his father, the ex-chief of the islands, had died), as well as several provinces (Satun and Perlis). Osborne (1987: 94–107) in 1838, reports visiting Perlis while under the control of, "Datoo Mahomet Ali" [sic] and holding regular meetings with his second in charge, "Haggi Loung" [sic].

The title given to Wan Mali, that of Datu, by Kedah's Sultan is indeed significant. According to Osborne (1987: 27) the title indicated Wan Mali as a "chieftain or lord." T. J. Newbold (1971: 19), a British officer who had met the ex-Sultan in the 1830s further reports that other than the four principal ministers of Kedah, power was further enforced by the "eight Dattus, or heads of tribe" [sic]. Hence, the title was likely conferred to Wan Mali by Kedah's ex-Sultan and would have therefore meant that he was able to operate as a sea lord amongst the sea peoples and their chiefs in exile, whilst enforcing the Sultan's control and power over them. But this did not mean that he was appointed to the position of the Laksamana of Kedah. Indeed it seems that Ishmahel (presumably Ismail), the son of the previous Laksamana of Kedah, was already appointed to his father's position in 1822 after he was killed during the Siamese invasion (see "Norton-Kyshe Cases" 1885: 4–12).

The Siamese naval attack on the Langkawi Islands was indeed more brutal than their invasion of mainland Kedah six months earlier (in November 1821).[65] In the words of Bonney (1971: 157) Langkawi's defenses were "greatly helped by those who escaped the initial onslaught" and thus it "proved to be the strongest centre of resistance and which was to suffer the ravages of two brutal Siamese assaults and further attacks in later years." The Siamese were therefore determined to put down any form of resistance in the Langkawi Islands. A dispatch received at Bangkok on the 24th of May 1822 from the Raja of Ligor, outlines some of the reasons for their recent capture of the Langkawi Islands.[66] According to the dispatch:

> The people of the island Langkawi having rebelled, the army went thither, beat them, and obtained possession. I sent news of this to Penang, accusing the King of Quedah of having stirred up the Malays of Langkawi to rebellion . . . The Governor of Penang replied saying that the English would not encourage the Raja of Kedah contrary to the

interests of the Great King . . . , nor permit the King of Kedah to send
our stores or ammunition to assist the rebels of Langkawi. (1915: 48–50)

In consequence, the population of the Langkawi Islands appear to have remained loyal to the ruler of Kedah even though he was no longer residing at the royal capital, and despite the fact that the Laksamana had been earlier killed by the Siamese (Anderson 1824: 3–4; Begbie 1834: 109; "Norton-Kyshe Cases" 1885: 4–5; Bonney 1971: 167n; Rubin 1974: 190; Sheppard 1984: 2). With the May 1822 Siamese capture of the Langkawi Islands much of its population were therefore killed, taken prisoners or forced to escape (with only a small proportion of an estimated island population of 3,000–5,000 people, before the invasion, remaining after 1822; see Anderson 1824: 9–10, 142, Crawfurd 1830 I: 461; Newbold 1971 II: 4, 14).[67] The captured prisoners were then sent by their Siamese captors to populate the sparsely populated coastal areas around Trang (and the nearby coastal regions of Kubong Boya and Batu Ampar) in order to be employed in the construction of boats, see Anderson 1824: 142.

Nevertheless, with the Siamese invasion of the Langkawi Islands in 1822 it appears that its population or the *suku pulau* (i.e., clans of the sea peoples in the islands) that were able to escape the onslaught headed for safety in three directions. Indeed each of these three locations was strategically important. Foremost the majority of the refugees seem to have gone north into the complex network of islands in the Bay of Bengal, extending to the Mergui Archipelago. They were accompanied by Wan Mali. Then there were those that left for Sungei Penaga or Timian (contemporary Tamiang) in Aceh. Anderson (1826: 235–236) who visited Timian in 1822–1823 reports that amongst the 1,000 inhabitants there was a large colony of Langkawi refugees, presumably sea peoples, residing there. These refugees were led and accompanied by Sultan Ahmad's nephews, Tengku Muhammad Saad (the leader of the 1838–1839 Malay rebellion) and his brother Tengku Muhammad Taib. Indeed Tengku Muhammad Saad was reported to be pirating in the Straits of Melaka in the 1830s, with about forty to fifty boats under his command (*PGSC* dated 3rd of November 1838; Asiatic Intelligence in *AJMR* 1840: 27; "Quedah, and Tuanku Mahomed Saad" in *AJMR* 1841: 114; Winstedt 1936: 185; Khan 1939: 41, 43; Gullick 1983: 47–48, 75n). His brother Tengku Muhammad Taib and Wan Mali were in about 1837–1838 believed to have jointly coordinated a naval attack against the Siamese at Kedah and defeating their fleet at Kuala Merbok (Winstedt 1936: 184; Khan 1939: 41).

Finally, Sri Johan Perkassia (also referred to as Seri Pekerma Jaya, Tunkoo Johan, and Johar Perkassa in the *Straits Factory Records*) the ex-chief of the Langkawi Islands and father of Wan Mali, decided to move to the coast of Kedah with the remaining refugees. There they settled in the Kerian district to the south of Province Wellesley.[68] The British meanwhile in about 1823 accused these Langkawi Islanders, without mentioning Seri Pekerma Jaya, of joining other Kedah refugees and committing piracy (see Anderson 1824: 171).[69] In 1825 the ex-ruler of Kedah successfully requested permission for Sri Johan Perkassia to be allowed to travel to Phangnga and Phuket but the same request a year later to proceed to Tavoy in the Mergui Archipelago met initial hesitation (SSFR 106, Index 1825: November 1825, To inform Raja of Kedah that permission is granted to Sri Johan Perkassa; SSFR 106, Index 1825: 24th of November 1825, Judicial: Superintendent of Police replies to permission respecting Sri Johan Perkassa; SSFR 113, Index 1826: 22nd of July 1826, Raja of Kedah requesting permission to send Sri Johan Perkassa to Tavoy). The 1826 opposition to his travel to Tavoy was likely due to the British failing a year earlier to persuade him to settle permanently in Province Wellesley simultaneously after he requested payment for one of his boats being seized and taken away to Rangoon by the British (SSFR 106, Index 1825: 4th of January 1825, Tunkoo Johan Perkassa; SSFR 106, Index 1825: January 1825, Superintendant of Province Wellesley). Meanwhile, the British simultaneously accused him of being behind a piratical seizure of a boat in 1825 (SSFR 106, Index 1825: 15th of January 1825, Superintendent of Police submits deposition as to the piratical seizure of a boat by Tuanko Johan Perkassa).

Little is heard from the ex-chief of the Langkawi Islands after the above references. It is possible that he spent much of his time with his son, Wan Mali, at Ko Yao or other nearby islands but continued to visit the ex-Sultan of Kedah. Nonetheless, it is possible that the enclave of Langkawi *sukus* at Kerian continued to 1829 when the British decided to send notices to the Malay *prahus* at Province Wellesley to stop "plundering the birds' nest islands" in the Tenasserim coastline (contemporary Tanintharyi region, southeast of Burma), in an area ceded to the British by Burma circa 1826 (SSFR 131, Index 1829: 19th of November 1829, Letter from Tenasserim; SSFR 131, Index 1829: 16th of December 1829, Birds Nests orders issued to the collector, master attendant, and superintendent of Province Wellesley).

Without a doubt, the Langkawi refugees by moving themselves to the three strategically locations of Aceh, the islands in the Bay of Bengal and Kerian they could maintain pressure, economically and politically, on the Siamese fleet and coastline by blocking ships and stopping them from farming the birds' nests or acquiring other resources. What's more the Siamese seem to have the disadvantage that their navy in the Bay of Bengal was not a permanent one. Thus they had to construct the boats locally or purchase them from elsewhere, as well to rely on the Malays, sea peoples and the Chinese to construct, maintain and operate them. Furthermore the Siamese were dependent on a number of their coastal vassals (including Kedah, see *Syair Sultan Maulana* 1985) or recruited pirates (particularly the Chinese) for directing trade to its ports, naval expeditions or for protection of its maritime lines of communication. Besides the Siamese navy was composed of larger boats, that were likely unable to keep up with the pace and maneuvering of the Malay *prahus*.

The population number of the Langkawi Islands only began to recover after the return of the ex-Sultan to Kedah in 1841–1842 largely due to the settlement of the islands by predominantly Sumatran migrants, with virtually no record or evidence that the sea peoples ever returned to any of the islands (Bird 1989: 7; Carsten 1995: 317–335). Writing three decades later than his first reference to the *orang laut* and Tarutao Island, Crawfurd (1856: 440) notes that the island was no longer inhabited thus suggesting that following the restoration of the monarchy the sea peoples did not return to Kedah. Reasons behind their choosing of not to return to Kedah or the Langkawi Islands are not known and difficult to speculate. It could be that the Siamese upon allowing the return of the ex-ruler to Kedah in 1841–1842 set a prerequisite on not allowing the Langkawi *suku pulau* to return (as punishment). This perhaps explains the fact that some of the *Urak Lawoi suku* of Trang and southern Thailand were only allowed to return to the islands in the Adang Archipelago and the nearby Tarutao Island (north and west of the Langkawi Islands) at the beginning of the twentieth century (Hogan 1972: 225; and Wongbusarakum 2007: 11).

KEDAH'S SOUTHERN CORRIDOR: FOREIGN-BORN SEA LORDS

To the south of Kedah it seems that from the late seventeenth to the first half of the nineteenth century consecutive rulers of Kedah were able to rely on the naval power of the wandering or foreign born sea lords as well as their allied sea peoples. This alliance for Kedah meant protecting and defending its southern maritime lines of communications, directing and assisting shipping to its ports as well as for gaining political or economic leverage against its enemies and pirates. The recruitment of foreign born sea lords during this period also enabled Kedah to attack or threaten its enemies further south of the Melaka Straits and to the east of the Malay Peninsula. Furthermore, the help of foreign born sea lords and their sea peoples was rendered in the early eighteenth century to expel a colony of pirates on Penang Island. While the same non-indigenous sea peoples and their chiefs were then allowed by the ruler of Kedah to settle and use the Island and the adjacent coastline as a base.

On the other hand, the presence and influx of these foreign sea lords and their peoples at Kedah further complicated internal politics. They consisted of a well-armed and external force that was paid for their services and thus had little loyalty for the political institution of Kedah, rather to their own chiefs and sea lords. Hence, these sea lords in time of internal strife or a succession dispute would simply reassess their presence there or shift their allegiance to any of the contending sides and often offering their services to the highest bidder. Besides many of these chiefs had their own motives for being at Kedah, and often came with their own political baggage, e.g., the Siak and Bugis-Makassar rivalry with each other or political ascendancy.

It is no wonder then that in order to further protect their political and personal interests the foreign born sea lords, the Laksamana and the ruler of Kedah often resorted to traditional and symbolic forms of agreements or bonds. Some of these relationships have been discussed earlier but marriage too was an important aspect of forming alliances amongst themselves or their immediate relations. These marriages are significant in interpreting seventeenth to the nineteenth century history of Kedah, its court politics as well as in understanding the internal involvement of the foreign born sea lords to the north of the Melaka Straits. They are similarly important as they shed further light into seeing how these alliances were maintained. They also help in understanding the extent of the Siak and Bugis-Makassar rivalry in the Melaka Straits. In fact it seems that even the nineteenth century Siamese invasion of Kedah did not put an end to politically and strategically motivated marriages between the family of the ex-ruler of Kedah and his officials to the chiefs, families, and tributary allies of Siak. This would explain the marriage of Wan Achan, referred to as a "piratical adventurer" and a brother of Rajah Pulo Baria based at the town of Medan (north Sumatra) and a tributary ally to Siak, to a Kedah woman soon after the Siamese invasion of Kedah (Anderson 1826: 9, 25–26, 79, 95).

In consequence, Kedah's rulers and high ranking officials were historically sure to both gain and lose, militarily and politically, from economic, family or economic links to the powerful sea lords. This followed several decades of internal political turmoil, a succession crisis, with several revolts orchestrated by members of the Kedah royal household who had recruited mercenaries and independent sea lords from amongst the Siak people, the Bugis and their allies. Indeed these, so-called times of turmoil and family disputes at Kedah can be traced to 1681–1684 and continued in the years 1711, 1713–1715, 1722–1725, 1759–1762, and 1770–1771.[70]

In the first instance (1681–1684) Minangkabau[71] men, supporting the Sultan, were reported to be "in the vanguard of the battle" (i.e., "*bahwa akan Raja Indera Negara jadi panglima cucuk, kapitnya Tun Bijaya Indera d-a-n Minangkabau*") against a rebel Kedah *anak raja* (likely Dato" Padang Seri Jana the younger brother of the Sultan), his allies and his Bugis-Makassar relations (thought to be from his wife's side) at Kuala Muda, Kedah (*Commission of Sultan Muhyiddin Mansur Syah* 1985). The opposing forces supporting the rebel Kedah prince included the Makassarese from Billiton that were led by a Bugis, Haji Besar, and one Daeng Tollolo (Muhammad Hassan 1968: 86–90 88n; Bonney 1971: 21; Andaya 1975: 173; Andaya 1976: 163, 170, 170n).

This event in 1681 is important in the history of Kedah as it is the earliest documentation of the historic Siak-Minangkabau/Bugis-Makassar rivalry in the northern Melaka Straits and at Kedah. Moreover, there may in fact be some truth in the story of a marriage between this *anak raja* and Makassar or Bugis refugees, at Kedah. A Dutch letter for 1658 reports that three Makassar Haji's helped to burn the Dutch factory at Phuket, kill some of the Dutch and their employees and then escaped to Kedah never returning or being arrested (Governor General Gerard Reynst to the Heren XVII, 14th of December 1658, in *Generale Missiven* 1968 III: 220).[72] Likewise, there are numerous reports of Makassar chiefs (and/or their allies, the Bugis) together with their followers settling around the Malay Archipelago, as well as in Siam in the second half of the seventeenth century.[73] It is therefore likely that the Kedah *anak raja* had married a person connected to one of these Makassar drifters.

It is possible that such marriages with the wandering sea lords or their relations were attempts by Kedah's rulers to extend their influence, prestige, and authority outside their traditional power base into neighboring *negeri*. Hence Kedah's ruler may have viewed the marriage of Raja Kecik to Tenghku Masuna in the 1720s as an attempt to connect himself to a powerful sea lord, with many sea peoples and chiefs under him. Furthermore, the marriage to Raja Kecik would have meant to Kedah's ruler and his Laksamana further leverage and power to offset the growing Bugis-Makassar power in the region. Indeed one may question the motivation behind several rulers of Kedah in the late eighteenth and early nineteenth century linking their lineage to the Minangkabau, although Kedah's literary sources gave a different version of their origins (Francis Light in the late eighteenth century mentions that the Sultans of Kedah came originally from Minangkabau, cited in Maier 1988: 15, 92–93; a similar report was also reported by Anderson 1824: 45, 152; Malcom 1840: 33).[74] Was this alleged Minangkabau connection an attempt by Kedah's rulers to legitimize themselves amongst the growing numbers of Siak and Minangkabau sea peoples at Kedah? Besides one wonders if the marriage was the reason, or an attempt, by the ruler to reassert, legitimize, and reiterate Kedah's royal control, loyalty, and power over the disinherited indigenous *orang laut* that had earlier deserted the throne in the 1670s.

It also appears that the marriage for Raja Kecik meant another step in his prolonged struggle to procure legitimacy and support amongst the old royal households in the Malay Peninsula, as well amongst the chiefs and sea peoples under him. Certainly in the case of Sultan Berkabat or Cabo, the offspring to Raja Kecik and Tenghku Masuna (born—possibly—in the second half of 1720s) he is reported in 1746, by a Dutch visitor, to be betrothed to the only daughter of Sultan Muzafar, the ruler of Perak. Likewise he was reported to be considered to succeed the throne there (Andaya 1979: 75–76, 119n–120n, 160, 168–170).[75] Although the marriage never materialized yet the mere consideration of Sultan

Berkabat as a legitimate suitor by the ruler of Perak may further indicate the approval and growing acceptance of Raja Kecik, his descendants and his cause, arguably after connecting himself to Kedah line, amongst the Malay ruling class. Besides, the proposed marriage is significant as the Perak royal line considered itself as descending from Alexander the Great and the Palembang-Melaka line. Hence the marriage with Sultan Berkabat would have further cemented Perak's genealogical line to that of the claimant of Johor dynasty, as well as the Minangkabau-Siak and Kedah.

Consequently marriage was imperative for gaining further legitimacy and power in the Malay world. And it appears that the connection to the supposed purity of the Kedah royal lineage was an important aspect in the indigenous political culture, after the 1699 turmoil and regicide of the Johor line, and was highly sought after.

Indeed the proposed 1767 marriage between prince Abdullah of Kedah (later Abdullah Mukarram Shah, 1778–1798), to a daughter of the Bugis chief of Selangor was highly desirable for both parties. For Kedah the marriage was an attempt to seek out a new and powerful ally amongst the powerful Bugis-Makassar sea lords a few years after having suffered a major revolt and invasion in 1759–1762 at the hands of Raja Alam[76] (1712–1779) of Siak.[77] Whilst for the chief of Selangor the marriage meant getting further legitimacy amongst the old Malay rulers and peoples after having proclaimed himself as Sultan Salih al-Din (Winstedt 1936: 178; Andaya 1976: 175–176; Ali Haji Ibn Ahmad 1982: 139–140; Hooker 2003: 87).[78] Hence, the tension in relations between Kedah and Siak further explains the 1767 decision for a marriage between prince Abdullah of Kedah and the daughter of the Bugis ruler of Selangor.[79] Nevertheless, the 1767 failure of the marriage may have in reality smoothed the progress of the marriage of the daughter, Wan Mas, of Kedah's Laksamana to the future ruler of Kedah, prince Abdullah.[80] Thus furthering the Laksamana's consolidation of power, and family connections to Kedah's ruler well into the first half of the nineteenth century (see comments by Skinner, as well as family connections, between the Sultan and the Laksamana, mentioned in *Syair Sultan Maulana*, 1985: 48–49, 62–63, 264, 266).

Furthermore, there is the possibility that the Siak sea lords were once again recruited by Kedah in threatening or attacking Selangor in 1775, Songkhla in 1789, the British in 1791, Perak in 1780 and 1816 and the 1821–1841/1842 attempts to regain Kedah from the Siamese.[81] The mere rumor of a naval attack orchestrated on behalf of Kedah in 1780 by the Siak sea lords, was in fact so real that Selangor's Bugis and their ally, Perak's ruler, were forced to move their small settlement of former Kedah rebels from Bernam in Perak much further south to Tanjung Tarung near Sungei Jeram (Andaya 1976: 184, 184n).[82] This preventative measure reflects an awareness of a similar attack on the Bugis enclave at Selangor by the Siak sea lords five years earlier in 1775.

In effect, Raja Ismail's (the Siak sea lord) readiness in 1775 to attack the Bugis enclave at Selangor on behalf of the raja of Kedah indicates the extent to which these alliances were exploited (Lewis 1975: 40; *VOC* 3470, Secret letters from Malacca to Batavia for 1775, cited in Barnard 2003: 138). Then again, this move by the ruler of Kedah, in procuring the traditional services of the sea lords in times of its emergency, also reflects his earlier failed negotiations and hollow promises by the British to deliver him the means to attack Selangor or help him to attack there (Lee 1995: 41–44, 50–51; Bonney 1971: 47–48, 48n). Perhaps, the unsuccessful attempts by Kedah's ruler to procure large number of mercenaries and weapons from European powers, was an expression of his original intention of seeking help from the sea peoples. Also he attempted to bolster Kedah's forces with recruited European officers and their skilled native Indian sepoys (Reid 1969; Bonney 1971; Lee 1995). As a result, this event in 1775 not only indicates the traditional reliance on the sea lords but also the difficulty in seeking similar alliances with Europeans or others from outside the indigenous political systems. Alternatively, the notion of being replaced by European officers and soldiers, as well jeopardizing his control of the maritime trade routes henceforth prompted the Laksamana to oppose the establishment of a British Settlement in 1772 Kedah (Turnbull 1980: 90–91; Bassett 1990: 69).

The recruitment and the presence of these foreign born sea lords and their followers at Kedah however do not necessarily indicate that they themselves stayed there for long durations. Indeed as Barnard (2003, 2007) argues in the case of the Siak sea lords and their followers they controlled no land, and continued to shift from one island or coastal area to another, in either mainland or island Southeast Asia. To this insight it may be added that these chiefs, married to local women, were away for long periods from their wives and families. But this did not limit their interest in Kedah's affairs or involvement in its internal politics. Anderson in travelling to Bukit Batu in 1823 Siak reports that:

> Here we were met by Tuanko Long Putih, a man of celebrity in these seas. He had been expelled from Jambi about eight months before, and had lost three of his sons in one day, who were suddenly attacked while bathing in the river and stabbed. He sent his writer on board to inquire if a visit would be agreeable. When he came on board, his first inquiries were respecting one of his wives, who had been carried off by the Siamese from Quedah. He had three prows, and was about to sail for Singapore, to see Sir Stamford Raffles and intends shortly visiting Pinang. [sic] (1826: 160–161)

This report by Anderson is important as Long Putih was in fact married to the sister of Kedah's Sultan, Tunku Jam Jam, circa 1815–1816 (*SSFR* 54, 14th of January 1816, Raja of Kedah to the Governor of Penang). Furthermore, Long Putih was Siak's powerful chief *Panglima Besar*, who was also a confidant and friend to the Siak Chief Syed Ali and had family connections to Palembang and Jambi, as well the powerful and affluent Arab Syed community (Anderson 1826: 160–161, 186; Ali Haji Ibn Ahmad 1982: 189–190, 206; Gullick 1983: 35, 77n).[83] Although the marriage to Long Putih would have meant his absence from Tunku Jam Jam, to Kedah the marriage was politically a significant one. Long Putih was frequently reported to have a leading role in the political affairs of Kedah for much of the first half of the nineteenth century. Thus in 1816, together with Syed Zein (with the official Siak title of *Tuanku Pangiran*), he was in charge of the Siak fleet threatening Perak on behalf of Kedah and later he was involved as the second in charge in the 1831–1832, and possibly in the 1838–1839, wars against Siam. (*SSFR* 50, 22 June 1815, Raja of Kedah to Governor of Penang; *SSFR* 54, 14 January 1816, Sultan Ahmed of Kedah to Governor of Penang; Anderson 1840: 72–74; Low 1849b: 364; Wynne 1941: 209; Bonney 1971: 128–155; Gullick 1983: 35, 77n; Osborn 1987: 94, 99).[84] Consequently Long Putih was deeply involved in any new development at Kedah that could threaten his own interests.

Moreover, there is evidence to suggest that toward the end of the eighteenth century the Siak sea lords had acquired the assistance of other sea peoples distinct from their original followers. Thus in the case of Kedah in 1790 the then chief of Siak, Syed Ali, and his allies, the Ilanun, were in fact just south of Kedah, supposedly in pursuit of Dutch ships and looting coastal areas in Perak, when Sultan Abdullah of Kedah tactfully asked for their assistance to help to drive the British out of the Penang Island settlement (*SSFR* 4, 22 December 1790, Francis Light to General of India; Gullin and Zehnder 1905: 6; Barnard 2003: 152–162).[85] The Siak sea lords in their attempts to seek alliances along the eastern Malay Peninsula enlisted these Ilanun sea peoples and their chiefs in the last two decades of the eighteenth century (Warren 1981: 158; Barnard 2003: 154). Hence, the recruitment of the Ilanun by Siak sea lords indicated the transformation of their original sea peoples at that point in history. It also raises the possibility that there were often other groups in Southeast Asia attached to the Siak or Bugis-Makassar sea lords in their quests for power and wealth. This includes the attachment of a number of *anak rajas* as well as opportunistic Malay officials and their followers. For one thing in the 1770–1771 Bugis attack on Kedah, the Raja Muda of Perak is said to have personally accompanied the expedition (Andaya 1976: 182).

The background of the previously expelled pirates in the early eighteenth century Penang Island and surrounding areas is unknown but may include remnants of the earlier Bugis invaders or *orang laut*. Similarly, it is not clear if the pirates resided at Penang permanently, temporarily or if they just visited the region from other areas during the "*musim perompak*" or "pirate season" in the Straits of Melaka between November and April (Sopher 1977: 98). There is a royal order by Sultan Ahmad Tajuddin Halim Syah, dated 1133 Hijri (i.e., 1720–1721 CE) and a year or two prior to the Bugis invasion of Kedah and the arrival of Raja Kecik, to quash piracy that may possibly correspond to those at Penang and the surrounding southern districts of Kedah (Andaya 1975: 318n).[86] From various reports it is possible to speculate that they may have began settling or temporarily using Penang regularly sometime during the late seventeenth to the time of the royal order by Sultan Ahmad in the early 1720. For one thing Count Claude De Forbin (*The Siamese memoirs of Count Claude de Forbin, 1685–1688* 1996: 144) the French visitor to the island circa 1685–1688, as well as earlier reports point-out that it was uninhabited.[87] But the use of Penang in order to hide and prey upon unsuspecting maritime traffic would make sense. There is a Portuguese report from the 1630s that the island was popular with Portuguese boats that were sent there annually to use the island as a cover in order to gather intelligence and monitor the nearby shipping traffic to Kedah's harbor (Barretto de Resende's account of Malacca 1911: 6).

The pirates at Penang were likely *orang laut* or Bugis-Makassar with their own chiefs, who often shifted allegiances between various sea lords. They were noted for kidnapping people from the coastline and islands in Southeast Asia to sell as slaves (Forrest 1792: 68; Dampier 1931: 91; Vos 1993: 198). Assuming that the pirates were at Penang and that they were able to escape it is possible that they escaped south, perhaps to Dinding (i.e., to the contemporary island of Pangkor, located in the Manjung district of Perak) and the nearby Sembilan Islands (or Pulau Sembilan, consisting of nine islands), or north possibly to one of the Langkawi Islands. For one thing J. G. Koenig (1894: 128) visiting Dinding on his way to Kedah in 1779 noted that hardly anyone wanted to live on those islands since they feared "slave dealers," a fact that normally indicated pirates. It was therefore imperative for Kedah to protect its southern maritime routes, harbors, trade, and coastal settlements from a potential piratical attack.

It is likely that with the expulsion of the pirates from Penang in the eighteenth century the Sultan of Kedah then allowed Siak "sea people" and their allies, the Ilanun, to settle there. Following the settlement of Penang in 1786, by the British; it is believed that there were Minangkabau people, aligned traditionally to Siak, on the island. According to the local traditions the Minangkabau settlement on Penang Island was carried out by, Nakhoda Intan Ibn al-Marhum Nam Tungku Patis Batang originally from Pagar Ruyung in Sumatra. He was joined by two of his brothers, Nakhoda Kechil and Bayan, with the permission of the ruler of Kedah, sometime before 1734 (*HSMKP* 1974: 9, 34, Appendix 5; Zulkifli Khair and Badrol Hisham Ibrahim 1994: 1–24; Khoo Su Nin 1994: 91).[88] There is little documentation to support the above claims; yet, there are reports of about fifty-eight people already living on the island of Penang, upon the British arrival in 1786, as well as an alleged meeting between Light and a Malay headman, named Nakhoda Kechil (Macalister 1803: 23; Gullin and

Zehnder 1905: 5; Garnier 1923: 5; Stevens 1929: 388–389; Wong 1958: 29–30; Hoyt 1991: 5). Furthermore, there are reports of Minangkabau settlements on the mainland at Kedah opposite to Penang at Sebrang Perai and Batu Bahara areas (both areas in Province Wellesley) in about 1780 (Andaya 1976: 183).[89] There is a strong possibility that the previously mentioned Ilanun, were living amongst the Minangkabau people on Penang or the opposite coastal areas. This may further explain early European reports that the coastline opposite Penang Island, at Perai, was being used for shelter, equipment and repair by the Ilanuns in the "early days" of the British settlement of Penang in 1786, see Anderson (1824: 8–9) and Cameron (1865: 329–330). Assuming N. Macalister's informant, s to be correct, about sixty years earlier Penang had a population of about 2,000 but soon: "These people who were settled upon the island, having given themselves up to piracy and plunder, which disturbed the commerce of Quida, the king fitted out an armament and expelled every soul from the island" [sic] (1803: 23).

Consequently, it is likely that Kedah's ruler acquired the assistance of the Siak "sea people" and their allies the Ilanun in expelling the local pirates (the Bugis or *orang laut*) from Penang and they themselves founded the settlement. Alternatively it is probable that in the first half of the eighteenth century Penang was invaded by pirates, *orang laut* or Bugis sea men and hence Nakhoda Intan's men asked for the help of Siak's sea lord or Kedah's ruler. This may thus explain Vaughan's (1970: 161) mid-nineteenth century account of the presence of a 100 year old native woman from "Borneo or one of the Philippine Islands" that was left on the island "by pirates before the English settled therein." Indeed Borneo and the nearby Philippine Islands are traditionally areas associated with the historic origin of the Ilanun. In any event, the subsequent peace, tranquility, and prosperity (especially the abundance of food) at Penang are likely the reasons for the author, or authors, of the mid-eighteenth century Acehnese epic, *Hikajat Potjut Muhamat*, to consider the island a safe place to settle, particularly in times of starvation in their own homelands (*Hikajat Potjut Muhamat* 1979: 7, 168–169). Similarly Peter Osbeck (1771 II: 216–20, 234) a Swedish visitor to Kedah in 1751 praised its security, prospects, trade, safety, tolerance, and the multiethnic composition of its population. From Kedah Osbeck travelled south to Selangor but mentions no difficulty in getting there nor reports of seeing pirates.

The probability of small isolated pockets of followers and relations of the eighteenth century Siak sea lords at Kedah cannot be ruled out. This includes the previously mentioned Syed and his wife, connected to Raja Alam, at Kedah, as well as the Minangkabau at Seberang Perai, Batu Bahara and Penang. Indeed the legend surrounding Nakhoda Intan, his brothers and their supposed place of origin at Pagar Ruyung, is of interest and is overlooked by other scholars. Particularly since Pagar Ruyung, in highland Minangkabau region of Sumatra, is central to indigenous traditions about the life, power, and the rise of Siak's infamous sea lord, Raja Kecik, believed to have visited Kedah personally and married the Sultan's niece circa 1720–1725.[90] The presence of Minangkabaus and a possible Siak refitting or naval base at Kedah is indeed significant. For Kedah this was important as it effectively blocked foreign intrusion or pirates into its southern districts. It is no wonder then that with the lease and handover of the Seberang Perai coastal area to the British in 1802 the second article in the agreement demands that "The English Company are to protect this coast from all enemies, robbers, and pirates that may attack it by sea, from south to north" [sic] (DMCMW 1837 IV: 647).

The pirates meanwhile were determined to take the risk and plunder ships or coastal settlements, particularly when there was turmoil or conflict at Kedah. There is a report that when the steamer *Diana* went to Riau in 1838 it picked up 27 freed Kedah slaves that were living at the nearby Linggin Island (Asiatic Intelligence, Singapore: Piracy and Slavery, *AJMR* 1838: 24–25). According to the report they were simple men, women, and children that had in 1831 escaped mainland Kedah by sea following the failed Malay revolt there, but were:

> captured by pirates inside of Pulau Bunting,[91] which is only a short distance from the northern entrance to the harbor, and were afterwards conveyed by the pirates to the Dinding and Sembilan (Islands). . . . Subsequently, they represent themselves as being sold to the Ilanun people. The Sultan did not purchase any of their number, although his subjects did. (Asiatic Intelligence Singapore: Piracy and Slavery, *AJMR* 1838: 24–25)

Around the same time of the report the Dinding and the Bunting Islands were likewise reported as "noted haunts for pirates on the western coast" by a former Malay pirate from Selangor (Newbold 1836: 634n–635n). Similarly George Finlayson (1826: 35) and Crawfurd (1830 I: 46) visited the Dinding in the mid and late 1820s and noted that although it had an excellent harbor the islands were uninhabited and only known to be used as a temporary base and refuge by the pirates.[92] Consequently it seems that with the turmoil at Kedah and the departure of foreign born sea lords to protect its southern corridor, during the Siamese invasion, pirates once again took the opportunity to plunder Kedah. It is also of interest that the pirates were able to evade the British at Penang and travel north to the Bunting Islands. The Siamese were likewise unable to effectively patrol Kedah's coastline during this period. This report is in contrast to the fact that eyewitness reports on the last days of the Malay rebellion in areas adjacent to the Bunting Islands tell of the presence of a number of British frigates in the area as well as forty two Siamese boats there (*Singapore Chronicle*, 24th of November 1831; Asiatic Intelligence in *AJMR* 1832: 26–27). Moreover they continue that the British frigates successfully thwarted a group of fifteen *prahus* from the Langkawi Islands (likely *orang laut*) in the same vicinity. Thus the presence of pirate boats in and around the Bunting Islands during the same period shows the extent of the risk that they had taken.

The above report of the pirates preying on the refugees at the Kedah coastline during the Siamese invasion is also significant as it is a rare documentation of an actual event. This is because British sources of the time often tend to exaggerate or be selective or unclear about their definition of piracy. For example an attack on the British gun boat of *Hawk* in 1834 was reported in the *Prince of Wales Island Gazette* (7th of December 1834) to have been orchestrated by pirates from "Linga, Siak, Galang, and other ports in the vicinity of Singapore" and that "a reinforcement is expected which, if reports are to be depended on, will make the fleet 160–170!" [*sic*]. The same newspaper a week later (14th of December 1834) admitted that the pirate fleet was in fact *orang laut* that headed back to the Langkawi Islands.

The foreign born sea lords were thus able to monitor and control Kedah's southern maritime lines of communication and direct safe passage for Kedah's trade or traffic. Alternatively having a base and being linked to Kedah meant for the traditional rulers and sea lords of Siak an ally and recognition in their struggle to establish their ruler's presence in the Melaka Straits. Furthermore, it gave them the ability to control the seas to the north of the Melaka Straits, something that the Bugis and their main rivals never managed to achieve.

CONCLUSION

The maritime and riverine systems were therefore an integral part of any traditional Malay polity. Trocki's (1979) study of Johor has in fact aptly argued that traditionally all Malay political, economical and social structures exploited the maritime or the riverine systems. Hence it is important to understand how each of these structures functioned individually and how they contributed to the indigenous socioeconomic and political systems. In particular it is significant to understand how the Malay ruler traditionally controlled the maritime routes, directed shipping to the entrepot, as well as maintaining the vitality of the sea lines of communication for the economic and political survival of an entrepot. The sea routes were in reality the paths that traditionally connected a Malay domain to the outside world.

In this context it is noteworthy that Kedah's historic infrastructure embodied both the riverine and the maritime domains. A study of Kedah is therefore imperative in understanding the similarities or differences in the indigenous Malay systems and structures. Similarly it can shed further light into how the Malay rulers traditionally maintained their control of the maritime lines of communication. Additionally, it offers an insight into the delicate, but essential, relationship that existed between the ruler, the sea lords and the sea peoples. This relationship is also significant as it helps to expose the forces that traditionally bound or separated them and in return ensured the prolongation and defense of the Malay monarchy.

Indeed by examining seventeenth to the early nineteenth century historic records it emerges that many of Kedah's sea peoples were often distinct from each other. With the seventeenth century sea routes of Kedah dominated by indigenous Straits-born sea peoples and their chiefs, originating from the southern half of the Malay Peninsula. And the eighteenth century saw the rise in importance of non-native chiefs and sea peoples from Siak, Bugis-Makassar and elsewhere in the Malay world. In the mid-eighteenth century to the beginning of the nineteenth century however it is apparent that Kedah's coastline and islands were divided into two corridors or zones. The northern zone of Kedah was dominated by the indigenous *orang laut* that operated in and around the Langkawi Islands; and the southern zone in and around the Penang Island was controlled by the foreign sea lords and their sea peoples. This arrangement appears to have continued well into the nineteenth century and only disappeared following the 1821–1842 Siamese occupation of Kedah after which virtually nothing is heard from them. Nonetheless, the historic presence of the sea peoples in the more remote, strategically located and resource rich islands and coastlines enabled their protection from the more immediate dangers (e.g., pirates or foreign intrusion). It also enabled the sea peoples to act for the realm and to be the Laksamana's eyes and ears as a source of intelligence

It also seems that the Laksamana acted as the undisputed sea lord of Kedah at least from the eighteenth century onward. He was thus the key official at the court that acted as a link between the ruler and the indigenous *orang laut* and their chiefs. Likewise, it is possible that he was often working together with regional men of prowess or wandering sea lords (e.g., the *anak raja* and the wandering or foreign born sea lords, such as Bugis-Makassar or Siak chiefs), that were often recruited together with their followers and sea peoples on behalf of Kedah's ruler at least from the 1680s onward. Local or foreign born Syeds (often born at Palembang from Arab ancestry) were another group of such men of prowess, with a high social and spiritual standing amongst the Muslim population, whom the Laksamana and the ruler often exploited by forming family alliances particularly from the mid-eighteenth century onward. From an indigenous point of view it could even be argued that the British, or other European powers, were perhaps considered in the context of these wandering sea lords by Kedah's rulers and the Laksamana.

In consequence, the Laksamana looked after the economic, social and political interests of the indigenous sea peoples and their chiefs, as well as the recruited men of prowess in the royal court. Furthermore, he supervised the sea peoples and their chiefs' control of the maritime and riverine lines of control, as well as in maintaining their loyalty to the ruler. The Laksamana however was kept loyal to Kedah's ruler through economic incentives, family politics, as well as symbolic means. Additionally he was one of the few officials in the realm to be allowed to own ships, trade and collect tolls and dues. Indeed, in the words of an early nineteenth century Kedah document the Laksamana's undisputed political position is even equated to that of a Raja on land. But this did not mean that he was the second in command after the ruler in the realm. As in the events of the 1809–1811 war against Burma, the success of the Laksamana against the enemy and his relentless loyalty or *bakti* to the ruler meant being promoted to the office of *Bendehara* (see *Syair Sultan Maulana* 1985: 252–253).

On the other hand, the relationship between the wandering sea lords and Kedah's royalty can be best described in economic or political terms. Their loyalties toward the Kedah monarchy, in times of turmoil or succession crisis, can in the interim be questioned, and they appear to easily switch among the contending sides. Nonetheless, Kedah's strategic geography (at the northern end of the Melaka Straits and linked to the Bay of Bengal) in controlling traffic, its elaborate link to overland and sea routes, and the prestige associated with the royal house of Kedah appear to have attracted foreign born sea lords to its shores.

Bugis chiefs in particular seem to have based their services to Kedah on economic or financial payments. Moreover, their presence at least in the 1722 civil war at Kedah can also be partly explained (according to *Tuhfat al-Nafis*, see Ali Haji Ibn Ahmad 1982: 44, 65–67) in the context of their historic rivalry with the Siak chiefs. Hence eighteenth century Kedah became a battleground between the Bugis and the Siak chiefs. Both determined to win over support, influence, recognition, and allies at Kedah.

Relations with Siak chiefs at Kedah were somewhat similar to those with the Bugis. Economic benefits and restricting Bugis presence were thus traditionally important in obtaining their services. But these were not the only reasons that appear to have motivated the Siak chiefs to be active at Kedah. It seems that they were keen to seek allies in their quest to attain recognition as the true heirs to the Palembang, Melaka, and Johor dynasty amongst the Malay royalty, peoples, and *orang laut* following the 1699 regicide at Johor. Hence reported marriages between the Siak chiefs, officials, and their relations to those of Kedah's royalty were more frequent than to the Bugis.

In fact it could be argued that Kedah's royalty were the first major polity in the Malay Peninsula to acknowledge the royal claims of Raja Kecik. This can be demonstrated in the 1722 royal marriage of Raja Kecik to a close relation of Kedah's ruler. Undoubtedly this marriage provided Raja Kecik further prestige and support amongst the Malay population, the *orang laut suku* in the Melaka Straits and his followers. Meanwhile, it is likely that Kedah's royalty appreciated the rise of the Siak chiefs as they could be used to balance off the Bugis or Dutch power on its southern borders. They were also happy to be connected to powerful sea lords that commanded large followings amongst the indigenous *suku* of the Straits sea peoples, as well as being able to extend their influence and support to both sides of the Malay Peninsula (as in the case of Raja Ismail and Syed Ali). This was important to Kedah as its trading ports and centers were linked by land to the other side of the Malay Peninsula. Besides it could be argued that the eighteenth century regal institution at Kedah, with its unique genealogy and traditions, was already well established and did not feel threatened by the claims, or presence, of Raja Kecik and his chiefs that frequented the realm. Hence Raja Kecik's claim to the Palembang-Melaka-Johor genealogy was no threat to Kedah's royal genealogy that traced itself to Rum and Persia. This was in contrast to Kedah's southern neighbor Perak, or perhaps aspects of Patani's royal genealogy, that could have been easily exploited by Raja Kecik in order to establish him there.

On the other hand, Kedah's ability to obtain the help of the sea peoples and their chiefs following the 1821 Siamese invasion and occupation is remarkable. For one thing it is believed that the Siamese killed the Laksamana of Kedah early in the invasion, and with the Sultan on the run it would have been extremely difficult to rekindle the former support. Furthermore, the ability of Wan Mali and Tengku Mohammed Saad to successfully seek support from the sea peoples and in controlling Kedah's maritime lines of communication may further indicate the continuance of the covenant and sacred links between the ruler and his subjects. Indeed there was little in immediate economic and material wealth that the ex-Sultan was able to offer the sea peoples and their chiefs in order to entice them to support him. This unswerving loyalty to the Kedah ruler and his influence over the *orang laut* resonates with the 1619 Acehnese occupation of Kedah and the Langkawi Islands. At the grassroots level it therefore appears that the *orang laut* were little interested in financial or material wealth. In fact in line with Vivienne Wee's (1985, 1986) argument on the indigenous *orang laut* in the Riau Archipelago it seems at Kedah they were similarly interested in a moral economy. Hence loyalty or the act of *bakti* to the ruler and the principles of a sacred pact with the monarchy may have fuelled their continuing support.

NOTES

1. See regional studies of the sea peoples by Warren (1981) on the Ilanun, Barnard (2003, 2007) on Siak and sea peoples in the southern Melaka Straits and anthropological works on the Riau sea peoples by Wee (1986) and Chou (2003).

2. For a discussion on the spread and variant names given to the "sea peoples" in Southeast Asia refer to the studies by W. G. White (1922), D. Hogan (1972: 205–235), Sopher (1977), and J. Ivanoff (1997).

3. Refer to the undated indigenous source of *"Hukum Kanun Dato Kota Setar"* (i.e., "the laws and regulations of the chief of Kota Setar," likely written in the 1740s) and *"Bunga Mas, Alat Kerajaan Pada Masa Tabal, Orang Besar-Besar, Adat Meminang"* (roughly translated as "the tributary, silver flower, royal instruments/regaliaused used during the beating of the drum [during the royal installation], important/high ranking people, custom of engagement/proposal," written in about 1222 Hijri/circa 1807 CE). Both sources are reproduced at length and partially translated in Winstedt (1928: 11, 35, 40, 44).

4. Being related to Malay rulers the *anak rajas* often amassed much power, followings and influence in the realm. Furthermore, they were allowed to wear the royal yellow color, but not the white color, see Andaya 1979: 90. Andaya (1976: 167) has discussed how the *anak rajas* in western Malay Peninsula attempted to *"mencari rezeki"* or "seek their fortunes" by legitimate trade soon fell apart and they ultimately had to resort to piracy.

5. The financial situation for the ex-Sultan became dire following the 1826 Burney treaty, held between the British and the Siamese. Having concluded a favorable treaty with the Siamese—at the expense of the ex-Sultan of Kedah—the British begun restricting him to his own money, as well any claims that he had for collecting the rent for Penang and Province Wellesley. This became apparent in the 1829 when a judge at Penang in a civil case refused to recognize the ex-Sultan and his officials as the legitimate government of Kedah, and thus threw out their claim to 5,000 dollars that had been deposited with the British government in 1809 on behalf of the Sultan (SSFR 131, Index 1829: July 1829, Mr. Trebek claims amount of the late Laksamana of Kedah; *Ishmahel Laxamana v. East India Company* in "Norton-Kyshe Cases" 1885: 4–12). For their objections to the ruling the judge then had the ex-Sultan's lawyer, Mr. Trebeck, severely reprimanded and permanently struck off the rolls.

6. The license demanded by the *penghulu* was from Tengku Raya Udin Muhammad Shah, the son of Kedah's former ruler that was earlier in the year—1619—captured and taken to Aceh with his family. Tengku Raya Udin Muhammad Shah was somehow able to elude his captors at Aceh, and escaped back to Kedah and take refuge inland at Perlis (Beaulieu 1705: 245, 247; *Phongsawadan Muang Zaiburi* 1990: 95).

7. Andaya (1975: 319n) suggests that "the fact that Raja Kecik married the niece, and not the daughter, of the ruler of Kedah may be interpreted as indicating that the elder brother supported by the Bugis was still ruling when the war ended in 1724." But it is also possible that the ruler of Kedah did not have a marriageable girl or that he intentionally did not want to be directly related to Raja Kecik as his father-in-law. Direct connection to Raja Kecik would have not only isolated and displeased key officials, or other neighboring rulers but also threaten or complicate Kedah's monarchy hierarchy in the long run. It is possible that Kedah may have followed indigenous custom popular in other parts (e.g., in neighboring Perak) that enabled succession to pass through an only royal daughter and that thus enabled her husband to rule (see Andaya 1979: 75–76 and also the marriage of Sri Tribuana to Wan Sundaria in *Sejarah Melayu* -in which the father of the bride stepped aside and asked his son in law to rule in his place, see *Malay Annals* 2001: 25–27 and Brown 1970: 16).

8. *SSR* 2, 12 September 1786, Francis Light to Cornwallis; *SSFR* 2, 22 January 1787, Letter received from Francis Light at Fort William; *SSFR* 4, 19 March 1791, Letter received from Francis Light to the Governor General of India; Andaya 1976: 176n; Anderson 1824: 153; also comments by Skinner in *Syair Sultan Maulana* 1985: 264, 266, 292 and Bassett 1990: 69, 71.

9. The Laksamana in the time of Sultan Muhammad Jiwa Zainal Abidin Muazzam Shah (1723–1778) was reported to be his brother, see *SSFR* 2, 22 January 1787, Letter received from Francis Light at Fort William. Following the death of Sultan Muhammad Jiwa Zainal Abidin Muazzam Shah in 1778 the Laksamana became the brother-

in-law of Sultan Abdullah (1778–1798), see *SSFR* 4, 19 March 1791, Letter received from Francis Light to the Governor General of India. The Laksamana seems to have died at the turn of the century and replaced by his son. In about 1809–1810 the Laksamana was said to be the young "nephew" of Sultan Ahmad's (ruler from 1803 to about 1845) mother, (i.e., "*anak saudara kepada bunda,*" see *Syair Sultan Maulana* 1985: 48–49, 62–63). But with the death of the *Bendehara* and the fall of grace of his replacement, Datuk Maharaja, for when he failed to attack Patani in time, the Laksamana was thus raised in about 1810 to the higher rank/position of the *Bendehara* (other reasons for the elevation of his position were given as to the Laksamana's former success against Burma and his *bakti*, see *Syair Sultan Maulana* 1985: 252–253 and a note by Skinner in *Syair Sultan Maulana* 1985: 315n). Following this another Kedah official, the *Paduka Seri Raja*, was then promoted to the office of Laksamana (see stanza 21 and 834–835 in *Syair Sultan Maulana* 1985: 49, 207). He was related to Sultan Ahmad and the Laksamana's cousin (by having the same grandfather). The new Laksamana remained at Kedah until his death at the hands of the Siamese invaders in about 1821/1822. His son Ishmahel (presumably Ismail) was then appointed as the new Laksamana by the ex-Kedah ruler in the same year as was argued unsuccessfully in a civil case ("*Ishmahel Laxamana v. East India Company*" in " Norton-Kyshe Cases" 1885: 4–12.

10. This includes a 1664 report of a sale of a large ship build for Mr. Edward Lock, an English private trader, and big enough to carry 9–10 elephants and a large quantity of tin (*Dagh-Register* 1664 [1893]: 82, 267; Winstedt 1936: 159–161).

11. There were however smaller dockyards reported at Satun, Sungei Lingow, Sungei Perlis and the Langkawi Islands, at least from the eighteenth century onward.

12. The reports continue that the Dutch interest in controlling this industry was denied by Kedah's ruler in fear of Siamese objections. It is unclear if attacks in 1644 on these pearl islands by "Johorese Saletters" and kidnapping of people were conducted on behalf of Kedah, see *Dagh-Register* 1644–1645 (1903): 78–79. Little is mentioned about this form of industry at Kedah in later periods and it is likely that the islands were controlled by Siam. This may thus explain the attack by Kedah sea peoples and rebels on the Siamese military posts on the islands in the late 1820s (Winstedt 1936: 183; Wynne 1941: 209; Burney 1971 V Part 1: 139). Smyth (1895b: 522–523, 532) visiting the area two centuries later notes the continuation of the pearl industry in that region as well as the involvement of the *orang lauts* in procuring it.

13. The Kedah ruler similarly owned ships. In the seventeenth century he is thought to have owned as many as 40 trading ships that visited ports in Southern India, Sumatra and other ports on the Bay of Bengal (*Original Correspondence* [No. 3917], 1st of January 1674, Kedah General to Surat; Bowrey 1905: 282–283; Winstedt 1936: 171; Subrahmanyam 1990: 310n, 310–311). Similarly at the seventeenth century Patani the Queen and the Laksamana had their own ships and traded directly with Siam and other places (Letter from Batavia, 17th of April 1617, in *Bescheiden omtrent zijn Bedrijf in Indie* 1920 II: 226–230; Floris 1934: 81; Bradley 2009: 282).

14. But it is unclear if the Laksamana would receive a share of the tin tolls and customs. Swedish traveler Peter Osbeck (1771 II: 220) that visited Kedah in 1751 reports, on the tin trade, that the ruler has "the toll and custom of what is brought here" [*sic*].

15. Also Kuala Batang, both names refer to the contemporary Kuala Kedah (Khan 1939: 13; Adil 1980: 1; note by Skinner in *Syair Sultan Maulana* 1985: 263n; Sharifah Zaleha 2004: 422n).

16. One wonders if Kedah's ruler by granting this permission to the British was indeed viewing them as a replacement for the *orang laut*.

17. According to the indigenous source of *Sejarah Melayu* the *orang laut* were summoned to fetch their ruler, the ex ruler of Melaka, who fled as an exile from his capital in Bentan after a Portuguese attack in 1526 CE, see Andaya 1975: 48. Similarly the *orang lauts* were reported, by an anonymous European eyewitness, in the early part of the nineteenth century to be obliged to transport the people of Rotti and Savu to

Timor, "when required and ordered to do so by the ruler," see "Short Account of Timor, Savu, Solor, and c" cited at length in *AJMR* 1822: 534.

18. It should be noted that attacks outside of Kedah (e.g., the 1810/1811 attack against the Burmese in the Bay of Bengal) were sometimes carried out on behalf of Siam.

19. See a discussion on issues surrounding this incident and its connection to Kedah in the next chapter.

20. There was however complexities in distribution of booty, particularly when wandering sea lords were involved. In the case of booty taken from Kedah by the Bugis (circa 1715–1720) a confrontation erupted between their chiefs and the Sultan of Johor. This conflict proved disastrous for the Kingdom of Johor and marked the beginning of a permanent Bugis political and social role on the Malay Peninsula, Straits of Melaka and the south-west coast of Borneo, see Andaya 1975: 230–231.

21. Twelve cannons were given to the Bugis chief, Daeng Merewa, in 1716 as part payment for his help and the Bugis success in the succession crisis of 1713–1715, see Andaya 1975: 229.

22. Swearing oath of loyalty was traditionally common and popular amongst the Malay rulers. According to the indigenous source of *Tuhfat al-Nafis* when Kelantan was defeated, by a join Trengganu and Siak force, its ruler presented himself to the ruler of Trengganu and hence an oath of loyalty was sworn, see Ali Haji Ibn Ahmad 1982: 147.

23. The object used for the oath taking ceremony at Kedah could have be anything that had symbolic or historic significance. The swearing on an object is indeed very old, dating to the pre-Islam period. A pre-Islamic ruler of Patani is according to *Hikayat Patani* (1970: 73–74, 150) said to swear by the idols that he worshipped, or in another version of the same story he swore by the "image of the Lord Buddha," see comments by D. K. Wyatt to the passage in *Hikayat Patani* (1970: 43). In the case of Prince Muhammad and the influential *uleebalang* in the mid-eighteenth century Acehnese epic of *Hikajat Potjut Muhamat* (1979: 22, 151–163) the swearing of the oath was simply taken "on the bullet" [sic]. But at Johor the taking of an oath was over a piece of rusted iron, the *"besi kawi"* (i.e., obligatory force of iron), that was attributed to have magical powers (see notes by Matheson and Andaya in Ali Haji Ibn Ahmad 1982: 69, 333n–334n; Cummings 2002: 175). Unlike Johor, the *"besi kawi"* at the Minangkabau region of Sumatra refers to the curse of the royal family especially if anyone defaults royal oath or agreement (Drakard 1999: 6, 153, 157).

24. Similarly the Johor's oath taking ceremony involved the symbolic sipping of water after the rusted iron (i.e., the *"besi kawi"*) was dipped into the water, see notes by Matheson and Andaya in Ali Haji Ibn Ahmad 1982: 333n–334n.

25. The Malay word *"bakti"* is derived from the Sanskrit word of *"bhakti"* or *"bhakta"* (i.e., duty, serve, unconditional devotion, commitment or homage) and its usage can be documented to the seventh century CE "Kota Kapur" (or Bangka) inscription of Srivijaya, see the romanised version of the inscription and its translation in G. Coedes (1918: 54–56) whereby the word is mentioned four times. In the inscription Srivijaya attacked the land of Java for not showing *bakti*, i.e., *"yam bhumi jawa tida bhakti ka sriwijaya"* [sic]. I like to thank Professor Pierre-Yves Manguin for drawing my attention to this passage.

26. It is located to the west of the Timor Island, in the Indian Ocean, and is part of Indonesia's East Nusa Tenggara province.

27. From the passage it is unclear if the government was the Portuguese, the Dutch or a native ruler.

28. For British intentions in establishing themselves at Kedah during this period see the studies by C. S. Wong 1958: 29–30, Bonney 1971, L. A. Mills 1971: 15–27, and Hing Kam Lee 1995: 41–44, 47–49, 51, 54.

29. The connection of *Saletters* to Johor and the southern half of the Malay Peninsula are indeed no surprise. They were the *orang Selatan*, or people of the Straits. Chinese sources, compiled from twelfth to the thirteenth century reports, similarly acknowl-

edge the presence of "Men of the Sea" [sic] in the southern half of the Malay Peninsula that would plunder ships and sell them to Java, or "*Sho-P'o*," see Chau Ju-Kua 1966: 150, 261. Furthermore, Melaka (predecessor to Johor) is believed to have been founded, in about 1240 CE, by the help of the *Saletters* or *orang lauts* (Winstedt 1979: 6). And the sea peoples and their chiefs are reported to be in alliance and control much of the Melaka Straits and Johor's maritime routes in the sixteenth to the nineteenth century (see John De Barros cited in Crawfurd 1830 I: 81–82; Crawfurd 1839 I: 65–66; Seventeenth century visitors 1934: 103; Floris 1934: 102; Cortesao 1944). In any case, not all the *orang lauts* rendering their services to the rulers of Melaka and Johor were indigenous. Traditions amongst the *Orang Suku Mepar* of Lingga traces their origin to Trengganu, on the east coast of the Malay Peninsula, before moving to Lingga and entering into an arrangement with the rulers of Melaka, see Andaya 1975: 47.

30. From the report it is not clear if the people returned were sea peoples, officials, emissaries or chiefs. Thus assuming that the forty were chiefs or officials then it is likely that together with their followers, family and peoples their numbers would have been much higher. The Dutch at Melaka further report that there were envoys exchanged between Kedah and Johor in 1680 and 1682 (see Winstedt 1936: 174–175).

31. There is however no record that Kedah was, prior to the 1680 return of the Johor refugees, openly antagonizing or fighting against Johor. Johorese ships were reported by the Dutch to visit and trade at Kedah in the 1640s and in the 1660s (January–March 1645 entry in *Dagh-register* (1644–1645) 1902: 73–74; 9th of July entry in *Dagh-Register* [1664] 1893: 268, 338, 347; and Winstedt 1936: 167). Thus, it is possible that the Johor refugees came to Kedah following the destruction of its capital, Johor Lama, by Jambi in 1673 or a few years later (see Andaya 1975a: 7 and Trocki 1979: 1n). Although Johor recovered quickly, threatening Jambi with a naval attack and blockade a year later in 1674, yet it is possible that some sea peoples may have left Johor for Kedah.

32. By the mid 1670s Johor pursued a policy of intercepting Siamese and Dutch ships, as well redirecting ships destined away from their ports to Johor and Riau (Andaya 1975: 107–108). Hence it is highly likely that Kedah realized the potentials of forming an alliance with Johor against the Dutch and the Siamese.

33. In November 1668 the Dutch governor at Melaka noted that the "*Saletters* or pirates who infested the Straits, those from Kedah were by no means the fewest in number," cited in Winstedt 1936: 168.

34. Indeed Mt Jerai is also significant to the foundation myth of several *orang asli* groups at Kedah; see Evans 1926: 81, and Hogan 1972: 219–220.

35. In reporting on the sea peoples of southwest Thailand, Nelson Annandale and H. C. Robinson (1902: 407–417) observed that the Muslim and non-Muslim *orang lauts* near Trang were of the same subgroups but were given different names indicating their historic conversion to Islam. Indeed the authors are one of the earliest observers to notice the religious division between the two groups. Hence it is possible that the conversion to Islam amongst the *orang lauts* of Trang happened late in the nineteenth century.

36. Indeed their departure may reflect Kedah's decision in 1646 to join Songkhla against Ayutthaya.

37. Pulaw and Tamab were historically districts belonging to Phuket, see Anderson 1824: 128.

38. Similarly in the first half of the seventeenth century it was common for the Portuguese to yearly spy and gather intelligence at Kedah, by using some of the islands (e.g., Penang Island) as a hideout, see Barretto de Resende's account of Malacca (1911: 6).

39. The factory was eventually disbanded in early 1674 or 1675. K. G. Tregonning (1959: 8) in his article suggests the English factory was at Kedah for only two years. Other factors for the English to disband their trading factory at Kedah were two fires and other damages to their goods. Bassett (1990: 4) however believes the English factory to have operated at Kedah from 1669 to 1676. The discrepancy of dates to the closure of the English factory at Kedah in 1674 is due to the fact that the Kedah king

treacherously rejected the idea and refused to allow the English to leave, as well did not repay his debts to them (Surat Factory Records [volume 107], 28th of October 1674, Joshua Burroughs at Kedah to the President and Council at Surat, cited at length in *Records of the R elations* 1915/1917 II: 111). Ultimately and with great difficulty it seems the English were allowed to leave in 1676 (*Original Correspondence* [No. 4163], 17th of January 1676, The Council at Surat to the East India Company).

40. The Dutch in 1672 praised Perak for not allowing the British to go there, see *Dutch Documents* (M 546), 14th of May 1672, Letter to the Governor General and the Council for India.

41. Bonney (1971: 20) believes Kedah's preparations for defense were the main reasons for its success. On the other hand, Bonney interprets the Dutch independent involvement and blockading force at Kedah, as cited by Bowrey, to have in reality "further strengthened" Kedah's position against the Siamese attack.

42. In the same letter Capell and Burroughs further report of a second fire in May of that year. This fire destroyed the English factory at Kedah, as well most of the goods at their warehouse.

43. See letters dated 17th of May 1673 and 19th of May 1679 in *Dutch Documents* (M 546), Letter to the Governor General and the Council for India, for the General Dutch Chartered Company at Batavia.

44. This period also saw the beginning of the strained relationship between the Siamese and the British. This eventually led to the Anglo-Thai war of 1686–1688 that persisted into the 1690s (Records of Fort St. George. Sunday Book. 12th of August 1686, Letter from the Council at Fort St. George to the Rt. Worshipful Job Charnock at Hugli, cited at length in *Records of the R elations* 1915/1917 V: 29; Bassett 1989b: 633).

45. Kedah's involvement in 1679 Phuket against the Siamese, was more than likely in conjunction with Songkhla and Patani revolts in that year (Factory Records Siam [volume 1], letters dated 22nd of January and 9th of August 1679, Samuel Potts at Singora to Richard Burnaby at Siam, cited at length in *Records of the Relations* 1915/1917 II: 214, 237–239; Dutch Records [volume 881], 3 March 1680, The Council at Batavia to the Dutch East India Company, cited at length in, cited at length in *Records of the Relations* 1915/1917 II: 267).

46. In the same entry for 1680, to the dismay of the Siamese, the King of Kedah began harboring two fugitive chiefs and their two hundred followers from Phuket. Moreover, in a January 1682 letter the king of Siam proclaimed that the Dutch would no longer be allowed to take tin from Phuket or Bang Khli since they already had been granted a monopoly at Nakhon Si Thammarat. It therefore seems that the Siamese were in control of Phuket and Bang Khli at that time. Similarly a request by the British at Siam in 1683/1684 to build a "fortified settlement" on the Langkawi Islands, or another nearby island, may point out to the Siamese firm control of the maritime routes to the north of the Melaka Straits (Letter Book [vol. 7], 29 February 1684, General Letter from the Court of Committees to the Council at Fort St. George, cited at length in *Records of the Relations* 1915/1917 III: 294).

47. Anderson (1824: 128) suggests that Ban Takua was at that time already a district belonging to Phuket. The district was likely a combination of contemporary Thai districts of Takua Thung and Takua Pa.

48. The *Dagh-Register* entry for January 1682 reports that a number of Dutch visitors to Phuket had suffered harm following the killing of the Muslim governor, sent there by Kedah, by the people of Phuket and Takua.

49. In 1697 two Acehnese pirates were arrested at Tenasserim after they had assisted a number of mutineers in a Danish ship on its way from Tharangambadi (or Tranquebar, south India) to China, see Fort St. George Factory Records (volume 33), 17 April 1697, Claus Voogt and Council for the Danish East India Company at Tranquebar to Nathaniel Higginson and Council at Fort St. George, cited at length in *Records of the R elations*1915/1917 V: 138.

50. Yam and sago were the staple food diet for all the sea peoples, see Finlayson 1826: 74 and various references in Sopher (1977) and Ivanoff (1997). Northern and

eastern Sumatra, as well as the nearby Nicobar and Andaman Islands were traditionally reported to have been a fertile ground for these food articles that was procured by the sea peoples, see Anderson 1826: 283–284, Crawfurd 1830 I: 83–84 and Hamilton 1995 II: 71. Writing in circa 1678 Balthasar Bort, the Dutch governor at Melaka, notes that the *Saletters* regularly frequent Bengkalis in Sumatra see *Report of Governor Bort on Malacca 1678* 1927: 177, 182.

51. Kedah's control of the former Siamese provinces and the birds' nests trade appears to have occurred due to the fall of the Ayutthaya kingdom by the Burmese forces in 1767. But, with the reconsolidation of Siamese power, under the Chakri dynasty in 1782, it seems that Kedah's hold and control of several key islands and coastal areas in the Bay of Bengal began to diminish (Anderson 1824: 69; Simmonds 1963: 596).

52. In the above dispatch the peoples poised to attack by land and sea were in fact the former Kedah refugees and their allies that planned to return and free the realm from the Siamese.

53. The Siamese in fact had captured Kedah in 1821 by sea; see Anderson 1824: 2–10; Newbold 1971 II: 7–8; Gullick 1983: 31.

54. J. S. 1200 corresponds to 1838 CE, see conversion of the Thai date by Kobkua Suwannathat-Pian in *Phongsawadan Muang Zaiburi* (1990: 115n).

55. The Siamese/Thai name for Kedah.

56. For a number of reasons, the ex-Sultan avoided being directly connected to Saad and the Malay rebels. Foremost the British had threatened him with stopping his pension and in removing him further away from Kedah if he was involved. Besides at the time of the 1839 uprising he was at Melaka, removed there earlier allegedly for planning attacks on Siam.

57. Sea peoples still reside on Ko Yao. The islands caves are popular tourist destination as they are considered the burial places for the sea peoples, as well containing their bones/remains. It seems this practice predates the twentieth century (Annandale and Robinson 1902: 413)

58. His European contemporaries also praise Wan Mali's military and naval prowess (*PGSC*, 16th of March 1839; see also *AJMR* 1839: 124, Adil 1980: 69–70, and Osborne 1987: 95). According to the *PGSC* article 1,000 Siamese soldiers captured the village of Alloo Ganoo but "the hero with a small number of his men went to their assistance, and WAN MAT ALLI a brave Warrior soon dispersed the enemy" [sic]. He also defeated the Siamese fleet at Kuala Merbok and again at Langkawi Island (Winstedt 1936: 184 and Osborne 1987: 334–335). Osborne (1987: 95) in 1838 refer to Wan Mali as "one of the most enterprising of pirates."

59. Various reports estimate that the island was retaken from the Siamese with the use of about 25–60 boats and a force of 500–2,000 men (Supplement to Asiatic Intelligence in *AJMR* 1837: 48).

60. Siamese even panicked believing that Wan Mali was preparing a surprise attack on the key town of Chaiya, located on its east coast and about 600 kilometers to the south of Bangkok (2nd Dispatch, Udomsombat et al. 1993: 86). For a discussion on this please refer to the next chapter.

61. It is also possible that some of his followers may have escaped into Sumatra as was suggested by Osborne (1987: 325, 329, 349), the English captain whom chased Wan Mali and his followers away from Perlis toward the Langkawi Islands.

62. It seems however unlikely that he was the nephew of the ex-Sultan of Kedah. In the indigenous work of *Syair Sultan Maulana* (1985: 84–85), Seri Pekerma Jaya, Wan Mali's father and the chief of the Langkawi Islands, is only referred to as: "*Panglimadi Pulau Langkawi itu; Seri Pekerama Jaya digelar ratu; turun temerun semerab di situ; benih baik bangsa pun tentu*" [i.e., The Chief on Pulau Langkawi; had been granted the title of Seri Pekerma Jaya; he was descended from one of the island families; of good stock and noble birth]. The author of the text was quite adamant making family connections known. Thus there is no indication that Seri Pekerma Jaya and his son were related to Sultan Ahmad.

63. He is likely the same as "Che Allang" reported to the British by the Siamese in 1825 of committing piracy at the Langkawi Islands, see Burney 1971 II: part 1: 36, part 2: 35.

64. See also *SSFR* 94, 5th of February 1824: 62–64, "King of Kedah seeking help from Burma and Cochin China."

65. The Siamese invasion and its devastation of the Langkawi Islands is still recounted in one of its tourist sites, the burned rice village, in which according to the local tradition when the news of Siamese invasion arrived the villagers burned all their rice to starve the invaders. Burned rice, apparently dating from the period, was displayed in the village during my visit there in 2005.

66. According to Crawfurd (1830 I: 113, 146, 255–256) a copy of the letter was handed to him during his visit to Bangkok (the dispatch is now part of the *Crawfurd Papers* 1915, and can also be found in *SSFR* 87, 28th of November 1822, Fort Cornwallis: Translation of a letter from the Rajah of Ligor to the Siamese Government). The dispatch was given to Crawfurd by a Siamese Muslim official "Ko-chai-sahak" [sic], formerly Nakhoda Ali. He was originally a South Indian but said to speak Malay "tolerably" after having visited Kedah and Penang. George Finlayson (1826: 202) who knew Crawfurd and accompanied him to Bangkok writes that "Mr. Crawfurd at length discovered that this man (i.e., Ko-chai-sahak) was totally unworthy of his confidence and that his conduct was altogether worthless."

67. Following the Siamese invasion of 1822 there was an attempt by them to repopulate the islands. In patrolling Kedah's coastline Osborne (1987: 79–80) reports in 1838 intercepting a boat carrying a Bangkok father and his son that were escaping the Malay recapture of the Langkawi Islands. The father had earlier moved to the island to work as a barber and a painter.

68. There is also a short reference to a group of these refugees at Kuala Muda, to the north of Province Wellesley But since there is no further reference to them in the sources hence it is possible that they later moved south, further away from the Siamese, and to the Kerian district or simply joined the other refugees there.

69. It seems that by then Tengku Din, a nephew of the ex-Sultan had reached an agreement with the Siamese to control the Kerian region and areas outside Province Wellesley. It is however more likely that the real intention of relocating close to Penang by the ex-chief of the Langkawi Islands was to be closer or in protecting the ex-Sultan of Kedah.

70. Winstedt 1936: 177; Bastin 1964: 147–148; Muhammad Hassan 1968: 86–89, 88n; Bonney 1971: 21–22, 27–36; Andaya 1975: 229, 301–303, 318n–319n; Lewis 1975: 38–39; Andaya 1976: 170n, 173, 179; Turnbull 1980: 71–72, 76, 79, 90–91.

71. The Minangkabau were traditionally attached to the rulers of the Siak polity, from the 1680s onward, and later to Raja Kecik and his descendants throughout the eighteenth century, see Barnard (2003).

72. Dutch attempts in 1660 and 1661 to seek the help of Phuket and Siamese officials in apprehending these fugitives failed (see Letters from the Governor General Gerard Reynst to the Heren XVII" dated 16th of January 1660, 16th of December 1660, and the 26th of January 1661 in the *Generale Missiven* 1968 III: 294, 326, 354; also *Dagh-Register* for September 1661 cited by Winstedt 1936: 166).

73. For various reports and studies on the Bugis-Makassar diasporas, see Muhammad Ibn Ibrahim 1972; Andaya 1975: 116–117, 202–203; Trocki 1979: 8n, Turnbull 1980: 69–71; Scupin 1980: 55–66; *The Siamese Memoirs of Count Claude de Forbin, 1685–1688* 1996: 97–119; Kaempfer 1998: 36–37; Cummings 1998: 107–121. It is not entirely clear if there were any Bugis or Makassar amongst the 200 Phuket refugees that came to Kedah in the early 1680s; see translation of passages in *Dagh-Register* dealing with Kedah for the period 1680–1682 in Winstedt 1936: 174–175.

74. There is also an obscure comment by Newbold (1971 II: 20) after meeting the ex-ruler of Kedah that "The Malays are generally thought to be a colony from Melaka; though, as the ex-King informs me, the inhabitants pretend to be descended in a direct line from Alexander the Great." It is likely that the Minangkabau too may have at-

tempted to highlight a royal link to Kedah. The Minangkabau source of *Tromba Minangkabau*, dating to the seventeenth or eighteenth century, refers to the island of Langkawi to be solely created by the almighty "for the original sovereigns of the world, viz. the descendants of Sultan Hidayet Allah Taala, whom he had brought down from the clouds" [sic] (*Tromba Minangkabau* produced at length in Moor 1837: 261–263). The Sultan is according to the source an ancestor of Alexander the great. It is possible that the ex-ruler of Kedah and his predecessors were aware of this link or source. The centrality of the Langkawi Islands to the Minangkabau traditions (and perhaps their Ilanun allies) may partly explain Jadee's earlier reference of the islands being the traditional home of Kedah's ruler (chapter 1).

75. Due to a succession crisis and internal politics at Perak this marriage never materialized, the Perak princess instead married the rival Sultan Iskandar. By 1750 Sultan Berkabat had established himself to the upstream region of Perak, with his stronghold at Larut. He was involved there in the tin trade to Kedah and had also married a Kedah princess; see Andaya 1979: 111–113, 119n–120n, 281–283. Hence he continued his relations and family connections to Kedah.

76. Raja Alam was the eldest son of Raja Kecik and married to Daeng Khadijah (the daughter of the Bugis prince Opu Daeng Parani, see Ali Haji Ibn Ahmad 1982: 24). Opu Daeng Parani was the eldest of the five famous Bugis brothers that was in fact killed at Kedah by Raja Kecik circa 1723–1724; see Andaya 1975: 301–302, Ali Haji Ibn Ahmad 1982: 44, 65–67 and notes by Matheson and Andaya in Ali Haji Ibn Ahmad 1982: 332n–333n.

77. Raja Alam invaded to help Raja Nambang (the Kedah ruler's half brother) and a powerful Kedah Syed (an uncle to Raja Alam's Arab son-in-law, Syed Othman b. Abd al-Rahman bin Shihab/Syahab, for more see Andaya 1976: 173, 1979: 144, 245–246; comments by D. J. Goudie in *Syair Perang Siak* 1989: 38–40, Ali Haji Ibn Ahmad 1982: 24–25, 368n and Ho 2006: 163). Indeed in the ensuing civil war at Kedah, Syed Othman was designated by Raja Alam as the head of the Siak fleet and was accompanied by Siak's *Shahbandar*, or the harbor master (Andaya 1979: 218, 253n; Barnard 2003: 93). The revolt was short lived and Raja Nambang was ultimately forced to flee with his followers to Perak, see Andaya 1979: 245–246.

78. The marriage was one of the many vigorous attempts by the new Bugis Sultan of Selangor to establish his ruler and legitimize himself amongst the Malay royalty. This may further explain Sultan Salih al-Din's unexpected letter of friendship to Perak, after being at odds for more than twenty years, see Andaya 1979: 261–263.

79. The marriage was short and with a bitter ending resulting in a further Bugis invasion of Kedah in 1771–1772.

80. SSR 2, 12 September 1786, Francis Light to Cornwallis; SSFR 2, 22 January 1787, Letter received from Francis Light at Fort William; SSFR 4, 19 March 1791, Letter received from Francis Light to the Governor General of India; Anderson 1824: 153;

81. SSFR 2, 17th July 1789, Francis Light to Governor Genera; SSFR 4, 1791, "Treaty of Peace and Friendship," reproduced at length in Bonney 1971: Appendix 3 (c); SSFR 4, 31st May 1791, Francis Light to Hay; SSFR 50, 22nd June 1815, Raja of Kedah to Governor of Penang; SSFR 54, 14 January 1816, Sultan Ahmed of Kedah to Governor of Penang; Anderson 1840: 72–74; Low 1849b: 364; Wynne 1941: 209; Bonney 1971: 87n, 128–155; Gullick 1983: 35, 77n; Osborn 1987: 94, 99. Regarding the possibility of Siak's attack on Songkhla being on behalf of Kedah please see a discussion in the next chapter.

82. One wonders if Kampong Kedah visited in 1876 by W. Barrington D'Almeida (1876: 371) in south Selangor and near Klang is remnant of this event in history.

83. These "Syeds" were considered foreigners, though sometimes born locally or else in Arabia or Persia or India, and often worked as traders, teachers or clergymen. Moreover, their supposed genealogical connection to the prophet was seen spiritually and generally, by most Muslims, as highly desirable and often led to marriages with Muslim royal households throughout Southeast Asia and beyond (Omar Farouk 1978; introduction by G. W. J. Drewes in *Hikajat Potjut Muhamat* 1979: 16–18, 20, 22; Andaya

1979: 165; Adil 1980: 28–29, 50; Arjomand 1984: 105–210; Khoo 1991: 60; *Hadhrami Traders* 1997; Sharifah Zaleha 2004: 401–424). Thus they appear to have been allowed to operate semi-independently of the ruler or the Laksamana, and were allowed to own ships and carry out their own trade. From an eyewitness report of Kedah in about 1759–1761 by Charles Miller, an English sea-captain of the ship *Helena snow*, it is evident that the "Syeds" of Kedah were highly organized, with a "head Siad" [sic] amongst them, and were influential at the royal court often acting as, what can be best described as lobbyists (Bassett 1989a: 11–12). Hence, Miller in his own dealings at Kedah in order to get around the bureaucratic hurdles had the "Syeds" "making frequent application" on his "behalf" and once attempted to "bribe" the "head Siad" [sic] (Bassett 1989a: 11, 1990: 51–52). Miller in the same account further notes that the King's sister had married "Syed Mahomet Jarr" [sic] thus indicating the extent of the influence of such families and family politics then at Kedah.

84. Virtually nothing more is heard about Tengku Putih after this incident; although it is possible that he left for the *hajj* to Mecca and that he joined the 1838–1839 rebellion against Siam. In blockading the northern coast of Kedah Sherard Osborn (1987: 94, 99) reports meeting Haji Long, an older man, who was second in charge to Dato Ali or Wan Mali (he had liberated much of northern Kedah including Perlis and the Langkawi Islands). At the end of the 1839 rebellion Haji Long and the other Malay forces escaped north from the Langkawi Islands. If the connection is correct then Tengku Putih must have in his late 60s or in his 70s.

85. It is possible that Ilanun sea peoples were involved at the 1770s disputes at Kedah, see Khan 1939: 25. Apparently originating from central Mindanao it is thought that a volcanic eruption in 1765 was the catalyst for their relocation elsewhere into Southeast Asia (Andaya 1993: 224).

86. The order is part of Raffles collection at London. But unfortunately I have been unable to consult it and see whether Penang or any other district and island of Kedah are mentioned.

87. See accounts of visits to Penang by Captain James Lancaster in 1591(Kerr 1824 IV: 22); *Dutch Records* 1–3, 23 November 1608, Willem Verhoef to Melaka; Floris in 1613 (1934: 106–107); and a Portuguese report in the 1630s by the Portuguese Pedro Barretto de Resende (1911: 6).

88. The Batu Uban mosque at Penang is believed to have been built by Nakhoda Intan in 1734 CE.

89. Perhaps Batu Bahara was named after Batu Bara a trading port at Siak, eastern Sumatra, see Anderson 1826: 312. It is therefore possible that it was frequented by people and traders from Batu Bara at Siak.

90. Winstedt 1936: 177; Andaya 1975: 265; Trocki 1979: 8–9; Ali Haji Ibn Ahmad 1982: 332n; Bassett 1989a: 14n; Vos 1993: 66; Drakard 1999; Andaya 2001b: 328; Barnard 2003: 62–63, 63n.

91. The Bunting Islands consist of four islands with an islet between them (Horsburgh 1852 II: 231). The islands can be found just south of contemporary Alor Setar opposite to Kedah Peak with the main island connected to the mainland by a 2.3 km bridge.

92. There was evidence of two temporary huts on the coast when Crawfurd (1830 I: 44–46) visited the island. It was pointed out to him by his native companions that they belonged to pirates. Finlayson (1826: 35) goes on to say that there is little advantage of a stopover on the island and that the taste of the water is "bitter and disagreeable." These reports are in contrast to William Dampier (1931: 117–118) that visited and stayed on the same island in 1688. During his visited the Dutch maintained a small garrison and a factory there. Additionally Dampier praises the island, its location, safety, and quality of water.

FOUR

Bay to Gulf or Gulf to Bay

The Sultan and the Trans-Peninsular Routes of Kedah

The areas under the control and influence of Kedah's ruler were quite extensive. This is shown in both indigenous sources as well as contemporary European reports. The areas of control involved both riverine and maritime domains, including hundreds of islands (*Hikayat Merong Mahawangsa*; *Syair Sultan Maulana*; *SSFR* 1, 1786, Accounts of Kedah and adjacent countries by Michael Topping; Larenaudiere 1822: 33; Anderson 1824; Crawfurd 1830 I: 42–43; Low 1849; Bowrey 1905; Floris 1934: 42; Topping 1970: 43–44; Bonney 1971: 5; Ahmet 1984). At the height of its power, to the north it extended to the Trang River, to the south to the Kerian River (refer to Map 3).[1] And inland it extended all the way to the Titi Wangsa range that divides the east and west coast of the Malay Peninsula (Daly 1882: 406; Bacon 1892: 14; Floris 1934: 69; Dobby 1951: 299; Newbold 1971 II: 22, 69; see Map 6).

A number of more recent Southeast Asian scholars have worked on inland routes between river systems in Malay Sumatra (e.g., Bronson and Wisseman 1976; Miksic 1989; Drakard 1990; Andaya 1993; Barnard 2003).[2] While these authors do not focus on Kedah, they do discuss similar circumstances in Sumatra in considerable detail and provide considerable information about inland routes between river systems and the Minangkabau highlands. Nevertheless, the view of a traditional maritime or riverine domain, with few lines of communications inland, as argued by Gullick (1958) is held to be true for Kedah by most scholars. Consequently, it has been argued that the maritime lines of communication were more important, rather than inland or overland routes.

It is often argued that, in contrast to the common use of the maritime lines of communications, the use of the overland and trans-peninsular routes in the Malay Peninsula were more expensive, riskier, less functional, and that they were only popular prior to the fifteenth century or during short intervals in the nineteenth century (Sullivan 1957; Wheatley 1961; Sopher 1977: 286; Gothamasan 1984: 141–142; Hall 1985: 325n; Benjamin 1986; Miksic 1989; Drakard 1990: 11; King 2006: 4–6, 4n). Banks (1983) and Carsten (1995) in their respective studies of Sik and the Langkawi Islands further argue that Kedah's ruler had traditionally little political or economic control in the outer fringes of his realm. Similarly, a recent but relevant study of Siam by Dhiravat Na Pomberja (2003: 279, 282, 295) also claims a similar degree of autonomy existed in the territorial fringes of historic Siam, particularly in areas that overlapped with the Malay population, as far as the sale of tin was concerned. Thus confirming Gullick's (1958) argument on the ruler's diminishing control and power outside the riverine system.

But Kedah's unique geography, or location, and its ability to be connected to a complex network of overland and trans-peninsular trade routes meant that it traditionally did not rely solely on the maritime and riverine trade routes and structures. This further meant that Kedah was historically less susceptible to environmental, political, and economic changes than other Malay territorial units since there was a larger interplay of systems. Hence it could more easily continue to function as an independent political, social, and economic unit.

Besides, the complex network of lines of communications allowed Kedah to have multiple coastal and inland trading centers, with a relatively good harbor and secure from monsoon winds, that were separate and often some distance from the royal *kota* or capital at Langgar (a short distance from Alor Setar), as was the case of Kuala Kedah (on the coastline), Satun (to the north of Perlis), Baling (an affluent inland trade centre), the Langkawi Islands (including the island of Tarutao and the nearby twenty five smaller islands in the Adang Archipelago and the Bay of Bengal), Kuala Muda (to the south of Kedah adjacent to Penang Island), and Kuala Perlis (to the north of Kuala Kedah). This was in contrast to most other parts of the Malay world that there was one trading centre that was generally adjoined to the royal *kota* (Gullick 1958; Milner 1982; Colombijn 2004). Indeed, attempts by Siam and the Dutch for much of the second half of the seventeenth century to jointly and continuously block the coasts and borders of Kedah and thus force it into submission had limited success. A regular visitor to Kedah, from 1669 to 1681, Bowrey (1905: 259–282) describes its commerce as "little by Sea and much less by Land." This comment may in reality suggest the continuation and survival of Kedah's maritime and the overland trade in its worst case scenario.

In addition, it appears that Banks's (1983) and Carsten's (1995) assertion about control in the periphery was of a physical rather than a perceived or unseen form of control. But central to the ruler's unseen control over his subjects was a sense of an unconditional devotion *"bakti"* toward the ruler, as was mentioned with respect to the sea lords in the previous chapter. This was reinforced through a historic notion of a prototypical covenant between the ruler and his subjects that extended to the *orang asli*, or aboriginal tribes, and sea peoples. The sense of loyalty was possibly further emphasized through the extensive network of *mukim* at Kedah. In a short note in his book, *Kedah 1771–1821*, Southeast Asian scholar Bonney (1971: 9n) argues that the *mukims* were an intricate and dynamic indigenous system that Gullick's (1958) study failed to evaluate. Citing John Anderson (1824: 147–148) on Kedah, Bonney (1971) then continues that the *mukims* were parish style divisions based largely on "Muslim ecclesiastical division of people," which "must consist of not less than forty-four men" who were qualified to perform the "ceremonies of their religion at a mosque" (see also Newbold 1971 II: 20; Hamilton 1984 II: 438; Lee 1995: 8–9). Hence Kedah was believed to include a total of 128 *mukims* prior to the Siamese invasion of 1821.[3]

To this insight it must be added that in such a system, at least in the case of Kedah, a *penghulu* (i.e., a chief) or *penghulu mukim* would preside over the *mukim* with a *kweng*, or *toh kweng*,[4] that acted as district headmen over groups of villages and or districts comprising one or more *mukims* (Logan 1885: 176; Winstedt 1928: 9, 29; Yegar 1979: 60, 74; notes by Skinner in *Syair Sultan Maulana* 1985: 302; Sharifa Zaleha 1985: 48; Lee 1995: 8–9, 304).[5] These individuals were generally men of prowess in their own right and had influence over their people. Thus, in the 1839 Malay uprising against the Siamese at Kedah it was reported that several of the "Penghulu Mukims" that had formerly taken refuge at Province Wellesley returned together with their people, of about 4,000 Malays ("Quedah, and Tuanku Mahomed Saad" in *AJMR* 1841: 114).

The people in such a system, that of "*Kampong* or *Mukim*,"[6] alternatively were to observe a traditional set of customs and rules (Alwi bin Sheikh Alhady 1967: 3–6). Thus according to the indigenous "*Adat Bersekampong*," people had to observe the welfare of the community, attend local mosque, render mutual assistance to all (i.e., "*bergotong-royong*") and help visitors to the area. Under these conditions the people were expected to render their service, loyalty and devotion (*bakti*) to the ruler as a means of acquiring the charisma of the latter (Sharifa Zaleha 1985: 48). Consequently the ruler would have possibly expected an equal devotion and loyalty from his subjects, in the fringes of the realm, with the *mukim* acting as another avenue through which loyalty toward the monarchy was emphasized, especially with the help of the religious leaders. Nevertheless, it is difficult to know if there was traditionally a religious official at the court through whom the Sultan could command the villages, although it is possible that the *Kathi* (i.e., Muslim judge) held that post.

A study of historic Kedah therefore offers yet another political model, a mixture of riverine, maritime and inland systems, to our understanding of the "Malay world." It is noteworthy that in contrast to Sumatra most recent scholars have neglected Kedah's traditional network of inland, including overland and trans-peninsular, routes and its development of a distinctive political structure (see Map 6).

This is in contrast to European reports from the sixteenth to the nineteenth century on the significance and magnitude of Kedah's vibrant trans-peninsular routes (Crawfurd 1830 I: 21–22, II: 154; Claine 1892: 389–396; Norman 1895: 529; Floris 1934: 42, 69; Hamilton 1922: 389–392; Cortesao 1944 I: 105–106). Furthermore, nearly all reports and eyewitness accounts of Kedah's trans-peninsular routes in fact confirm that they were relatively safe, well-maintained, monitored and that merchants and traders, in order to lower risks, often used them in conjunction with maritime routes circumnavigating the Malay Peninsula. Remarkably the

Map 6. The Malay Peninsula and Kedah's network of overland and trans-peninsular routes.

French in 1685 wanted to establish a factory in Siam, hoping they could avoid the Dutch at Melaka. They were promised a base in Kedah:

> the King of Siam has promised to give the French Company a port in the Kingdom of Kedah which is tributary to him, on the same side as Junk Ceylon (i.e., Phuket), and in this way those in Singora (i.e., Songkhla) could trade overland by river with those in Kedah without passing through the straits of Sunda or Malacca. (*Chaumont and Choisy* 1997: 178)

Kedah's connection to the trans-peninsular route was high on the French agenda in their decision to establish a trading factory in Southeast Asia.[7] In any event, several more recent scholars have, in the context of other studies on Southeast Asia, briefly examined aspects of Kedah's inland and trans-peninsular routes.

SCHOLARLY STUDIES OF KEDAH'S OVERLAND LINES OF COMMUNICATION

Paul Wheatley is possibly the earliest scholar to consider the economic viability of historic inland lines of communication in peninsular Southeast Asia. According to Wheatley (1961: xxi–xxxi) the interior of the Malay Peninsula consists of a virtually continuous mountain range that has traditionally divided the peninsula into two separate regions. These two regions he (1961: xxvi–xxvii) continues were, however, interconnected through a network of river and stream valleys and mountainous passes that acted in effect as "trans-peninsular route ways."

Of these, Wheatley (1961: xxvii–xxix) identifies eleven traditional routes in the peninsula operating from "Isthmus of Kra" to the north all the way south to the state of Johor. These routes he argues were in common use at least to the fifteenth century. Furthermore Wheatley (1961) continues that out of the eleven route-ways in the Peninsula six can be found from Kedah south: Kedah-Patani, Perak-Patani, Bernam-Pahang, Muar/Melaka-Kelantan, Muar/Melaka-Pahang, and finally the Sembrong route in Johor. Wheatley (1961: xxvii, 320) then considers the Kedah-Patani route to be the most northerly trans-peninsular route, as well the most prosperous route in the Malay Peninsula. Furthermore, Wheatley notes that parts of the Kedah-Patani route traditionally may have consisted of fully overland routes rather than partially overland and partly riverine. At any rate, Wheatley (1961: xxvii, 320) affirms that prior to the sixteenth century the chief commodities of rice and pepper could easily travel from the Kedah River into neighboring Patani, and thence to China using the trans-peninsular routes.

The six route-ways of the Malay Peninsula, as discussed by Wheatley (1961), were further investigated several decades later in 1986 by Geoffrey Benjamin. Benjamin, by examining the substance and quantity of archaeological remains found on each of the six route-ways, agrees with Wheatley on the economic precedence of the Kedah-Patani route.

In addition to Wheatley and Benjamin's arguments, Phan-ngam Gothamasan in a 1984 article entitled *"Some Aspects of the Political and Economic Systems of the Nineteenth Century Northern Malay States: Kedah, Kelantan and Trengganu A Comparative View"* suggests that the trans-peninsular routes to and from Kedah were not merely designed for trade and economic objectives. Rather Gothamasan (1984: 141–142) asserts that the inland routes, from the thirteenth century onward, were further instrumental in effecting Kedah's political dependency and tributary status on its northerly neighbor, Siam.[8] Thus, by drawing on Kedah's historic link with Siam he further asserts the political significance of the inland routes to other parts of mainland Southeast Asia. According to Gothamasan:

> By the end of the thirteenth century, the evidence indicates that Kedah had recognized the sovereignty of Siam. The dependency of Kedah on Siam can be attributed largely to the former's political-geographical setting which made her an important part linking of the trade routes between the Bay of Bengal and the Straits of Malacca to the land route of the Southern Siamese States. (1984: 141–142)

Furthermore, Gothamasan (1984: 142) further identifies other trade routes from Kedah to neighboring centers. These were the land routes to Nakhon Si Thammarat, Songkhla and Trengganu. Consequently, Gothamasan also reveals Kedah's elaborate network of trade routes that were alternatives to the trans-peninsular Patani route, as in the case of Songkhla, and other regional centers. R. K. Hall (1985: 325n) similarly notes that the uses of the trans-peninsular routes are quite ancient and may predate a 983 CE reference to an overland route at Songkhla. It is likely that this route had its western terminus at Kedah and was historically an alternate route connecting the east and west coasts of the Malay Peninsula.

More recently Phil King (2006: 4–6, 4n; 2006b: 87–88, 93) has discussed how in the nineteenth century a local knowledge of this complex network of overland routes assisted in the movement and ambush of invading Siamese forces, disruption of trade, and attacks on neighboring territories by Tengku Muhammad Saad/Sa'ad and the Kedah rebels. In addition King (2006: 8–10, 8n) is perhaps the only scholar to have, in the context of Kedah's nineteenth century history, drawn attention to the vitality and effectiveness of elephants in transporting tin to the coastal centers from tin mines further inland. King (2006b: 84–86, 89–90, 258–259) asserts that with the demise of Patani and its break up into federated territories by Siam in 1808/1810 it merely sponsored the rise of dynamic new polities such as the productive inland tin centre of Raman in its periphery, located between Kedah, Patani and upper Perak. King (2006b: 145–147, 149–151, 159, 162) then discusses Raman's nineteenth century Raja or chief seeking political and economic independence from Siam by exploiting the transportation and export of tin overland to Penang via Kedah, from the Klian Intan and Kroh mines. This route he argues was shorter and more economical than through the complex pathways and waterways linking Raman to upper Perak, as was realized by native or British traders and officials.

In addition, to the above scholars Michael Sullivan (1957), David E. Sopher (1977), and Lorraine Gesick (1995) assert that the inland routes, besides having an economic and political significance for Kedah and its neighbors, were also important in transmitting cultural and social aspects amongst the people concerned. Sullivan (1957) in particular argues for the possible historic connection or origin of a Kedah legend, of a tusked and bloodthirsty ruler called Raja Bersiong, to that of a similar tradition at Champa, in contemporary southern Vietnam. Thus he (1957: 290–293) suggests that this tradition may have traveled through the trans-peninsular routes that run between Merbok, in southern Kedah, to the region of Songkhla or Patani on the east coast of the Malay Peninsula and hence through the sea routes to Funan and Champa.

In a similar manner, Sopher (1977: 286) and Gesick (1995) believe that land routes from Kedah were partly the means for transmitting to Kedah legends and fables from Funan and possibly Champa, particularly the legend surrounding the rulers' possession of white blood, stories which are deeply rooted in neighboring Songkhla and Phattalung.[9] Sopher (1977: 286) even goes as far as to claim land route crossings from the towns of Kedah and Alor Setar, in northern Kedah, as the main avenues in the spread of the white blood legend to neighboring Songkhla and Phattalung. Consequently, Sopher identifies trading centers in northern Kedah, rather than coastal centers to the south as argued earlier by Sullivan (1957), as the terminus of the trans-peninsular routes.

KEDAH'S OVERLAND LINES OF COMMUNICATION

Shortly after arriving at Penang in 1821 Crawfurd, a British official, reports that on the 28th of December: "Juragan Soliman, an old Malay trader, came to call upon me. He had traveled into several parts of the interior of the Malayan peninsula, and often gone across it to the opposite coast" (Crawfurd 1830 I: 21).

Soliman gave Crawfurd an eyewitness account of two trans-peninsular routes that he had personally used, as well as an overland route to the tin mines of Patani that he frequented. According to him the trans-peninsular route:

> from Trang, on the western coast, to Ligor on the eastern, the distance, by elephants, is but three days' journey: and a man on foot can travel despatch in two. From Queda to Sungora,[10] the nearest Siamese province to the Malays, on the side of the Gulf of Siam, he says that merc-

handize is carried on elephants in five days. This last route is so safe and expeditious, that a great deal of merchandize is sent by it; and it is not uncommon for native vessels from Siam, to send back half their returns in this direction, as well for expedition as to divide the risk. [*sic*] (Crawfurd 1830 I: 21–22)

The complexity of the terrain and the difficulty of getting to the rich tin mines of Kroh, at Patani, were then explained by Soliman to Crawfurd:

> From the mouth of the river Muda, in the territory of Kedah, . . . to nearly the foot of the Patani hills, is a voyage of ninety-six hours in boats, by a very winding course. From thence four hours' journey on elephants carries the traveler across the mountains to Kroh, in the Patani territories, where there are tin mines. (Crawfurd 1830 I: 22)

Soliman's report on the trans-peninsular routes, at Trang and Kedah, and his vivid description of the overland route to Patani is unprecedented. In particular his report sheds further light into the trans-peninsular route ways, the modes of transport and the duration of the trips. Similarly it signifies that Malay traders, like Soliman, as well as foreign traders, e.g., the Siamese, would regularly use more than one trade route, in conjunction to the maritime routes, and had substantial knowledge about the time, risk factors and costs involved. Conversely, the timing of the meeting between Crawfurd and Soliman is significant since it only happened a month after the 1821 Siamese invasion of Kedah, which meant a disruption to the trans-peninsular and overland routes. Hence Soliman's comments reflect his knowledge and use of the trans-peninsular and overland routes prior to the Siamese invasion.

Besides in describing his use of the trans-peninsular routes at Kedah, Soliman suggests that the route to Songkhla was "safer" than a similar but shorter route operating further north at Trang. Yet he provides no explanation on what he meant by the term, or on why the Kedah route was safer. Thomas Forrest, an eighteenth century English visitor to Southeast Asia, reports on the failures of the Siamese to establish a trans-peninsular route in 1782 at Phuket to the north of Trang. According to Forrest: "About the year 1782, in return for many China articles they got from Siam partly over land, they returned tin, the same way; but the project was given up in 1784, it not answering the expense to send tin across the isthmus" (Forrest 1792: 33).

In consequence Forrest attributes the failure of Phuket's trans-peninsular route to be predominantly due to the high expenses involved. It is therefore possible that part of the expense of sending tin, along the trans-peninsular pathways, at Phuket involved safety factors, such as the loss of merchandise due to theft and robbery. Theft and robbery along the trans-peninsular routes may have been why Soliman felt the Kedah route was safer. Alternatively it is possible that there were more bureaucratic hurdles, tolls (e.g., tolls levied on boats to dredge and clear the silting of the waterways, as noted by Smyth 1895: 402, 404, 409), customs or taxes (and possibly bandits) in the Siamese provinces to the north of Kedah, e.g., at Nakhon Si Thammarat, thus hampering trade. Certainly a seventeenth century English report, by a Mr. Bladwell, on the viability of using the Tenasserim to Patani trans-peninsular route rejected the idea solely based on its high charges. According to the report: "the Muslims at Patani do supply that place, with fine goods per via Tenasserim, but they carry them 40 days by land, and pay several Customs and are at above 50 percent charges more than the goods that go by shipping so that if we used that trade, we shall quickly beat them" (*Original Correspondence* [No. 2983], 10th of December 1663, Fort St. George to the East India Company).

It is difficult to speculate on the reasons behind Soliman's earlier remark although royal patronage in providing security and regular control or maintenance of the pathways, as well as a support and emergency system in place, e.g., travel lodges or access to elephants, buffaloes and bulls used in transport, seem to have been paramount factors in the routes' viability.[11]

Soliman's report also makes a distinction between the trans-peninsular routes and the shorter routes to the tin mines inland at Patani. Both routes were significant to the trade of Kedah but unique in their own ways, although the trans-peninsular route appears to have been more accessible. Hence, the hindrance to the safe passage to the tin mines at Patani had more to do with the use of complex river passageways and the land paths than robbery or theft. The tedious and timely method of procuring tin from the Kroh mines at Patani is similarly deprecated in an 1821 official dispatch letter from Penang that coincides with Soliman's report (*SSFR* 83, 27th December 1821, Letter to Lord Minto the Governor General in Fort William).[12] According to this information the only viable option of procuring tin from the Kroh mines at Patani was through the use of the Kuala Muda River system as it extended all the way from Kedah's coastline into Patani territory. In Patani the tin then was "conveyed on elephants" for six miles to get to the banks of the river "being about six hours journey."[13]

Certain facts appear to be missing from Soliman's account by Crawfurd. For example Crawfurd does not elaborate why the meeting with Soliman took place, why the detailed and descriptive reports were told or how he was acquainted with him. Skinner (see notes in *Syair Sultan Maulana* 1985: 270n) speculates that the person mentioned by Crawfurd as "Juragan Soliman" is one and the same as "*Jeragan* Sulaiman" [*sic*], a Malay skipper involved in the joint Kedah-Siamese naval battle of 1809/1811 against Burma, and referred to in the indigenous source of *Syair Sultan Maulana* (1985: 86–87).[14] Further to Skinner's insight it must be added that *Jeragan* Sulaiman was Malay but not a native of Kedah. In a subsequent verse in *Syair Sultan Maulana* (1985: 215) the author praises

"Jeragan Sulaiman" but emphasizes that *"sugguh pun dia dagang pinjaman"* [i.e., "although he was a foreigner on loan to us"]. Thus if Skinner is correct in identifying *Jeragan* Sulaiman then he must have been a man of much influence, with substantial knowledge of Kedah and the Siamese coast on the Bay of Bengal. Furthermore, he seems to have been popular with Penang's Governor John Bannerman as he was entrusted with his negotiations with the Kroh chiefs in 1818 Patani (King 2006b: 86n).

The trans-peninsular routes at Kedah would therefore enable the "Inland Merchants" [sic] such as Soliman, and the local caravan trade, referred to in the early part of the seventeenth century as *"caffala"* [sic], to cross from one side of the Malay Peninsula to the other, in a relatively short space of time (Floris 1934: 69).[15] Trading with the "Inland Merchants" of Kedah was similarly on the agenda, when in 1668 the British begun to reassess their strategy and trade in Southeast Asia. According to the report: "we are informed by a merchant that is well acquainted with the country, there may be a great trade driven, and very profitable when once the Inland Merchants shall find they may be yearly furnished with goods proper to them" [sic] (*Factory Records Miscellaneous* [volume 2], November 1668, General Letter from Surat to the Factory Court).

Little is known however about the early history and use of the trans-peninsular routes between Kedah, on the west coast, and the east coast of the Malay Peninsula, although Hall's (1985: 325n) earlier reference to the usage of an undetermined overland route in about 983 CE to Songkhla may in fact suggest its connection to Kedah. What is more, is Benjamin's (1986) archaeological study of numerous artifacts, predominantly pottery, found along the historic pathways from Kedah to Songkhla. These may imply the operation of a vibrant east-west route for more than a thousand years. Much evidence and clues have however been destroyed due to environmental factors, as well as the fact that settlements on the east and west coasts of the Peninsula have continuously shifted sites. In the case of Songkhla it is therefore thought that only in the past four centuries the town has moved about three times (Stargardt 1973: 5–29; Choungsakul 2006: 45–46).[16] Similarly at Kedah there were multiple overland routes that separately, or simultaneously, extended and operated to the centre/s at Songkhla (such an ancient route between Songkhla reaching Perlis River, see Choungsakul 2006: 52). Hence complicating the understanding of a single trans-peninsular route, that connected Kedah's entrepot to Songkhla.

Tome Pires, a Portuguese visitor to Kedah circa 1512–1515, is perhaps the earliest European to make a reference to Kedah's overland routes. According to him goods to Siam from Kedah generally took "three or four days by land" (Cortesao 1944 I: 106).[17] The remark by Pires is indeed ambiguous and is not entirely clear if he was referring to the trans-peninsular route, from the coast of Kedah across the Peninsula, e.g., into Patani or Songkhla, or the overland route from northern Kedah into Siamese territories. Nevertheless, a century later, in about 1613, Peter Floris, a Dutchman working for the English and perhaps the first European to give an eyewitness account of the Kedah-Patani trans-peninsular route, suggests that it is a "ten-day journey" (Floris 1934: 69). Here the ten-day journey was between the main ports of Kedah, likely Kuala Kedah, and Patani's main port. The Kedah to Patani route was also reported to be popular with Muslim and Portuguese traders and much cloth brought to Patani from Kedah, as reported by an English trader in 1614 Patani (see *LREIC* 1 [No. 167], 5th of October 1614, Adam Denton to the East India Company). The connection of Kedah's trans-peninsular routes to a network of overland routes in Southeast Asia further enhanced its popularity for traders and travelers. This connection meant their avoiding of delays, problems, and risks often associated with sea travel as a result of the monsoon season, piracy and colonial or indigenous political rivalries. A combination of these factors and Kedah's link to a network of overland routes may thus best explain the choice by Samuel Baron, a Dutch trader working for the British to travel in the early 1690s by ship from Madras to Kedah in order to continue by land to Nakhon Si Thammarats and his final destination at Ayutthaya (Dutch Records [volume 50], 24th of January 1695, The factors at Batavia to the Council of Seventeen, cited at length in *Records of the Relations* 1915/1917 V: 132).

From various reports and accounts on Kedah it appears that there were traditionally two routes commonly used in the east-west trade in the north of the Malay Peninsula: Kedah/Songkhla and Kedah/Patani. Essentially, the use of these trans-peninsular routes was further enhanced through a number of valleys or defiles, in particular "Genting Pahat" in the case of Patani that cut through the continuous and high mountain ranges in the Malay Peninsula (Low 1837: 103; Bowring 1857 II: 49; Hamilton 1922: 388).[18] There were also shorter land routes connecting Kedah to Patani, Perak, Trang or further away to Phattalung, Nakhon Si Thammarat, Kelantan and Pahang, although some of these routes may have linked to other pathways and with the popularity of some of them are questionable.

In the case of Perak it seems Kedah's inland town of Baling, a large inland trade center, and its southern coastal towns benefited from a combination of direct overland routes, especially through the lowest pass of the Kroh Plateau near Padang Niring Todok, and river based lines of communication, at least from the seventeenth century onward (Birch 1910: 142–145; Winstedt 1936: 166; Memorandum by Albinus 1954: 28). The rich Perak tin mines of Larut and Klian Intan were also easily reachable and the trip was brief. Thus the Intan tin mine was said to be "only two days travel away" from Kedah, or about 12 miles to Baling, and the distance for tin to be transported from the headwaters of the Larut tributaries to Kedah was only fifteen miles (Andaya 1979: 112, 148; King 2006b: 147). But the trip to the inland centers and mines of Patani, e.g., the

Kroh tin mines or the gold mines at Ulu Sai, would take roughly four to six days as reported elsewhere (*SSFR* 83, 27 December 1821, Letter to Lord Minto the Governor General in Fort William; Crawfurd 1830 I: 22; *Syair Sultan Maulana* 1985: 56–57; Brailey 1999: 537). Conversely, the inland route to Kelantan or Rahang [sic] (likely Pahang) involved travelling by boat from Kedah's Muda River, in the south, and then to Kuala Kupang taking the overland route (Daly 1882: 404).[19] This likely followed a similar path to that of Kroh, cited earlier by Soliman, but may have diverged along the way. It was also possible to take the overland routes from Kedah to Patani and then take the overland route south into Raman, Ligeh, *ulu* Kelantan and up the Lebih into Pahang, as was taken in 1900 by members of the Cambridge Exploring Expedition (The Cambridge Exploring Expedition to the Siamese-Malay States 1900: 915–916; Skeat 1900: 73–77).

In consequence, the extended network of overland, riverine and maritime trade routes further supplemented Kedah's trans-peninsular routes and trade to the nearby regions on both sides of the Malay Peninsula and beyond. As a result, in the case of the town of Songkhla, it is said that its safe harbor historically received and sent ships to China; while, its network of waterways and pathways (see Figure 3) enabled goods and people to easily travel north, west and south (into Bangkok, Trang, Nakorn Sri Thammarat, Phattalung and south to Patani). (See Moor 1837: 110–117; Smyth 1898: 465–489; Light 1938: 123; Stargardt 1973: 5–29; Choungsakul 2006: 44–65.)[20]

The Thai source of *Phongsawadan Muang Zaiburi* (1990: 100), written predominantly in the nineteenth century, similarly refers to the mid-nineteenth century visits by Kedah's ruler, "Phraya Zaiburi," to Bangkok as part of royal audiences. Kedah's rulers therefore traveled to Songkhla by the land route from Kedah. From there he traveled south to Singapore in order to catch a steamer from there to Bangkok. It was therefore not unusual for goods imported through Kedah's maritime trade routes to end up in Trang, Bangkok or China through the trading centre of Songkhla.

Alternatively, it is possible that the Malay, Siamese, and/or Chinese traders—referred to by Soliman, Crawfurd and others—would take their merchandise to Songkhla and then travel overland to the ports, or inland centers, of Kedah in order to sell, transfer or trans-ship their goods using the maritime and inland lines of communication.

The complex nature of travel on Kedah's network of overland routes did not necessarily mean that they were tedious. Rather as was noticed by Anderson in 1824, Logan in 1850, and D. D. Daly (nineteenth century visitors to the area) even in shallow parts of rivers, such as in ascending Kedah River or Muda River, passed a large network of small *kampongs* or villages (Anderson 1824: 168–169, 173; Daly 1875: 403; Logan notes at Kedah in 1850 cited by Ahmat 1984: 2). Hence, they were not remote,

Figure 3. The Harbor of Songkhla. Smyth, W. H. (1898). Journeys in the Siamese East Coast States. *The Geographical Journal*, 11 (No. 5, May), 465–489.

depopulated or rundown routes. W. G. Maxwell (1882: 52–53) reports that a *kampong* on a trade route to Patani, during his visit in 1876, had shifted site as its inhabitants were fed up with the continuous travelers and the traffic.

The Kedah ruler further controlled and monitored his outer areas and settlements, including the inland rivers and pathways, through the appointment of a network of loyal chiefs and officials. Traditionally regional chiefs or *penghulus* of Kedah's 128 *mukims*, were therefore assigned by Kedah's ruler to oversee the well being, agreements (for rent of animals, boats and/or porters) and security of the expeditions inland, as was observed by Maxwell in 1876, Jules M. Claine (a late nineteenth century French traveler to Kedah in 1889–1890) and separately in 1899 by F. F. Laidlaw on border areas between Upper Perak and Kedah (Maxwell 1882: 62; Claine 1892: 394–396; Laidlaw 1953: 158–159; Newbold 1971 II: 20, 22; Bonney 1971: 9n). But the elephants, the dugouts, the bulls and buffaloes used for transportation, did not necessarily belong to the Sultan or the *penghulu* as was observed by Maxwell (1882: 62) and Laidlaw (1953: 159). Hence the travelers had to negotiate with the owners of the animals separately. Additionally, there were traditionally caravanserai, or lodges, and stations along the main pathways whereby the inland *caffula*, or expeditions, could exchange, leave behind or recruit elephants, buffaloes, and bulls used to transport goods, as well as porters and guides (see Figure 4).

Other than the *penghulu mukim* and his people who assisted, monitored and kept security for inland expeditions it in remoter pathways the *orang asli* of Kedah played a similar role. Traditionally *orang asli* of Kedah consisted of several groups, particularly Semang, Bila/Wila, Pangan and Kensieu/Kensiu, each with modest numbers (Roberts 1837: 410–415; Lo-

Figure 4. Expedition preparing to depart from "maison de voyageurs" (i.e., a travelers lodge) in Kedah on its way to Songkhla. Smyth, W. H. (1898). Journeys in the Siamese East Coast States. *The Geographical Journal*, 11 (No. 5, May), 465–489.

gan 1881: 83–92; Skeat and Blagden 1906; Evans 1937: 12–20, 24). They were also active inland and on the peripheral areas, thus it would have made sense for the ruler and his officials to seek their strategic allegiance (Banks 1983: 23).[21] In order to further obtain the loyalty of these *orang asli* groups in Kedah, *datus*, or tribal chiefs, were appointed amongst them.[22] Newbold (1971 II: 19) reports, from information supplied to him by the ex-Sultan of Kedah, that power was traditionally divided at Kedah amongst the four principal officials (i.e., the *Bendahara, Laksamana, Maharajah Lela* and the *Temenggong*) but it was the "eight *datus*," or "tribal chiefs," that enforced the rules amongst their peoples. Thus it is likely that the *orang asli* tribes had chiefs amongst themselves and were recognized by the Malay rulers of Kedah. There is indeed a 1870s report of an anonymous European visitor and his party meeting the chief of the Semang tribe at a remote and desolate inland route along Kedah and Patani territory (Miscellaneous Notices 1878: 111–113). According to the report the Semang chief had previously been given the title of *"datu"* and "protection" of the Raja of Kedah "by whose orders they roamed unmolested through his country." The chief was also contrary to his people wearing a symbolic "sarong" given to him by the ruler of Kedah. Consequently the *orang asli* chief and his peoples appear to have been given substantial recognition and protection by the ruler. Likewise, they were active in patrolling remote and isolated outposts in the fringes of the realm. Hence it is likely that traditionally chiefs were appointed amongst the *orang asli* and that their alliances, survival techniques, knowledge, and expertise were sought by the ruling elites of Kedah.

On the other hand, the loyalty of the *orang asli* peoples to the ruler at Kedah can be further explained through indigenous traditions, oath taking, *bakti*, a foundation or covenant myth and popular stories. Andaya (2002: 33) in his study of *Orang Asli and the Melayu in the History of the Malay Peninsula* has gone as far as suggesting that *Hikayat Merong Mahawangsa* "best captures the tone of mutual respect in the early relationship between the *orang asli* populations and the Melayu." Nevertheless, aspects of *Hikayat Merong Mahawangsa* (Low 1849: 3, 9) continue to remain ambiguous when dealing with the *orang asli* and their relationship to the *raksasas* or the *gergasis*. Hence the *raksasas* and the *gergasis* in a number of stories have the undertone of being one and the same as the *orang asli* and at other times are different to them. In consequence in the *Hikayat* it was wrong for a person of pure royal blood to have married a *gergasi* woman (such as in the case of Raja Bersiong's father) as it ended in disaster when their child developed tusks and became a cannibal. Yet Merong Mahawangsa, the founder of the dynasty, came to power only after he was invited by the *penghulu* of the *gergasis* and *raksasas* to rule over Kedah. Similarly Merong Mahawangsa's son, who became Kedah's second ruler, was the offspring of Merong Mahawangsa having married a wife, back in Rum, that had a *"gergasi"* as a father and a mother descended from a *"raksasa."*

Alternatively, there is the *Hikayat's* story of Raja Kelana Hitam's attempt to become ruler of Kedah because it had no King. He therefore asked the chiefs of the Semang, Bila, *rakyat bukit* (the hill people) and the Sakai ethnic groups (or *"bangsa"* in Malay) of Kedah to help him find a settlement there. They performed this task, and then came to serve him faithfully. Raja Kelana Hitam's kingdom was then later attacked by monsters (i.e., *gergasi*) and the four *bangsa* suffered the brunt of the fighting and their dead were piled in heaps like mountains to measure their bravery (Andaya 2002: 34–35). In this aspect of the *Hikayat* the *gergasi* are considered the enemy.[23] Newbold (1971 I: 330–331) also conveys a summary of *Hikayat Proat Nang Meri*, a Malay text, given to him by the secretary of the ex-ruler of Kedah in which the prince hero of the story successfully and heroically opposes the persecution of the *raksasas* and *gergasis* and finally marries their queen. Thus these stories and royal traditions further emphasized the traditional bond between the ruler, the *orang asli* and the Malay population. Likewise, they would have reasserted their loyalty toward the ruler and his chiefs in supporting the inland *caffulas*, gathering intelligence, guiding, and patrolling the more remote routes (particularly against foreign kidnappers and foreign troop movements).

The complex network of small streams and rivers in combination with mountains, hills and thick forests meant unnecessary hazards and time consuming travelling complications. Additionally the rivers were winding as was the case of the Kuala Muda River noted earlier in Soliman's (Crawfurd 1830 I: 22) report and Ketil River connecting to Baling, as noted by an eyewitness report by E. W. Birch in the nineteenth century that it took between six to eleven nights travel from Kedah's southern coastline (Birch 1910: 145). Hence, most of these were only navigable upriver for short distances; whereas, the rest of the river was restricted to low stout dug-outs, flat bottomed boats and bamboo rafts (Daly 1882: 403; Logan 1885: 174; Koenig 1894: 129, 131; Mohamed Radzi 1956: 27; Dobby 1951: 314). This employment of bamboo rafts and smaller vessels was also true for inland rivers and streams that were considered as shallow (Daly 1882: 407–408). Meanwhile, many smaller rivers and streams on Kedah's coastline were not navigable even with small canoes. This includes Kuala Yen, a small rivulet close to Kedah Peak or *Gunong* Jerai. According to an 1894 account by F. W. Irby and G. A. Lefroy the Kuala Yen was "the shore is so shallow that it is not possible to approach even with a small launch, within half a mile, and even native canoes cannot be paddled into the stream at low water" (1905: 76).

Alternatively, some of these smaller rivers, such as Sungei Kiti, were so narrow that they were easily blocked by fallen timber (Daly 1882: 403). Correspondingly, the travel between the two termini of the trans-peninsular and overland routes does not necessarily mean that they were not susceptible to environmental challenges and regional conflicts or tensions.

Foremost to the environmental disruption of Kedah's trans-peninsular routes were the seasonal floods, the thick or impregnable forests, wild animals, the terrain, the heat, silting of rivers and diseases.[24] These floods were often caused by the monsoon storms occurring at different times, on either the east or west coast of the Malay Peninsula. Nonetheless, in the case of Kedah the rains associated with the monsoon storms were normally spread out during the season, with little destruction or flooding (Koenig 1894: 129; Dobby 1951: 305). In contrast, more destructive monsoons and floods seem to be recorded to the east of the Titi Wangsa range, particularly at Patani, on the east coast of the Malay Peninsula (Daly 1882: 406; Floris 1934: 69; Dobby 1951: 299). In surveying the mining areas of Siam in the 1890s, H. W. Smyth (1895: 421) reports that "the east coast of the peninsula are completely shut up by bad weather the whole of the north-east monsoon season, and the only way out of them is thus across the country to the west coast" [sic]. In consequence, traders and travelers by travelling in different times seem to have generally avoided the possible floods as well as the monsoon season on either side of the Malay Peninsula.[25] But, there were instances whereby both sides of Titi Wangsa range were flooded concurrently thus disrupting the trans-peninsular routes. Hence, Floris in 1613 reports that the floods between Kedah and Patani were so bad in that year that rather than the 10 day journey he had received a letter that took 36 days to travel across the

Peninsula (Floris 1934: 69). Reports of a flood of that magnitude in Kedah may seem rare; but undoubtedly it had a profound effect on the transpeninsular trade and movement of people. On the other hand, one wonders if the 1617 report of disease at Kedah and the death of two thirds of its 40,000 population was a direct result of the devastation caused by the 1613 floods (Beaulieu 1705 I: 246).

Despite the consequences, Kedah's historic connection to the transpeninsular routes meant that its politics and economy were simultaneously intertwined with events on the east coast of the peninsula. Often this meant the continuance or disruption of the flow of key commodities for both local consumption and re-export, such as the overland gold and tin trade from Kelantan and Patani (Low 1837: 103n; Bowrey 1905: 280; Cortesao 1944 I: 106; Bassett 1989b: 626).

In consequence, Kedah's 1646 decision to join Songkhla against Ayutthaya and its subsequent 1647 capture of Phattalung can be partly interpreted as a result of its connection with its trans-peninsular partner (Smith 1977: 32; Choungsakul 2006: 45; Bradley 2009: 279; see Maps 6 and 7).[26] Meanwhile, the Kedah ruler's vigorous attempt in 1671 to negotiate a peace treaty between Patani and Songkhla, both on the east coast of the Malay Peninsula, was less of being a "Good Samaritan" and more to do with the disruption of its trans-peninsular route trade.[27] No wonder then that in February 1671 in the report of two British agents from Kedah, Portman and Davis, about the Sultan's recent dispatch of peace envoys to both Patani and Songkhla were crucial: "as indeed it concerned him; for unless ye way be clear between those two places no Cloth can be carried up or Elephants brought down with safety which will be a great hindrance to this trade" [sic] (Surat Factory Records [volume 105], 3rd of February 1671, George Davis and John Portman at Kedah to the President and Council at Surat, cited at length in *Records of the Relations* 1915/1917 II: 101).

Similarly it is most likely that the 1789 attack on Songkhla by Syed Ali, the Siak sea lord based on Siantan Island,[28] was orchestrated on behalf of the Kedah Sultan. According to the incident Syed Ali and his Ilanun allies attacked Songkhla in June of that year. Then burned the city, seized two Chinese junks, and carried off a large number of people (Warren 1981: 158; Barnard 2003: 154). Barnard (2003: 154) speculates that the raid may have been an attempt by Syed Ali to "force more traffic and goods toward Siak's ports or raiding vessels." But it is equally possible that the attack was carried out on behalf of Kedah. Following the attack on Songkhla the British governor of Penang, Sir Francis Light, in a dispatch to the Governor General of India suggested that the Siamese would hold Kedah and Terengganu responsible for the attack and indicated the strong possibility of Siamese punitive action (*SSFR* 2, 17th July 1789, Francis Light to Governor General; also Bonney 1971: 87n).[29] It is therefore possible that Kedah and Trengganu (and possibly Kelantan) were in

Map 7. The Kedah-Songkhla trans-peninsular route, as traveled by Jules M. Claine (1892: 389) in 1889–1890 CE.

fact behind the attack and in recruiting Syed Ali and his forces. All these territories had in fact witnessed Siamese wrath and retaliatory reprisals a few years earlier in 1786 against their neighbor Patani after it had refused to recognize Siamese suzerainty and control.[30] The Siamese incursion into Patani that year was so devastating that it resulted in about 15,000 people taking refuge in Kedah and possibly more in other territories, as well as disrupting the flow of tin (*SSFR* 1, 1786, Accounts of Quedah and adjacent countries by M. Topping; *SSFR* 2, 22nd of January 1787, Letters from Fort Cornwallis to Fort William; *SSFR* 2, 17th July 1789, Francis Light to Governor General). Certainly by attacking Patani the Siamese appear to have wanted to make its desolation an example to its neighbors and in reasserting their power and control in the region, following Burma's defeat of Ayutthaya in 1767.

Consequently Kedah and Trengganu had good reasons to fear Siam and in doing so attempted to shift attention away from their borders. In addition, Songkhla's overland routes acted as a gateway to Siamese forces and supplies in the event of war. Hence the intention by Kedah and Trengganu may have been to ultimately force the Siamese troops to stay on the east coast and defend Songkhla, rather than planning further attacks elsewhere. The perception of a Siamese invasion of Kedah, diminishing or loss of control over the birds nest islands in the Gulf of Bengal, as a result of Siamese demands and their ensuing war with Burma, together with the Siamese unrelenting demands for men, arms and money, as argued by Bonney (1971: 84), was in fact so real that its ruler, Sultan Abdullah, may have contemplated in 1788 to make a surprise attack on Phattalung, Songkhla, and Nakhon Si Thammarat. Similarly the recruitment of the Siak sea lord may have heralded Kedah's attempt to seek further protection, defense treaties or allies after failing to gain similar support amongst European nations against a possible Siamese attack. Few months prior to the June 1789 attack on Songkhla, in April, Light (*SSFR* 2, 17 July 1789, Francis Light to Governor General) reported that the Sultan had approached the British, Dutch, and the French in seeking support, alliance, and weapons against a foreign attack on its territory. Conversely, it is also possible that the attack on Songkhla was part of a well-coordinated and clandestine plan by Kedah and Trengganu—and perhaps Kelantan and Patani—to overthrow Siamese control in the region.[31] This may further explain the concurrent 1789–1791 rebellion against the Siamese authorities at Patani (Syukri 1985: 58–59; Yegar 2002: 75; Choungsakul 2006: 47; Bradley 2009: 291).

In addition, Kedah's complex network of overland routes and waterways often resulted in kidnapping, foreign intrusion, ambush, smuggling, and refuge inland at times of confusion and turmoil. Kidnapping of women and children was not only confined to the coastal and island regions of Kedah and at the hands of pirates, as argued in the previous chapter, but involved areas that were further inland as well in the periphery (such as the more remote fruit or rice-fields). Anna Harriette Leonowens (1870: 18–21), the English governess that in the 1860s spent six years at the royal palace at Bangkok recalls a number of conversations she had with an older woman that was the custodian of the harem. The woman was a native of Kedah but about sixty years ago she was together with her sister and some other girls kidnapped by "a party of Siamese adventurers" when they were working in the fields. The girls were then taken back to Siam and sold as slaves. What is interesting is that the woman and the other girls were kidnapped several years prior to the 1821 Siamese invasion. It is thus possible that the same roads were used by the Siamese in 1821 to make their surprise attack on Kedah. The use of the overland routes for smuggling or a surprise attack was not only a concern to Kedah but also its neighbors.[32] In January 1628 the Dutch reported that the news of Aceh preparing an invading armada in Sumatra was indeed taken seriously at Patani as it was interpreted to suggest the possible invasion of Kedah by sea and push into Patani by land (Letter from Batavia, 6th of January 1628, in *Bescheiden omtrent zijn Bedrijf in Indie* 1920 V: 64).[33] In the case of Perak in 1749 and 1768–1769 however it was claimed that tin was taken and smuggled into Kedah from the tin mines of Larut, Rui, and Indah in *ulu*[34] Perak (Andaya 1979: 111–113, 281–283, 291; Bassett 1990: 68).[35] Thus, Perak's ruler and his Dutch partners accused Kedah's ruler of being behind the smuggling. The same smuggling route was perhaps taken in 1822 by eighty Siamese and 300 Malays entering Perak overland clandestinely and capturing a "military post" on behalf of the Raja of Ligor (*SSFR* 99, 28th February 1825, Fort Cornwallis to the Governor General in Council in Fort William).[36] Furthermore, during the 1838–1839 uprisings in Kelantan, Patani and other Malay territorial units in Siam's southern areas, as well as their success in outmaneuvering Siamese assaults it was believed that intelligence received from emissaries to the Kedah's Sultan's nephew, Tengku Muhammad Saad, was instrumental to their success.[37] These emissaries were believed to have made effective use of the complex network of overland routes from Kedah in order to reach their destinations, exchange or gather intelligence, and incite further rebellion against the Siamese elsewhere. Consequently when in 1839 the Siamese planned a surprise attack on Kelantan, the Siamese ruler, Rama III, acknowledged the possibility that "Wwen Tengku Mat Saad[38] learns that the army is going down to Kelantan, he will send someone to incite them to rebellion and the trouble will break out again. We cannot afford to be careless in dealing with the situation. If they rebel again, we shall really be up against it" [sic] (9th Dispatch, Udomsombat et al. 1993: 188).

But the Malay uses of the complex network of the overland and transpeninsular routes against the Siamese forces were not restricted to Kedah and its neighbors. From the comments by Soliman and Crawfurd (1830) it is clear that local traders were familiar with the use of a number of transpeninsular routes across the Malay Peninsula. With the liberation of Kedah by the Malays in 1839 the Siamese ruler, Rama III, received intelligence from Chaiya, a key town about 600 kilometers south of Bangkok on the Gulf of Siam and on the east of the Malay Peninsula, that Wan Mali, a relation of the Sultan, had captured Trang and other key Siamese ports, on the Bay of Bengal. Then there was further panic in Bangkok a few days later when there was no longer any form of communication arriving from Chaiya. Rama III in addressing his ministers then said, "As regards Chaiya, there's no news either — I wonder if Wan Mali will attack there? It was reported that thirty Malay ships had been seen at Ko Yao.[39] Here I am waiting for news but so far I have heard nothing — no one sends in any reports. What is going on?" (2nd Dispatch, Udomsombat et al. 1993: 86).

This was significant news at Bangkok as historically none of Siam's rebellious southern Malay states had little interest in threatening its central territories. The ambush on Chaiya never materialized. But the remarks by the Siamese ruler are indeed significant since Ko Yao is on the west coast of the Peninsula while Chaiya is on the east coast. Hence implying the possible use of the trans-peninsular route, such as the one mentioned by Crawfurd (1830 II: 154) from Pun-Pin to Chaiya or a path noted decades later by Smyth (1895: 421) from the Paklao village (to the north-east of Phuket) into the valley of the Bandon River and into Chaiya, by Wan Mali and his followers.[40]

The use of inland routes and waterways in Kedah was not only popular for trade and exploited in times of war and conflict, but they were also a source of refuge and avenues of escape in times of invasion. Kedah's rulers thus traditionally used the overland routes and pathways as avenues to sanctuary inland in times of political turmoil or emergency.

In consequence, Kedah's indigenous source, the *Hikayat Merong Mahawangsa* (Low 1849: 264–269, 314–316; Hikayat Merong Maha Wangsa or Kedah Annals 1916: 74–75; Winstedt 1938: 34) refers to Kedah's vampire style ruler, Raja Bersiong, escaping from his palace on the coastline deep into the forest and then taking refuge inland, close to Patani, following a successful and popular uprising against his tyranny.

In the same way, in 1619 the son of Kedah's ruler, was captured and taken alive to Aceh. He later managed to escape and take refuge inland at Perlis "about three days journey further into the country, for fear of the King of Aceh's army" (Beaulieu 1705: 245, 247). Remarkably he was able to rule and control much of the affairs of Kedah from this outpost. Similarly, the threat of an imminent attack by the Siamese or the Dutch in the latter part of the seventeenth century was likely the reason behind the remote location of Kedah's capital. On a visit to Kedah's ruler in circa 1669–1679, an English merchant Bowrey, was therefore required to be accompanied by an *"orang kaya"* (i.e., a nobleman or literary "a man of wealth or power"), travel upriver, then mount on elephants and travel quite a distance inland in order to arrive at the palace (Bowrey 1905: 271–272). On the other hand, there is the question of whether the escape of Kedah's Sultan to Penang Island to seek protection with the British went against the indigenous norms and traditions.[41] In fact in line with the above examples it would have been expected that the Sultan, upon the intelligence of a Siamese assault on Kedah, would have taken refuge inland, rather than escape into Penang. A parallel thus may be drawn between the 1821 events, that of Sultan of Kedah removing himself to Penang and Sultan Mahmud Syah of Johor in the early part of the sixteenth century. According to the *Sejarah Melayu* when Sultan Mahmud

Syah was urged by a faithful servant to abandon Bentan Island to escape from the Portuguese the events unfolded as follows:

"But Sultan Mahmud Shah refused to leave the palace: his intention was "if the Franks come, I will fight them here." The Sri Nara "diraja urged him to leave Bentan now that the city had fallen. But he replied, "When I came here, Sri Nara "diraja, I knew full well that Bentan was an island; and it was because I was determined that there should be no retreating that I took up my abode here! If I had thought of retreating, I should have done better to stay on the mainland. (But I did not do that), for it is the custom of Rajas that when their country falls to the foe, they die." And the Sri Nara "diraja said, "Our Highness is mistaken. Every country has a Raja, and if your Highness is granted length of days, we can find ten countries for you!" But Sultan Mahmud Shah answered, "Say no more, Sri Nara "diraja. Retreat from here I do not!" (Brown 1970: 184–185).

Bonney (1971), in his study of the pre-1821 Siamese invasion of Kedah, has effectively argued the legal possession of Penang Island and Province Wellesley by Kedah following its lease to the British in 1786. A similar argument was also put forward in the nineteenth century by leading British officers, residents, and merchants of Penang (Anderson 1824; Crawfurd 1830; Begbie 1834; Beighton 1888; Newbold 1971; Osborne 1987).[42] The ex-Sultan and his relations, particularly those leading the numerous uprisings at Kedah (1821–1842) likewise would reiterate this reality in most of their communications to the British, as well as in their quest to liberate Kedah. Thus the Sultan by removing himself to Penang was effectively on his own turf and with his peoples. What's more, there was always the possibility that he could get help from the British—or at least be in a position to buy arms from European merchants. This was in line with the words reiterated by Sultan Mahmud Shah at Bentan, and points toward an indigenous political system that the ruler by moving to an island in his domain demonstrated his intention not to flee from an invasion. Consequently, by removing himself to Penang the ex-Sultan was perhaps making a powerful statement to his own peoples of his intention to liberate Kedah at all costs and that he had not yet abandoned them.

The destruction of a trading centre did not necessarily mean the end of Kedah's trade or political infrastructure. Hence, both the riverine and maritime centers, including large islands, through their maritime and overland trade routes were able to quickly rise from the ashes and reclaim their former trade and political influences in the same vicinity. This is especially true in the aftermath of the seventeenth and eighteenth century Bugis invasion of the southern half of Kedah, as well as the 1821 Siamese invasion (Bastin 1964: 147n, 146–147; Lewis 1970: 120–121, 1975: 39; Bonney 1971: 29–40; Turnbull 1980: 80; Ali Haji Ibn Ahmad 1982: 147–150).[43]

Understandably in the aftermath of the 1821 Siamese invasion and the escape of Kedah's ruler to Penang it appears that the popularity of its routes began to wane.[44] In a number of "communications" received from "Siamese and Chinese traders" at Bangkok and Singapore by Crawfurd (1830 II: 152, 154), circa 1822–1826, he continues that the Kedah to Songkhla trans-peninsular route was still in use but the Trang to Nakhon Si Thammarat route was now being "the most frequented."[45] Hence, suggesting that the Kedah to Songkhla route was now less popular, or perhaps safer, with traders. The uncertainty or the mixed reports on the functionality and safety of the Kedah to Songkhla trans-peninsular route may explain the decision by W. E. Medhurst, of the London Missionary Society, in planning to cross the Malay Peninsula to Kedah from Songkhla in 1828. Tomlin (1831: 46) of the London Missionary Society mentions receiving a letter at Bangkok from Medhurst, dated Trengganu 1st of September 1828, of his future intention to proceed to Songkhla and hence to cross the Malay Peninsula to Kedah. With the ensuing rebellions in the 1830s it is however unlikely that any of Kedah's trans-peninsular routes were frequented by traders (King 2006: 87, 93). Indeed, the Siamese would have done their utmost to redirect traffic to their own routes to the north of Kedah (Rungswasdisab 2004: 101–118).[46] This may also explain Medhurst's decision (1838: 349–350) to rethink his original travel plan, instead taking a boat from Songkhla to the town of Pontianak in Borneo.

With the return of the royal house of Kedah in the early 1840s, however it seems there was an attempt to restart the trans-peninsular route. But Kedah had not only shrunk in area (especially with the loss of Perlis, Satun, Penang Island, and later the Krian region to Perak, see Gullick 1983: 42–82) it had also lost its regional niche particularly with the rise of British and other colonial powers, and their traders and shipping in South Asia, Southeast Asia, and the Far East. Hence the return of Kedah's ruler in 1841/1842 came into a completely different sociopolitical and economic setting than what was common previously. From the Thai source of *Phongsawadan Muang Zaiburi* (1990: 94) it appears that the trans-peninsular route to Songkhla was still functioning, in the mid-nineteenth century, and was used at least once by the ruler of Kedah in his travels to Bangkok. There is also a report by Fred A. Neale (1852: 122), an Englishman in the services of the Siamese ruler circa 1850–1852, that upon travelling by sea, south from Bangkok to Singapore, stopped briefly at Songkhla to meet the Raja there "so simply begging of him to forward our letters that we entrusted to his care, overland to Queda and Penang" [sic]. This report by Neale is significant too as it indicates the extensive knowledge of the Kedah-Songkhla trans-peninsular route in the mid-nineteenth century, although Neale does not specify where his knowledge of the route came from. But in the two reports mentioned in *Phongsawadan Muang Zaiburi* (1990) and Neale (1852) there is no mention of traders or other travelers taking the Kedah-Songkhla route. It seems that in the second half of the nineteenth century the Trang to Songkhla trans-peninsular route had become more popular with traders and travelers. Writing from India in 1878 but relying on sources collected earlier at Burma, Henry Croley reports that the Kedah to Songkhla road is still popular and remains one of the three remaining trans-peninsular routes connecting the Bay of Bengal to the Gulf of Siam. Croley (1878: 189) then continues that despite this the road from Trang to Nakhon Si Thammarat is the "more frequented" in the peninsula. Then there is a letter from Penang dated 8th of April 1883 by the French Commander Alfred J. Loftus (1883: 19–20) to Lieutenant Bellion, in charge of the French Government Kra (Survey) Expedition in the Siamese southern provinces. It appears that Loftus was well acquainted with the Malay Peninsula and its trans-peninsular routes. In reporting his expert assessment and the viability of a canal across the Malay Peninsula, Loftus mentions that his knowledge of the area extends for the past twenty-eight years. And that his knowledge of the trans-peninsular routes in the Malay Peninsula similarly extends beyond the Kra Expedition that he had participated in. Loftus then continues with an eyewitness report of the Kedah-Songkhla trans-peninsular route:

> I may say that such a scheme is impossible, for it is well known, that there is only one road, and very few jungle tracks across the Peninsula. The road I speak of extends from Songkhla to Kedah and is very serpentine and undulating among the hills in the interior, where it reaches an elevation of 1,100 to 1,300 feet. It is scarcely worth the name of a road, but it is the best across the Peninsula. The jungle tracks are very narrow and whilst running in various direction, are exceedingly tortuous and undulating, sometimes in valleys, and by the slopes of hills, and in some parts over their tops, at elevations from 50 to 800 feet. (1883: 19)

The eyewitness report by Loftus is significant. It not only confirms the continuation of the Kedah-Songkhla trans-peninsular route, but also implies that it remained the only surviving road across the Peninsula. A. H. Keane (1887: 16) reports that during the time of writing his book there was only a "rough road" across the Malay Peninsula, that went from Kedah's royal capital at Kota Star, i.e., Alor Setar, to Songkhla (see Map 7 of an 1889–1890 use of the same route by a French visitor). This road Keane (1887: 17) continues was relatively recent, dating to 1871 when it was officially opened at the time of the King of Siam's visit to Kedah. *Phongsawadan Muang Zaiburi* (1990: 100–102, 116n) similarly reports on the existence of a new "highway" between Kedah and Songkhla in the "Year of the Dog, Jattawa Saka, J. S. 1234" [sic] (i.e., 1872 CE).[47] This date corresponds to Keane's report, although it suggests the building of a new highway rather than a rough road. But there is no mention in the Siamese version of the event that the road was officially opened. Rather the report continues that the Siamese ruler noted the new highway when he took the overland route together with Kedah's ruler, to Songkhla, after the former had returned from Calcutta and was on his way back home to Bangkok. Furthermore, the *Phongsawadan Muang Zaiburi* continues that the Siamese ruler was pleased with Kedah's ruler, or "Phraya Zaiburi," as he was the driving force behind the construction of the new highway since he had:

> urged other Phraya and state councils of the neighboring tributaries together with Malay subjects to join efforts in constructing the new highway from Muang Zaiburi to the boundary of Muang Songkhla. This has been done with efficiency and without delay. Presently, the road serves as a route for traders and common people who can communicate with one another with much ease [sic]. (1990: 102)

This remark is of further interest as it also suggests that traders and people would make use of the new highway between Kedah and Songkhla two decades after the return of the royal family from exile. Additionally, it further proves the interest that Kedah's ruler continued to have with the continuance of the trans-peninsular roads. Smyth (1895: 414–415, 420) similarly reports the continuation of the Kedah-Songkhla trans-peninsular route and that during his visit "it is still much frequented by Siamese and Malays for purposes of local trade." Furthermore, he gives an eyewitness account of meeting an eclectic array of "Siamese-speaking Burmans, Tailings (or Mons), and Karens" [sic] traders at Songkhla that had also arrived there, to sell merchandise and purchase elephants, using a number of other routes. Nevertheless, Smyth (1895: 421) continues that the Kedah-Songkhla route "is on the line of the proposed railway, now just begun." Jules Claine (1892: 392–398), a French traveler, in about 1890, also took the previously mentioned Alor Setar to Songkhla route and further comments that the pathway was popular, well maintained and safe.[48] But the trip to Songkhla required him to travel all the way from Penang Island north by boat, to the Kedah River estuary and then upriver to Alor Setar in order to link to the trans-peninsular route (see Figure 5, Map 7). The tenuous and complex form of travel to Alor Setar, and hence to Songkhla, therefore meant valuable time loss and outlay for travelers from Penang. This may explain the building of the 1907 Kedah road linking Penang to Songkhla directly. But the road seems to have been of little practical use, since it was only two meters wide, as well as expensive to maintain (Choungsakul 2006: 56–57).[49]

Then again, it could be argued that the new road between Alor Setar and Songkhla, built in the second half of the nineteenth century, simply replaced an older path to Songkhla. Likewise, it seems that this road became the only trans-peninsular route to and from Kedah. Indeed with the return of Kedah's royalty in 1841/1842 the previously significant trans-peninsular routes between Kedah and Patani appear to have fallen

Figure 5. Kedah River at Alor Star. Claine, J. (1892). Un an en Malaisie, 1889–1890. *Le Tour Du Monde* (Paris), 63, 369–400.

into limited use, with only a mention of its existence in the 1890s by Smyth (1895: 420). A. W. Hamilton (1922: 389–392) in his 1922 study of the "The Old Kedah-Patani Trade-Route" asserts that this pathway across the peninsula had not been in use for some time. But the abandoning of the Kedah-Patani trans-peninsular route in the nineteenth century did not however mean an end to the combination of the shorter overland and riverine routes to Patani. In particular the route to the tin mines at Raman appears to have survived during and after the 1821 Siamese invasion of Kedah. Likewise, it was still possible to cross into Patani using the overland routes in *ulu* Perak at the turn of the nineteenth century and thereof to Songkhla, as was undertaken by Annandale and Robinson (1902: 407).

Anderson (1824: 171, 171n) reports on the transport of tin from the Kroh mines soon after the Siamese invasion "There are great obstructions at present to bringing the Tin down the Kwala Muda, being infested by Pirates some of the refugees from Quedah and the Lancavy Islands" [*sic*]. In a later note to this passage, likely in 1824, however Anderson continues that "considerable supply of Tin has been obtained from the Patani Country through the judicious arrangements of Mr. Maingy, the Superintendent of Wellesley Province and there is every prospect of an increasing Trade" [*sic*]. But the British success in obtaining tin from Patani was only short-lived. In an 1827 General Letter from the Superintendent of Province Wellesley it was remarked that the tin trade with Patani is no longer "profitable because of the Siamese restrictions" (*SSFR* 185, 25th of January 1827, General Letters: Received from Province Wellesley). The Siamese restrictions combined with the ensuing Malay rebellions on both sides of Titi Wangsa range similarly continued to disrupt the flow of tin and other commodities to the coast of Kedah and Penang (King 2006, 2006b). In the 1830s Low (1837: 101–102, 103n), attributed the disruption of overland trade to Siamese politics. According to Low (1837: 101–102, 103n) the Siamese intervention resulted in the "avenues to the tin mines" to be "blocked up" and that "gold dust" brought overland from Kelantan and Patani to be similarly stopped.

Nevertheless, with the 1840s return of peace and tranquility to the Malay territories of Kedah, Patani, and Kelantan, as well as the end of Perak's attempts to reclaim the mines at Raman, as argued by King (2006b: 89), it seems that there was a resumption of the overland trade.[50] The overland trade between Kedah to Raman in particular continued to prosper despite stiff competition in the 1850s onward from newly discovered or expanded tin mines in Perak (Khoo 1972; King 2006b: 89–90). But, Maxwell (1882: 59) reports that the Kroh mines "mentioned by Anderson" in 1824 "are now abandoned, probably the result of the liberal Malay policy of driving the hardest possible bargain with the Chinese." Nevertheless, Maxwell (1882: 59–60) during his visit to Patani in 1876 was astonished that despite the hefty tin tax, almost equal to the price paid for the metal before transport, the Kedah route continued to be the tin trade's choice from the Patani mines as it was the "safest route" to the market in Penang. Indeed the safety of the overland route in transporting tin from Raman to Kedah could be further explained by the nature of the alternate route through upper Perak. Travel through Kedah depended upon elephants, or was conducted on foot, while the connecting raft trip down the Perak River was a hazardous one given the various rapids (King 2006b: 150–151). In 1900 a border agreement with Siam shifted the borders of Perak all the way to the Kroh plateau. A 1905 prospectus gave licenses to British companies over large tracks of land at Raman (that of "Rahman Hydraulic" and "Rahman Tin"). This meant the annexation of Raman by Perak in July 1909. The transfer of Siamese control of Kedah to the British in 1909 gradually meant the beginning of the end for Kedah's overland routes (King 2006b: 145–146, 159).[51] In particular, the Siamese Railway Department signed an agreement in 1909 with the Government of the British Federated Malay States by which it secured a loan of four million sterling for the purpose of extending the railway from Petchaburi, southwards through southern Siam, to link up with the Federated States railway and Penang (Graham 1913: 423; Ratanapun 1961: 26–27; Brailey 1999: 536). By 1913 the survey work for the southern extension was completed and the section which crossed the peninsula from Trang on the west to Songkhla was open for traffic. Smyth (1895: 418) further argues that the growth of "English power" was combined with the development of the "steam navigation" which has "robbed the overland routes of the peninsula of their value."

British intervention in Kedah meanwhile came with the introduction of colonial residents at the royal court. Furthermore, the residents had to be consulted in all matters except religion and Malay customs, which became the responsibility of the Sultan. Hence the control, maintenance, monitoring, and economic benefits of the overland routes of Kedah were no longer associated with the Malay ruler. This loss of socioeconomic and political control of the realm to the British resident may further elucidate the Sultan's diminishing *bakti*, amongst his local chiefs and peoples on the periphery, as argued earlier by Banks (1983) and Carsten (1995). It is therefore not so coincidental that in his study of colonial Police records between 1909 and 1927, Cheah Boon Kheng (1981: 98–130) discovered that crimes such as theft (including that of bulls and elephants), gang robbery, and social banditry committed in Kedah had increased exceedingly, outweighing the combined total of the Federated Malay Sates (i.e., Perak, Pahang, Selangor, and Negeri Sembilan). The unprecedented rise in crime at the early part of the twentieth century Kedah differs radically to the relative peace, safety and order that reportedly it experienced years earlier (refer to the studies by Ratanapun 1961: 13–24, Ahmat 1970: 115–128; Haji Mahmud 1972a: 196–200). In the early 1890s, the Secretary of the Federated Malay States, Sir John Frederick Dickson, after visiting Kedah commented that it "stands out conspicuously above all the other states of the Peninsula (excepting one or two which have been long under British protection) in all the signs of successful and intelligent administration" [*sic*]. (See CO 273/168, 1890, Report of Sir F. Dickson's Visit to Kedah.)

Certainly, the colonial residents were able to expand their authority with roles no longer restricted to "advice" and "consultation" to the Sultan. In reality according to Syed Husin Ali (1975: 26–27), a noted Malay scholar: "Sultans became only symbols of Malay political sovereignty but without any authority to make decisions." Thus the colonial authorities provided the Rajas with protection and support. And for its finances and development the political institution of Kedah and its peoples came to rely on loans from European, Chinese and Indian financial institutions, pawnshops, and moneylenders (Wu 2003: 7, 57, 59, 92, 160, 184).

CONCLUSION

Undeniably Kedah has benefited immensely from its commanding links to a number of trans-peninsular routes that have historically connected the Bay of Bengal to the Gulf of Siam. The trans-peninsular routes were indeed enhanced through a number of valleys or defiles that effectively connected the east and west coasts of the Malay Peninsula. Of these trans-peninsular routes the Kedah-Patani and Kedah-Songkhla appear to have been the oldest and the most active. The routes are believed to have been in operation for more than 1,000 years and they appear to have impacted virtually all aspects of Kedah's economy as well as its sociopolitical infrastructure. The overland Kedah to Songkhla route in fact seems to have continued to the present time in the form of a highway and train (the trans-peninsular railway between Kedah and Songkhla was completed in 1918; see Ratanapun 1961: 71–72).

The elaborate network of Kedah's trans-peninsular routes and their ability to effectively link up with the maritime and overland lines of communications on both sides of the Malay Peninsula is unprecedented. Thus reports of peoples and merchandise being discharged or unloaded at the ports of Kedah, for the overland travel to Bangkok, Pahang, China, or other destinations are not unusual and can be further explained through a complex network of overland and sea based lines of communications.

To the maritime merchants and travelers to Kedah the overland routes offered yet another passage to avoid sailing around the Malay Peninsula. This alternative therefore enabled them to further avoid risks associated with the maritime travels, such as environmental factors (e.g., the destructive months of the monsoon winds) or other dangers (e.g., pirates or being intercepted by an unfriendly European or native fleet demanding a license to trade). Then there were perhaps the more experienced, cautious or wealthier merchants, as reported by Crawfurd (1830 I: 21–22), that preferred to lower the risk factor by sending their goods both ways.

On the other hand, it could be argued that Kedah was also attached to shorter pathways and routes that often complemented the trans-peninsular routes and were significant to the trade and economy of Kedah in general. These included the pathways and routes that terminated at a particular destination either within or outside the realm. The short routes to upstream destinations in neighboring domains of Patani and Perak traditionally provided Kedah with much of its tin ore for export. Nevertheless, the pathways to these destinations seem to have been more intricate than the trans-peninsular routes involving an admixture of travel partly on foot, boats, and elephants. Conversely, it is possible that the short routes within the realm were for inland trade or pathways to the collection centers, such as the inland town of Baling or the smaller rice collection centers. Products and goods from these centers similarly complemented the maritime or the overland trade and sustenance of Kedah.

Kedah's entrepots did not therefore simply act as centers whereby commodities, travelers and supplies were unloaded locally or transferred to other destinations by boats, as was traditionally the case in most other Malay realms. Rather the goods and the peoples were able to continue to their destinations overland, to either side of the Peninsula. This is indeed a significant aspect of a traditional Malay polity that was able to maintain its maritime system, or outlook, but also complement it with a complex network of trans-peninsular routes and overland lines of communications.

What is intriguing however is Kedah's ability to be able to monitor, operate, and keep these overland routes secure and viable over the period of several centuries, as reported by a number of eyewitnesses. Then there is the question that if such an elaborate system of overland routes was able to continue to function in Kedah, then why was it less successful for Siam or elsewhere in the Malay Peninsula? Indeed the report by Crawfurd that Siamese traders would choose Kedah as a destination, rather than using the Siamese ports and their overland routes further north of Kedah, may appear strange. This is against a backdrop of nineteenth century attempts by the Siamese to redirect traffic to their own routes north of Kedah (Rungswasdisab 2004). Although a detailed study of Siamese trans-peninsular routes is beyond the scope of this study yet it is possible to speculate that security, taxes or tolls (e.g., tolls levied on boats to dredge and clear the silting of the waterways), physical aspects of the route, royal protection or bureaucratic hurdles may have been behind the unpopular trans-peninsular routes of Siam.[52] It is also possible that Kedah's sea peoples would have traditionally directed traffic to Kedah's ports. Nevertheless, there seems little evidence that the traditional rulers of Kedah were concerned with competition from other trans-peninsular routes to the north, or in the south, of the Malay Peninsula, although it kept a watchful eye for the movement of troops. In opposition it could even be argued that Kedah was concerned about their well being, or at least some of them, since they may have ultimately linked to its own overland routes and/or were destinations for its trade items. This may further explain its interference as well as contributions toward regional politics, peace and negotiations often on behalf of its neighbors, including the Malay realms or Siamese ports on the other side of the Malay Peninsula. Then again in order to protect its interests and the continuation of its routes Kedah was not afraid to get involved militarily, including making use of the services of foreign-born or native sea lords and sea peoples.

From numerous records and eyewitness reports it is evident that Kedah's monarchy was traditionally central to the overall operation, security, and the safety of its overland routes. But the rulers were not merely patrons of the overland routes or their duties were not limited in appointing officials or district chiefs (*penghulu mukims*) in order to protect and be in command of the routes. In fact the rulers' historic and direct involvements in diplomatic negotiations or military forays in order to protect the overland routes are powerful statements of their personal attachment to virtually all aspects of the realm. Furthermore, it may draw attention to the Malay rulers' moral obligation and attachment to the land that is reiterated in indigenous sources. The fate of the realm and the ruler therefore seem to be intertwined. On the other hand, it is apparent that the ruler of Kedah was able to further seek the assistance and loyalty of the tribal peoples and their chiefs, i.e., the *orang asli*, to help monitor and patrol the fringes of the realm. Indeed this devotion by the *orang asli* toward the monarchy and the relative peaceful relationship with the Malay population could be further explained through an indigenous foundation myth and literary sources that connects them together. Similarly the inland Malay population of Kedah and their chiefs were enticed to remain loyal to the ruler as reflected through oral and literary traditions, as well as the unseen power that protected the monarchy and the realm.

NOTES

1. Also spelt as Krian or Creang in Malay, British, and archival sources.

2. I would like to thank Dr. Timothy Barnard (National University of Singapore) for his insights and comments on the study of inland routes in Sumatra.

3. John Crawfurd (1830 I: 43, 49) reports that in 1821 Kedah and its neighbor Perak each had 105 "*mokims*, or petty parishes" [sic]. At the end of the 1838–1839 Malay rebellion the Siamese decided to divide Kedah into 12 *mukim*, see *Phongsawadan Muang Zaiburi* (1990: 97). But the plan was eventually disbanded. It is not possible to say if the mukim division and system at Kedah resembled that of historic Aceh. In the eighteenth century Aceh the realm was composed of three federations, each with their own chief that were identified by the original number of *mukims* that had been placed under them, see Lee 1995: 8–9.

4. The term in Javanese and Thai means "a district headman," see notes by Skinner in *Syair Sultan Maulana* (1985: 302).

5. The *penghulu* was further to assist the *Temmengung*, the minister for defense or the police chief.

6. *Kampong* is translated as a village in Malay.

7. Due to a combination of political factors in Siam and France the plan of establishing the factory at Kedah never materialized.

8. The thirteenth century political rise of Siam and Kedah's recognition of its sovereignty are further mentioned by Wheatley (1961: 301).

9. Certainly a Thai version of Lady White Blood refers to her arriving at the port of Trang from Nakhon Si Thammarat riding an elephant, see Diller 1998: 234.

10. That is Singora or contemporary Songkhla.

11. According to Anderson (1824: 171) an elephant could carry about one *bahara* (about 400 lbs or 181.44 kilograms, see Newbold 1971 I: 25, Andaya 1975: 334; Trocki 1979: Currencies and Weights) of tin while a bull could only carry about half a *bahara*.

12. See also a somewhat similar report on procuring tin from Kroh and its nearby Intan mines of Patani by Anderson (1824: 170–171).

13. The report does not go into the difficulty of sending the tin in the river system and the time involved. For a similar report on the transportation of tin from the Larut tin mines at Perak to the coast and hence overland to Kedah see Andaya 1979: 112.

14. *Jeragan*, also spelt *Juragan*, means a ship skipper in Malay.

15. Indeed the use of the Perso-Arabic term "*caffula*" [sic], pronounced "*ghaafeleh*" in Persian, corresponding to the long distance caravans by Floris in about 1613, is remarkable. But regrettably, there is no indication whether Floris used this term because of his knowledge of Persian, Indian languages or Arabic or whether this was a term already in use by local Kedah-Patani merchants. Nevertheless, *Syair Sultan Maulana* (1985: 216–217), an early nineteenth century Kedah source, does use the term "*dalam kafilah*" [sic] translated as "in the expedition." Hence, it is likely that it was a term commonly used in Kedah referring to the expeditions inland.

16. Similarly for political and environmental factors the royal capital and trade ports of Kedah are believed to have historically shifted sites on numerous occasions, see Low 1848: 62–66; Irby 1905: 76–81; Quaritch-Wales 1040: 1–85; Sastri 1954: 11–14; Lamb 1961b: 12–17; Colless 1969: 1–9; Peacock 1970: 20–23; Treloar and Fabris 1975:

74–76; Christie 1988/1989: 39–54; Allen 1998: 261–288. The shifting of sites, e.g., royal capital, is not unusual in the Malay world. Trocki (1979: 1n) has discussed reasons behind the shifting of Johor's capital twenty times between 1512 and 1682. In the late nineteenth century the Raja of Trang similarly moved his capital down river (Smyth 1895b: 529).

17. Tome Pires (Cortesao 1944 I: 107) further notes that Kedah was then a purchasing destination for cloth in which it was "worth the same as in Malacca."

18. A. W. Hamilton (1922: 392) continues that Genting Pahat is about "fifty yards long by ten feet deep and though only three feet broad at the bottom widens gradually form the height of a man's shoulders until it merges into the slopes of the hill on either hand."

19. It is possible that this route was also another—less popular—trans-peninsular trade route that may have linked to pathways further south and continued to the trade entrepot at Kelantan or Pahang.

20. Please note that the geography and landscape of the port of Songkhla and nearby areas were historically different to its contemporary outlook. This can be explained through the silting of a number of waterways, personal communications with Professor Craig Reynolds (Australian National University).

21. John Bradley (1876: 295–320) crossing the border area between Patani and Province Wellesley in the 1870s reports meeting different groups of *orang asli*.

22. According to Edmund Roberts (1837: 412), the Semang of Kedah "have chiefs among them, but all property is in common."

23. This incident happened after Raja Bersiong deserted the throne, after a coup, and escaped into the country thus disappearing from the public eye. Hence it is possible that the gergasi saw their duty to protect the land and await his return or one of his descendants return. Particularly since the *gergasi*, and not the four-*bangsa* groups, are said to be the first people according to the *Hikayat* who invited Bersiong's ancestor, i.e., Merong Mahawangsa, to ruler over them.

24. An important source of information regarding problems and difficulties associated with crossing the Malay Peninsula, from Patani to Province Wellesley, is given in the 1870s eyewitness account by Bradley (1876: 241–323). Annandale and Robinson (1902: 409) similarly note that malaria, small-pox, ulcers, and skin diseases were common in the inland areas and overland routes. Maxwell (1882: 65) meanwhile reports of swarm of bees taking the river course when they migrated upstream, as well their danger to travelers.

25. The heavy seas and unpredictable currents blown up by the monsoon winds effectively closed the east coast of the Peninsula to shipping.

26. Songkhla became politically independent from Ayutthaya circa 1642 to 1680, see Choungsakul 2006: 45. During that period it appears that Kedah periodically, particularly in 1655 and the 1670s, joined Songkhla to attack the Siamese forces and positions at Nakhon Si Thammarat and other areas, see Governor General Gerard Reynst to the Heren XVII, 24th of December 1655, in *General Missiven* 1968 III: 19–24; also the entries for May 1648 in *Dagh-Register* 1903: 70; Governor General Gerard Reynst to the Heren XVII, 1676, 1969 IV: 160.

27. A similar intention may explain Kedah's mediations between Patani and Siam to settle for peace in 1635 (Governor General Gerard Reynst to the Heren XVII, 1635, 1960 I: 516; the year 1636 is however suggested by Bonney 1971: 17).

28. The island of Siantan is part of a cluster of islands called Anambas located in South China Sea, between the Malay Peninsula and Borneo, see Crawfurd 1830 I: 455, 1856: 12.

29. In the nineteenth century indigenous source of *Tuhfat al-Nafis* (Ali Haji Ibn Ahmad 1982: 188–189) however the Trengganu Sultan and his officials were unaware of Syed Ali's plan to attack Songkhla. Consequently there was panic at Trengganu when the news of the attack arrived and thus war preparations were made in the possibility of a similar attack by Syed Ali's fleet.

30. There was further rebellion at Patani between 1789 to 1791, see Yegar 2002: 75. To the ruler of Kedah the Siamese attack on Patani was of a special concern and interest. His sister was married to Tuanko Rajah Chara, the Rajah of Patani, see Anderson 1824: 154.

31. Ibrahim Syukri (1985: 58–59) and Thai sources report that (Suhrke 1970/1971: 534) in a bid to fight off the Siamese, the Patani ruler, Tunku Lamidin, in 1789 wrote a letter to seek help and alliance from Annam. But the ruler of Annam informed Siam of the plan. Nonetheless, Tunku Lamidin successfully attacked and assaulted Songkhla.

32. Indeed the 1941 joint Thai and Japanese surprise land invasion of the western Malay Peninsula was by the use of the Songkhla to Kedah trans-peninsular route.

33. Similarly the Dutch were alarmed soon after the Acehnese attack and devastation of Kedah in 1619, see Fort Jakarta to the yacht "Cleen Hollandia," 2nd of June 1619, in *Bescheiden omtrent zijn Bedrijf in Indie* 1920 II: 560. Although the 1628 attack on Kedah did not materialize, yet there was some truth to the Dutch intelligence of a looming Acehnese naval assault on the Malay Peninsula. Iskandar Muda of Aceh attacked the Portuguese to the south of Kedah at Melaka only a year later in 1629, but suffered a major defeat including the loss of 19,000 men (Ricklefs 1986: 31–32).

34. *Ulu* means upriver in Malay.

35. In 1768, Kedah had taken the border areas of Batu Kawan and Kerian that were relatively close and accessible to the tin mines; see Andaya 1979: 281, 332. Avoiding a severe smallpox epidemic in the down river (i.e., *hilir*) areas of Perak in 1768–1769, where the Dutch fort was, was likely another factor for the upriver (i.e., *ulu*) miners preferring to take their tin directly overland to Kedah see Andaya 1979: 282.

36. This was likely orchestrated on behalf of the Siamese by Tengku Din, a nephew of the ex-Sultan of Kedah, see Chapter 3.

37. The 1831 and 1838–1839 rebellions at Kedah may have contributed to similar events at Patani, Kelantan and Trengganu, see Begbie 1834: 131, Skinner 1964: 178–177; Syukri 1985: 50, 62–67. In most instances Kelantan and Trengganu supported the Malay rebellions at Kedah and Patani without officially declaring war against Siam.

38. That is Tengku Muhammad Saad.

39. Pulau Panjang is the Malay name of the island.

40. It is also possible that this was the overland route between Chaiya and Phangnga used by Bangkok army in the war against Burma in circa 1810–1811, see *Syair Sultan Maulana* 1985: 138–139. But it is possible that this route was linked to the one mentioned by Crawfurd (1830 II: 154). Besides Skinner (notes in *Syair Sultan Maulana* 1985: 281), suggests that in the nineteenth century there was an overland tin route from Phangnga, close to Ko Yao, to Chaiya.

41. Initially the Sultan of Kedah resided at Penang Island but was later moved to Province Wellesley and then Melaka.

42. See also a discussion and communications by the London Missionary Society, the Kedah Sultan and British officials in Milner 1979/1980: 5, 9–12.

43. Indeed the Bugis acknowledged their inability to be able to "weaken Kedah" during their assault in about 1771–1772 since "Kedah had a large population and sufficient food provided by extensive tracts of land and by the interior," see Ali Haji Ibn Ahmad 1982: 149.

44. The disruption of the trade routes not only affected the transportation of minerals and goods but also saw the decline of the live elephant trade. This may further explain the attempt by the Sultan of Deli, in eastern Sumatra, to woo Kedah's former elephant catchers to his domain. In meeting Sultan of Deli in 1823, Anderson (1826: 40) reports that he "begged I would endeavor to persuade some of the Kedah people who had been accustomed to catch elephants, to go over to Deli, where there is no doubt that an immense quantity of ivory might be collected."

45. Crawfurd (1830 II: 154) further identifies a third trans-peninsula route in the Malay Peninsula, that of "Pun-Pin" (opposite to Phuket) to Chaiya.

46. The Siamese policy may have had initial success. An eyewitness report by Medhurst (1838: 349) in 1832 Songkhla has its port busy with "files of Siamese junks

moored along the shores" [sic]. I would like to thank Professor Trocki for bringing into my attention this source and his insight into the Siamese policies of the period.

47. See conversion of the Thai date by Kobkua Suwannathat-Pian in *Phongsawadan Muang Zaiburi* (1990: 116n).

48. The same route was taken in 1900–1901 by Annandale and Robinson (1902: 407–417) of the Cambridge Exploring Expedition.

49. The difficulty of maintaining and constructing the road was chiefly the result of the pathway having to cross through sixty-nine creeks, waterways, and river systems.

50. Maxwell (1882: 57) reports the continuance of Perak claims over the tin mines of Patani in about 1876.

51. The agreement and shift of borders was allowed by the Siamese under the signing of the *Anglo-Siamese Secret Convention* in 1897 whereby British firms were granted exclusive access to Siamese Malay states such as Raman and Kelantan, see Ratanapun (1961: 15–20), Roff (1974: 54–57), Kobkua Suwannathat-Pian (1988: 141–142) and King (2006b: 145). At least in the case of the Rahman Tin Company it seems that they preferred to use the more economical overland route to Kedah. Consequently, in 1908 they completed, at their own expense, the construction of a twelve mile road from Klian Intan to Baling in Kedah, see King 2006b: 147.

52. For a number of reasons hampering overland trade in Siam see Smyth (1895: 402, 404, 409).

Conclusion

In the past several decades a number of historical, social, and anthropological studies on Southeast Asia have uncovered a comparable political, social, and cultural structures or models amongst the Malay people in what constitutes the historic "Malay world." These studies have contributed to an increased awareness, among scholars, of indigenous political systems, lines of communication, motivation, and mechanisms that traditionally held together and shaped the *negeri*. Consequently, these studies have reemphasized a historically cohesive perception of a "Malay model" for the region's political and cultural system, as discussed in detail by Gullick's study of 1958 and Milner's 1982 research into the subject.

On the contrary, Trocki's 1979 discussion on the distinction between riverine and maritime systems, and several more recent scholarly publications, that of Miksic (1989), Drakard in 1990 and Barnard in 2003, have effectively drawn attention to a number of variations and tensions in a number of Malay territorial units, generally viewed as belonging to the "Malay model." Thus these scholars argue from their studies of other Malay territorial units, societies and patterns that they have identified a variety of indigenous structures that contradict aspects of the cohesive perception of a single type of Malay political and cultural system, as mentioned earlier by Gullick and Milner. In the light of the above-mentioned studies, research, and the "Malay model," this study has focused primarily on the traditional political and cultural systems of the pre-twentieth-century north-western Malaysian state of Kedah.

Kedah's geographical location at the northern end of the Melaka Straits linking it to the Bay of Bengal; its proximity to the Siamese, Burman, and Acehnese empires; its lines of communication both maritime and trans-peninsular in the midst of a complex network of shorter overland routes, its economic and agricultural environment, its rich cultural and literary traditions and its political structure and independence show aspects that do not entirely follow, and often contradict, the commonly perceived "Malay model." In addition, Kedah's traditional political structure and its historic endurance demonstrate patterns of both a riverine and a maritime system. Besides the local literary version (*Hikayat Merong Mahawangsa*) of events and political emergence contradict that of the popular *Sejarah Melayu*, written outside of Kedah at the Melaka, Aceh and/or Johor courts. It is noteworthy that Kedah's traditional socioeconomic and political infrastructure has continued to withstand the calamities of over one thousand years of history, with only short intervals of disruption, and remain in more or less in the same geographical space. This is in contrast to other Malay domains on the Peninsula that were constantly invaded, shifted their powerbase or had their royal dynasties terminated or replaced.

Consequently, a study of premodern and historic Kedah offers yet another political model. It was a mixture of riverine and maritime systems as well as the terminus of important trans-peninsular routes. As such, it adds to our understanding of the "Malay world." What's more the Malay ruler of Kedah not only enforced his power and authority to those lower in the social hierarchy, traditionally through a network of loyal chiefs and officials, as argued by Gullick (1958), but it was further enhanced with the help of unconventional modes, myths and traditions. Indigenous traditions, concepts of loyalty and customs therefore reemphasized the ruler's role and his royal place amongst the Malay populace, the realm, and the world in general. But then these were concepts that were by tradition entwined and embedded in each Malay individual no matter where they resided or belonged in the domain, including the ruler. In this book I have therefore examined the physical and spiritual attributes of Malay kingship in Kedah together with forms of power that cemented the ruler, the peoples, and the environment.

One feature of this study is its attention to Kedah's role as a terminus of trans-peninsular trade routes. It is noteworthy that most recent scholars have neglected Kedah's traditional network of inland, including overland and trans-peninsular, routes and its development of a distinctive political structure. Likewise there has been virtually no scholarly study or research on the historic presence, loyalty or politico-economic, significance of the sea peoples and the sea lords of Kedah or to the areas north of Melaka Straits. Furthermore, popular studies of indigenous Malay political systems by Gullick (1958) and Milner (1982) mainly emphasize the indigenous political system from the royalist and urban point of view. Hence they place less stress on what the Malay peoples in general perceived as important limitations on royal power. Whatever the case may be, the symbolic association of the Malay ruler with religion further complemented his control of the economy, trade routes and the political infrastructure of the maritime and riverine systems that connected the territorial unit. This association is important since virtually all Malay indigenous sources point out that it was the moral duty of the ruler to seek out and implement the best ethical system that would ensure prosperity and harmony between the *negeri*, the monarchy and the people. The Malay ruler was thus a moral or a spiritual being whose personal actions and rule of law had a direct effect on the sociopolitical and economic survival of the realm. Moreover, the variant conversion stories at Kedah and its comparison to other similar traditions elsewhere in the Malay world enables us to better comprehend the forces involved in its political survival, as well as its ability to function as a regional economic powerhouse. In certain respects, the religious transformation of the Malays and the accounts of their modes of conversion to Islam act as gateways into the regions' past and at the same time set the scene for the future development of Malay social and political systems. This is significant as we know little about pre-Islamic history, political systems and belief systems that traditionally persisted in the Malay world. Hence the conversion traditions of the Malay rulers and peoples help us to further understand the indigenous view of their origins, political and social infrastructure, belief systems and aspects of religion that were deemed significant to keep or change.

Furthermore, the various Malay conversion stories, often with their own unique peculiarities, in the literary and oral sources enable us to ascertain whether there is a similarity or pattern emerging amongst them. Besides the stories can shed additional light into the extent of indigenous or foreign influences that have impacted the Malay society and systems of government in the pre and post-Islamic periods.

In the case of Kedah, the account of the conversion to Islam, in indigenous sources, follows a similar pattern to the rest of the Malay-speaking Southeast Asia. With its main literary source of *Hikayat Merong Mahawangsa* and an early nineteenth century oral report suggesting that Kedah's Hindu-Buddhist and Siamese styled Raja, adopted Islam as the official religion for himself and for his people. The association of Kedah's ruler directly with religion and as the source of change would have indeed provided the moral foundation for the acknowledgement of the monarchy in evoking the loyalty of the populace.

Nonetheless aspects of the *Hikayat* closely follow and resemble those of Persian (particularly *Shah Nameh* or book of Kings and *Hekayateh Simrugh*), South Asian (*Ramayana* and *Jataka* stories). There are references to other Southeast Asian sources or traditions (e.g., the Naga worship and *wayang kulit*). Hence, indicating an attempt by its authors to construct a text and a theme that would appeal to a wider audience without compromising Kedah's unique foundation myth, royal genealogy or prestige. Conversely, the mode of conversion of the Kedah ruler and peoples to Islam, as suggested in the *Hikayat*, and the fact that the text was first in the possession of Sultan Ahmad, the early nineteenth century ruler of Kedah, is a powerful testament to the way the monarchy and the political infrastructure viewed this historic event from within, or alternatively wished to be viewed by the indigenous population and foreign visitors. Hence the *Hikayat* should be considered as a relevant and serious source for the study of Malay and Southeast Asian history. Besides upon further investigation into the various stories within *Hikayat Merong Mahawangsa* it is event that it acts as a repository for a combination of sources.

It is also significant that key aspects of the *Hikayat* are comprised of foreign elements, pre-Islamic, as well as popular characters and indigenous stories from shadow puppets or oral traditions. This certainly indicates the popularity of such stories and traditions amongst the general population and at the court. It may also point to the numerous authors and compilers of the *Hikayat*. What's more the inclusions of Persian, Indian, Chinese and Thai elements in the text also give further prestige to the construction of a theme for the *Hikayat Merong Mahawangsa*. This inclusion may not only refer to the knowledge of such stories and traditions by the native Malay or foreign author/s or copyist/s at Kedah but also their elegant integration into the indigenous context and worldview. In particular the integration of stories traditionally associated with Persia, e.g., from *Shahnameh* and *Hekayateh Simrugh*, in *Hikayat Merong Mahawangsa* are unprecedented in the Malay world. The *Hikayat Merong Mahawangsa*'s inclusion of the story of Garuda, Prophet Solomon and the marriage of a prince and princes, from the east and the west, in fact run parallel to the little known Persian story of *Hekayateh Simrugh*. *Simurgh* is the Persian equivalent of Garuda and a mystical bird.[1]

The oral report, outlined in the book, may in fact have been one of the many circulating amongst the population and in areas outside of the urban centers. Nonetheless, it is a significant aspect for understanding the sociopolitical climate of the general population. The ruler does not appear as a supernatural or as a powerful spiritual being. Thus he was able to only temper the wrath of the monstrous snake temporarily by sacrificing a royal virgin. It is possible that this aspect of the story is a remnant of older traditions in Southeast Asia (possibly Angkorean or Southern Indian stories of a ruler in a covenant with a powerful female Naga spirit or her father). Conversely it could also be argued that the report portrays the ruler as a caring and thoughtful individual who is not afraid to seek out or consult with men of religious/spiritual prowess in his domain in order to combat evil powers from the past that had continued to persist.

The Sultan's decision to convert to a new religion therefore serves as a powerful statement of transition from the old to the new realities in Southeast Asia and the outside world known to them. This further meant that the people had to follow suit and adhere to the new principles of the religion. But it also meant that the Sultan had to reinvent himself by handpicking pre-Islamic aspects that were popular and easily understood at various levels. Furthermore, the ruler had to highlight aspects of the imported religion that ensured the endurance of the monarchy and further strengthened his power. The socioeconomic and political divisions amongst the Sultan's peoples also meant that their expectations from him and Kedah's political entity were different. Indeed a comparison of the literal and oral sources in this chapter highlights a certain cultural and moral baggage that was intentionally, but necessarily, carried into Islam.

What's more, from the conversion stories of Kedah and the covenant tradition and its familiarity amongst the Malays we find that the ruler, important as he may have been, was nothing without a people and that it was the people and their traditional leader/s who choose their ruler, and who decided freely to whom they would offer their total obedience. Indeed in the tradition of Kedah it was the *menteri* or court ministers that appear to have been the traditional representatives of the people. Hence the newly converted ruler decided to address them first. Similarly they were the first group in the palace to oppose Raja Bersiong when it became known to them that he had violated the sacred Malay ethos. In fact the circumstances surrounding the incident ensured that they themselves did not commit *derhaka* or sacrilege against the ruler by breaking any rules. In *Sejarah Melayu* and other traditions that connect themselves to the royal house of Palembang-Melaka-Johor however the representative of the people is in fact the chief of Palembang (possibly connected to the sea peoples) and father-in-law of a girl that is about to marry a magical being and a descendant of Alexander the Great. By demanding a covenant as a precondition of the marriage he therefore ensured the moral rights of the population and set the future basis for subject-ruler relationship.

As part of the covenant according to *Sejarah Melayu* there is of course a price that the two parties have to pay and share. With the covenant between the ruler and the subjects limiting and putting conditions on the political powers exercised by the ruler on the one hand, and at the same time controlling and dictating the duties and actions of the peoples towards their superiors. Alternatively it could be argued that the rulers' acknowledgement of the people's rights is of historic relevance since it adds a new component to the Malay ruler's traditional relationship with the living realm. Thus the royal curse associated with the *negeri* now extended to the ruler's treatment of his subjects.

Although the reciprocal nature of the terms and the social contract between the ruler and the chief of Palembang appears to be unique to *Sejarah Melayu*, in fact, from oral and literary reports in Kedah, and a number of other Malay domains, it appears that there was a traditional familiarity with a similar covenant, or aspects of it, between the Malay rulers and their subjects. Indeed the understanding of what constituted humiliation, or shame, appears to have been universal amongst the Malay populace and well embedded in their traditional political and social worldview. The persistence of the covenant at Kedah is of particular significance as its royal genealogy, foundation myth, conversion story, history, and traditions are much different to most Malay domains. It therefore appears that the covenant story as reiterated in *Sejarah Melayu* was part of Malay indigenous political system, as well as the likelihood of a prototypical foundation myth persisting in the Malay world. Furthermore, it seems that the Malays expected this consideration from their rulers, no matter if he/she was Malay or not. It seems this expectation was part of the Malay worldview of a universal regal quality that included the correct etiquette and chivalry towards the subjects. This may further explain the fact that the Malay indigenous traditions as well as historic reports (e.g., Arab rulers in eighteenth century Aceh) demonstrate the ability of foreigners to ruler over them. Arguably this aspect of Malay political system was indeed indigenous to the Malays (also parts of India) and is an aspect that is not found in the Chinese, Indian, and Persian traditions. Conversely, it is likely that these qualities were set in place in order to explain the moral explanations of having foreign rulers, or their acceptance amongst the population.

On the other hand, a study of historic Kedah can shed further light into how the Malay rulers traditionally protected and maintained their control of the maritime lines of communications. In line with Gullick (1958) and Trocki's (1979) independent studies of the Malay indigenous political systems, it is apparent that maritime and riverine systems were an integral part of the political and economic structure of Kedah. Kedah was a maritime state in the sense that traditionally the centre of power and the "trading city" or the entrepot, were located at or close to the river-mouths, or near the coastline. Moreover, its historic lines of control included the "sea routes" that also expanded to a number of river systems and river estuaries within its domain, as well as several large and small islands.

What's more, Kedah's "sea routes" were controlled and defended, as discussed with respect to Johor by Trocki, at least from the seventeenth to the nineteenth century by the ruler in conjunction with a number of sea lords and their followers, the "sea peoples" that were the backbone of the realm's navy. Reasons behind their recruitment could vary and may have included financial benefits, symbolic acknowledgements, or were done as a loyal act of devotion (*bakti*) by the Malay subjects towards their ruler. Equally royal marriage and family alliances were further means of seeking alliances and friends amongst the sea lords and the sea peoples. In fact marriage alliances could benefit the sea lords by politically allowing them to get public or regional recognition (e.g., in the case of Raja Kecik of Siak), as well as enabling the royal house of Kedah to call upon the support and assistance of powerful regional men of prowess. The 1821 Siamese invasion of Kedah is a testament to the continuing support and devotion of its sea peoples and well-connected sea lords (e.g., Tengku Long Putih) with family connections to the ex-ruler of Kedah. In fact according to the Siamese sources, the 1838–1839 Malay uprising at Kedah was equally conducted by land and sea. Furthermore, the eighteenth and nineteenth century attempts by the ruler of Kedah to marry his close family relations, but apparently not himself, to people claiming to be descendants from Prophet Muhammad, or Syeds, deserves notice and may even suggest the new realities in the socioreligious make-up in the Straits of Melaka. Indeed many of the Syeds married into the royal house of Kedah and appear to have been close or distantly related to the sea lords of Siak or other parts of Sumatra. Besides, connections to the line of the Prophet may have given more leverage, legitimacy, and moral authority to the ruler of Kedah in seeking support not only amongst the Malays but also foreign Muslims visiting and trading with the realm.

In any case, the Laksamanas in particular acted as Kedah's undisputed sea lords for much of the seventeenth to the early nineteenth century. They were powerful officials with a hereditary position at the royal court of Kedah. The fortunes of the Laksamana rose in the second half of the eighteenth century when his daughter married the heir apparent. The traditional recruitment of the sea peoples and their chiefs by Kedah's sea lords therefore enabled them to strengthen and protect Kedah's sea routes from foreign or pirate attacks. Moreover, the sea peoples contributed extensively to the economy of the realm. In particular they would assisted by directing shipping to Kedah's ports, in gathering intelligence or news, collecting birds' nests or other products from often remote islands and in supplying the entrepot or other centers with fish or other seafood items.

But, by examining the historic records of the seventeenth to the early nineteenth century it becomes apparent that many of Kedah's sea peoples were often distinct from each other. The seventeenth century appears to have been dominated by the indigenous or straits-born sea peoples, who are thought to have come originally from the southern half of the Straits of Melaka. The eighteenth century, on the other hand, saw the rise in importance of foreign-born sea lords together with their followers, chiefs, and sea peoples such as Makassarese and Bugis from Sulawesi or else Selangor. There were also important groups of sea-farers from Siak, and the Minangkabau areas as well as Ilanuns from the Southern Philippines. Indeed the indigenous sea peoples and the Siak sea lords continued to play significant roles in the first half of the nineteenth century and during the Siamese occupation of 1821–1841/1842.

At any rate, it seems that by the eighteenth century there was a power-sharing arrangement in Kedah's traditional maritime lines of communications. In consequence the indigenous *orang laut* thus began to render their services to the Sultan and the Laksamana in the northern half of the maritime domain of the realm, extending all the way to the Mergui Archipelago, with their powerbase in the Langkawi Islands. And the foreign born sea lords and their followers dominated its southern corridor/zone, extending to the Kerian River, with refitting settlements in and around Penang.

On the other hand, the view of a traditional maritime or riverine structure, with few lines of communications inland, as argued by Gullick (1958) is also held to be true for Kedah, by most Southeast Asian scholars. But Kedah's unique geography and its ability to be connected to a complex network of overland and trans-peninsular trade routes meant that it did not solely rely on the maritime trade routes. Furthermore, historic reports and accounts of Kedah's trans-peninsular reach demonstrate that it offered an alternative to the maritime routes, as well as having a lower risk factor for sending goods from the Bay of Bengal into the Gulf of Siam. Besides it appears that the trans-peninsular routes of Kedah similarly connected the two cultures on the other side of the Malay Peninsula together. They were each further linked and influenced by their connections to other overland and sea routes. Hence, Kedah was culturally and socially linked by land to its neighbors (e.g., Siam, Songkhla, Nakhon Si Thammarat, and the Malay territories mostly to its south and south-eastern borders) and beyond by sea to Sumatra, Burma, Angkor, the Mon principalities, Europe, China, India, Persia and elsewhere. Meanwhile, it could further be argued that Kedah traditionally acted as a regional exchange-hub in which an eclectic admixture of people, goods, and cultures intermingled. Thus Kedah's commanding link to the sea and overland routes enabled a regular exchange of traditions, literary sources, education, languages, sciences, and inventions to travel to and from Kedah, with only short periods of disruption. Kedah's society was therefore continuously transformed and had to cope with the new changes and political realities in Southeast Asia and beyond.

Kedah's ability to cleverly interconnect its maritime lines of communication with those of the trans-peninsular routes is indeed remarkable. Control of these alternate routes arguably gave Asian or other foreign traders' further choices of in directly selling their goods, cutting costs, and ensuring a safe return of their investments. Moreover, this further meant that Kedah was historically less susceptible to environmental, political, and economic changes than other Malay territorial units. Consequently there were numerous instances in which the ruler of Kedah and his subjects could take refuge inland (including the 1821 escape to Province Wellesley and the Penang Island) to escape their enemies. Moreover, the overland routes were significant when Kedah attempted to avoid a blockade of its coastline, smuggling of minerals and other goods, ambushing enemies and in seeking assistance or help from neighboring territories (including Siam) against foreign intrusions. Hence the kingship could continue to function as an independent political and economic unit.

Additionally there are many examples in which Kedah would peacefully or militarily interfere in regional politics, e.g., with regard to Patani or Songkhla, in order to ensure the safe passage of goods and continuation of its trans-peninsular routes. It is noteworthy that in doing so they were ardent in making use of the services of sea lords their followers. Indeed assuming that Syed Ali, the Siak sea lord, left Siak in the Straits of Melaka (according to the indigenous sources of *Tuhfat al-Nafis*, Ali Haji Ibn Ahmad 1982: 188) solely to ambush Songkhla, in the Gulf of Siam, on behalf of Kedah then it highlights the extent that it would go to protect its trade routes.

Little is known however about the actual history, archaeology, control, maintenance and the traditional monitoring of the overland routes. Similarly the extent and motivations of the *orang asli* and their chiefs in assisting with the monitoring of the routes remains ambiguous. Beside many of the reports of the overland routes come from the nineteenth century and it is not known if the same order of things persisted prior to that date. Nonetheless, further archaeological study of the remaining, or known, overland routes of Kedah may indeed shed light into its past.

Finally, the study of Kedah is important as it tells us about the internal and external forces that have facilitated, or shaped, the durability and the resilience of a traditional royal dynasty. This is significant as Kedah's royalty is in fact the oldest surviving lineage in the Malay and the Islamic world. A comparative study of a number of other Malay royal dynasties would therefore shed further light onto regional similarities and differences. Furthermore, a study of Kedah helps us in comprehending the delicate relationship of the ruler-subject relationship in premodern Malay society. Hence an attempt has been made to study what was traditionally deemed as noteworthy about the relationship between a Malay ruler or dynasty and the Malay population. This would therefore further clarify reasons for the customary loyalty of the Malay subjects towards their rulers.

Then there is the question on the dynamics of why Kedah's royal dynasty and its sociopolitical infrastructure which were able to persist while other royal Malay dynasties was less successful. Similarly there is the question of indigenous control of their lines of communications in the Malay world. Without a doubt Kedah's historic connection to a diverse array of trade routes as well as the ruler's traditional attempts to be the pinnacle of the realm's spiritual hierarchy were important factors in its survival. These links were therefore essential in its economic and sociopolitical arena as well as its worldview. Likewise, the prestige associated with the prosperity of the realm and the unseen spiritual power of the ruler would further draw attention to the loyalty of the indigenous population towards their ruler and in their assistance in controlling Kedah's lines of communication. Nevertheless, by studying the traditional control of the maritime and/or the overland lines of communications by the Malay domains in island and mainland Southeast Asia we gain further insight into indigenous political, economical and social systems. Indeed it could be argued that the 1821 Siamese invasion of Kedah combined with a rise in colonial expansion and power in the region signals the beginning of an end to the indigenous political systems, education, and governments in Southeast Asia. The new realities for the region includes the gradual end for the Burman empire (following the Anglo-Burman wars, 1824–1886), the Dutch and French expansion into mainland and island Southeast Asia, the British settlement of Singapore (in 1822) and the rise in British influence and interference in the Malay Peninsula. The return of the ex-Sultan to Kedah also came at a high price. Kedah not only lost nearly half of its total land area (including any further claims to Penang and Province Wellesley) but also its historic links to the sea peoples. Furthermore, the introduction as well the presence of Siamese and, later, British advisers in post 1842 Kedah arguably complicated its internal affairs, political infrastructure, economy and view of its own history and the independence of its rulers (Ratanapun 1961; Allen 1968; Ahmat 1970, 1984; Haji Mahmud 1972a; Gullick 1983, 1991; Kobkua Suwannathat-Pian 1988).

On the other hand, insufficient scholarly attention has been given to Malay indigenous literary, oral or other historic and cultural sources. In the case of Kedah most scholars have argued against the credibility of its indigenous sources. Yet these sources, as argued by Maier (1988) in the case of Kedah, are also important avenues for understanding indigenous thought patterns and practices. They also highlight what was important to the Malay ruler and his subjects. It is therefore hoped that this study would inspire further scholarly inquiry to enhance our understanding of the political culture the Malay world.

NOTE

1. But it can also be said that the inclusion of *Hekayateh Simrugh* in *Hikayat Merong Mahawangsa* also creates several problems. Foremost, the Persian story only survives in a handful of sixteenth century documents, attributed to the courts of Persia, collected at the time by an official from central Iran [A version of the story is also found amongst Persian stories (attributed to the same Persian official) collected in the seventeenth century Mogul court, see Safa 1994 v Pt3: 1530]. Thus the story is not widely known, cited or popular (as are stories from *Shahnameh*). Alternatively it can also be argued that *Hekayateh Simrugh* has its origin in Indian sources or traditions that were later translated in Islamic Persia and then made their way to Kedah. If so then is it possible that the story was part of a combination of official documents and traditions exchanged directly between Persia and Kedah?

Bibliography

ARCHIVAL SOURCES

Newspapers

Penang Gazette and Straits Chronicle (1838–1934)
Prince of Wales Island Gazette (1805–1828, 1833–1835)
Singapore Chronicle (1824–1837)
Singapore Free Press (1835–1962)
The Asiatic Journal and Monthly Register for British and Foreign India, China and Australasia (1816–1843)
The Oriental Herald and Colonial Review (1824)
The Straits Times (1845–)

Official Documents

Colonial Office Records

Crawfurd Papers: A collection of official records relating to the mission of Dr. John Crawfurd sent to Siam by the government of India in the year 1821. (1915). Bangkok: National Library.
Dagh-register gehouden int Casteel Batavia vant passerende daer ter plaetse als over geheel Nederlandts-India (31 vols.), (1887–1931). The Hague: Martinus Nijhoff.
Dutch Records at The Hague (Vols. 1–70) [IOL/M/2/259]
Generale Missiven van Gouverneurs-Generaal en Raden aan Heren XVII der Verenigde Oostindische Compagnie Indie. Edited by W. Ph. Coolhaas (9 vols.), (1960–1997). The Hague: s-Gravenhage.
Straits Settlements, Original Correspondence (CO 273)

India Office MS Records

China and Japan (IOR/G/12/13, IOR/G/12/15)
East India Records: [M470–535] 1769–1830
Jan Pieterszoon Coen: Bescheiden omtrent zijn bedrijf in Indie. Edited by H.T. Colenbrander and W. Ph. Coolhaas (8 vols.), (1919–1953). The Hague: s-Gravenhage.
Letters Received by the East India Company from Its Servants in the East: Transcribed from the "Original Correspondence" Series of the India Office Records, (6 vols.). (1968). Amsterdam: N. Israel.
Miscellaneous Records (Vol. 2)
Original Correspondence
Records of the Relations between Siam and Foreign Countries in the 17th Century (5 vols.). (1915–1921). Bangkok: Vajirana National Library.
Straits Settlements Factory Records (East India Company 1769–1795/1805–1830, Vols. 1–169)
Straits Settlements Records (Singapore Series A-I, 1804–1837)

Transcripts of selected Dutch documents relating to India and the East [M550–576] 1600–1699: Letters from India 1600–1699; Letters from the Dutch East India Company to India 1614–1700; Letters from the Governor General at Batavia to various factories 1617–1699

UNPUBLISHED ACADEMIC SOURCES

Granbom, Ann-Charlotte. (2005). Urak Lawoi: A Field Study of Indigenous People in Thailand and Their Problems with Rapid Tourist Development. *Lund University: Unpublished Master's Thesis*.

King, Phil. (2006b). From Periphery to Centre: Shaping the History of the Central Peninsula. *University of Wollongong: Unpublished Doctoral Dissertation*.

Lee Chye Hooi. (1957). The Penang Land Problem, 1786–1841. *University of Malaya (Singapore): Bachelor of Arts, Unpublished Academic Exercise*.

Ratanapun, Thamsook. (1961). The Development of the North-Western States of Malaya, 1909–1941. *University of Hong Kong: Unpublished Master's Thesis,*

Sharifah Zaleha Binte Syed Hassan. (1985). From Saints to Bureaucrats: A Study of the Development of Islam in the State of Kedah, Malaysia. *Cornell University: Unpublished Doctoral Dissertation*.

Trocki, C. A. (2000). Borders and the Mapping of the Malay World. *Paper presented at the Association of Asian Studies Annual Meeting,* San Diego: California. Retrieved November 22, 2010, from http://eprints.qut.edu.au/archive/00000092/01/trockiBorderline.pdf.

———. (2006). The Question of Pre-Colonial Borders and Malay Political Culture. *Report Prepared for Attorney General Office of Singapore,* Singapore: Unpublished Report Paper.

Wee, V. (1985). Melayu: Hierarchies of Being in Riau. *Australian National University: Unpublished Doctoral Dissertation*.

ARTICLES, MONOGRAPHS, AND WEBSITES

A Letter of Instructions from the East Indian Company to Its Agent, circ. 1614. Edited and notes by W. G. Maxwell. (1909). *JSBRAS*, (No. 54), 75–77.

Adler, W. (1986/1987). Abraham and the Burning of the Temple of Idols, Jubilees Traditions in Christian Chronography. *The Jewish Quarterly Review*, 77(2–3), 95–117.

Ahmat, Sharom. (1970). The Political Structure of the State of Kedah 1879–1905. *JSEAS*, 1/2 (September), 115–128.

Alatas, F. (1985). Notes on Various Theories Regarding the Islamization of the Malay Archipelago. *Muslim World*, 75/3–4, 162–175.

Algar, H. (1982). Eblis. In Ehsan Yashater (ed.), *Encyclopedia Iranica* (Vol. 6, pp. 660–661). New York: Bibliotheca Persica Press.

Allen, J. S. (1998). History, Archaeology, and the Question of Foreign Control in Early Historic-Period Peninsular Malaysia. *International Journal of Historical Archaeology*, 2 (No. 4), 261–88.

Allen, J. De V. (1968). The Elephant and the Mousedeer—A New Version: Anglo-Kedah Relations, 1905–1915. *JMBRAS*, 41/1 (July), 54–94.

Alor Star Through the Ages. (1953). *The Gate* (Being the Magazine of S. A. H. College Historical Society, T. T. Printers, Alor Star), Special Edition (Number 4).

Andaya, B. W. (1976). The Role of the *Anak raja* in Malay History, A Case Study from Eighteenth-Century Kedah. *JSEAS*, 7 (No. 2, September), 163–186.

———. (1978). The Indian Saudagar Raja in Traditional Malay Courts. *JMBRAS*, 51 (Part 1), 13–35.

Andaya, L. Y. (1975a). The Structure of Power in Seventeenth-Century Johor. In Anthony Reid and Lance Castles (eds.), *Pre-Colonial State Systems in Southeast Asia*. Monographs of the Malaysian Branch of the Royal Asiatic Society (No. 6, pp. 1–11).

———. (2001). The Search for the "Origins" of Melayu. *JSEAS*, 32/3, 315–330.

———. (2001b). Aceh's Contribution to Standards of Malayness. *Archipel*, 61, 37–63.

———. (2002). Orang Asli and the Melayu in the History of the Malay Peninsula. *JMBRAS*, 75/1, 23–48.

Annandale, Nelson, and Robinson H. C. (1902). Some Preliminary Results of an Expedition to the Malay Peninsula. *JAIGBI*, 32 (July–December), 407–417.

Archaimbault, C. (1957). A Preliminary Investigation of the Sam Sam of Kedah and Perlis. *JMBRAS*, 30 (Part 1), 75–92.

Awang, Omar. (1981). The Major Arabic Sources which Determined the Structure of Islamic Thought in the Malay Archipelago before the Nineteenth Century A. D. in the Fields of Law, Theology, and Sufism. In Lutpi Ibrahim (ed.) *Islamika: Esei-Esei Sempena Abad ke 15 Hijrah* (pp. 80–85). Kuala Lumpur: Serjana Enterprise.

Aye Chayan (2005). The Development of a Muslim Enclave in Arakan (Rakhine) State of Burma (Myanmar). *SOAS Bulletin of Burma Research*, 3/2 (Autumn), 396–420.

Baker, A. J. (1939). Notes on the Meaning of Some Malay Words, Part III (Kedah Words). *JMBRAS*, 17/1, 107–120.

Balfour, H. (1897). Life History of an Aghori Fakir; with Exhibition of the Human Skull Used by Him as a Drinking Vessel, and Notes on the Similar Use of Skulls by Other Races. *JAIGBI*, 26, 340–357.

Barnard, T. P. (2007). Celates, Rayat-Laut, Pirates: The *Orang Laut* and Their Decline in History. *JMBRAS*, 80 (Part 2, No. 293), 33–50.

Barretto de Resende's account of Malacca. Edited and translated by W. G. Maxwell, (1911). *JSBRAS* (No. 60), 1–24.

Bassett, D. (1989a). Anglo-Kedah Relations 1688–1765. *JMBRAS*, 62/2, 1–17.

———. (1989b). British Country Trade and Local Trade Networks in the Thai and Malay States c. 1680–1770. *MAS*, 23 (Number 4), 628–642.

Bastian, A. (1865). A Visit to the Ruined Cities and Buildings of Cambodia. *JRGSL*, 35, 74–87.

Bastin, J. (1964). Problems of Personality in the Reinterpretation of Modern Malayan History. In John Bastin and R. Roolvink (eds.), *Malayan and Indonesian Studies* (pp. 141–153). Oxford: Clarendon Press.

Beaulieu, M. (1705). Memoirs of Admiral Beaulieu's Voyage to the East-Indies. In *Navigantium atque Itinerantium Bibliotheca or a Complete Collection of Voyages and Travels* (Volume 1, pp. 238–255). London: Printed for Thomas Bennet et al. (Beaulieu reported from Kedah in 1621)

Behm, A. J. (1971). The Eschatology of the Jatakas. *Numen*, 18/Fasc. 1 (April), 30–44.

Benjamin, G. (1997). Issues in the Ethnohistory of Pahang. In Nik Hassan Shuhaimi bin Nik Abd. Rahman et al. (ed.) *Pembangunan Arkeologi Pelancongan Negeri Pahang* (pp. 82–121). Pahang: Lembaga Muzium Negeri Pahang.

Biran, M. (2002). The Chaghadaids and Islam, The Conversion of Tarmashirin Khan (1331–1334). *JAOS*, 122/4, 742–752.

Birch, E. W. (1910). My Visit to Klian Intan. *JSBRAS*, 141 (No. 54), 137–146.

Blackburn, S. H. (1981). Oral Performance, Narrative and Ritual in a Tamil Tradition. *The Journal of American Folklore*, 49/372 (April–June), 207–227.

Blagden, C. O. (1909). Marong Mahawangsa, The Kedah Annals. Translated by Lieut. Col. James Low. *Journal of the Royal Asiatic Society*, (April), 525–531.

———. (1917). Cannibal King in the Kedah Annals. *JSBRAS*, 79, 47–48.

Bland, R. N. (1909). Story of the Burong Geruda and the Raja Merong Mahawangsa. *JSBRAS*, 54, 107–115.

Bloomfield, M. (1924). On False Ascetic and Nuns in Hindu Fiction. *JAOS*, 44, 202–242.

Bloss, W. L. (1973). The Buddha and the Naga, A Study in Buddhist Folk Religiosity. *History of Religion*, 13/1, 36–53.

Bone, S. D. (1982). Islam in Malawi. *Journal of Religion in Africa*, 13/2, 126–138.

Bowen, R. (1999). Investing in Conrad, Investing in the Orient, Margaret Drabble's The Gates of Ivory. *Twentieth Century Literature*, 45/3 (Autumn), 278–298.
Braddell, R. (1936). An introduction to the study of ancient times in the Malay Peninsula and the Straits of Malacca. *JMBRAS*, 14(3), 10–71.
Braddell, T. (1851). On the History of Acheen, Translations from the Majellis Ache. *JIAEA*, V, 15–32.
Bradley, F. R. (2009). Moral Order in a Time of Damnation: The *Hikayat Patani* in Historical Context. *JSEAS*, 40/2 (June), 267–293.
Brailey, N. (1999). The Scramble for Concessions in 1880s Siam. *MAS* 33/3, 513–549.
Brakel, C. (1997). *Sandhang-pangan* for the Goddess, Offerings to Sang Hyang Bathari Durga and Nyai Lara Kidul. *AFS*, 56/2, 253–283.
Brewster, G. P. (1972). Some Parallels between the "Feng-Shen-Yen-I" and the "Shahnameh" and the Possible Influence of the Former upon the Persian Epic. *AFS*, 31/1, 115–122.
Briggs, L. P. (1951). The Syncretism of Religions in Southeast Asia, Especially in the Khmer Empire. *JAOS*, 71/4, 230–249.
Bronson, B. (1977). Exchange at the Upstream and Downstream Ends: Notes Toward a Functional Model of the Coastal State in Southeast Asia. In K. L. Hutterer (ed.), *Economic Exchange and Social Interaction in Southeast Asia: Perspectives from Prehistory, History and Ethnography* (University of Michigan Papers on South and Southeast Asia No. 13, pp. 39–52). Ann Arbor: Centre for South and Southeast Asian Studies.
Bronson, B., and Wisseman, J. (1976). Palembang as Srivijaya, The Lateness of Early Cities in Southern Southeast Asia. *Asian Perspectives*, 19(2), 220–239.
Brown, C. C. (1948). A Malay Herodotus. *BSOAS*, 12 (Nos. 3/4), 730–736.
———. (1952). The Malay Annals. *JMBRAS*, 25/2–3, 5–276.
Brown, R. G. (1921). The Pre-Buddhist Religion of the Burmese. *Folklore*, 32/2, 77–100.
Bruce, Allan (1996). Notes on early Mosques of the Malaysian Peninsula. *JMBRAS*, 69 (Part 2), 71–81.
Buddensieg, Tilmann (1965). Gregory the Great, the Destroyer of Pagan Idols. The History of a Medieval Legend concerning the Decline of Ancient Art and Literature. *Journal of the Warburg and Courtauld Institutes*, 28, 44–65.
Burghardt, R. (1978). Hierarchical Models of the Hindu Social System. *Man*, 13/4 (December), 519–536.
Cambell, J. (1860). Notes on the Antiquities, Natural History, &c., of Cambodia, compiled from Manuscripts of the late E. F. J. Forrest, Esq., and from information derived from the Rev. Dr. House, &c. &c. *JRGSL*, 30, 182–198.
Capwell, H. C. (1974). The Esoteric Belief of the Bauls of Bengal. *JAS*, 33/2, 255–264.
Carsten, J. (1995). The Politics of Forgetting, Migration, Kinship and Memory on the Periphery of the Southeast Asian State. *Journal of the Royal Anthropological Institute*, 1/2, 317–335.
Ceridwen, Amelia. (2001). The *Silsilah Raja-Raja Perak I*, An Historical and Literary Investigation into the Political Significance of a Malay Court Genealogy. *JMBRAS*, 74/2, 23–129.
Chambert-Loir, H. (2005). The Sulalat al-Salatin as a Political Myth. *Indonesia*, (Number 79, April), 131–160.
Chand Chirayu Rajani, MC. (1974). Review article, Background of the Sri Vijaya Story. *JSS*, 62/1, 174–211.
Chandler, D. P. (1974). Royally Sponsored Human Sacrifices in Nineteenth-Century Cambodia, the Cult of *Nak Ta Me Sa* (Mahisasuramardini) at Ba Phnom. *JSS*, 62/2, 207–222.
———. (1979). Folk Memories of the Decline of Angkor in Nineteenth-Century Cambodia, the Legend of the Leper King. *JSS*, 67/1, 54–62.
Chao, D. (1979). The Snake in Chinese Belief. *Folklore*, 90/2, 193–203.
Cheah, Boon Kheng (1981). Social Banditry and Rural Crime in North Kedah, 1909–1929. *JMBRAS*, 54/2, 98–130.

———. (1993). Power Behind the Throne, the Role of Queens and Court Ladies in Malay History. *JMBRAS*, 66/1, 1–21.
Choungsakul, Srisuporn. (2006). The Role of Chinese Traders on the Growth of Songkhla, 1775–1912. *MANUSYA, Journal of Humanities*, 9/2, 44–65.
Christie, J. W. (1988/89). The Sanskrit Inscription Recently Discovered in Kedah, Malaysia. *Modern Quartenary Research in Southeast Asia*, 11, 39–54.
Claine, J. (1892). Un an en Malaisie, 1889–1890. *Le Tour Du Monde* (Paris), 63, 369–400.
Coedes, G. (1918). The Kingdom of Sriwijaya. In George Coedes and Louis-Charles Damais (collected studies). (1992). *Sriwijaya: History, Religion and Language of an Early Malay Polity* (Monograph No. 20, pp. 1–31). Kuala Lumpur: Malaysian Branch of the Royal Asiatic Society.
Colless, B. E. (1969). The Early Western Ports of the Malay Peninsula. *The Journal of Tropical Geography*, 29, 1–9.
Colombijn, Freek. (2004). Islamic Influences on Urban Form in Sumatra in the Seventeenth to Nineteenth Centuries CE. *Indonesia and the Malay World*, 32 (No. 93, July), 249–70.
Croix, de Ste G. E. M. (1963). Why Were the Early Christians Persecuted? *Past and Present*, 26, 6–38.
Crowley, M. (1996). When the Gods Drank Urine, a Tibetan Myth May Help Solve the Riddle of Soma, Sacred Drug of Ancient India. *Fortean Studies*, 3. Retrieved July 20, 2008, from http://www.erowid.org/plants/amanitas/amanitas_writings1.shtml.
Cummings, W. (1998). The Melaka Malay Diaspora in Makassar, c. 1500–1669. *JMBRAS*, 71 (Part 1), 107–121.
D'Almeida, B. W. (1876). Geography of Perak and Salangore, and a Brief Sketch of Some of the Adjacent Malay States. *JRGSL*, 46, 357–380.
Daly, D. D. (1882). Surveys and Explorations in the Native States of the Malayan Peninsula, 1875–1882. *Proceedings of the Royal Geographical Society and Monthly Record of Geography* (New Monthly Series), 4 (No. 7, July), 393–412.
Daniels, F. J. (1960). Snake and Dragon Lore of Japan. *Folklore*, 71/3 (September), 145–164.
Day, T. (1996). Ties That (Un) Bind, Families and States in Premodern Southeast Asia. *JAS*, 55 (No. 2, May), 384–409.
de Jong J. W. (1994). The Story of Rama in Tibet. In K. R. Srinivasaiyengar (ed.), *Asian Variations in Ramayana: Papers presented at the International Seminar on "Variations in Ramayana in Asia: Their Cultural, Social and Anthropological Significance": New Delhi, January 1981* (pp. 163–182). New Delhi: Sahitya Akademi.
Dhiravat Na Pombejra. (2003). Toward an Autonomous History of Seventeenth-Century Phuket. In Abu Talib Ahmad and Tan Liok Ee (eds.), *New Terrains in Southeast Asian History* (pp. 247–300). Singapore: Singapore University Press.
Diller, Anthony. (1998). A Trang Cave Text of 1614 AD. *JSS*, 86/1–2, 232–234.
Dimand, S. M. (1933). An Indian Relief of the Amaravati School. *The Metropolitan Museum of Art Bulletin*, 28/2 (July), 124–125.
Dimock, C. E. (1962). The Goddess of Snakes in Medieval Bengali Literature. *History of Religions*, 1/2 (Winter), 307–321.
Dobby, G. H. E. (1951). The North Kedah Plain a Study in the Environment of Pioneering for Rice Cultivation. *Economic Geography*, 27 (Number 4, October), 287–315.
Dunalp, E. P. (1907). The Edible Bird Nest Islands of Siam. *JSS*, 4 (Issue III), 1–11.
Dupont, P. (1950). Les Buddha sur Naga dans l'Art Khmer. *Artibus Asiae*, 13, 39–62.
Duran, J. (1863). On the Shell-Mounds of Province Wellesley, in the Malay Peninsula. *Transactions of the Ethnological Society of London*, 2, 119–129.
———. (1990). The Nagaraja, Symbol and Symbolism in Hindu Art and Iconography. *Journal of Aesthetic Education*, 24/2 (Summer), 37–47.
Evans, N. H. (1926). Results of an Expedition to Kedah. *Journal of the Federated Malay States Museum*, 12, 71–82.
Farouk, Omar. (1978). The Arabs in Penang. *MIH*, 21/2, 1–16.

Fatwa and Archeology. (21 February 1989). New Straits Times. In *Kajian Malaysia, Journal of Malaysian Studies*, (December 1989), 6/2.
Foley, K. (2001). The Origin of Kala, A Sundanese Wayang Golek Purwa Play by Abah Sunarya and Gamelan Giri Harja I. *Asian Theatre Journal*, 18/1 (Spring), 1–58.
Frye, R. N. (1964). The Charisma of Kingship in Ancient Iran. *Iranica Antiqua*, 4, 36–54.
Garnier, Keppel. (1923). Early Days in Penang. *JMBRAS*, 1, 5–12.
Gaudes, R. (1993). Kaundinya, Preah Thaong, and the "Nagi Soma," Some Aspects of a Cambodian Legend. *AFS*, 52/2, 333–358.
Gerini, G. E. (1986). Historical Retrospect of Junk Ceylon Island. In *Old Phuket, Articles Reprinted from the Journal of the Siam Society 1905–1906*. Bangkok, The Siam Society. (This book is a reprint of the original articles published by Gerini in December 1905.)
Gibson-Hill, A. C. (1954). The Boats of Local Origin Employed in the Malayan Fishing Industry. *JMBRAS*, 27 (Part 2), 145–174.
Gladney, C. Dru. (1987). Muslim Tombs and Ethnic Folklore, Charters for Hui Identity. *JAS*, 46/3 (August), 495–532.
Gokhale, G. B. (1966). Early Buddhist Kingship. *JAS*, 26/1 (November), 15–22.
Goldberg, Ellis (1991). Smashing Idols and the State; The Protestant Ethic and Egyptian Sunni Radicalism. *Comparative Studies in Society and History*, 33/1, 3–35.
Golestan of Sa'adi. Translated by Richard Francis Burton (1821–1890). Retrieved September 2, 2008, from http://enel.ucalgary.ca/People/far/hobbies/iran/Golestan/.
Gopinath, K. (1950). The Malayan Purse Seine (Pukat Jerut) Fishery. *JMBRAS*, 23 (Part 3), 75–96.
Gothamasan, Phan-Ngam. (1984). Some Aspects of the Political and Economic Systems of the Nineteenth Century Northern Malay States, Kedah, Kelantan and Trengganu A Comparative View. *JSS*, 72, 140–165.
Grancsay, V. S. (1937). The George C. Stone Bequest, Chinese and Malayan Arms and Armor. *The Metropolitan Museum of Art Bulletin*, 32/6, 143–148.
Gullick, J. M. (1983). Kedah 1821–1855. Years of Exile and Return. *JMBRAS*, 56 (2), 31–86.
Hall, R. K. (2005). Traditions of Knowledge in Old Javanese Literature, c. 1000–1500. *JSEAS*, 36/1, 1–27.
Hamilton, A. W. (1922). The Old Kedah-Patani Trade-route. *JSBRAS* 86, 389–92.
———. (1923). Custom and Chanticleer. *JMBRAS*, 1, 250.
Hara, M. (1994). Rama Stories in China and Japan: A Comparison. In K. R. Srinivasaiyengar (ed.), *Asian Variations in Ramayana: Papers presented at the International Seminar on "Variations in Ramayana in Asia: Their Cultural, Social and Anthropological Significance": New Delhi, January 1981* (pp. 340–356). New Delhi: Sahitya Akademi.
Harman, W. (1985). Kinship Metaphors in the Hindu Pantheon, Siva as Brother-in-Law and Son-in-Law. *Journal of the American Academy of Religion*, (3), 411–430.
Harper, N. T. (1997). The Politics of the Forest in Colonial Malaya. *MAS*, 31/1, 1–29.
Heine-Geldern, R. (1942). Conceptions of State and Kingship in Southeast Asia. *The Far Eastern Quarterly*, 2 (November), 15–30.
Hervey, D. F. A. (1884). Valentyn's Description of Malacca, Translated from the Dutch by Mr. Muller. *JSBRAS*, 13, 49–74. (Valentyn visited Southeast Asia in the 1720s.)
———. (1885). Valentyn's Description of Malacca, Translated from the Dutch by Mr. Muller. *JSBRAS*, 15, 53–132.
Hikayat Iblis (Mss. Catalogue Number Cap. Schoemann V. 24). Berlin: Preussischer-Kultur-Besitz. Retrieved April 10, 2007, from http://www.geocities.com/Athens/6795/iblis.html.
Hikayat Marong Maha Wangsa or Kedah Annals, Edited by A. J. Sturrock. (1916). *JSBRAS*, 72, 37–119. (The romanized version of the *Hikayat Marong Mahawangsa*.)
Hikayat Raja-Raja Pasai, Translated and Revised by A. H. Hill. (1960). *JMBRAS*, 33/190 (Part 2), 3–208.
Hill, A. H. (1963). Islam Comes to North Sumatra. *JSEAH*, 4/1, 17–18.
Hindu-Buddhist Civilisation in South Kedah, (1958), *MIH*, 4/1 (January), 34.

Hogan, D. (1972). Men of the Sea, Coastal Tribes of Thailand's West Coast. *JSS*, 60/1, 205–235.
Hooker, Barry. (1993). Fatawa in Malaysia 1960–1985 Third Coulson Memorial Lecture. *Arab Law Quarterly*, 8/2, 93–105.
Hopkins E. W. (1906). The Buddhist Rule against Eating Meat. *JAOS*, 27, 455–464.
Horton, Robin. (1971). African Conversion. *Africa*, 41/2 (April), 85–108.
Hua Tao. (1993). Central and Western Tianshan on the eve of Islamization. *JAH*, 27/2, 95–108.
Indian and Colonial Intelligence. (1824). *OHCR*, 1 (January–April), 171.
Irby, F. W., and Lefroy, G. A. (1905). A short account of some 'ancient remains' found on Gunong Jerai, Kedah. *Journal of the Federated Malay States Museums*, 1 (No. 3), 76–81.
Irwin, C. J. (1982). The Sacred Anthill and the Cult of the Primordial Mound. *History of Religions*, 21/4 (May), 339–360.
Johns, A. H. (1957). Malay Sufism as illustrated in an anonymous collection of 17th century tracts. *JMBRAS*, 30/178 (Part 2), 5–111.
Jordaan, E. R. (1997). Tara and Nyai Lara Kidul, Images of the Divine Feminine in Java. *AFS*, 56/2, 285–312.
Josselin de Jong P.E. (1986). Textual Anthropology and History: The Sick King. In D. D. Grijns and S. O. Robson (eds.), *Cultural and Textual Interpretation* (pp. 218–32). Foris: Dordrecht-Cinnaminson.
Kadi, W. (2005). What Is Prophecy? Reflections on a Qur'anic Institution in History. In Michael Ipgrave (ed.), *Bearing the Word: Prophecy in Biblical and Qur'anic Perspective* (pp. 45–58). London: Church House Publishing.
Kartomi, J. M. (1973). Music and Trance in Central Java. *Ethnomusicology*, 17/2, 163–208.
Katz, N. (2000). The Identity of a Mystic, The Case of Sa'id Sarmad, a Jewish-Yogi-Sufi Courtier of the Mughals. *Numen*, 47/2, 142–160.
Kempe, E. J., and Winstedt, R. O. (1948). A Malay Legal Digest Compiled for 'Abd al-Ghafur Muhaiyu'd-din Shah Sultan of Pahang 1592–1614 A. D. with undated additions. *JMBRAS*, 21 (Part 1), 1–67.
Kersten, C. (2006). Cambodia's Muslim King, Khmer and Dutch Sources on the Conversion of Reameathipadei I, 1642–1658. *JSEAS*, 37/1, 1–22.
Kesan-Kesan Awal Islam Wujud Di Kedah. In *Sejarah Kemasukan Islam Dan Pekembangannya*. Retrieved December 21, 2007, from http://www.mykedah2.com/10heritage/102_1_p4.htm#sub10 ww.kwikx.com/index-islam4.html.
Khansor Johan (1999). The *Undang-Undang Melaka*, Reflections on Malay Society in Fifteenth-Century Malacca. *JMBRAS*, LXXII (Part 2), 131–150.
King, Phil. (2006). Reading nineteenth century history from a regional perspective: the central Malay Peninsula. *Draft paper prepared for 2nd Water Frontier Workshop* (18–19 February). Phuket.
Klimkeit, Hans-J. (1982). Manichaean Kingship, Gnosis at Home in the World. *Numen*, 29/Fasc. 1 (July), 17–32.
Koenig, J. G. (1894). Journal of a Voyage from India to Siam and Malacca in 1779. *JSBRAS*, (No. 27), 57–134.
Kratz, E. U. (1993). Durhaka, The Concept of Treason in the Malay *Hikayat Hang Tuah*. *South East Asia Research*, 1/1 (March), 68–97.
Kripal J. J. (1994). Kali's Tongue and Ramakrishna, Biting the Tongue of the Tantric Tradition. *History of Religions*, 34/2, 152–189.
Lai, W. (1992). From Folklore to Literate Theatre, Unpacking "Madame White Snake." *AFS*, 51/1, 51–66.
Laidlaw, F. F. (1953). Travels in Kelantan, Trengganu and Upper Perak, a Personal Narrative. *JMBRAS*, 26 (Part 4), 148–164. (The account dates back to 1899.)
Lamb, A. (1959a). The Kedah Casket, A Review of Its Contents. *MIH*, 5/1 (February), 13–20.

———. (1959b). Restoring the Temple on the River of Cut Stone. *MIH*, 5 (November), 5.

———. (1961a). A Model of the Temple on the River of Cut Stone. *MIH*, (April), 34–35.

———. (1961b). Pengkalan Bujang, An Ancient Port in Kedah. *MIH*, 7/1 (September), 12–17.

———. (1962). The Hermits of Perlis. *MIH*, 8/1 (December), 14–19.

———. (1966). Old Middle Eastern Glass in the Malay Peninsula. *Artibus Asiae, Supplementum*, 2, 74–88.

Lambton, A. K. S. (1962). Medieval Persian Theory of Kingship. *Studia Islamica*, XVII, 91–119.

Larenaudiere, M. (1822). Notice sur Le Royaume De Quedah. In *Nouvelles Annales des Voyages* (pp. 32–46). Paris: Gide fils.

Laufer, B. (1931). Inspirational Dreams in Eastern Asia. *The Journal of American Folklore*, 44/172 (April–June), 208–216.

Lawson, Todd. (2001). Fatima's Religious Authority in an Early Work by the Bab. In L. S. Walbridge (ed.), *The most learned of the Shi'a: the institution of the Marja'taqlid* (pp. 94–130). New York: Oxford University Press.

Le May, R. (1929). An Introduction to Sculpture in Siam. *The Burlington Magazine for Connoisseurs*, 55 (No. 320), 212–226.

Lewis, D. (1970). The Growth of the Country Trade to the Straits of Malacca, 1760–1777. *JMBRAS*, 43 (Part II), 114–130.

———. (1975). Kedah—The Development of a Malay State in the 18th and 19th Centuries. In Anthony Reid and Lance Castles (eds.), *Pre-Colonial State Systems in Southeast Asia*. Monographs of the Malaysian Branch of the Royal Asiatic Society (No. 6, pp. 36–43).

Light, F. (1938). A Brief Account of the Several Countries Surrounding Prince of Wales's Island with Their Production. Received from Captain Light. Enclosed in Lord Cornwallis's letter to Mr Dundas, dated 7th January, 1798. *JMBRAS*, XVI (Part I), 123–126.

Logan, J. R. (1846). Journal of an Excursion from Singapore to Malacca and Pinang. *JRGSL*, 16, 304–331.

———. (1851). Notes at Penang, Kedah etc. *JIAEA*, V, 53–65.

———. (1881). Memorandum of the Various Tribes Inhabiting Penang and Province Wellesley. *JRASB*, No. 7, 83–92.

———. (1885). Plan for a Volunteer Police in the Muda District, Province Wellesley, Submitted to the Government by the Late JR Logan in 1867. *JSBRAS*, 16, 173–202.

———. (1887). Journal of an Expedition from Singapore to Malacca and Pinang. In *Miscellaneous papers relating to Indo-China and the Indian Archipelago, Reprinted for the Straits Branch of the Royal Asiatic Society* (vol. 1, pp. 1–20). London: Trubner.

Low, J. (1837). History of Tenasserim. *JRASBI*, 4, 42–109.

———. (1848). An account of several inscriptions found in Province Wellesley, on the Peninsula of Malacca. *JASB*, 17/2, 62–6.

———. (1849). A Translation of the Keddah Annals. *JIAEA*, III (August), 1–23, 162–181, 250–270, 314–336, 467–488.

———. (1849b). An Account of the Origin and Progress of the British Colonies in the Straits of Malacca. *JIAEA*, III, 360–379.

———. (1851). On the Ancient Connection between Kedah and Siam. *JIAEA*, V, 498–527.

Mabbett, Ian. (1986). Buddhism in Champa. In David G. Marr and A. C. Milner. (eds.), *Southeast Asia in the 9th to 14th Centuries* (pp. 291–313). Australia: Institute of Southeast Asian Studies; Canberra: Research School of Pacific Studies, Australian National University.

Malay Concordance Project. Australia National University. Retrieved 2006 to 2008, from http://www.anu.edu.au/asianstudies/ahcen/proudfoot/MCP/.

Manguin, Pierre-Yves (1985). The introduction of Islam into Champa. *JMBRAS*, 58/1, 1–28.

———. (1993). Palembang and Sriwijaya, An Early Malay Harbour-City Rediscovered. *JMBRAS*, 66 (Number 1), 23–46.
Marrison, G. E. (1955). Persian Influences in Malay Life (1280–1650). *JMBRAS*, 28 (Part 1), 56–60.
———. (1995). Reviews: The System of Classical Malay Literature by V. I. Braginsky. *BSOAS*, 58/1, 210–212.
Maung Htin Aung (1931). Burmese Crocodile Tales. *Folklore*, 42/1 (March 31), 79–82.
Maxwell, W. E. (1882). A Journey on Foot to the Patani Frontier in 1876. *JSBRAS*, 9 (June), 1–68.
———. (1887). Pulau Langkawi. *JSBRAS*, 19, 27–33.
McKinnon, E. E. (1988). Beyond Serendib, A Note on Lambri at the Northern Tip of Aceh. *Indonesia*, 46 (October), 103–121.
Memorandum by W. B. Albinus, Governor of Malacca in 1750: Malacca in the Eighteenth Century, Two Dutch Governors' Reports. Translated by Brian Harrison. (1954). *JMBRAS*, 27 (Part 1), 24–34.
Miksic, J. N. (1989). Urbanisation and Social Change, the Case of Sumatra. *Archipel*, 37, 3–29.
Miller, E. H. (1941). Extracts from the Letters of Col. Nahuijs, *JMBRAS* 19/2, 169–209.
Milner, A. C. (1979/1980). The Sultan and the Missionary. *JEBAT* (Jabatan Sejarah, Universiti Kebangsaan Malaysia), Bil 9, 1–15.
———. (1981). Islam and Malay Kingship. *JRASBI*, 1, 46–70.
Misbana. (1954). Mengkaji Sejarah Trengganu. In Wan Hussein Azmi. (1980). Islam di Malaysia: Kedatangan dan Perkembangan (Abd 7–20M). In Khoo Kay Kim (ed.), *Tamadun Islam di Malaysia* (p. 145n). Kuala Lumpur: Persatuan Sejarah Malaysia.
Miscellaneous Notices, The Semang and Sakei tribes of the Districts of Kedah and Perak bordering on Province Wellesley. (1878). *JSBRAS*, 1 (July), 111–113.
Mohamed Radzi. (1956). Kota Kuala Muda, *The Malayan Historical Journal*, 3 (July), 26–34.
Newbold, T. J. (1835). On the Government and History of Naning in the Malay Peninsula. *JASB*, 42 (June), 297–319.
———. (1836). Outline of Political and Commercial Relations with the Native States on the Eastern and Western Coasts, Malay Peninsula. *JASB* 5 (January–December), 626–635.
Nihom, M. (1986). The Identification and Original Site of a Cult Statue on East Java, The Jaka Dolog. *JAOS*, 106/3, 485–501.
Nik Hassan Shuhaimi Nik Abdul Rahman (2007). Current Issues on Prehistory and Protohistory in Malaysian Archaeology. *JMBRAS*, 80 (Part 1), 41–57.
Norouzi, P. (2006). Baadeh Sufianeh [Sufi intoxicants]. *Sufi*, 71 (Summer 1385), 7–12.
Norris, W. (1849). Malay Amoks Referred to Mahomedanism. *JIAEA*, III (August), 460–463.
Oertel, H. (1897). Contributions from the *Jaiminiya Brahmana* to the history of the *Brahmana* literature. *JAOS*, 18, 15–48.
Othman, R. M. (1997). Hadhramis in the Politics and Administration of the Malay States in the Late Eighteenth and Nineteenth Centuries. In Ulrike Freitag and William G. Clarence-Smith (eds.), *Hadhrami Traders, Scholars and Statesmen in the Indian Ocean, 1750s–1960* (pp. 82–94). Leiden: Brill.
Peacock, B. A. V. (1970). New Light on the Ancient Settlement of Kedah and Province Wellesley. *MIH*, 13/2 (December), 20–23.
Persopedia (The Persian Poetry Online Library). (2011). Retrieved 2006 to 2011, from http://persopedia.com/show.aspx.
Petersen, R. (1991). The Role of the Raksasa, an Interview with Pak Asep Sunanda, Dalang of Wayang Golek Purwa. *TDR*, 35/2 (Summer), 129–137.
Pfeiffer, H. Robert (1926). Images of Yahweh. *Journal of Biblical Literature*, 45/3–5, 211–222.

Phongsawadan Muang Zaiburi (The Chronicle of Negeri Kedah), Translated and with an Introductory Note by Kobkua Suwannathat-Pian. (1990). *Jebat* (Kuala Lumpur), 18, 89–118.

Quaritch-Wales, H. G. (1940). Archaeological Researches on Ancient Indian Colonization in Malaya. *JMBRAS*, 18 (Part 1), 1–85.

Quedah, and Tuanku Mahomed Saad. (1841). *AJMR*, 110–114.

Ramos, M. (1969). The *Aswang* Syncrasy in Philippine Folklore. *Western Folklore*, 28/4 (October), 238–48.

Reck, S. C., and Reck D. (1981). *Naga-Kalam*: A Musical Trance Ceremonial of Kerala. *Asian Music*, 13/1, 84–96.

Reid, Anthony (1969). Sixteenth Century Turkish Influence in Western Indonesia. *JSEAH*, 10/3, 395–414.

———. (1990). An "Age of Commerce" in Southeast Asian History. *MAS*, 24/1, 1–30.

———. (1993). Kings, Kadis and Charisma in the Seventeenth Century Archipelago. In Anthony Reid (ed.), *The Making of an Islamic Political Discourse in Southeast Asia* (pp. 83–108). Clayton: Monash University Centre of Southeast Asian Studies.

———. (1994). Early Southeast Asian Categorizations of Europeans. In Stuart B. Schwartz (ed.), *Implicit Understandings: Observing, Reporting, and Reflecting on the Encounters between Europeans and Other Peoples in the Early Modern Era* (pp. 268–294). Cambridge: Cambridge University Press.

Report of Governor Balthasar Bort on Malacca 1678. Translated by M. J. Bremer with introduction and notes by C. O. Blagden. (1927). *JMBRAS*, 5, 134–182.

Richman, P. (1993). Veneration of the Prophet Muhammad in an Islamic *Pillaitamil*. *JAOS*, 113/1 (January–March), 57–74.

Roff, W. R. (1964). The Malayo-Muslim World of Singapore at the Close of the Nineteenth Century. *JAS*, 24/1 (November), 75–90.

Roolvink, R. (1967). The Variant Versions of the Malay Annals. *Bijdragen tot de Taal-, Landen Volkenkunde*, 123/3, 301–24.

Rungswasdisab, Puangthong. (2004). Siam and the Contest for Control of the Trans-Mekong Trading Networks from the Late Eighteenth to the Mid-Nineteenth Centuries. In Nola Cooke and Tana Li (eds.), *Water Frontier: Commerce and the Chinese in the Lower Mekong Region, 1750–1880* (pp. 101–118). Singapore: Singapore University Press and Rowman and Littlefield Publishers.

Saber, M., Tamano M. M., and Warriner, A. C. (1960). The Maratabat of the Maranao. *Philippine Sociological Review*, 8/1–2, 10–15.

Sahai, S. (1994). Indo-Chinese Geography as Described in the Phra Lak Phra Lam: A Laotian Version of the Ramayana. In K. R. Srinivasaiyengar (ed.), *Asian Variations in Ramayana: Papers presented at the International Seminar on "Variations in Ramayana in Asia: Their Cultural, Social and Anthropological Significance": New Delhi, January 1981* (pp. 221–229). New Delhi: Sahitya Akademi.

Salinger, G. (1956). A Muslim Mirror for Princes. *Muslim World*, 46/1, 24–39.

Santiko, Hariani (1997). The Goddess Durga in the East-Javanese Period. *AFS*, 56, 209–226.

Sastri, Nilakanta. (1954). Ancient Contacts between India and South East Asia. *MIH*, 1/1 (May), 11–14.

Scott, B. S. (1913). Mohammedanism in Borneo, Notes for a Study of the Local Modifications of Islam and the Extent of its Influence on the Native Tribes. *JAOS*, 33, 313–344.

Scott, D. (1995). Buddhist Responses to Manichaeism, Mahayana Reaffirmation of the "Middle Path." *History of Religions*, 35/2 (November), 148–162.

Scott-Kemball, J. (1959). The Kelantan Wayang Siam Shadow Puppets "Rama" and "Hanuman," A Comparative Study of Their Structure. *Man*, 59 (May), 73–78.

Scupin, R. (1980). Islam in Thailand before the Bangkok Period. *JSS*, 68/1, 55–66.

Sears, L. L. (1989). Aesthetic Displacement in Javanese Shadow Theatre, Three Contemporary Performance Styles. *TDR*, 33/3 (Autumn), 122–140.

Setudeh-Nejad, N. (2002). The Cham Muslims of Southeast Asia, A Historical Note. *Journal of Muslim Minority Affairs*, 22/2, 451–455.

Shahruddin, Inon. (1983). *Si Miskin A Structural Study* (Monograph No. 2). Malaysia: Universiti Kebangsaan Malaysia, Institut Bahasa Kesusasteraan dan Kebudayaan Melayu.

Sharifah Zaleha Binte Syed Hassan. (1989). Versions of Eternal Truth, Ulama and Religious Dissenters in Kedah Malay Society. *Contributions to Southeast Asian Ethnography*, 8 (December), 43–69.

Sheikh Niamat Bin Yusoff and Haji Wan Shamsudin Bin Muhammad Yusof. (1996). Sejarah dan Perjuangan Ulama Kedah Darul Aman: Suatu Muqaddimah. In *Biografi: Ulama Kedah Darul Aman* (vol. 1, pp. 1–15). Alor Setar: Sebuah Terbitan, Lembaga Muzium Negri Kedah Darul Aman.

"Short Account of Timor, Savu, Solor, &c" *Malayan Miscellanies*, cited at length in *AJMR*, 1822 (January–June), 529–536.

Shulman, D. (1978). The Serpent and the Sacrifice, An Anthill Myth from Tiruvarur. *History of Religions*, 18/2 (November), 107–137.

Simmonds, E. H. S. (1963). The Thalang Letters, 1773–1794, Political Aspects and the Trade in Arms. *BSOAS*, 26 (No. 3), 592–619.

Singaravelu, S. (1985). The Episode of Maiyarab in the Thai *Ramakien* and its Possible Relationship to Tamil Folklore. *AFS*, 44/2, 269–279.

Skeat, W. W. (1900). Report on Cambridge Exploring Expedition to the Malay Provinces of Lower Siam. *JAIGBI*, 30, 73–77.

Skinner, C. (1964). The Trengganu Leader of 1839. *JSEAH*, 5, 179–187.

Smit, J. (1997). "Do Not Be Idolaters." Paul's Rhetoric in First Corinthians 10, 1–22. *Novum Testamentum*, 39/1, 40–53.

Smyth, W. H. (1895). Notes on a Journey to Some of the South-Western Provinces of Siam. *The Geographical Journal*, 6 (No. 5, November), 401–421.

———. (1895b). Notes on a Journey to Some of the South-Western Provinces of Siam. *The Geographical Journal*, 6 (No. 6, December), 522–541.

———. (1898). Journeys in the Siamese East Coast States. *The Geographical Journal*, 11 (No. 5, May), 465–489.

Sohnen, R. (1991). Indra and Women. *BSOAS*, 54/1, 68–74.

Soon, Derek Heng Thiam. (2001). The Trade in Lakawood Products between South China and the Malay World from the Twelfth to Fifteenth Centuries AD. *JSEAS*, 32/2 (June), 133–149.

Spores, C. J. (1988). Running Amok: An Historical Inquiry. *Ohio University, Monographs in International Studies Southeast Asia Series (No. 82)*.

Sprunger, L. K. (1997). Puritan Church Architecture and Worship in a Dutch Context. *Church History*, 66/1, 36–53.

Stargardt, J. (1973). Southern Thai Waterways, Archaeological Evidence on Agriculture, Shipping and Trade in the Srivijayan Period. *Man*, New Series, 8 (No. 1, March), 5–29.

State of Education among the Malays in Malacca. (October 1818). *Indo-Chinese Gleaner*, cited at length in *AJMR* 1820, 345–347.

Steffen, A., and Annandale, N. (1902). Clay Tablets from Caves in Siamese Malaya. *Man*, 2, 177–180.

Stevens, F. G. (1929). A Contribution to the early history of Prince of Wales Island. *JMBRAS*, 2, 388–389.

Stokes, L. (2000). Langkawi, the Island of Legends, *Sawaddi* (Bangkok), 46/4, 12–16.

Suhrke, Astri. (1970/1971). The Thai Muslims: Some Aspects of Minority Integration. *Pacific Affairs*, 43/4, 531–547.

Sullivan, M. (1957). Raja Bersiong's Flagpole Base, A Possible Link between Ancient Malaya and Champa. *Artibus Asiae*, 20/4, 289–295.

Sweeney, A. (1967). The Connection between the Hikayat Raja Pasai and the Sejarah Melayu. *JMBRAS*, 40/2, 94–105.

———. (1971). Reviews, Hikayat Marong Mahawangsa by Siti Hawa Saleh. *BSOAS*, 34/2, 436–437.
Syair Perang Siak; A Court Poem Presenting the State Policy of a Minangkabau Malay Royal Family in Exile. Edited and translated by D. J. Goudie and with essays by Phillip L. Thomas and Tenas Effendy. (1989) (Monograph No. 7). Kuala Lumpur: Council of the Malaysian Branch of the Royal Asiatic Society. (M. B. R. A. S.)—Art Printing.
The Cambridge Exploring Expedition to the Siamese-Malay States. (1900). *Science* 11/284 (8 June), 915–916.
The Kedah Blockade. Retrieved September 5, 2008, from http://mizteryjw.blogspot.com/2007/10/kedah-blockade.html.
Three Seventeenth century visitors to the Malay Peninsula. Translated and edited by J. J. Sheehan (1934). *JMBRAS*, 12/2, 71–107.
Thompson, J. W. (1916). The German Church and the Conversion of the Baltic Slavs Concluded. *The American Journal of Theology*, 20/3, 372–389.
Thomson, G. (1868). Notes on Cambodia and Its Races. *Transactions of the Ethnological Society of London*, 6, 246–252.
Topping, M. (1970). Some Account of Kedah. *JIAEA*, IV, 43. (The JIAEA article was originally published in 1850 and is a reproduction of a study on Kedah by Michael Topping in 1786 CE.)
Tregonning, K. G. (1959). Penang and the China trade. *MIH*, 5/1, 8–12.
Treloar, F. E., and Fabris, G. J. (1975). Evidence for the Contemporary Existence of Two Kedah Sites. *JMBRAS*, 48 (Part 1), 74–76.
van der Tuuk, H. N. (1887). Account of the MSS Belonging to the Royal Asiatic Society. In *Miscellaneous Papers Relating to Indo-China and the Indian Archipelago: Reprinted for the Straits Branch of the Royal Asiatic Society* (Volume 2, pp. 1–56). London: Trubner.
Vaughan, J. D. (1970). Notes on the Malays of Pinang and Province Wellesley. *JIAEA*, 2, 115–175. (Originally published in 1858.)
Vincent, F. (1878). The Wonderful Ruins of Cambodia. *Journal of the American Geographical Society of New York*, 10, 229–252.
Visser, H. F. E. (1956). Naga Figures at Rotterdam, Amsterdam and Chicago. *Artibus Asiae*, 19/3–4, 374–377.
Wagoner, B. P. (1996). Sultan among Hindu Kings, Dress, Titles and the Islamicization of Hindu Culture at Vijayanagar. *JAS*, 55/4 (November), 851–880.
Walker, J. H. (2004). Autonomy, Diversity, and Dissent, Conceptions of Power and Sources of Action in the *Sejarah Melayu* (Raffles MS 18). *Theory and Society*, 33/2 (April), 213–255.
Wan Hussein Azmi. (1980). Islam di Malaysia: Kedatangan dan Perkembangan. (Abd 7–20M). In Khoo Kay Kim (ed.), *Tamadun Islam di Malaysia* (pp. 135–145). Kuala Lumpur: Persatuan Sejarah Malaysia.
Wasson R. G. (1971). The Soma of the Rig Veda, What Was It? *JAOS*, 91/2 (April–June), 169–187.
Waszink J. H., and Winden Van, C. M. J. (1982). A Particular Kind of Idolatry. An Exegesis of Tertullian, "De idololatria" ch. 23. *Vigiliae Christianae*, 36/1, 15–23.
Wayman, A. (1961). Totemic Beliefs in the Buddhist Tantras. *History of Religions*, 1/1, 81–94.
Webb, Gisela. (1994). Tradition and Innovation in Contemporary American Islamic Spirituality: The Bawa Muhaiyaddeen Fellowhsip. In Y. Y. Haddad and J. I. Smith (eds.), *Muslim Communities in North America* (pp. 75–108). Albany: State University of New York Press.
Wee, V. (1988). Material Dependence and Symbolic Independence: Constructions of Melayu Ethnicity in Island Riau, Indonesia. In A. Terry Rambo, Kathleen Gilloghy and Karl L. Hutterer (eds.), *Ethnic Diversity and the Control of Natural Resources in Southeast Asia* (pp. 210–213). Ann Arbor: Michigan Papers on South and Southeast Asia, No. 32.
Wessing R. (1990). Sri and Sedana and Sita and Rama, Myths of Fertility and Generation. *AFS*, 49/2, 235–257.

———. (1997). A Princess from Sunda, Some Aspects of Nyai Roro Kidul. *AFS*, 56/2, 317–353.
Wheatley, Paul. (1964). Desultory Remarks on the Ancient History of the Malay Peninsula. In John Bastin and R. Roolvink (eds.), *Malayan and Indonesian Studies*. Oxford: Clarendon Press.
Wieringa, P. E. (1994). The Javanese Story of Dewi Maleka, A Transformation of a Persian or Perso-Urdu Tale. *Bijdragen tot de Taal-, Land-, and Volkenkunde van Nederlandsch Indie*, 150/3, 584–587.
Wilkinson R. J. (1957). Papers on Malay Customs and Beliefs, Beliefs Regarding Life and Living Things (first published 1906). *JMBRAS*, 30/180 (Part 4), 24–32.
Winstedt, R. O. (1920a). The Genealogy of Malacca's Kings from a copy of the Bustanu's-Salatin. *JSBRAS*, 81, 29–35.
———. (1920b). The Indian Origin of Malay Folk-Tales. *JMBRAS*, 82, 119–126.
———. (1920c). History of Kedah. *JMBRAS*, 81, 29–35.
———. (1928). Kedah Laws. *JMBRAS*, 6/Part II, 1–44.
———. (1932). A History of Johor (1365–1895). *JMBRAS*, 10/Part 3, 1–159.
———. (1936). Notes on the History of Kedah. *JMBRAS*, 14/3, 155–189.
———. (1938). The Kedah Annals. *JMBRAS*, 16 /2, 31–5.
———. (1938a). The Chronicles of Pasai. *JMBRAS*, 16 /2, 24–30.
———. (1938b). The Malay Annals or Sejarah Melayu, The earliest recension from MS. No. 18 of the Raffles collection, in the Library of the Royal Asiatic Society, London. *JMBRAS*, 16 /3, 1–226.
———. (1939). A history of Malay literature with a chapter on modern developments by Zaba (Zain Al-Abidin Bin Ahmad). *JMBRAS*, 17 /3, 1–243.
———. (1940). Did Pasai Rule Kedah in the 14th Century? *JMBRAS*, 18/2.
———. (1947). Kingship and Enthronement in Malaya. *JMBRAS*, 20/1, 129–139.
Wolters, O. W. (1979). Studying Srivijaya. *JMBRAS*, 52/2, 1–33.
Wong, C. S. (1958). The Founding of Penang. *MIH* 4 (No. 1, January), 29–30.
Woodward, W. H. (1980). Some Buddha Images and the Cultural Development of the Late Angkorian Period. *Artibus Asiae*, 42/2–3, 155–174.
Yahya Abu Bakar. (1991). Kedah dan perdagangan Tradisi Di Asia Abad Ke-tujuh Hingga Abad Keenam belas Masihi. In *Biografi: Ulama Kedah Darul Aman*. Alor Setar: Sebuah Terbitan, Lembaga Muzium Negri Kedah Darul Aman.
Yarshater, E. (1960). The Theme of Wine-Drinking and the Concept of the Beloved in Early Persian Poetry. *Studia Islamica* 13, 43–53.
Yatim, Othman Mohd. (1985). Early Islamic Tombstones in Malaysia, Indian and Indonesian Origins. *Islamic Culture* (Hyderabad, India), LIX/2 (April), 143–152.
Yi-Liang, C. (1945). Tantrism in China. *Harvard Journal of Asiatic Studies*, 8/3–4 (March), 241–332.
Yousof, Ghulam-Sarwar. (1994). Ramayana Branch Stories in the Wayang Siam Shadow Play in Malaysia. In K. R. Srinivasaiyengar (ed.), *Asian Variations in Ramayana: Papers presented at the International Seminar on "Variations in Ramayana in Asia: Their Cultural, Social and Anthropological Significance": New Delhi, January 1981* (pp. 296–323). New Delhi: Sahitya Akademi.
Zaharah bt Haji Mahmud (1972). The Period and Nature of "Traditional" Settlement in the Malay Peninsula. *JMBRAS*, 43, 81–105.
———. (1972a). The Population of Kedah in the Nineteenth Century. *JSEAS*, 3/2 (September), 193–209.
Zakaria Ali (1993). Notes on the *Sejarah Melayu* and Royal Malay Art. *Muqarnas*, 10, 382–386.
Zakharov, O. Anton. (2007). The Political Organization of Crivijaya in Historiographic Perspective. In Anton O. Zakharov (ed.), *Essays on the History of Traditional Orient* [translated from the Russian title] (pp. 127–160). Moscow: Vostochnyi Universitet.
Zulkifli Khair and Badrol Hisham Ibrahim. (1994). Sejarah Awal Masyarakat Islam di Pualu Pinang dan Masjid Jamik Batu Uban. In *Sejarah Islam di Pulau Pinang: Islam dan Masyarakat* (Volume 1). Penang Island: Sinaran Bros. Sdn. Berhad.

BOOKS

Abdullah bin Abdul Kadir. (1970). *The Hikayat Abdullah*. Translated by A. H. Hill. New York: Oxford University Press.

Adil, Buyong. (1980). *Siri Sejarah Nusantara: Sejarah KEDAH*. Kuala Lumpur: Dewan Bahasa Dan Pustaka.

Ahmat, Sharom. (1984). *Tradition and Change in a Malay State: A Study of the Economic and Political Development of Kedah, 1878–1923*. Kuala Lumpur: Council of the Malaysian Branch of the Royal Asiatic Society. (M. B. R. A. S.) – Art Printing.

al-Attas, Syed Naguib. (1963). *Some Aspects of Sufism as Understood and Practiced among the Malays*. Singapore: Malaysian Sociological Research Institute Ltd.

———. (1969). *Preliminary Statement on a General Theory of the Islamization of the Malay-Indonesian Archipelago*. Kuala Lumpur: Dewan Bahasa Dan Pustaka.

Ali Haji Ibn Ahmad (Raja). (1982). *The Precious Gift (Tuhfat al-Nafis)*. Edited and translated by Virginia Matheson and Barbara Watson Andaya. Kuala Lumpur: Oxford University Press. (Raja Ali Haji Ibn Ahmad, the author of the text, lived circa 1809–1870 CE.)

Alwi bin Sheikh Alhady. (1967). *Malay Customs and Traditions*. Singapore: Donald Moore Press Ltd.

Andaya, B. W. (1979). *Perak, The Abode of Grace*. Kuala Lumpur: Oxford University Press.

———. (1993). *To Liver as Brothers: Southeast Sumatra in the Seventeenth and Eighteenth Centuries*. Honolulu: University of Hawaii Press.

Andaya, Leonard Y. (1975). *The Kingdom of Johor 1641–1728*. Kuala Lumpur: Oxford University Press.

Anderson, Benedict. (1983). *Imagined Communities: Reflections on the Origin and Spread of Nationalism*. London: Verso.

———. (1990). *Language and Power: Exploring a Political Culture in Indonesia*. Ithaca, NY: Cornell University Press.

———. (1998). *The Spectre of Comparisons: Nationalism, Southeast Asia, and the World*. New York: Verso.

Anderson, John. (1824). *Political and Commercial Considerations relative to the Malayan Peninsula and the British Settlements in the Straits of Malacca*. Unknown: William Cox.

———. (1826). *Mission to the East Coast of Sumatra in 1823*. London: William Blackwood, Edinburgh, and T. Cadell, Strand.

———. (1840). *Acheen, and the Ports on the North and East Coasts of Sumatra: With Incidental Notices of the Trade in the Eastern Seas, and the Aggressions of the Dutch*. London: W.H. Allen.

———. (1890). *The Selungs of the Mergui Archipelago*. London: Trubner.

Arberry, A. J. (1969). *Sufism*. London: Allen & Unwin.

Arjomand, A. S. (1984). *The Shadow of God and the Hidden Imam: Religion, Political Order, and Societal Change in Shi'ite Iran from the Beginning to 1890*. Chicago: University of Chicago Press.

Attar Neyshaburi, Sheikh Farid al-Din. (1359 *Shamsi*) [i.e., 1980 CE]. *Divane Attar-e Nayshaburi*. Edited and a forward by M. Darwish. Tehran: Sazmane Chap va Entesharate Javidan. (In Farsi.)

Awn, P. J. (1983). *Satan's Tragedy and Redemption: Iblis in Sufi Psychology*. Leiden: E. J. Brill.

Bacon, G. B. (1892). *Siam, the Land of the White Elephant: As It Was and Is*. New York: Charles Scribner's Sons.

Balkhi, M. J. (1366 *Shamsi*) [i.e., 1987 CE]. *Kuliyateh Mathnawiyeh Maanawi*. Tehran: Sazmaneh Entesharateh Javidan. (In Farsi.)

Banks, D. J. (1983). *Malay Kinship*. Philadelphia: Institute for the Study of Human Issues.

Barnard, T. P. (2003). *Multiple Centres of Authority: Society and Environment in Siak and Eastern Sumatra, 1674–1827*. Leiden: KITLV Press.

Barua, N. S. (1991). *Tribes of Indo-Burma Border: A Socio-cultural History of the Inhabitants of the Patkai Range*. New Delhi: Mittal Publications.

Bassett, D. (1990). *The British in Southeast Asia during the Seventeenth and Eighteenth Centuries* (Occasional Paper: No. 18). United Kingdom: The University of Hull, Centre for South-East Asian Studies. (A volume in memory of the late Dr. David Kenneth Bassett.)

Begbie, P. J. (1834). *The Malayan Peninsula*. Madras: Vepery Mission Press.

Beighton, T. J. (1888). *Betel-Nut Island: Personal Experiences and Adventures in the Eastern Tropics*. London: The Religious Tract Society.

Bella, B. (1989). *Langkawi—from Mahsuri to Mahathir: Tourism for Whom?* Kuala Lumpur: INSAN.

Benjamin, G. (1986). *between Isthmus and Islands: Reflections on Malayan Palaeo-Sociology*. (Working Papers: Number 71), Singapore: Department of Sociology, National University of Singapore.

Bennett, A. (1929). *The Religion of Burma*. Madras: Theosophical Publishing House.

Bharati, A. (1977). *The Tantric Tradition*. Westport: Greenwood Press.

Bill, A. J., and Williams A. J. (2003). *Roman Catholics and Shi'i Muslims, Prayer, Passion and Politics*. Chapel Hill and London: The University of North Carolina Press.

Bird, Bella. (1989). *Langkawi-from Mahsuri to Mahathir: Tourism for Whom?* Kuala Lumpur: Insan (Institute of Social Analysis).

Bonney, R. (1971). *Kedah 1771–1821: The Search for Security and Independence*. Kuala Lumpur: Oxford University Press.

Bowrey, T. (1905). *The Countries Around the Bay of Bengal 1669–1679*. Edited by Sir R. C. Temple. Cambridge: Hakluyt Society.

Bowring, J. (1857). *The Kingdom and People of Siam* (2 vols.). London: John W. Parker & Son.

Bradley, J. (1876). *A Narrative of Travel and Sport in Burmah, Siam, And the Malay Peninsula*. London: Samuel Tinsley.

Braginsky, V. I. (1993). *The System of Classical Malay Literature*. Leiden: KITLV Press.

Brown, C. C. (1970). *Sejarah Melayu "Malay Annals."* Kuala Lumpur: Oxford University Press.

Buckley, C. B. (1902). *An Anecdotal History of Old Times in Singapore, from the Foundation of the Settlement under the Honourable the East India Company, on Feb. 6th, 1819, to the Transfer to the Colonial Office as Part of the Colonial Possessions of the Crown on April 1st, 1867* (vol. 1). Singapore: Fraser & Neave.

Burney, H. (1910–1914). *Burney Papers*, Reprinted with an Introduction by D. K. Wyatt (5 vols.). Bangkok: Gregg International Publishers, 1971.

Cameron, J. (1865). *Our Tropical Possessions in Malayan India: Being a Descriptive Account of Singapore, Penang, Province Wellesley, and Malacca: Their Peoples, Products, Commerce, and Government*. London: Smith, Elder.

Cases Heard and Determined in Her Majesty's Supreme Court of the Straits Settlements 1808–1890, compiled by James William Norton-Kyshe (Straits Settlements Supreme Court). (1885). Singapore: Singapore and Straits Printing Office.

Chau Ju-kua, his work on the Chinese and Arab Trade in the Twelfth and Thirteenth Centuries, Entitled Chu-fan-chi. Translated from the Chinese and annotated by Friedrich Hirth and W.W. Rockhill. (1966). New York: Paragon Book Reprint Corp. (Chau Ju-kua, 1170–1231 CE, completed his text circa 1225–1226 CE)

Chaumont, de Chevalier, and Choisy, de Abbe. (1997). *Aspects of the Embassy to Siam 1685 Being Alexandre de Chaumont's Relation of the Embassy to Siam 1685 and Francois-Timol'eon de Choisy, Memoranda on Religion and Commerce in Siam and Reflections on the Embassy to Siam*. Edited and in part translated by Michael Smithies. Chiang Mai: Silkworm Books.

Cheah Boon Kheng. (2006). *To' Janggut (Old Long Beard): Legends, Histories and Perceptions of the 1915 Rebellion in Kelantan*. Singapore: Singapore University Press.

Chittick, C. W. (1992). *Faith and Practice of Islam: Three Thirteenth Century Sufi Texts*. Albany: State University of New York Press.

Chou, Cynthia. (2003). *Indonesian Sea Nomads: Money, Magic and Fear of the Orang Suku Laut*. London: Routledge.
Clodd, H. P. (1948). *Malaya's First British Pioneer: The Life of Francis Light*. London: Luzac.
Codrington, H. W. (1970). *A Short History of Ceylon*. London: Ayer Publishing. (First published in 1926.)
Croley, Henry. (1878). *Geography of the Eastern Peninsula*. Ootacamund: Neilgherry Courier Press.
Cortesao, A. (1944). *The Suma Oriental of Tome Pires: An Account of the East, from the Red Sea to Japan Written in Malacca and India in 1512–1515* (2 vols.). London: The Hakluyt Society.
Crawfurd, J. (1830). *Journal of an Embassy from the Governor-General of India to the Courts of Siam and Cochin China Exhibiting a View of the Actual State of Those Kingdoms* (2 vols.). London: Henry Colburn & Richard Bentley. (First published in 1828.)
———. (1856). *A Descriptive Dictionary of the Indian Island and Adjacent Countries*. London: Bradbury & Evans.
Cummings, W. (2002). *Making blood white: Historical transformations in early modern Makassar*. Honolulu: University of Hawaii Press.
Dampier, W. (1931). *Voyages and Discoverie*. With an Introduction and Notes by Clennell Wilkinson. London: Argonaut Press.
Davids, T. W. R., and W. Stede. (1991). *The Pali-English Dictionary*. New Delhi: AES.
Dehkhoda, A. A. (1325 *Shamsi*) [i.e., 1947 CE]. *Farhangi Dehkhoda* (15 Vols.). Tehran: Chap-Khaneyeh Majles. (Persian Lexicon.)
Douglas-Klotz, N. (2003). *The Genesis Meditations: A Shared Practice of Peace for Chritians, Jews and Muslims*. Wheaton, IL: Quest Books.
Dowson, J. (1888). *A Classical Dictionary of Hindu Mythology and Religion, Geography, History, and Literature*. London: Trubner.
Drakard, J. (1990). *A Malay Frontier, Unity and Duality in a Sumatran Kingdom*. Ithaca, NY: Cornell University Press.
———. (1999). *A Kingdom of Words: Language and Power in Sumatra*. Kuala Lumpur: Oxford University Press.
Earl, G. W. (1837). *The Eastern Seas*. London: W. H. Allen.
Eaton, R. M. (1996). *Sufis of Bijapur 1300–1700: Social roles of Sufis in Medieval India*. Reprinted New Delhi: Munshiram Manoharlal Publishers Pvt Ltd. (Originally published in 1978.)
Eggermont, P. H. L. (1993). *Alexander's campaign in Southern Punjab*. Leuven: Uitgeverij Peeters en Departement Orientalistiek.
Evans, C. (2006). *Thailand: Adventure Guide*. Edison, NJ: Hunter Publishing.
Evans, H. N. I. (1968). *The Negritos of Malaya*. Cambridge: Cambridge University Press.
Fatimi, S. Q. (1963). *Islam Comes to Malaysia*. Singapore: Malaysian Sociological Research Institute.
Finlayson, G. (1826). *The Mission to Siam, and Hue: The Capital of Cochin China, in the Years 1821–2*. London: J. Murray.
Floris, Peter. (1934). *Peter Floris: His Voyage to the East Indies in the Globe 1611–1615*. Translated and edited by W. H. Moreland. London: Hakluyt Society. (Floris reports from Kedah in 1613.)
Forrest, Thomas. (1792). *Voyage from Calcutta to the Mergui Archipelago, Lying on the East Side of the Bay of Bengal*. London: J. Robson.
Frye, R. N. (2004). *The Heritage of Persia*. California: Mazda Publishers, Inc.
Gerini, G. E. (1909). *Researches on Ptolemy's Geography of Eastern Asia (Further India and Indo-Malay Archipelago)*. London: Royal Asiatic Society and Royal Geographical Society.
Gresick, M. L. (1995). *In the Land of Lady White Blood: Southern Thailand and the Meaning of History*. Ithaca: Studies on Southeast Asia, Cornell University.
Gosling, D. L. (2001). *Religion and Ecology in India and Southeast Asia*. New York: Routledge.

Graham, W. A. (1913). *Siam: A Handbook of Practical, Commercial, and Political Information*. Chicago: G. G. Browne.
Groeneveldt, W. P. (1960). *Historical Notes on Indonesia and Malaya: Compiled from Chinese Sources*. Jakarta: C. V. Bhratara. (First published in 1880.)
Gullick, J. M. (1958). *Indigenous Political Systems of Western Malaya*. London: The Athlone Press.
———. (1991). *Malay Society in the Late Nineteenth Century: The Beginnings of Change*. Singapore: Oxford University Press.
Gullin E. G. and Zehnder, W. F. (1905). *The Early History of Penang*. Penang: The Criterion Press.
Hadhrami Traders, Scholars and Statesmen in the Indian Ocean, 1750s–1960. (1997). Edited by Ulrike Freitag and William G. Clarence-Smith. Leiden: Brill.
Hall, K. R. (1985). *Maritime Trade and State Development in Early Southeast Asia*. Honolulu: University of Hawaii Press.
Hamilton, Alexander. (1995). *A New Account of the East-Indies: Being the Observations and Remarks of Capt Alexander Hamilton from the Year 1688–1723* (2 Vols.). New Delhi/Madras: Asian Educational Services. (Originally published in 1744.)
———. (1997). *A Scottish Sea Captain in Southeast Asia 1689–1723*. Edited by Michael Smithies. Chiang Mai: Silkworm books.
Hamilton, W. (1984). *East-India Gazetteer* (2 Vols.). New Delhi: B. R. Corp. (A reprint of the 1828 edition.)
Hamzeh-Nameh (Gheseyeh Amir al-Muminin Hamzeh). Edited by Dr Jafaar Shoaar. (1362 Shamsi) [i.e., 1982 CE]. Tehran: Ketabeh Farzan. (The book includes the sixty-nine stories of the undated Amir Hamza manuscript, Number 4181, kept at the Berlin State Library, *Staatsbibliothek zu Berlin*.)
Heine-Geldern, R. (1956). *Conceptions of State and Kingship in Southeast Asia* (Southeast Asia Program, Data Paper: Number 18, April). Ithaca: Cornell University.
Hikayat Amir Hamza. Edited by A. S. Ahmad. (1987). Kuala Lumpur: Dewan Bahasa Dan Pustaka.
Hikayat Indraputra: A Malay Romance. Edited by S. W. R. Mulyadi. (1983). Holland: Foris Publications.
Hikayat Marong Mahawangsa yakni Silsila Negri Kedah Darulaman. Edited by Muhammad Yusuf b. Nasruddin. (1898). Penang: Kim Sik Hian. (J. R. Wilkinson's Jawi copy of the text acquired at Penang.)
Hikayat Merong Mahawangsa. Edited by Siti Hawa Saleh. (1970). Kuala Lumpur: University of Malaya Press.
Hikajat Potjut Muhamet: An Achenese Epic. Translated and edited by G. W. J. Drewes. (1979). The Hague: Martinus Nijhoff.
Historical Survey of the Mosques and Kramats on Penang Island. (1974). Penang: Malayan Teachers College.(Compiled by lecturers and members of the junior and senior history options.)
Ho, Engseng. (2006). *The Graves of Tarim: Genealogy and Mobility Across the Indian Ocean*. Berkeley: University of California Press.
Hooker, V. M. (2003). *A Short History of Malaysia: Linking East and West*. Singapore: Allen & Unwin.
Horsburgh, J. (1852). *The India Directory, or Directions for Sailing to and from the East Indies, China, Australia, and the Inter-jacent Ports of Africa and South America* (2 vols.). London: W. H. Allen.
Hoyt, H. Sarnia. (1991). *Old Penang*. New York: Oxford University Press.
Hurgronje, C. Snouk. (1970). *Mekka in the Latter Part of the 19th Century; Daily Life, Customs and Learning of the Muslims of the East-Indian archipelago*. Translated by J .H. Monahan. Leyden: E.J. Brill. (The book was first published in Dutch in 1889 and later in 1931 into English by J. H. Monahan.)
Husin Ali, S. (1975). *Malay Peasant Society and Leadership*. Kuala Lumpur: Oxford University Press.

Ibn Al-Farid, Umar Ibn Ali. (2001). *Sufi Verse, Saintly Life*. Translated by Emil Homerin. New York: Paulist Press. (Umar Ibn al-Farid died in about 1235 CE.)

Ivanoff, J. (1997). *Moken: Sea-Gypsies of the Andaman Sea Post-war Chronicles*. Bangkok: White Lotus Press.

Jessup, I. Helen. (1990). *Court Arts of Indonesia*. New York: The Asia Society Galleries.

John Leyden's Malay Annals. Translated by John Leyden. With an introduction by M. B. Hooker and V. M. Hooker. (2001). Reprint 20, Kuala Lumpur: Malaysian Branch of the Royal Asiatic Society.

Johns, A. H. (1965). *The Gift Addressed to the Spirit of the Prophet*. Canberra: The Australian National University.

Jones, R. (1979). Ten Conversion Myths from Indonesia. In Nehemia Levtzion (ed.), *Conversion to Islam* (pp. 129–158). New York: Holmes & Meier Publishers.

Kaempfer, E. (1998). *A Description of the Kingdom of Siam 1690*. Bangkok: Orchid Press. (Originally published in 1727 CE.)

Kashifi, Hussein Waiz. (1362 Shamsi) [i.e., 1982 CE]. *'Anwar-e Suhayl'i* or *'Kelileh va Demneyeh Kashefi'*. Tehran: Entesharateh Amir Kabir. (Persian text, first published in the fifteenth century by Kashifi, died 1503 CE.)

Keane, A. H. (1887). *Eastern Geography: A Geography of the Malay Peninsula, Indo-China, The Eastern Archipelago, The Philippines, and New Guinea*. London: Edward Stanford.

Kerr, R. (1824). *A General History and Collection of Voyages and Travels, Arranged in Systematic Order* (18 vols.). Edinburgh: William Blackwood.

Khan, G. M. (1939). *History of Kedah*. Penang: Penang Premier Press.

Khoo Kay Kim. (1972). *The Western Malay States, 1850–1873: The Effects of Commercial Development on Malay Politics*. Kuala Lumpur: Oxford University Press.

———. (1991). *Malay Society: Transformation and Democratisation*. Petaling Jaya: Selangor Darul Ehsan, Pelanduk Publications (M) Sdn Bhd.

Khoo, Su Nin. (1994). *Streets of George Town: Penang* (2nd edition). Penang: Janus Print & Resources.

Kobkua Suwannathat-Pian. (1988). *Thai-Malay Relations: Traditional Intra-regional Relations from the Seventeenth to the Early Twentieth Centuries*. Singapore: Oxford University Press.

Kokan, Y. Muhammad. (1974). *Arabic and Persian in Carnatic 1710–1960*. Madras: University of Madras.

Ladinsky, Daniel. (1999). *The Gift: Poems by Hafiz the Great Sufi Master*. New York: Penguin Group.

———. (2002). *Love Poems from God: Twelve Sacred Voices from the East and West*. New York: Penguin Group.

Lamb, A. (1960). *Report on the excavation and reconstruction of Chandi Bukit Batu Pahat, Central Kedah*. Kuala Lumpur: Museums Department, Federation of Malaya.

Lang, A. (1996). *Myth, Ritual and Religion* (2 vols.). UK: Random House. (Originally published in 1913.)

Lee, K. H. (1995). *The Sultanate of Aceh: Relations with the British, 1760–1824*. Kuala Lumpur: Oxford University Press.

Leonowens, Anna Harriette. (1870). *The English Governess at the Siamese Court: Being Recollections of Six Years in the Royal Palace at Bangkok*. Philadelphia: Porter & Coates.

Levtzion, Nehemia (ed.). (1979). *Conversion to Islam*. New York: Holmes & Meier Publishers.

Li, T. (1998). *Nguyen Cochinchina: Southern Vietnam in the Seventeenth and Eighteenth Centuries*. New York: Cornell University Southeast Asia Program.

Liaw Yoke Fang. (1976). *Undang-Undang Melaka (The Laws of Melaka)*. The Hague: Martinus Nijhoff.

Loftus, J. A. (1883). *Notes of a Journey across the Isthmus of Kra: Made with the French Government Survey Expedition January–April 1883*. Singapore: Straits Times Press.

Low, J. (1836). *A Dissertation on the Soil and Agriculture of the British Settlement of Penang or Prince of Wales Island in the Straits of Malacca including Province Wellesley on the Malayan Peninsula*. Singapore: Singapore Free Press Office.

Lu, H. G. (1969). *Old Burma-Early Pagan* (Vol. 1). New York: JJ. Augustin Publishers.

Lynch, J., and Talib, Shaharil. (1994). *Legends of Langkawi*. Hong Kong: Apa Publications.

Macalister, N. (1803). *Historical Memoir relative to Prince of Wales Island in the Straits of Malacca*. London: J. H. Hart.

Mackenzie, A. D. (1998). *Myths and Legends of India*. England: Cox & Wyman. (Originally published in 1913.)

Mahávansi, the Rájá-ratnácari, and the Rájá-vali: Forming the Sacred and Historical Books of Ceylon: Also, a Collection of Tracts Illustrative of the Doctrines and Literature of Buddhism: Translated from the Singhalese. (1833). (Vol. 1). London: Parbury, Allen, and Co.

Maier, M. J. Hendrik. (1988). *In the Centre of Authority: The Malay Hikayat Merong Mahawangsa*. Ithaca, NY: Cornell University, Studies on Southeast Asia.

Maitland W. F., and Pollock, F. (1898). *The History of English Law Before the Time of Edward I*. Cambridge: Cambridge University Press.

Malayan Literature; Comprising Romantic Tales, Epic Poetry and Royal Chronicles. Edited and translated by Chauncey C. Starkweather. (1901). London: The Colonial Press.

Malcom, Howard (Reverend). (1840). *Travels in Hindustan and China*. Edinburgh: William & Robert Chambers.

Marsden, W. (1975). *The History of Sumatra*. Kuala Lumpur: Oxford University Press. (Originally published in 1811.)

Masnavi i Manavi. Edited by E. H. Whinefield. (2001). Iowa: Omphaloskepsis.

Mawson, C. O. S., and Ehrlich, H. E. (1987). *The Harper Dictionary of Foreign Terms*. Ann Arbor, MI: Harper & Row.

Medhurst, H. W. (1838). *China: Its State and Prospects with Especial Reference to the Spread of the Gospel, Containing Allusions to the Antiquity, Extent, Population, Civilization, Literature, and Religion of the Chinese*. London: John Snow.

Milburn, W., and Thornton, T. (1825). *Oriental Commerce, or, the East India Trader's Complete Guide: Containing a Geographical and Nautical Description of the Maritime Parts of India, China, Japan, and Neighbouring Countries . . . with an Account of Their Respective Commerce*. London: Kingsbury, Parbury, and Allen.

Mills, L. A. (1971). *British Malaya: 1824–1867, with appendix by C. O. Blagden*. New York: AMS Press Inc. (First published in 1925.)

Milner, A. C. (1982). *Kerajaan: Malay Political Culture on the Eve of Colonial Rule*. Tucson: Published for the Association for Asian Studies by the University of Arizona Press.

———. (1995). *The Invention of Politics in Colonial Malaya: Contesting Nationalism and the Expansion of the Public Sphere*. Cambridge: Cambridge University Press.

Mirando, H. A. (1985). *Buddhism in Sri Lanka in the 17th and 18th Centuries, with Special Reference to Sinhalese Literary Sources*. Dehiwala, Sri Lanka: Tisara Prakasakayo.

Moebirman. (1973). *Wayang Purwa: The Shadow Play of Indonesia*. Jakarta: C. V. Anugerah. (First published in French and in 1961)

Mohamed Zahir Haji Ismail. (2000). *The Legends of Langkawi*. Kuala Lumpur: Utusan Publications & Distributors Sdn Bhd.

Moor, J. H. (1837). *Notices of the Indian Archipelago, and Adjacent Countries*. Singapore: n.p.

Muhammad Hassan Bin To'Kerani Mohd. Arshad. (1968). *Al-Tarekh Salasilah Negeri Kedah*. Edited by Mohd. Zahid bin Mohd Shah. Kuala Lumpur: Dewan Bahasa Dan Pustaka. (First published in 1927.)

Muhammad Ibn Ibrahim. (1972). *The Ship of Sulaiman*. Translated by John O'Kane (Persian Heritage Series No. 11). London: Routledge and Kegan Paul. (Ibrahim was heading a Persian delegation to Siam on behalf of the Safavid kings in the second half of the seventeenth century.)

Mutalib, H. (1990). *Islam and Ethnicity in Malay Politics*. Singapore: Oxford University Press.

Nabarz, Payam. (2005). *The Mysteries of Mithras: The Pagan Belief That Shaped theChristian World*. Rochester: Inner Traditions.

Nagata, A. J. (1984). *The Reflowering of Malaysian Islam: Modern Religious Radicals and Their Roots*. Vancouver: University of British Columbia Press.

Nahjul-Balagha. (The Style of Eloquence): The Written and Spoken Words of Imam Ali. Collected by Sharif Razi (395–440 Hijjri) in Arabic, translated into English by Dr. A. Pazargadi, (2001). Tehran: Rahnama Publication.

Neale, F. A. (1852). *Narrative of a Residence at the Capital of the Kingdom of Siam*. London: Office of the National Illustrated Library.

Newbold, T. J. (1971). *Political and Statistical Account of the British Settlements in the Straits of Malacca*, introduction by C. M. Turnbull (2 vols.). Kuala Lumpur: Oxford University Press. (Originally published in 1839.)

Nezamol Molkeh Tusi, Abu Ali Hasan.(1377 Shamsi) [i.e., 1998 CE]. *Siyasat-nameh (Seir al Moluk)*. Tehran: Sherkateh Entesharateh Elmi va Farhangi. (The text is in Farsi.)

Nizami Ganjavi, Ilyas. (1965). *Layli va Majnun*. Moskow: Idareyeh Entesharateh Danesh. (The text is in Farsi.)

———. (1388 *Shamsi*) [i.e., 2009 CE]. *Layli va Majnun*. Tehran: Entesharateh Qoqnoos. (The text is in Farsi) .

———. (1388 *Shamsi*) [i.e., 2009 CE]. *Khusrow va Shirin*. Tehran: Entesharateh Qoqnoos. (The text is in Farsi.)

Norman, Henry. (1895). *The Peoples and Politics of the Far East*. London: Fisher Unwin.

Northam B., and Olsen, B. (1999). *In Search of Adventure: A Wild Travel Anthology*. San Francisco: Consortium of Collective Consciousness.

Nurbakhsh, J. (1986). *The Great Satan "Eblis."* London: Khaniqahi-Nimatullahi Publications.

———. (1987). *Sufi Symbolism: The Nurbakhsh Encyclopedia of Sufi Terminology. (Farhang-E Nurbakhsh)* (2 vols). London: Khaniqahi-Nimatullahi Publications.

Osbeck, P. (1771). *A Voyage to China and the East Indies* (2 vols.). London: Benjamin White.

Osborn, Sherard. (1987). *The Blockade of Kedah in 1838: A Midshipman's Exploits in Malayan Waters*, introduction by J. M. Gullick. Oxford: Oxford University Press. (From a journal written by Sherard Osborn, at Kedah, between 1838 and 1839.)

Osborne, Milton. (1997). *Southeast Asia: An Introductory History*. Singapore: Allen & Unwin.

Pinto, Mendes Fernao. (1989). *The Travels of Mendes Pinto*. Edited and translated by Rebecca D. Catz. Chicago: The University of Chicago Press. (Originally published in Portuguese in 1614.)

Potter, D. S. (2004). *The Roman Empire at Bay: AD 180–395*. London: Routledge.

Purcell, Victor. (1951). *The Chinese in Southeast Asia*. Oxford: Oxford University Press.

Purnalingam Pillai, M. S. (1928). *Ravana the Great: KING OF LANKA*. Tinnevely District, India: The Bibliotheca.

Qanungo, B. S. (1988). *A History of Chittagong. (From Ancient Times down to 1761)* (Volume 1). Chittagong: Billah Printers.

Raffles, S. (1835). *Memoir of the Life and Public Services of Sir Thomas Stamford Raffles, F.R.S., &c. &c.* (2 Vols.). London: J. Duncan.

Rama III and the Siamese Expedition to Kedah in 1839, The Dispatches of Luang Udomsombat. Translated by C. Skinner and edited Justin Corfield. (1993). Clayton: Centre For Southeast Asian Studies, Monash University.

Ramayanam of Bhodhayanam: With an appendix and Critical and Explanatory Notes. (1840). Translated from the Sanskrit and published by E. A. Rodrigues. Madras: Oriental Lithographic Press.

Ras, J. J. (1968). *Hikajat Bandjar: A Study in Malay Historiography*. The Hague: Martinus Nijhoff.

Reid, Anthony. (1993b). *Southeast Asia in the Age of Commerce, 1450–1680*. New Haven: Yale University Press.

———. (2005). *An Indonesian Frontier: Acehnese and Other Histories of Sumatra*. Singapore: Singapore University Press.

Ricklefs, M. C. (1986). *A History of Modern Indonesia, c. 1300 to the Present*. Hong Kong: Macmillan.

———. (1998). *The Seen and Unseen Worlds in Java 1726–1749*. Australia/Honolulu: ASAA Southeast Asia Publications Series.

Riddell, P. (2001). *Islam and the Malay-Indonesian World: Transmission and Responses*. Honolulu: University of Hawaii Press.

Rizvi, A. A. (1986). *A History of Sufism in India* (2 vols). New Delhi: Munshiram Manoharlal Publisher Pvt. Ltd.

Roberts, E. (1837). *Embassy to the Eastern Courts of Cochin China, Siam, and Muscat: In the Sloop-of-War Peacock, David Geisinger, Commander, During the Years 1832–3–4*. New York: Harper & Brothers.

Roff, R. W. (1974). *Kelantan: Religion, Society, and Politics in a Malay State*. Kuala Lumpur: Oxford University Press.

Rubin, A. P. (1974). *The International Personality of the Malay Peninsula: A Study of the International Law of Imperialism*. Kuala Lumpur: Penerbit Universiti Malaya.

Rutnin, M. M. (1996). *Dance, Drama, and Theatre in Thailand: The Process of Development and Modernization*. Chiang Mai: Silkworm Books.

Saad Shukri Hajji Muda. (1971). *Detik-Detik Sejarah Kelantan*. Kota Bharu: Pustaka Aman Press.

Sa'di of Shiraz. (n.d.). *The Orchard of Sa'di*. Iowa: Omphaloskepsis.

Safa, Z. (1371–1373 *Shamsi*) [i.e., 1992/1994 CE]. *Tarikheh Adabiat dar Iran* [*A history of Iranian literature of the Islamic era*] (5 Vols.). Tehran: Entesharateh Ferdows. (In Farsi).

Sahai, S. (1996). *The Rama Jataka in Laos: A Study in the Phra Lak Phra Lam* (2 Vols.). New Delhi: B. R. Publishing Corporation.

Sarkar, H. B. (1985). *Cultural Relations between India and Southeast Asian Countries*. New Delhi: Indian Council for Cultural Relations & Motilal Banarsidass.

Sayles, G. W. (1999). *Ancient Coin Collecting VI: Non-Classical Cultures*. Iola, WI: Krause Publications.

Schimmel, Annemarie. (1975). *Mystical Dimensions of Islam*. Chapel Hill: The University of North Carolina Press.

Shadily, H., and Echols, J.M. (1994). *Kamus Indonesia-Inggris: An Indonesian-English dictionary* (3rd edition). Jakarta: Penerbit Pt Gramedia Pustaka Utama.

Shaghir Abdullah, M. (1998). *Tarikh Fatani*. Kuala Lumpur: Khazanah Fathaniyah.

Shah Nameh Hakim Abulghasim Ferdowsi [Book of Kings by Hakim Abulghasim Ferdowsi]. (1366 *Shamsi*) [i.e., 1988 CE]. Tehran: Sazmaneh Entesharateh. (In Farsi).

Sheppard, M. (1984). *Tunku, a Pictorial Biography, 1903–1957*. Kuala Lumpur: Pelanduk Publications Malaysia.

Siegel, J. (1979). *Shadow and Sound: The Historical Thought of a Sumatran People*. Chicago: The University of Chicago Press. (The text includes translations of *Hikajat Potjoet Moehamat*, Si Meuseukin's wedding, and *Hikajat Prang Sabil*.)

Sirdar M V K. (1947). *Location of Lanka*. Poona: Manohar Mahadee Kelkar.

Skeat, W. W. (1900). *Malay Magic: Being an Introduction to the Folklore and Popular Religion of the Malay Peninsula*. New York: The Macmillan Company.

Skeat, W. W., and C. O. Blagden. (1906). *Pagan Races of the Malay Peninsula*. London: Cass.

Slametmuljana B. Raden. (1976). *A Story of Majapahit*. Singapore: Singapore University Press Pte Ltd.

Sopher, E. David. (1977). *The Sea Nomads*. Singapore: Published by the National Museum Singapore. (First published in 1965.)

Stutley, M., and J. Stutley (1977). *Harper's Dictionary of Hinduism: Its Mythology, Folklore, Philosophy, Literature and History*. New York: Harper & Row.

Subrahmanyam, Sanjay. (1990). *The Political Economy of Commerce: Southern India 1500–1650*. Cambridge: Cambridge University Press.

Suhrawardi, Shahab al-Din Yahya. (1375 *Shamsi*) [i.e., 1996 CE]. *Gheseha-yeh Sheikh-eh Eshragh* [Stories by *Sheikh-eh Eshragh*]. Edited by Jafar M. Sadeghi. Tehran: Nashr-eh Markaz. (In Farsi).

Sweeney, A. (1972). *Malay Shadow Puppets: The Wayang Siam of Kelantan*. London: Trustees of the British Museum.

———. (1972b). *The Ramayana and the Malay Shadow-Play*. Kuala Lumpur: Universiti Kebangsan Malaysia.

———. (1987). *A Full Hearing: Orality and Literacy in the Malay World*. Berkeley: University of California Press.

Swettenham, F. A. (1906). *British Malaya: An Account of the Origin and Progress of British Influence in Malaya*. London: G. Allen and Unwin.

Syamananda, R. (1986). *A History of Thailand*. Bangkok: Chulalongkorn University.

Syukri, Ibrahim. (1985). *History of the Malay Kingdom of Patani*. Translated by Conner Bailey and John N. Miksic. Athens: Ohio University Centre for International Studies

Tagliacozzo, Eric. (2005). *Secret Trades, Porous Borders: Smuggling and States along a Southeast Asian Frontier, 1865–1915*. New Haven, CT: Yale University Press.

Thant Myint, U. (2001). *The Making of Modern Burma*. Cambridge: Cambridge University Press.

———. (2006). *The River of Lost Footsteps: Histories of Burma*. New York: Farrar, Straus and Giroux.

The Battle for Junk Ceylon: The Syair Sultan Maulana. Edited and translated by C. Skinner. (1985). Holland: Foris Publications, Bibliotheca Indonesica. (The text was originally written circa 1810/1811 at Kedah.)

The Buddhist Legend of Jimutavahana: From the Katha-Sarti-Sagara [The Ocean River of Story] Dramatised in the Nagananda [The Joy of the World of Serpents]. Translated from Sanskrit by B. H. Wortham. (1911). London: George Routledge & Sons.

The Bustan of Sheikh Molehedin Saadi Shirazi. Translated and a forward by H. Razmjou. (1985). Tehran: Sepehr Printing House for Iranian National Commission for UNESCO.

The Crystal Sands: The Chronicles of Nagara Sri Dharrmaraja. Translated by David K. Wyatt. (1975). (Southeast Asia Program, Data Paper: Number 98, April). Ithaca: Cornell University.

The Despatches, Minutes, and Correspondence, of the Marquess Wellesley (5 vols). (1836–1837). London: W. H. Allen.

The Epic of Kings or Shahnameh by Ferdowsi. Translated by Helen Zimmern (2000). Iowa: Omphaloskepsis.

The Green Sea of Heaven: Fifty Ghazals from the Diwan of Hafiz, translations by T. Gray. (1995). Ashland, OR: White Cloud Press.

The Gulistan or Rose Garden by Musle-Huddeen Sheikh Saadi, of Shiraz. Translated by Francis Gladwin. (1865). Boston: Ticknor and Fields.

The Jataka: Or Stories of the Buddha's Former Births Translated from the Pali by Various Hands. Edited by E. B. Cowell (1994) (6 Vols.). Delhi: Motilal Banarsidass Publishers Private Limited. (First published in 1895)

The Jataka: Together with its Commentary Being Tales of the Anterior Births of Gotama Budda. Translated by V. Fausboll (1963) (Volume 5). London: Luzac and Company, Ltd. (First published in 1891.)

The Koran: With Parallel Arabic Text. Translated by J. Dawood. (1990). London: Penguin Classics.

The Pararaton: A Study of Southeast Asian Chronicle. Translated by I Gusti Putu Phalgunadi. (1996). New Delhi: Sundeep Prakashan.

The Rama Saga in Malaysia: Its Origin and Development. Translated by P. W. Burch and with a forward by C. Hooykaas. (1963). Singapore: Malaysian Sociological Research Institute Ltd.

The Siamese Memoirs of Count Claude de Forbin, 1685–1688, introduced and edited by Michael Smithies. (1996). Chiang Mai: Silkworm Books.

Thomson, J. T. (1991). *Glimpses into Life in Malayan Lands*, introduction and annotations by John Hall-Jones. Singapore: Oxford University Press. (Originally published in 1864.)

Tomlin, Jacob. (1831). *Journal of a Nine Months Residence in Siam.* London: Frederick Westley & A. H. Davis.
Trocki, A. C. (1979). *Prince of Pirates.* Singapore: Singapore University Press.
Tuckey, H. James. (1815). *Maritime Geography and Statistics, or, a Description of the Ocean and Its Coasts, Maritime Commerce, Navigation* (4 Vols.). London: Printed for Black, Parry, and Co.
Turnbull C. M. (1980). *A Short History of Malaysia, Singapore and Brunei.* Australia: Cassell.
Vashmgir Ibn Ziyar. (1378 Shamsi) [i.e., 1999 CE]. *Qabus-nameh.* Tehran: Sherkateh Entesharateh Elmi va Farhangi. (In Farsi.)
Vishnu Purana: A System of Hindu Methodology and Tradition. Translated by H. H. Wilson and edited by F. Hall (1864) (Volume 1). London: Tubner & Co.
Vogelsang, W. (2001). *The Afghans.* Malden: Blackwell Publishers.
Vos, Renout. (1993). *Gentle Janus, Merchant Prince: The VOC and the Tightrope of Diplomacy in the Malay World, 1740–1800.* Leiden: KITLV Press.
Wan Yahya bin Wan Muhammad Taib. (1911). *Salasilah atau Tarikh Kerajaan Kedah.* Alor Setar: n.p.
Warren, J. F. (1981). *The Sulu Zone, 1768–1898: The Dynamics of External Trade, Slavery and Ethnicity in the Transformation of a Southeast Asian Maritime State.* Singapore: Singapore University Press.
Wheatley, Paul. (1961). *The Golden Khersonese: Studies in the Historical Geography of the Malay Peninsula before 1500 A.D.* Kuala Lumpur: University of Malaya Press.
White, Walter. G. (1922). *The Sea Gypsies of Malaya: An Account of the Nomadic Mawken People of the Mergui Archipelago.* London: Seeley, Service.
Wilkinson R. J. (1901). *A Malay-English Dictionary,* Part I. (Alif to Za). Singapore: Kelly & Walsh Ltd.
Winstedt, R. O. (1925). *The Malay Magician: Being Shaman, Saiva and Sufi.* London: Constable & Company.
———. (1964). *Practical Modern Malay-English Dictionary* (4th edition). Kuala Lumpur: Marican & Sons.
———. (1972). *The Malays, a Cultural History.* London: Rutledge & Kegan Paul.
———. (1979). *A History of Johor (1365–1895).* Kuala Lumpur: Malaysian Branch of the Royal Asiatic Society.
Wolters, O. W. (1970). *The Fall of Srivijaya in Malay History.* Kuala Lumpur: Oxford University Press.
———. (1982). *History, Culture, and Region in Southeast Asian Perspectives.* Singapore: Institute of Southeast Asian Studies.
Wongbusarakum, Supin. (2007). *Urak Lawoi'of the Adang Archipelago.* Bangkok: Themma Group.
Wu, Xiao An. (2003). *Chinese Business in the Making of a Malay State, 1882–1941: Kedah and Penang.* London and New York: Routledge Curzon.
Wyatt, D. K., and Teeuw, A. (1970). *Hikayat Patani. The Story of Patani,* (2 Vols.). The Hague: Koninklijk Instituut voor Taal-, Land- en Volkenkunde.
———. (1984). *Thailand: A Short History.* New Haven: Yale University Press.
Wynne, L. M. (1941). *Triad and Tabut: A Survey of the Origin and Diffusion of Chinese and Mohamedan Secret Societies in the Malay Peninsula, A.D. 1800–1935.* Singapore: Government Printing Office.
Yegar, Moshe. (1972). *The Muslims of Burma: A Study of a Minority Group.* Wiesbaden: Otto Harrassowitz.
———. (1979). *Islam and Islamic Institutions in British Malaya: Policies and Implementation.* Jerusalem: The Magnes Press.
———. (2002). *between Integration and Secession: The Muslim Communities of the Southern Philippines, Southern Thailand, and Western Burma/Myanmar.* Lanham: Lexington Books.
Yousof, Ghulam-Sarwar. (1994b). *Dictionary of Traditional South-East Asian Theatre.* Kuala Lumpur: Oxford University Press.

Index

Abani, 29
Abbasid, 37
Abdullah, Sheikh, xvi, 22, 25, 26, 29, 33n26, 39, 40, 41, 42, 43, 44, 51, 52, 53, 54, 59
Abhiseka, 104
Aboriginal, 16, 46, 144
Aceh, 107, 108, 113, 119, 120, 128, 133, 134n6, 136n23, 138n49, 161, 163, 173n3, 175n33, 177, 181. *See also* Jawi
Adang. *See* Archipelago
Adat, 103; Adat bersekampong, 145; Adat meminang, 101, 134n3; Adat minangkabau, 94n34
adil, 43, 44
Adil, Buyong, 28, 63n13
Africa, 62n4, 63n12, 67n57, 67n58; African, 22
Aghori Fakirs, 49
Agni, 50
agreement, 59, 70, 72, 76, 77, 85, 88, 90, 106, 122, 128, 136n23, 140n69, 155, 169, 176n51. *See also* Contract; Covenant; yaum al-mithak
akal, 44
Al-Tarekh Salasilah Negeri Kedah, 23, 27, 30. *See also* Muhammad Hassan Bin To'Keranni Mohd. Arshad
Alexander the Great, 3, 29, 57, 63n21, 69, 70, 75, 92n12, 123, 140n74, 181
Alloo Ganoo, 139n58
Alor Setar, 27, 142n91, 144, 149, 166, 167
Amir Hamza, 65n41. *See also* Hamzeh-Nama; Hikayat Amir Hamza
amok, 51, 80, 93n22, 94n33, 80. *See also* Farquhar, William,
Andaman, 68n71, 138n50; Andaman Sea, 109. *See also* Nikobar

Andaya, Barbara W., 32, 74, 134n4, 136n23, 141n75
Andaya, Leonard Y., 74, 97, 104, 134n7, 136n21, 157
Anderson, Benedict, 12, 20
Anderson, John, 137n37, 138n47, 142n89, 144, 154, 168, 169, 173n11, 173n12, 175n30, 175n44
Angkor, 59, 183
Angkorean, 180
Arab, 25, 26, 37, 55, 80, 141n83; Arab ancestry, 80, 131, 141n77, 181; Arab Syed community, 125; Arabian Peninsula, 37, 40; Arabic, 36, 50, 66n55, 76, 77, 92n7, 92n8, 93n18, 109, 173n15. *See also* Perso-Arabic
Arakan, 36
Archipelago: Adang, 109, 121, 144; Malay, 107, 113, 114, 123; Mergui, 98, 109, 113, 114, 117, 119, 183; Riau, 133
Attar Neishaburi/Neyshaburi, Sheikh Farid al-Din, 53
Australian, 67n58
Ava, 20. *See also* Burma
Avalokitesvara, 64n29. *See also* Bodhisattva
Ayutthaya, 20, 108, 137n36, 139n51, 152, 159, 174n26. *See also* Siam; Thailand

Bab al-nikah, 40, 66n55
Badju, 105. *See also* orang laut
Baghdad, xvi, 26, 29, 37, 43, 44, 51
Bahara, 173n11
Baishe zhuan. *See under* snake
bakti, 99, 105, 131, 133, 134n9, 136n25, 144, 145, 157, 169, 182; bhakta, 136n25; bhakti, 136n25; homage, 99, 136n25; kebaktian, 105; nama

211

Index

kebakti, 105; unconditional devotion, 99, 105, 136n25, 144, 145, 172, 182; unconditional loyalty, 90
balai, 101, 104; audience hall, 42, 88; balai rong, 42, 44; durbar, 41
Baling, 144, 153, 157, 171, 176n51
Balkhi, Muhammad Jalalludin, 45, 53. See also Rumi
Balthasar, Bort, 138n50
Bandar Abbas, 33n21; Gambarun, 33n21; Gumarun, 24
Bandjar, 85, 91n4
Bandon River, 163
Bang khli, 108, 112, 138n46
Bangka, 92n9, 95n49, 136n25. See also Kota Kapur
Bangkok, 7, 20, 89, 118, 139n60, 140n66, 140n67, 154, 161, 162, 163, 165, 166, 171, 175n40
Bangladesh, 66n53; Dhaka Armenian Church, 66n53
Banks, J. David, 100, 143, 169
Barnard, Timothy P., 18, 125, 133n1, 159, 173n2, 177
Batak, 55
Batta, 55
Batu Ampar, 119
Batu Bahara, 127, 128, 142n89
Bauls of Bengal, 49
Bay of Bengal, 4, 102, 103, 109, 113, 117, 119, 120, 132, 135n13, 136n18, 139n51, 144, 148, 151, 162, 165, 170, 177, 183
Beaulieu, M., 85, 86, 91, 99, 100, 105, 134n6, 158, 163
Beighton, Thomas, 35
Bengal, 64n28, 68n68, 161. See also Bay of Bengal
Bengkalis, 138n50
Benjamin, G., 32n9, 147, 148, 152
Bentan, 135n17, 163, 164. See also Sejarah Banten
Berlin, 64n30, 65n41
Bersiung. See Raja Bersiong; Tantric; Vampire
besi kawi, 95n49, 136n23, 136n24. See also curse
betel-nut, 42. See also sireh
Bhagavata Purana, 68n72, 94n35

Bhogavati or Put-Kari, 59
bhuta, 65n40
Billiton, 122. See also Bugis-Makassar
blood, 43, 46, 47, 48, 49, 50, 52, 65n42, 83, 85, 93n26, 97, 99, 100, 149, 157; white blood, 94n38, 149, 173n9
boa, 55, 67n57. See also Naga; snakes
Bodhisattva, 45, 49, 50, 37; God-like, 49, 50; Maha-Bodhisattva, 45. See also Tantric Buddhism
Bonney, R., 11, 14, 15, 17, 18, 118, 136n28, 138n41, 141n81, 144, 161, 164, 174n27
Book of Kings. See Ferdowsi, A. G.; Firdausi, A. G.; Shah-Nameh
Boostan/Bustan of Saadi, 54
border/s, 4, 8, 10, 11, 132, 144, 155, 161, 169, 174n21, 175n35, 176n51, 183
border markers, 11. See also boundaries
Borneo, 12, 45, 128, 136n20, 165, 174n28; Pontianak, 165
boundaries, 7, 167; boundary-marks, 32n8
Bowrey, Thomas, 110, 112, 138n41, 144, 163
Brahman, 46, 65n36, 93n19
Britain, 1, 11; British, 1, 5, 6, 7, 8, 9, 10, 21, 25, 26, 33n17, 78, 80, 90, 91, 99, 102, 103, 106, 110, 111, 116, 118, 119, 120, 124, 125, 126, 127, 128, 129, 130, 131, 134n5, 135n16, 136n28, 138n40, 138n44, 138n46, 139n56, 140n63, 148, 149, 152, 159, 161, 163, 164, 165, 168, 169, 173n1, 175n42, 176n51, 185. See also England
Brown, C. C., 41, 69, 70, 71, 75, 83, 88, 93n19, 164
Brunei, 36
Buddha. See Buddhism
Buddhism, 12, 25, 33n18, 45, 46, 57, 58, 59, 60, 61, 62, 67n59, 67n60, 68n65, 68n71, 68n74, 94n35, 136n23; four poisons, 45; Mahayana, 45, 57, 68n65; Tantric, 45, 49, 50, 57, 64n28, 64n32, 68n65; Theravada, 46, 49, 57, 66n45, 68n64, 68n65, 57, 68n64, 68n65
Bugis. See Bugis-Makassar

Index

Bugis-Makassar, 3, 10, 18, 25, 67n61, 81, 93n29, 98, 103, 106, 107, 110, 112, 114, 121, 122, 123, 124, 125, 126, 127, 128, 130, 131, 132, 134n7, 136n20, 136n21, 140n73, 141n76, 141n78, 141n79, 164, 175n43, 183; diasporas, 140n73; drifters, 123

Bukhari, Muhammad Ibn Ismail, 66n55

Bunga Emas dan Perak, 20, 134n3, 101, 111

Bunting Islands, 129, 142n91

Burma, xv, 19, 20, 36, 49, 64n28, 66n45, 109, 117, 120, 131, 135n10, 140n64, 151, 159, 161, 165, 167, 175n40, 183, 177, 185; Burmese, 4, 11, 59, 68n64, 68n71, 94n35, 117, 136n18, 139n51. *See also* Myanmar

Burney, H., 32n10, 63n14, 114, 134n5, 140n63

Bustan al-Salatin, 66n48

buta. *See* bhuta

Byzantium, 37

caffula, 155, 173n15; caffulas, 157; caffala, 152; kafilah, 173n15. *See also* caravan

Calcutta, 116, 166

Cambodia, 67n61, 68n64, 68n65, 91n4; Cambodian, 62n5

Cambridge Exploring Expedition, 153, 176n48

cannons, 82–83, 103, 136n21

caravan, 152, 173n15; caravanserai, 155

Carsten, Janet, 20, 100, 143, 169

Celebes, 81

Cetupuranam, 49

Ceylon, 33n18. *See also* Sri Lanka

Chaghadai, 63n12

Chaiya, 139n60, 162, 163, 175n40, 175n45

Champa, 36, 62n5, 63n10, 149; Cham, 11, 57, 59

Che Mali. *See* Wan Mali

Cheah Boon Kheng, 81, 85, 93n25, 169

China, xv, 1, 8, 23, 47, 56, 60, 62, 67n58, 68n66, 102, 138n49, 147, 150, 154, 171, 183; Chinese, 9, 34n34, 49, 58, 60, 66n48, 93n19, 103, 120, 136n29, 154, 165, 169, 170, 179, 181. *See also* Cochin China; junks; South China Sea

Christianity, 37, 61, 82

Chulias, 112

Cochin China, 107, 140n64

colonial, xvi, 1, 4, 13, 30, 80, 99, 152, 165, 169, 170, 185; colonies, 90; colonization, 10

contract, xvi, 3, 65n42, 71, 73, 74, 75, 76, 85, 92n5, 92n8, 181. *See also* agreement; covenant; yaum al-mithak

conversion, 22, 24, 25, 27, 28, 29, 31, 32n11, 33n32, 35, 36, 37, 38, 39, 40, 41, 42, 43, 44, 51, 52, 53, 54, 55, 56, 60, 61, 62, 62n1, 62n2, 62n5, 63n8, 63n12, 63n13, 64n22, 66n49, 52, 68n64, 94n36, 109, 137n35, 139n54, 176n47, 178, 179, 181; Islamization, 1, 36; smashing of statutes, 61, 68n65

copyists, 35, 46, 47, 48, 49, 50, 54, 61, 76, 179

Coromandel, 112

covenant, xvi, 3, 70, 71, 72, 73, 74, 75, 76, 77, 78, 81, 82, 83, 84, 85, 86, 87, 88, 89, 90, 92n5, 92n6, 93n20, 99, 133, 144, 157, 180, 181. *See also* agreement; contract; yaum al-mithak

Crawfurd, John, 22, 107, 121, 129, 136n29, 140n66, 142n92, 149, 150, 151, 154, 162, 163, 165, 171, 172, 173n3, 174n28, 175n40, 175n45

Culvamsa, 66n45

curse, 65n39, 69, 71, 83, 86, 89, 94n32, 95n49, 99, 136n23, 181. *See also* besi kawi

Dampier, William, 142n92

Danish, 138n49

Dato Ali. *See* Wan Mali

daulat, 13, 20, 98, 100

Dawei, 109. *See also* Tavoy

debt-slave, 81. *See also* slave

Deli, 13, 103, 175n44

Demang Lebar Daun, 69, 70, 71, 74, 75, 76, 77, 89, 91, 91n1, 92n14, 93n19, 93n20

derhaka, 14, 61, 72–73, 74, 85, 92n9, 106, 181; crimem laesae maiestatis, 72, 106; drohaka, 92n9
Detik-detik Sejarah Kelantan, 62n1
Dinding, 127, 129
Dipawamsa, 67n60, 59
disaster, 72, 86, 100, 157. See also divine wrath
disease, 57, 91n2, 158, 174n24; chloasma, 69; illness, 40; kedal, 69, 91n2; leper, 67n59; leprosy, 69, 91n2; malaria, 174n24; smallpox, 174n24, 175n35; ulcers, 174n24
district, 6, 7, 13, 98, 100, 109, 119, 126, 127, 128, 137n37, 138n47, 140n68, 142n86, 145, 172, 173n4; daerah or jajahan, 13. See also mukim
divine attributes, 12
divine ecstasy, 50
divine retribution, 72, 83, 85, 91; divine wrath, 86; plague, 69, 86
dragon, 57, 67n58, 67n59, 67n62. See also Naga; serpent; snake
Drakard, Jane, 4, 12, 17, 18, 19, 23, 73, 77, 94n35, 95n49, 177
drohaka. See derhaka
Dutch, xx, 26, 31, 33n30, 80, 88, 95n40, 102, 103, 107, 108, 110, 111, 112, 123, 126, 135n12, 136n27, 137n30, 137n31, 137n32, 137n33, 138n40, 138n41, 138n43, 138n45, 138n46, 138n48, 138n50, 140n72, 142n87, 142n92, 144, 146, 152, 161, 163, 175n33, 175n35, 185; Dutch-Siamese, 111

Eblis, 22, 26, 39. See also Iblis
education, 21, 183, 185; educational systems, 21; intellectuals, 21; Western-oriented education, 23
Egypt, 67n58, 71
elephant, 81, 102, 135n10, 148, 149, 150, 151, 155, 159, 163, 167, 169, 171, 173n9, 173n11, 175n44; Elephant Gate, 82; ivory, 175n44
England: English, 5, 9, 21, 22, 26, 27, 29, 30, 33n12, 33n30, 33n31, 35, 39, 55, 64n26, 86, 91, 91n2, 102, 106, 110, 111, 116, 118, 128, 135n10, 137n39, 138n42, 139n61, 141n83, 150, 152, 161, 163, 165, 169. See also Britain
Ensani/Insani Kamil, 50
entrepot, 4, 15, 16, 102, 105, 111, 114, 130, 152, 171, 174n19, 182, 183; maritime-entrepot, xv
environment, 1, 3, 4, 18, 19, 20, 59, 100, 144, 152, 158, 171, 173n16, 177, 178, 184
Esfahan, 48; Kaveh of Esfahan, 48
Europe, 1, 10, 11, 23, 25, 26, 31, 36, 81, 89, 90, 102, 111, 125, 127, 131, 135n17, 139n58, 143, 146, 152, 155, 161, 164, 170, 171, 183
exorcist, 47, 48, 65n40. See also lakon; selembit; wayang kulit

fadzhihat, 92n8. See also humiliate; malu; shame
Farsi. See Persian
Farquhar, William, 80
Fatimi, S. Q., 27, 33n27, 39, 53, 63n13, 63n13
Fatimid dynasty, 71; Fatimid mirror, 71
fatwa, 30, 34n34
Fei Hsin, 49
Feng-Shen-Yen-I, 66n48
Ferdowsi, A. G., 22, 47, 65n38. See also Shah-Nameh
Finlayson, George, 129, 138n50, 140n66, 142n92
Firdausi, A. G. See Ferdowsi, A. G.
Floris, Peter, 142n87, 152, 158, 173n15
Forrest, Thomas, 150
foundation: foundation myth, 2, 19, 72, 73, 89, 137n34, 172, 179, 181; foundation story, 73; foundation tradition, 99
France, 173n7; French, 91n1, 85, 99, 126, 146, 147, 155, 161, 165, 166, 167
Fujian, 56
Funan, 57, 93n19, 149

Galang, 130
Gambaroon. See Gambarun
Gambarun, 33n21. See also Bandar Abbas
Garuda (Gerda, Geroda, Girda), 26, 29, 33n16, 37, 59, 60, 179; Geruda, 23

gergasi, 46, 64n34, 157, 174n23;
  girgassi, 64n34; ogre, 46, 58, 60;
  raksasa, 46, 64n34, 65n35, 65n39,
  157. *See also* Ravana
Ghazali, Ahmad, 53
Gheseyeh Soleyman va Simurgh, 24.
  See also Hekayateh Simrugh
Gothamasan, Phan-Ngam, 148
grave, 3, 28, 30, 37, 63n20, 70, 80, 84,
  94n31; Acehnese graves, 41; grave-
  posts, 94n31. *See also* Keramat
Guanyin/Kuan Yin, 58
Gujarati, xx, 22
Gullick, J. M., 3, 5, 8, 9, 12, 13, 14, 19, 73,
  143, 144, 165, 177, 178, 182, 183
Gumarun, 24. *See also* Bandar Abbas;
  Gambaroon
Gumpar. *See* Kampar: Kedah Peak,
  109, 142n91, 157

Hall, K. R., 21, 148
Hallaj, Mansour, 53, 66n54
Hamzeh-Nameh, 65n41. *See also* Amir
  Hamza; Hikayat Amir Hamza
Hanuman, 58, 64n32; monkey god, 58,
  64n32. *See also* Raja Handuman;
  Ramayana
Hatim Tai, 64n31
hawa nafsu, 51; carnal and lustful
  desires, 51; hawa-yeh nafs, 51–52;
  nafs, 43; satanic lust, 56
Hekayateh Simrugh, 179, 186n1. *See
  also* Gheseyeh Soleyman va
  Simurgh
Hevajra, 49
Hikajat Potjut Muhamat, 63n20, 66n51,
  82, 128, 136n23, 141n83
Hikajat Potjoet Moehamat, 95n39,
  95n48
Hikayat Aceh, 62n1
Hikayat Amir Hamza, 65n41
Hikayat Bandjar, 47, 62n1, 62n5, 62n7,
  65n40, 65n43, 66n52, 67n61, 91n3,
  95n48
Hikayat Deli, 67n63, 91n3
Hikayat Hang Tua, 87, 95n45
Hikayat Iblis, 45, 64n30
Hikayat Inderaputra, 21, 22, 63n21,
  67n61, 67n63, 95n39

Hikayat Iskandar, 66n48
Hikayat Koris, 67n61
Hikayat Merong Mahawangsa, xvi, 19,
  21, 22, 23, 25, 26, 27, 28, 29, 30, 31,
  33n12, 33n14, 37, 38, 39, 40, 41, 42,
  45, 47, 48, 50, 51, 52, 53, 54, 55, 56,
  57, 59, 61, 63n14, 64n22, 64n34, 84,
  91, 157, 163, 177, 179, 186n1;
  orthodox versions, 53; orthodox
  view, 59
Hikayat Patani, 35, 62n1, 62n5, 62n7,
  64n22, 64n25, 68n74, 82, 87, 88,
  93n16, 93n26, 93n30, 94n38, 136n23
Hikayat Proat Nang Meri, 157
Hikayat Raja Akil. *See* Hikayat Siak
Hikayat Raja Babi, 47
Hikayat Raja-raja Pasai, 35, 41, 42, 56,
  59, 62n1, 66n52, 67n63, 83, 84, 88,
  94n38
Hikayat Si Miskin, 65n35
Hikayat Siak, 92n10, 92n15; Siak
  Chronicles, 74, 75, 78, 88, 92n12,
  92n13
Hikayat Sri Rama, 22, 59
hilir, 17, 175n35
Hindu, 12, 33n14, 33n16, 34n34, 45, 46,
  49, 50, 57, 61, 62, 63n10, 66n46,
  67n60; Hindu-Buddhist, xv, xvi, 3,
  12, 38, 66n44, 179; Hindu-Javanese,
  48; icons, 64n29; Vaishnava branch
  of Hinduism, 65n37
Hooker, Virginia Matheson, 11
Hugli, 138n44
humiliate, 72, 74, 77, 78, 80, 82, 83, 84,
  87, 88, 89, 91, 92n8, 110, 181;
  disgrace, 70, 72, 74, 77, 78, 81, 82, 87,
  91, 93n26. *See also* fadzhihat; malu;
  shame; punishment

Ibbetson, Robert, 91
Iblis, 22, 26, 27, 29, 39, 40, 45, 47, 51, 52,
  53, 54, 66n54; demon, 47, 58, 65n39,
  65n40; devil, 22, 26, 27, 39, 47, 53, 56,
  59, 61, 78; Satan, 39, 45, 51, 52, 53, 56;
  shaitan, 51. *See also* Eblis
Ibn Arabi, 53
Ibn Battuta, 23
Ilanun, 3, 55, 103, 126, 127, 128, 129,
  133n1, 140n74, 142n85, 159, 183;

volcanic eruption in, 142n85. *See also* orang laut
Imam Ali, 71, 92n6
Imam Sayid, 56
Imam Wagga, 56
Inchi Laa, 78, 80, 81
Indah, 161
India, xix, 8, 23, 33n16, 37, 49, 53, 57, 62n4, 63n10, 64n30, 65n43, 68n72, 71, 80, 91n4, 94n35, 95n39, 102, 103, 106, 107, 112, 125, 135n13, 138n49, 140n66, 141n83, 159, 165, 170, 173n15, 179, 180, 181, 183, 186n1; British India, 90; Indian Ocean, 4, 93n28, 136n26; Indian subcontinent, 71
Indonesia, 28, 36, 62n5, 62n6, 93n28, 136n26
Insani Kamil. *See* Ensani/Insani Kamil
intoxicants, 22, 43, 45, 46, 50, 66n47, 66n50; wine, 22, 39, 40, 43, 46, 47, 49, 50, 52, 65n42, 66n50; arak, 39, 40, 43, 45, 46; arak tadi, 63n15; karana, 50; palm-wine, 45
Iran, 48, 186n1. *See also* Persia
Iran Rajadhamma. *See* Nithan Sibsawng Liam
Isthmus, 147, 150

Jaffna Peninsula, 68n71
Jain, 49
Jambi, 67n61, 73, 107, 125, 137n31
Jamshid, 50
Japan, 58, 60, 62, 67n58, 175n32
Jataka, 46, 59, 64n33, 67n60, 179; Bhuridatta-Jataka (no. 543), 68n70; Harita-Jataka (no.431), 46; Jayaddisa-Jataka (no. 513), 47; Kikati-Jataka (no. 327), 68n73; Kotisimbali-Jataka (no. 412), 68n70; Kumbha-Jataka (no. 512), 46; Maha-Sutasoma-Jataka (no. 537), 47, 65n40; Mahabodhi-Jataka (no. 528), 46; Pandara-Jataka (no. 518), 68n70; Samugga-Jataka (no. 436), 65n39; Sussondi-Jataka (no. 360), 60, 68n73
Java, 16, 20, 21, 36, 45, 48, 62n2, 62n6, 64n24, 65n40, 68n68, 72, 95n49, 136n25, 136n29, 173n4; Sho-P'o, 136n29
Jawi, 39, 40, 45, 48, 52, 63n14. *See also* Aceh; Perso-Arabic
Jeddah, 35
Jeragan Sulaiman, 151, 173n14
Johor, 3, 15, 16, 18, 19, 36, 55, 63n9, 67n61, 73, 74, 75, 76, 77, 80, 85, 86, 87, 88, 89, 92n12, 92n13, 92n15, 95n40, 95n47, 97, 98, 100, 107, 108, 109, 123, 124, 130, 132, 135n12, 136n20, 136n23, 136n24, 136n29, 137n30, 137n31, 137n32, 147, 163, 173n16, 177, 181, 182
Jonah, 68n67
junks: Chinese, 103, 159; Siamese, 175n46
Junk Ceylon, 113, 147. *See also* Phuket

kakawin, 21
Kala, 47, 48, 65n40; Indra Barma Kala, 47. *See also* wayang kulit
Kalah, 26
Kali, 49
Kalimantan, 94n36
Kalinga, 88
Kalmasha-Pada, 65n39
Kampar, 48, 84, 85, 91. *See also* Esfahan; Kaveh of Esfahan
Kampong Kedah, 141n82
Kandy, 68n64
Karens, 167
Kathi, 109, 145
Kaveh of Esfahan, 48. *See also* Esfahan; Shah-Nameh
Kawi text, 45–46
Kedah Laws, 26, 29, 32n8, 38
Kedah Annals. *See* Hikayat Merong Mahawangsa
Kelantan, 68n67, 80, 89, 136n22, 147, 153, 159, 161, 168, 169, 174n19, 175n37, 176n51
Keramat, 80, 93n24, 94n31
Khmer, 32n9, 57, 59
Khoo Kay Kim, 30, 34n33, 63n13, 73
Khorasan, 53
King, Phil, 148, 169, 176n51
Klian Intan, 149, 153, 173n12, 176n51
Ko Lanta Yai, 109. *See also* Pulau Lantar
Ko Talibong. *See* Talibong Island

Ko Yao, 116, 175n39
Kobkua Suwannathat-Pian, 139n54, 176n47, 176n51
Ko-chai-Sahak, 140n66
Koenig, J. G., 127
kota, 102, 144
Kota Kapur, 92n9, 95n49, 136n25
Kota Star, 166; See also Alor Star
Krian, 165, 173n1
Krishna, 49, 50
Kroh: Kroh mines, 148–149, 150, 151, 153, 168, 169, 173n12; Kroh plateau, 153, 169
Krtanagara, 64n32, 45, 46
Kuala: Kuala Bahang, 102; Kuala Batang, 135n15; Kuala Kedah, 4, 102, 135n15, 144, 152; Kuala Kupang, 153; Kuala Merbok, 102, 119, 139n58; Kuala Muda, 122, 140n68, 144, 151, 157; Kuala Pasai, 84; Kuala Perlis, 102, 144; Kuala Yen, 157
Kuan Yin. See Guanyin/Kuan Yin
Kubong Boya, 119
Kubang Pasu, 7
Kumbha-Karna, 64n32
Kupang (west Timor), 105
Kutai, 62n1, 94n36
kweng/toh kweng, 145
Kyshe cases. See Norton-Kyshe

lakon (plots), 47; Murwa Kala, 47; See also exorcist; wayang kulit
Laksamana, 97–98, 99, 100, 101, 102, 105, 107, 109, 113, 114, 116, 118, 119, 122, 123, 124, 125, 131, 133, 134n5, 134n9, 135n13, 135n14, 141n83, 155, 183. See also orang laut; panglima; raja di laut
Lanao, 95n46
Langgar, 144
Langka, 23
Langkapuri, 24, 60, 94n35
Lanka, 24, 33n18, 59, 60, 68n71, 68n72, 94n35
Langkawi Islands, 20, 23, 32n6, 41, 55, 56, 59, 62, 63n19, 65n35, 68n72, 83, 85, 94n32, 94n35, 94n37, 99, 100, 102, 105, 109, 114, 116, 117, 118, 119, 120, 121, 127, 129, 130, 131, 133, 135n11, 138n46, 139n58, 139n61, 139n62, 140n63, 140n65, 140n67, 140n69, 140n74, 142n84, 143, 144, 183
Laos, 59, 68n64; Laotian, 89
Laxamana. See Laksamana
Liaw, Y. F., 77, 78, 94n33, 76, 77
Ligeh, 154
Ligor, 57, 101, 118, 140n66, 149, 162. See also Nakhon Si Thammarat
Ligor, inscription. See Wiang Sa
Lilit Nithra Chakhrit, 66n48
Limbong, 101; Limbong Kapal dockyard, 101
Lingga, 136n29
Linggin Island, 129
Long Putih. See Tengku: Tengku Long Putih
Low, James, 5, 6, 22, 32n10, 33n12, 33n18, 38, 39, 48, 63n14, 64n26, 67n62, 68n72, 78, 80, 84, 94n35, 102, 104, 114, 117, 168, 173n16
Luoyang qielan ji, 47

Mabangers, 108
Madjapahit. See Majapahit
Madras, 153
Mahabharata, 67n60, 47, 49, 59, 65n40
Mahayana. See Buddhism
Mahavamsa, 66n45, 67n60
Mahavansi, 33n18
Mahsuri, 83, 94n32, 94n37, 94n38
Maier, Hendrik J. M., xix, xxii, 2, 21, 22, 33n13, 33n20, 53, 68n72, 94n35, 123
Majapahit, 12, 45, 62n7, 66n52
Makassar. See Bugis-Makassar
Makota Raja-Raja, 64n31. See also Raniri; Taj-i-Salatin
Malacca. See Melaka
Malay Annals. See Sejarah Melayu; Sulalat al-Salatin
malu, 72, 77, 78. See also fadzhihat; humiliate; shame; punishment
Maluku Island, 62n5, 62n6
mangkubumi, 91n3, 71
Manichaeism, 37, 49, 61
Manjung, 127
maratabat, 95n46. See also fadzhihat; malu; shame

218 *Index*

maritime, 2, 3, 15, 16, 17, 19, 20, 36, 37, 49, 54, 93n19, 97, 98, 100, 101, 102, 106, 108, 111, 112, 114, 116, 120, 121, 125, 126, 127, 130, 131, 133, 136n29, 138n46, 143, 144, 145, 146, 150, 154, 164, 171, 177, 178, 182, 183, 184, 185
Maroni, 57
Marrison, G. E., 21, 22, 44, 66n48
Masulipatnam, 111
Mathnawi, 45
Maxwell, G., 68n72, 75, 90, 94n35, 154, 155, 169, 174n24, 176n50
Mecca, 142n84, 35, 40. *See also* dragon; Naga; serpent; snake
Medan, 122
Medina, 40, 56
Melaka, xv, 3, 16, 18, 19, 26, 29, 33n32, 38, 63n9, 71, 73, 74, 75, 76, 77, 80, 82, 85, 87, 88, 89, 92n12, 92n15, 93n17, 95n40, 97, 99, 100, 102, 103, 104, 105, 108, 112, 114, 123, 126, 132, 135n17, 136n29, 137n30, 137n33, 138n49, 139n56, 140n74, 142n87, 146, 147, 175n33, 175n41, 177, 181
Melaka Straits, xv, 1, 3, 19, 20, 41, 55, 82, 98, 102, 105, 107, 109, 111, 121, 122, 123, 130, 132, 133n1, 136n20, 136n29, 138n46, 177, 178, 183, 184
menteri, 25, 30, 43, 44, 49, 75, 181. *See also* ministers
Mergui. *See* Archipelago
Miksic, J. N., 4, 17, 18, 19, 177
Milner, A. C., 3, 12, 13, 14, 17, 19, 35, 36, 73, 91, 175n42, 177, 178
Minangkabau, 3, 12, 17, 36, 63n8, 63n21, 67n61, 67n63, 73, 77, 82, 92n12, 94n34, 95n49, 98, 107, 110, 112, 122, 123, 127, 128, 136n23, 140n71, 140n74, 143, 183. *See also* Siak-Minangkabau
Mindanao, 142n85
ministers, 7, 8, 25, 41, 42, 43, 60, 64n25, 64n26, 71, 75, 84, 85, 89, 91, 118, 162, 173n5, 181
Misa Melayu, 32, 42
Misbana Mengkaji Sejarah Trengganu, 62n1
Mithra. *See* Mitra/Mithra
Mitra/Mithra, 49, 65n42, 92n5

Mogul, 53, 186n1
Moken, 109; Moken Pulaw, 109, 137n37; Moken Tamab, 109, 137n37; Moklen, 109; Selung, 109. *See also* orang laut
Mon, 32n9, 59, 68n64, 167, 183; Mon-Khmer, 32n9
moneylenders, 170
Mongolia, 37, 60, 62, 63n12
monsoon, 16, 144, 152, 158, 171, 174n25
mosque, 14, 55, 142n88, 144, 145
Mt Jerai. *See* Gunong Jerai
Muhammad Hassan Bin To'Keranni Mohd. Arshad, 27, 28, 33n29, 53, 63n13. *See also* Al-Tarekh Salasilah Negeri Kedah
mukim, 8, 14, 144, 145, 155, 172, 173n3
Myanmar, 19. *See also* Burma; Rangoon

Naga, 57, 58, 59, 60, 61, 62, 67n58, 67n59, 67n61, 68n71, 68n73, 94n35, 179, 180. *See also* dragon; Maroni; serpent; snake; Wiang Sa
Nagadipa, 68n71
nagari, 17
Nagarakertagama, 21
Nahjul-Balagha, 71, 92n7
Nahuijs, Colonel, 80, 93n21
Nakhon Si Thammarat/Dhammarat/Dharrmaraja, 57, 138n46, 148, 150, 152, 153, 161, 165, 173n9, 174n26, 183. *See also* Ligor
Naning, 94n34
Newbold, T. J., 94n34, 118, 139n53, 140n74, 155, 157, 173n11
Nezamol Molkeh Tusi, Abu Ali Hasan, 22
Nicobar. *See* Nikobar
Nikobar, 68n71, 138n50. *See also* Andaman
Nithan Sibsawng Liam, 66n48
nobat, 25, 27, 28, 29, 64n24, 104
Norton-Kyshe, 118, 119

oath, 57, 66n51, 76, 77, 103, 104, 136n22, 136n23, 136n24, 157; Telaga Batu Inscription, 57. *See also* pact
opium, 102

oral, 21, 82, 88, 89, 94n32, 109, 172, 179, 180, 181, 186
orang asli, 3, 11, 13, 16, 19, 102, 107, 137n34, 144, 155, 157, 172, 174n21, 185; Bila/Wila, 155, 157; Kensieu/ Kensiu, 155; Pangan, 155; Semang, 155, 157, 174n22
orang kaya, 163
orang laut: Orang Lonta/Urak Lawoi, 109; Orang Selatan, 136n29; Orang Suku Mepar, 136n29. *See also* Bugis-Makassar; Ilanun; Laksamana; Moken; panglima; Palimajatti; raja di laut; Sakais; Siak-Minangkabau
orthodoxy, 30, 67n56; orthodox critique, 54; orthodox Gujarati, 22; orthodox Islam, 51, 53, 67n56; orthodox Muslims, 22; orthodox Sufi, 54; orthodox Theravada, 49, 57
Osbeck, Peter, 128, 135n14
Osborne, Sherard, 55, 56, 78, 118, 139n58, 139n61, 140n67, 142n84

pact, 71, 75, 76, 77, 88, 89, 90, 103, 133. *See also* oath
Padma-Purana, 59
Pagan, 59, 64n28, 67n59, 68n64
Pagar Ruyung, 127, 128
Pahang, 13, 49, 73, 77, 80, 90, 94n34, 95n49, 105, 147, 153, 169, 171, 174n19
Pajajaran, 62n2
Pakistan, 63n18
Paklao village, 163
Palembang, xv, 3, 18, 19, 57, 67n61, 69, 71, 73, 75, 85, 89, 93n19, 100, 123, 131, 132, 181
Pali, 45, 57
Palimajatti, 110. *See also* orang laut
Pallava, 57
Pan-Islamic, 30
Pangkor, 127
panglima, 15, 103, 110, 122, 125; Panglima di Pulau Langkawi, 139n62; panglima laut, 97. *See also* Laksamana; raja di laut
Parameswara, 104
Pararaton, 45, 46
Parsi. *See* Persian

Pasai, 35, 36, 41, 42, 56, 59, 62n1, 62n7, 64n22, 66n52, 67n63, 83, 84, 88, 94n38
Patala, 59
Patani, 35, 36, 62n7, 63n9, 64n22, 68n74, 82, 85, 87, 88, 93n26, 94n31, 132, 133, 135n13, 136n23, 138n45, 147, 148, 149, 150, 151, 152, 153, 154, 155, 158, 159, 161, 163, 167, 168, 169, 170, 171, 173n12, 173n15, 174n21, 174n24, 174n27, 175n30, 175n31, 175n37, 176n50, 184
path/pathways, 18, 148, 150, 151, 152, 153, 154, 155, 163, 167, 171, 174n19, 176n49. *See also* trans-peninsular; waterways
pearl, xxii, 102, 107, 109, 135n12
Pegu, 111
Penang, xix, xxi, 1, 5, 6, 8, 9, 10, 21, 32n1, 35, 48, 55, 63n14, 78, 80, 89, 94n31, 119, 103, 106, 118, 121, 125, 126, 127, 128, 129, 131, 134n5, 137n38, 140n66, 140n69, 141n81, 142n86, 142n87, 142n88, 144, 148, 149, 151, 159, 163, 164, 165, 167, 168, 169, 175n41, 183, 184, 185. *See also* Pulau Pinang
penghulu, 8, 15, 94n34, 99, 100, 103, 105, 134n6, 145, 155, 157, 172, 173n5
pepper, 99, 105, 147
Perak, 13, 16, 31, 34n34, 73, 75, 77, 93n27, 94n31, 103, 104, 107, 108, 123, 124, 125, 126, 127, 132, 134n7, 138n40, 141n75, 141n77, 141n78, 147, 148, 153, 155, 161, 165, 167, 169, 171, 173n3, 173n13, 175n35, 176n50
Percut, 91n3
perfect man. *See* Ensani/Insani Kamil
periphery, 1, 16, 100, 144, 148, 155, 161, 169
Perlis, 7, 8, 41, 63n19, 64n29, 85, 99, 102, 105, 117, 118, 134n6, 135n11, 139n61, 142n84, 144, 152, 163, 165
Persia, 31, 33n21, 37, 47, 63n18, 67n56, 92n5, 111, 132, 141n83, 179, 183, 186n1; Persian, xix, xx, 3, 22, 23, 24, 26, 28, 31, 32n5, 33n16, 33n19, 37, 44, 45, 48, 50, 51, 53, 61, 63n18, 64n30, 65n41, 66n48, 66n50, 66n55, 90,

92n5, 92n8, 173n15, 179, 181, 186n1
Persian Gulf, 33n21
Perso-Arabic, 63n16, 173n15
Petchaburi, 169
Phangnga, 175n40, 120
Pharaoh, 53, 66n54
Phattalung, 108, 149, 153, 154, 159, 161
Philippines, 12, 47, 62n1, 65n39, 95n46, 98, 128, 183
Phongsawadan Muang Zaiburi, 116, 134n6, 139n54
Phuket, 94n37, 107, 112, 113, 114, 116, 119, 123, 137n37, 138n45, 138n46, 138n47, 138n48, 140n72, 140n73, 147, 150, 163, 175n45. *See also* Junk Ceylon
Pinto, Fernao Mendes, 87, 88, 95n44
piracy, 119, 126, 127, 129, 130, 134n4, 140n63, 152; pirate, 19, 94n36, 98, 100, 103, 107, 108, 116, 117, 119, 120, 121, 122, 126, 127, 128, 129, 130, 131, 137n33, 138n49, 139n58, 142n92, 161, 168, 171, 183
Pisitasanas/Pisitasins, 46
Portuguese, 29, 74, 76, 82, 87, 105, 108, 126, 135n17, 136n27, 137n38, 142n87, 152, 163, 175n33
prahus, 112, 120, 129
Province Wellesley, 116, 119–120, 127–128
Pulau: Pulau Bunting. *See* Bunting Islands: Pulau Langkawi; Langkawi Islands: Pulau Lantar; Ko Lanta Yai: Pulau Mutia, 107; Pulau Panjang; Ko Yao; Pulau Pinang, 32n1, 125; Pulau Sembilan; Sembilan Islands
punishment, 10, 57, 72, 78, 80, 81, 82, 84, 85, 88, 110, 121; behead, 74, 84; execution, 53, 72, 74, 78, 81, 82, 83, 84, 87, 88, 93n26, 94n34, 95n44, 95n49; gregoge, 87; hang, 80; impale, 72, 81, 84; quick death, 78, 80, 81, 91; torture, 78, 80, 81, 166
python. *See* snake

Qabus-nameh, 22

Raffles, Stamford, 80, 90, 92n8, 125, 142n86

railway, 167, 169, 170
Raja: Raja alam, 18, 124, 128, 141n76, 141n77; Raja Ali Haji Ibn Ahmad, 74; Raja Alif, 63n21; Raja Bersiong, 22, 33n14, 43, 46, 47, 48, 49, 50, 52, 84, 85, 86, 91, 149, 157, 163, 174n23, 181; Raja Bongsu of Pasai, 62n7, 66n52; raja di laut, 97; Raja Handuman, 23; Raja Ismail, 125, 132; Raja Kecik, 18, 92n12, 100, 123, 126, 128, 132, 134n7, 140n71, 141n76, 182; Raja Kelana Hitam, 157; Raja-less, 14; Raja Mahmud, 18, 92n12; Raja Muda of Perak, 126; Raja Nambang, 141n77; Raja Peranggi Dewa, 51; Raja Sangsapurba, 67n63, 69, 70
Rajatarangini, 67n60
rakyat, 8, 10, 32n7, 38, 81; rakyat bukit, 157
Rama, 22, 23, 48, 50, 59, 68n68, 92n11
Rama III, 6, 7, 114, 116, 161, 162
Ramakrishna, 50
Raman, 148, 153, 167, 169, 176n51
Ramayana, 23, 46, 53, 58, 59, 60, 64n32, 68n68, 68n70, 68n72, 94n35, 179; Rama story, 23, 48, 60; Ramayanam of Bhodhayanam, 68n70
Rangoon, 119
Raniri, Sheikh Nur al-Din Ibn Ali, 22, 37, 64n31, 66n55. *See also* wujudiya
Ravana, 33n18, 46, 60, 64n32, 65n36. *See also* gergasi; Ramayana
Reameathipadei I, 62n5
regalia, 7, 25, 67n63, 104, 134n3
regicide, 18, 86, 87, 95n40, 124, 132. *See also* wujudiya
Riau, xv, 15, 16, 73, 74, 92n13, 92n15, 129, 133n1, 137n32. *See also* Archipelago
rice, 4, 16, 20, 32n9, 57, 65n39, 140n65, 147, 161, 171, xv; rice-fields, 32n9, 161; rice-grass, 68n67
Risalat Hukum Qanun, 26, 29. *See also* Undang-undang Melaka
robbery, 169, 150, 151
robes, 105; Robes of honor, 104
Roolvink, R., 73, 77
Rotti and Savu, 135n17

Index

royal genealogy, 19, 25, 28, 29, 31, 41, 67n61, 73, 92n12, 92n15, 123, 132, 141n83, 179, 181
rum, 3, 23, 26, 29, 41, 52, 63n21, 64n34, 132, 157
Rumi, 45, 53, 45. *See* Balkhi
Rustam, 49. *See also* Shah-Nameh

Saadi, Sheikh, xxii, 53; Boostan/Bustan of Saadi, 53
Sadhyana, 49
Safavid, 23
sago, 114, 138n50
Sahih Bukhari. *See* Bukhari, Muhammad Ibn Ismail
Sakai, 157; sea-Sakai, 24. *See also* orang asli; orang laut
Salasilah atau Tarikh Kerajaan Kedah, 25, 27. *See also* Wan Yahya bin Wan Muhammad Taib
Saletters, 107, 109, 110, 111, 112, 113, 136n29, 137n33, 138n50; Johorse Saletters, 107, 135n12. *See also* orang laut
Sana'i, 54
sandalwood, 65n43
Sanrabone, 37–38, 62n1, 62n3, 63n9
Sarawak, 59
Sarmad, Sa'id, 53, 66n53
Satan. *See* Iblis
Satun, 7, 8, 110, 117, 118, 135n11, 144, 165
Savu/Sawu, 81, 105
sea lord, 18, 97, 100, 101, 102, 103, 118, 123, 125, 128, 131, 159, 161, 184
sea people. *See* orang laut
Seberang Perai, 32n1, 128. *See also* Province Wellesley
Seir al Moluk/Siyasat- nameh, 22
Sejarah Banten, 62n2
Sejarah dan Perjuangan Ulama Kedah Darul Aman, 30
Sejarah Kelantan, 62n1
Sejarah Melayu, xvi, 19, 21, 26, 29, 31, 35, 41, 56, 62n1, 64n24, 66n48, 66n49, 67n63, 68n67, 69, 70, 71, 72, 73, 74, 75, 76, 77, 78, 83, 84, 87, 88, 91, 92n8, 92n14, 93n20, 94n36, 134n7, 135n17, 163, 177, 181. *See also* Malay Annals;

Sulalat al-Salatin
Sejarah Trengganu, 62n1
Selangor, 10, 13, 16, 73, 106, 124, 125, 128, 129, 141n78, 141n82, 169, 183
selembit, 31, 48. *See also* exorcist; wayang kulit
Sembilan Islands, 127
serpent, 57, 58, 67n58, 67n61, 67n63, 166; Serpent-King. *See* Zahak. *See also* Naga; snake
shadow-puppet. *See* wayang kulit
Shah-Nameh, 22, 47, 48, 50, 66n48
shaitan. *See* Iblis
shame, 70, 72, 77, 78, 81, 82, 83, 87, 88, 89, 95n46, 181. *See also* fadzhihat; malu; maratabat
Sharifah Zaleha (Binte Syed Hassan), 29, 32n10, 105
Sheikh Abdullah. *See* Abdullah
Shiite, 71, 92n6
Shiva/Siva, 49
Siak, 3, 12, 18, 19, 73, 75, 92n12, 98, 100, 103, 106, 107, 114, 121, 122, 123, 124, 125, 126, 127, 128, 130, 131, 132, 133n1, 136n22, 140n71, 141n77, 141n81, 142n89, 159, 161, 182, 183, 184
Siak Chronicles. *See* Hikayat Siak
Siak-Minangkabau, 3, 123. *See also* orang laut
Siam, 4, 8, 16, 20, 25, 32n3, 36, 48, 52, 89, 91, 107, 108, 109, 111, 112, 114, 123, 125, 135n12, 135n13, 136n18, 138n45, 138n46, 139n56, 142n84, 143, 144, 146, 147, 148, 149, 150, 152, 158, 161, 162, 165, 169, 170, 172, 173n7, 173n8, 174n27, 175n31, 175n37, 176n52, 183, 184
Siantan, 67n61, 159, 174n28
Sik, 100, 143
silver, 40, 134n3
Singapore, 55, 72, 74, 75, 80, 83, 89, 90, 91, 93n22, 125, 129, 130, 154, 165, 173n2, 185
Singora, 138n45, 147, 173n10. *See also* Songkhla
Sinhalese sources, 68n71
Sirat al- Mustaghim, 22, 32n11, 40, 54, 66n55

sireh, 41, 42, 64n24. *See also* betel-nut
Siva 48, 49, 68n65. *See* Shiva,
Siyasat-nameh/Seir al Moluk, 22
Skinner, C., 20, 57, 83, 109, 114, 117, 124, 134n8, 134n9, 135n15, 145, 151, 173n4, 175n40
slave, 6, 32n3, 77, 78, 81, 82, 89, 94n34, 113, 127, 129, 161. *See also* debt-slave
smuggling, 161, 184
Smyth, W. H., 107, 109, 135n12, 150, 155, 154, 158, 163, 167, 169, 173n16, 176n52
snake, 47, 56, 57, 58, 59, 60, 62, 67n58, 67n59, 67n61, 67n63, 180; Baishe zhuan, 58; lambu, 67n63; little green snake, 58; Madam White Snake, 58; mamlud, 67n61, 67n63; Oular-besar/Ular-besar, 55, 56, 59, 67n57; python, 55, 56, 59, 67n57; Sacatimuna, 67n63; Sicatimuna, 67n63; Ur-myth, 58
Sohrab, 49. *See also* Shah-Nameh
soma, 49, 50; soma-juice, 66n47
Songkhla, 6, 78, 103, 108, 124, 137n36, 138n45, 141n81, 147, 148, 149, 150, 152, 153, 154, 155, 159, 161, 165, 166, 167, 169, 170, 173n10, 174n20, 174n26, 174n29, 175n31, 175n32, 175n46, 183, 184. *See also* Singora
South China Sea, xv, 4, 174n28
Spanish dollars, 114
Sri Lanka, 64n33, 66n45, 68n64, 68n71. *See also* Ceylon
Srivijaya, xv, 12, 15, 16, 57, 77, 92n9, 92n15, 95n49, 104, 136n25
staff 39, 53. *See* tongkat,; gading cane, 66n52; Sulam, 53
Sufi, 22, 39, 49, 50, 53, 54, 64n30, 66n50, 71, 92n6, 93n18, 94n31
Suhrawardi, Shahab al-din Yahya, 53
Sulalat al-Salatin. *See* Malay Annals; Sejarah Melayu
Sulawesi, 56, 62n1, 62n3, 62n5, 63n8, 63n9, 98, 183; Tallo, 62n1, 62n3, 63n8, 63n9; Gowa, 62n1, 63n9
Sulu, 15, 55
Sumatra, 8, 11, 12, 17, 18, 19, 41, 55, 57, 63n21, 67n61, 67n63, 69, 73, 91n3, 98, 102, 107, 109, 121, 122, 127, 128, 135n13, 136n23, 138n50, 139n61, 142n89, 143, 145, 163, 173n2, 175n44, 182, 183

Sumbawa, 81
Sunda, 48, 62n2, 65n40, 147
Sungei Jeram, 124
Sungei Kiti, 158
Sungei Lingow, 135n11
Sungei Penaga, 119
Sungei Perlis, 135n11
Sungei Susat, 9
Sunni, 92n6
Surat, 111
Swedish, 128, 135n14. *See also* Osbeck, Peter
Sweeney, Amin, 23, 48, 68n68, 68n72, 94n35
Swettenham, Frank, 9
Syair Perang Siak, 67n59, 75, 88, 92n12, 141n77
Syair Sultan Maulana, 11, 20, 57, 105, 114, 120, 134n8, 134n9, 135n15, 139n62, 151, 173n4, 173n15, 175n40
Syed, 35, 93n26, 125, 128, 131, 132, 141n77, 141n83, 182; Syed Ali, 103, 125, 126, 132, 159, 174n29, 184; Syed Asmayu'd din, 83, 84; Syed Husin Ali, 170; Syed Mahomet Jarr, 141n83; Syed Othman b. Abd al-Rahman bin Shihab/Syhab, 141n77; Syed Yasin, 80, 81, 90, 93n26; Syed Zein/Tuanku Pangiran, 125

Tai-ping-yu-lan, 93n19
Taj-i-Salatin, 64n31, 66n48. *See also* Raniri
Talibong Island, 107, 109
Tamiang, 119
Tanintharyi, 120
Tantric, xvi, 12, 43, 45, 49, 57, 64n28, 64n29, 64n32, 68n65; cakra Tantrism, 64n32; cannibalism, xvi, 46, 47, 48, 49, 65n39, 65n40, 84, 157; drunkenness, 49, 50; feces, 49; urine, 43, 49, 52
Tarutao Island, 121, 144
Tavoy, 110, 119. *See also* Dawei
Tenasserim, 120, 138n49, 150

Tengku: Tengku Anom, 7; Tengku Daud, 116; Tengku Din, 140n69, 175n36; Tengku Hasan, 7; Tengku Long Putih, 125, 142n84, 182; Tengku Masuna, 100; Tengku Mat Akip, 7; Tengku Mohammad Saad, 8, 78, 116, 117, 119, 133, 148, 161, 175n38; Tengku Mohammad Taib, 119; Tengku Raya Udin Muhammad Shah, 134n6

Terengganu, 73, 159

terminus, 148, 149, 178. *See also* trans-peninsular

Ternate, 62n5, 62n6

Thailand, 7, 25, 59, 64n29, 94n38, 109, 121, 137n35

Tharangambadi, 138n49

Theravada. *See* Buddhism

Tibet, 49, 59

timber, 101, 102, 158

Timian. *See* Tamiang

Timor, 93n28, 105, 135n17, 136n26

tin, 102, 103, 111, 112, 135n10, 135n14, 138n46, 141n75, 143, 148, 149, 150, 151, 153, 159, 161, 167, 168, 169

Titi Wangsa, 143, 158, 168. *See also* trans-peninsular

toh kweng. *See* kweng

tolls, 102, 103, 131, 135n14, 150, 172

To'Janggut, 80, 81, 93n25

Trang, 64n29, 107, 108, 117, 119, 121, 137n35, 143, 149, 150, 153, 154, 162, 165, 169, 172, 173n9, 173n16

Trangphura district, 109

Tranquebar. *See* Tharangambadi

trans-peninsular, xv, 2, 19, 20, 143, 144, 145, 146, 147, 148, 149, 150, 151, 152, 153, 154, 158, 159, 162, 163, 165, 166, 167, 170, 171, 174n19, 175n32, 175n45, 177, 178, 183, 184. *See also* path; waterways

treason. *See* derhaka; punishment

Trengganu, 36, 62n1, 136n22, 136n29, 138n41, 148, 159, 161, 165, 174n29, 175n37

tributary flower. *See* Bunga Emas dan Perak

tribute, 20, 25, 59, 90, 101, 111, 122, 134n3, 136n20, 147, 148, 167. *See also* Bunga Emas dan Perak

Trocki, A. Carl, 4, 10, 11, 12, 15, 16, 17, 18, 19, 93n19, 97, 98, 130, 173n16, 175n46, 177, 182

Tromba Minangkabau, 63n21, 67n63, 140n74

Tuanko, 42; Tuanko Johan Perkassa, 119; Tuanko Long Putih. *See* Tengku Long Putih; Tuanku Pangiran; Syed Zein; Tuanko Rajah Chara, 175n30; Tuanku Mahomed Saad; Tengku Mohammed Saad. *See also* Tengku

Tuhfat al-Nafis, 67n61, 74, 75, 76, 78, 86, 88, 92n11, 92n13, 92n15, 132, 136n22, 174n29, 184

Tunku Jam Jam, 125

Turkic, 63n12, 63n18

ular-besar. *See* snake

uleebalang, 66n51, 136n23

Undang-undang Kedah, 26, 29, 81

Undang-undang Melaka, 26, 29, 76, 77, 78, 82, 88. *See also* Risalat Hukum Qanun

Undang-undang Pahang, 49, 94n34, 95n49, 105. *See also* Pahang

upstream, 17, 141n75, 171, 174n24; Hulu, 17

Urak lawoi. *See* orang laut: Orang Lonta

vampire, 33n14, 43, 46, 47, 163; Ratu Anom, 65n40; tusks, 22, 47, 65n40, 84, 149, 157; human brains, 47, 65n40; human flesh, 48, 65n39, 65n40; human heart, 43, 46, 84; liver, 46, 84, 46, 49. *See also* blood; Raja Bersiung; Tantric

Vasishta, 65n39

Vietnam, 11, 149

Vijayanager, 63n10

Vinaya, 59, 67n60

Vishnu Purana, 47, 58, 65n39, 65n40

Wan Ali. *See* Wan Mali

Wan Hussein Azmi, 28

Wan Mali, 102, 116, 117, 118, 119, 120, 133, 139n58, 139n60, 139n61, 139n62, 142n84, 162, 163

Wan Sendari, 70, 71
Wan Sundaria. *See* Wan Sendari
Wan Yahya bin Wan Muhammad Taib, 22, 24, 25, 26, 27, 28, 31, 33n29, 34n35, 53, 63n13, 116. *See also* Salasilah atau Tarikh Kerajaan Kedah
waterways, 18, 148, 150, 154, 161, 163, 172, 174n20, 176n49. *See also* path; trans-peninsular
wayang kulit, 23, 31, 47, 60, 65n40, 179; wayang gedek, 48; Wayang golek purwa, 48; Wayang kulit Siam, 48, 53. *See also* exorcist; lakon; selembit
Wee, Vivienne, 133n1
Wheatley, Paul, 173n8, 147, 148
Wiang Sa, 57
Wila. *See* orang asli
Wilkinson, R. J., 30, 39, 46, 52, 63n14, 67n63, 93n24
Winstedt, R. O., 26, 27, 28, 32n8, 33n23, 33n29, 33n30, 34n35, 46, 63n13, 65n38, 68n67, 75, 85, 88, 91n1, 92n8, 93n19, 93n20, 94n33, 101, 103, 105, 108, 134n3, 137n31, 137n33, 140n70, 140n73
Wolters, W. Oliver, 15, 16, 64n29, 77, 91n2, 92n14, 104
wujudiya, 53; anti-wujudiya, 54. *See also* Raniri

yams, 113
Yasastilaka, 49
yaum al-mithak, 76, 77, 92n6, 93n18. *See also* agreement; covenant; contract
Yemen, 25, 26, 28, 29, 33n26

Zahak, 47, 48. *See also* Kaveh of Esfahan; Shah-Nameh; snake
Zaharah bt Haji Mahmud, 8
Zaiburi, 10, 116, 154, 166, 167. *See also* Phongsawadan Muang Zaiburi
Zakaria Ali, 87
Zoroastrian, xx, 37, 49

About the Author

Maziar Mozaffari Falarti is a visiting fellow at the Queensland University of Technology (Australia). He teaches history and Asian studies at the School of Arts, Humanities, and Social Sciences at the Habib University (Karachi).

www.ingramcontent.com/pod-product-compliance
Lightning Source LLC
Chambersburg PA
CBHW050325020526
44117CB00031B/1800